Cast for a Revolution

CAST

for a Revolution

SOME AMERICAN
FRIENDS AND ENEMIES
1728–1814

———•◦•———

JEAN FRITZ

Illustrated with Photographs

———•◦•———

Boston

HOUGHTON MIFFLIN COMPANY

1972

First Printing W

Copyright © 1972 by Jean Fritz
All rights reserved. No part of this work may be
reproduced or transmitted in any form by any means,
electronic or mechanical, including photocopying and recording, or by any information storage or retrieval system,
without permission in writing from the publisher.
ISBN: 0-395-13945-7
Library of Congress Catalog Card Number: 72-515
Printed in the United States of America

For Betty and Sig

CONTENTS

ILLUSTRATIONS

FOLLOWING PAGE 244

James Otis, Sr., by John Singleton Copley. *Courtesy, the Roland P. Murdock Collection, Wichita Art Museum, Kansas*

Mary Allyn Otis by John Singleton Copley. *Courtesy, the Roland P. Murdock Collection, Wichita Art Museum, Kansas*

James Warren by John Singleton Copley. *Courtesy, the Museum of Fine Arts, Boston*

Mercy Otis Warren by John Singleton Copley. *Courtesy, the Museum of Fine Arts, Boston*

James and Mercy Warren's house at Eel River, Plymouth. *Courtesy, the Charles R. Strickland Collection*

Manikin in Mercy Warren's dress poses beside Mercy's teapot and table. *Courtesy of Pilgrim Society, Plymouth, Massachusetts. Display in Pilgrim Hall*

James Otis, Jr., by Jonathan B. Blackburn. *Courtesy, the Boston Athenaeum*

Thomas Hutchinson by Edward Truman. *Courtesy, the Massachusetts Historical Society*

Abigail Adams by Mather Brown. *Courtesy, New York State Historical Association, Cooperstown*

AUTHOR'S NOTE

FOR ANYONE who has to make Dewey decimal decisions and may wonder whether this book should be classified as history or biography, let me say that I think of it as a collective biography, the story of a group of friends and enemies in Massachusetts before, during, and after the American Revolution. Although I have been interested in what this group did to shape the history of our country, I have been even more interested in what the business of fighting a revolution and founding a nation did to this group — how their private and public lives reacted on each other and how, as individuals, they interacted, sometimes as friends, sometimes as enemies, drawn together and pushed apart by the exigencies of their times. It is a passionate group, including such well-known leaders as John and Abigail Adams, Samuel Adams, and John Hancock, and also a few whose names and activities may be well known but who as personalities have never been explored as they deserved — James Otis, Jr., for instance, Mercy Otis Warren, James Warren, and Thomas Hutchinson. Had the colonial period been prolonged or had the members of this group lived a generation or two earlier, they might never have given their passions full play. As it was, each member of the cast played a different role in the American Revolution and represented a different psychological approach; to feel the full impact of the times on any one of these people, it seemed to me that it was necessary to explore them all, some in more detail, some in less.

Yet there is a central character. Mercy Otis Warren (sister of

James Otis and wife of James Warren, one-time president of the Massachusetts provincial congress and at the heart of the revolutionary movement) does not really assert herself until the early 1770s, when, apparently impressed by the historic nature of the times, she began to preserve her correspondence; nevertheless, her life, spanning the whole period from colonial dependence on England to 1814 and what has been called the second war of independence, forms a natural framework for this story. To follow Mercy Warren's life is to be, if not in the center of political activity, never more than a step away, for the men who were close to her — her father, her brother, her husband, her son Winslow, and her close friend John Adams — were all engaged in one way or another in the great events of their day. As a result, her private drama paralleled the drama of the nation.

But Mercy Warren was a major character in her own right as well. Unlike any other American woman of her day, she not only entered the political and literary worlds, she made a considerable contribution to them. Finally, Mercy Warren is important to this book for the simple reason that over my years of research she became important to me, and it was through her that I became fully acquainted with the others in the cast.

For help in the research stages of this book, I would like to thank the ever-cooperative staff at the Massachusetts Historical Society, Rose Briggs, Larry Geller, and Jane Strickland Hussey at Plymouth, James Ellis at West Barnstable, Virginia Hauhart at the Dobbs Ferry Public Library, and Donald Anthony at the Butler Library at Columbia University. I am grateful to Jean Whitnack for the many ways in which she has helped me and especially grateful to my husband, Michael, for his unfailing support.

JEAN FRITZ

September 25, 1971
Dobbs Ferry, New York

Prologue

James Otis

Jas: Warren

Mercy Warren

James Otis

Thos. Hutchinson

Samuel Adams

John Adams

John Hancock

Some Members of the Cast

I

———◆◆◆———

REVOLUTIONARY GENERATIONS are apt to think on a grand scale and in dramatic terms. It was so in Massachusetts. The leading figures all fancied themselves actors, and, indeed, they scarcely approached a crisis without reminding each other that they were onstage. Not that they expected acclaim. This group had little confidence in the judgment of their contemporaries; they played for posterity and listened to the dead. Old John Winthrop might still have been directing them from his grave. "For wee must consider that we shall be as a citty upon a hill," he had said a hundred years earlier. "The eies of all people are uppon us."

It was when they were tired of their roles and sick of their villains — Thomas Hutchinson, George III, and the rest — that they looked back wistfully to what they called "the good old days before the French and Indian War," when, as they remembered, life was simpler, morals purer, and England was minding her own business. At the time, of course, no one saw anything especially good about the days, and James Otis, twenty-six years old in the fall of 1728, was no different from the rest. Indeed, he could have pointed out that, far from pure, the morals of the province had so declined that it was necessary to raise the fine to fifteen shillings for anyone working or playing games on the Lord's Day and to thirty shillings for anyone traveling on that day. Nor were people happy with England. The new royal governor, William Burnett, just arrived in Boston, was already making himself objectionable. He had barely settled down and stationed his Negro valet, Andrew the Trumpeter, at the door of the Province House when he began making demands. A fixed salary was what he wanted, even though Massachusetts had been adamant in refusing a previous governor. The only way to keep a royal governor interested in serving the people, Massachusetts said, was to pay him as the people saw fit, according to his services.

As for his own life, James Otis of Barnstable would not have said it was simple, but then life is never simple for ambitious men and James Otis was ambitious. His father had died the year before and left him the family homestead along with some old chests, three mirrors, and a clock. It was a fine double house with a gambrel roof and three dormer windows; the Great Marshes swept away from the back door and the county road ran past the front door. It is hardly likely that James Otis, with no inclination to learning, would have wished to change places with his older brothers, both of whom had been given a Harvard education. Still, his brothers had something he did not have, and he felt the lack of it. Beneath his sociability, James Otis always seemed fearful that there was an ignorance in him that showed, and apparently there was. Over thirty years later, John Adams recorded in his diary that he had traveled with Colonel Otis. "He is vastly good humored and sociable," he wrote. "Learned he is not."

James Otis could not have contested this judgment (there is no evidence that he ever read, except strictly in the interests of politics or business), but he would have been hurt by it. Even in the portrait that Copley painted of him in his middle age, his eyes betray his vulnerability. He is the image of a prosperous country squire, yet his eyes are worried, as if he were afraid one would find something wrong with him. At the same time, his chin, thrust out in characteristic Otis aggressiveness, dares one to find it.

At twenty-six, however, James Otis was starting out. Trained as a tanner, busy with commercial ventures, he had no clear idea what kind of success he was after except for one thing: he would leave the family better off than he had found it. Each of the three Johns of the past century had in his turn increased the Otis holdings and

improved their status, and so would James. And his sons after him
— James, Jr., who was three now, Joseph, who was two, and, since
his wife, Mary, was pregnant, perhaps another son soon.

Most Barnstable people would have said that their town was well
suited for growing up and growing old in. It was far enough from
the main part of the province to escape much of the foolishness that
swept across it from time to time. Cape Codders, for instance, had
never raged as fiercely against the Quakers as other people in Massachusetts Bay. On the other hand, Barnstable was only half a day's
ride from Plymouth and there was a loyalty to Plymouth as the
center of the old colony that had not worn off yet. Women felt they
were due a visit to Plymouth at least once a year, and one John
Bacon even provided for his wife's annual visit in his will. As for
Boston, Barnstable was not so close as to be corrupted by big-city
ways, yet close enough so that the men, bound there on business,
could take with them their wives' and neighbors' shopping lists. In
James Otis' papers there is such a list, which includes rose water,
green tea, a pair of brass chafing dishes, currants, and some dark-
purple-and-yellow or dark-brown-and-yellow changeable crepe, "if
to be had without too much trouble if not any other dark crepe or
stuff — fourteen yards if half yard wide."

Barnstable was a pretty town too, boasting a hill from which, the
residents liked to point out, the ocean could be seen from both sides.
The view was best in the fall, when sumac flamed on the hillsides and
was mirrored in the ponds below. Twenty-five ponds nestled in the
hollows, glacial kettle holes where ice blocks had once melted.
Reminiscent also of an earlier America were the wigwams over by
Scorton's Hill. Old Hagar lived in one as late as 1767, Old Mookis
in another — the last of an Indian community which had once accepted three coats and four axes for the hayfields and cleared land of
Barnstable. By fall, the Great Marshes on the north shore, four
thousand acres, would be dotted with circular stacks of salt hay
waiting for the big autumn tide to sweep them to shore. And as one
looked beyond the marshes, there was Sandy Neck, a seven-mile-

long strip of land, home of night herons, resting place for what Cape people called the "flight birds" of the fall. The masts of Barnstable's ships could be seen from the hill, fishing boats and trading vessels, but the most prominent feature of the entire area was certainly West Barnstable's church steeple crowned with its gilded weather-vane cock. Five feet, five inches from bill to tip of tail, the cock, as it swung slowly about scanning the horizon, was the first sight returning sailors had of home.

This, then, was Barnstable in the year 1728, and if there needs to be an opening day for a prologue, let it be the twenty-fifth day of September. The buttonwood trees were turning to gold before the Otis house, and over the house triangles of geese honked their way south. Inside, in a room off the warm kitchen, Mary Allyne Otis had just given birth to her third child. It was a girl. With two boys before her, a girl was a welcome addition to the family. For Mary, she would in time be a helper and a companion. For James, whose life was already extending itself like the roots of a tree around the lives of his sons, a girl could be taken more lightly; she could be indulged. They named her Mercy after James's mother and his sister, wife of their minister, Jonathan Russell, who was to play such a prominent part in Mercy Otis' early years.

There is always in the presence of new life an aura of mystery — a sudden invasion of the future and a quickening of the past. It is as if all the unknown people yet to come and those unremembered who have gone before crowd into the presence of new life, eager to touch it. There is, as the myth-makers know, a visitation of spirits at this time, and surely it was a strange and distinguished group that assembled at Mercy Otis' birth.

The past would have been well represented. The three John Otises would have been there on one side of the family and Mercy's great-great-grandfather, Edward Dotey, on the other, all of them with the gift of quick wits and hot tempers. Edward Dotey, an indentured servant who threatened mutiny on the *Mayflower*, took part in America's first duel, but, once he had his heels and hands tied together for a while, he settled down and became, as far as one can tell, a good and certainly a prolific citizen.

But it was the spirits of the future that were most prominent, and not just those in the family, although there was no mistaking the husband and the sons dominating the room. There were friends whose destinies would be bound together in the days to come: Samuel Adams, for instance, and spirits not yet born — John and Abigail Adams, Elbridge Gerry of Marblehead, Hannah Winthrop, and John Hancock. Thomas Hutchinson, who had just graduated from Harvard, would be there too, an enemy, but very much a part of this cast of characters. And George III. He would not be born for ten years but he threw a long, a very long shadow before him.

In addition, there were two rather unlikely spirits for a Barnstable bedroom. One was an absent-minded bachelor who had died the year before, Sir Isaac Newton, and the other was his friend John Locke. They represented Reason and Rights and together they were, perhaps, more responsible than any other two men for what the eighteenth century, frankly enamored of its own image, called the Age of Enlightenment. And if Americans gave them seats on the right and left side of God Himself, it is no wonder. Each in his own way said exactly what Americans wanted to hear and, unlike God, they could be quoted. For Puritans who wanted God to be reasonable, here was Isaac Newton to prove that God's plan was, indeed, so perfect that stars obeyed the same laws as falling apples. And here was John Locke to show that natural laws applied even to people and among these laws was the inherent right to life, liberty, and property. So of course they would be here, for if Mercy Otis was the child of Puritans — passionate, turbulent-tempered Puritans, as it happened — she was also the child of her own age.

But ghosts drift away unrecognized and Mercy Otis began life, as we all do, by turning to her mother. We know little about Mary Allyne and only a little more about her family. Her father, Captain Joseph, commanded a sloop between Wethersfield, Connecticut, where Mary grew up, and Boston. Her grandfather Samuel had died only recently in Barnstable at the age of eighty-two and her great-grandfather Thomas, for some obscure reason, had in his possession at the time of his death two suits of armor. Actually, Lizzy Tower-hill, a servant girl in the home of Mary's cousin James, has won as much space in historical records as any of the Allynes, but since Lizzy was supposed to be a witch who could turn a house topsy turvy even when she was not present, it was only natural that she would be remembered.

Mary Allyne, referred to as Mrs. Molly by Mercy's friends, survives in a single memory and a portrait. She was able, according to Mercy, to console her children with religious arguments appropriate to every adversity and, indeed, she looks capable of it. In Copley's portrait, she is a buxom, shrewd, severe, peasant-faced woman who looks capable of doing anything once she got out of her silks and her stays. Certainly she was well acquainted with the meaning of *duty,* that abrasive word, that insatiable task master at the core of a New England woman's life, and Mercy learned from her.

But Mercy did not stop there. What interested her, once she was old enough, was what her brothers did, particularly her brother James, and what went on at the kitchen table when the dishes had been cleared away and the books brought out. In her early years, by a curious accident, there was a brief time when her father was also at that study table.

It began one day at the courthouse when a neighbor found himself without a counselor. His case was coming up and on the spur of the moment he turned to James, who happened to be there, and asked him to plead the case.

Any Otis would have enjoyed the experience — a chance to match wits, to spar, to declaim, to expand, to exploit, to take up for the wronged. James would have looked upon the venture as a lark, but when he had won the case, when the men in the courtroom gathered around, as they must have, slapping him on the back, congratulating him, telling him he should take up law, he would have asked himself — opportunist that he was — why not? Law was the most direct route to politics and it was primarily in elected office that a man attained status in the colonies. More and more lawyers, James Otis realized, were Harvard graduates like his brother John IV, fifteen years his senior and a justice of the peace. But James's own father, John III, had not had a college education. And John III had been elected not only to the House of Representatives but even to the more exclusive Council. So why not?

James Otis secured the necessary books, gave himself a course of home study, and the following year took the oath as attorney before Justice Benjamin Lynde of the Superior Court. The next ten years he spent dealing with debt actions, settling neighbors' quarrels, representing the most troublesome groups of poor whites, Negroes, and Indians, and occasionally handling a paternity suit, as when he defended a boy who claimed that he was "out a whalon" at the time the girl was "gitton" with child. As for Mary Allyne Otis, she spent the same years bearing children and burying them: seven more children were born before 1740, and of them only Mary, Hannah, and Elizabeth survived.

Mercy took her place at the study table. When her brothers went across the road to the parish house, where their uncle, Reverend Jonathan Russell, was preparing them for college, she went along. And here, as she grew up, she found the sustaining joy and moral ammunition for her years ahead.

Indeed, how fortunate it was that Mercy Otis, the zealous Puritan with her love of books and her preoccupation with morality, lived in an age when good literature was so often didactic. She followed the taste of her time and adopted its heroes: Cicero and Shakespeare for the sweep of their ideas, Brutus and Cromwell for their stand against tyranny, Alexander Pope for his clear-cut, black-and-white morality. Pope had everything his contemporaries admired, especially an ability to round off truth in couplets, and he had one thing more. Unlike the loftier poets, there was something almost reachable about Alexander Pope, something that impelled people to try their own hands at verse, and so they did — the whole generation and Mercy among them.

It was, however, when she took Sir Walter Raleigh's *History of the World* from her uncle's bookshelf that she found what she later considered to be the perfect literary form — the most moving, the most instructive. Here was the Word itself: God's own pattern revealed in the actions of men, the recurring story of the rise of men and kingdoms and their fall through greed and avarice, and who could tell it more dramatically than Sir Walter Raleigh writing in the Tower of London? His view of history coincided with that of the Puritans; it was, indeed, only a sophistication of the idea that one of the first Pilgrims, Robert Cushman, had expressed in 1620. "A Commonwele," he had said, "is readier to ebb than to flow, when once fine houses and gay cloaths come up." A sentiment that Mercy would herself subscribe to.

At just what particular point of her youth Mercy read these books is not recorded, but by the end of the decade (1739) she was a confirmed student. Uncommon as it was for a girl to go so far with reading, her uncle supported her. And Mercy's father, with his reverence for education, would have been proud — a girl, no less, *his* daughter, sailing head-on into study as if it could get her someplace — ironically, since the boys, with rewards waiting and college ahead, had to be prodded and pushed all the way. Joseph finally quit school and went into the family business, but he felt just as defensive about his lack of education as his father did. Perhaps more so. Joseph was more fiery.

James, Jr. (or Jemmy as he was called), was the center of his father's hopes and he was a worry. Less overtly rebellious than his brother, Jemmy stayed in school but did the minimum amount of work, just enough to complete his entrance requirements to Harvard. Still, one allowed that boys were apt to be lazy, but there was more to this worry. There was something strange about Jemmy. Magnetic, gay, boisterous, entertaining, he could be the life of a party and he could also walk out of that party suddenly and without any accounting for it. Once, while a student at Harvard, he was playing his violin at a dance when without warning he flung his violin aside. "So Orpheus fiddled," he cried, "and so danced the brutes!" And he rushed out into the night.

Everything about young James was larger than life — his body, his talents, his temper, his likes, his hates, his melancholy, his wit; he could not stay still. "He springs, and twitches his Muscles about in thinking," John Adams reported later. Indeed, James Otis was a storm of unpredictability and contradictions and at the center of this storm was his father with his high expectations both for his son and himself. Jemmy loved his father, he hated him; he wanted to fulfill his claims, he resented the claims; he wanted to abandon him, he wanted to protect him. With the acute sensitivity of an eldest son, he saw his father's vulnerability; he suffered for it and sometimes he even felt guilty. No one, however, least of all Jemmy, suspected what was brewing.

They were all busy the summer of 1739 getting ready for Barnstable's centennial celebration which took place on the Otis and adjacent Hinckley properties. If it was held on the actual day of the anniversary, it would have been on October 31 and Jemmy, who had entered Harvard only a few months before, would surely have come home for it. The preparations had been going on for weeks. The women had gone into their kitchens and the men had taken their fishing lines and their guns and had gone to the sea, the ponds, the marshes, and the hills. The result was clams, ducks, pies, oysters, bread, puddings, fish, venison, heaped high on outdoor tables.

Jonathan Russell would have played a prominent part in the day's services. His was not one of the first families to come to Barnstable, but his father had been the minister before him and was very much a part of Barnstable's history. It was his grandfather, however, whose story, although it had no specific relevance to Barnstable, linked New England history to the Stuart kings in such a curious way that it deserves to be recalled. For fifteen years in the cellar of his home in Hadley, Connecticut, Jonathan Russell's grandfather had hidden William Goffe and Edward Whalley, two of the judges who ordered Charles I beheaded, and who in consequence had been forced to run for their lives at the Restoration.

But William Goffe had been dead for sixty years now, the last of the Stuart kings and queens had been gone for twenty-five, and

Barnstable, in the eleventh year of the reign of George II, was saying good-bye to its first century. Before its second century was half over, there would of course be years when such a friendly gathering would be impossible, but no one guessed that now. Joseph Otis, for instance, who would be at the center of feuds that were later to rock Barnstable, was only a thirteen-year-old boy with nothing more on his mind than a community feast. At eleven, Mercy was undoubtedly more excited about the homecoming of her brother Jemmy than about Barnstable's past or future. A thin, plain, intense, and sober-looking girl, Mercy was not the type, nor would she ever be the type, to attract a bold, colorful kind of man as friend or lover, yet there were two such men in her life. Her brother Jemmy was the first; later she would have a son, Winslow, whom she would idolize in the same way.

II

THE EIGHTEENTH CENTURY, having decided that the world was governed by rules, found rules for everything and set young people to copying them. At Harvard University in James Otis' day, there were twenty-two rules for humbling freshmen and all of them had to be copied before a student could be officially admitted to the college. A freshman could not, for instance, wear a hat in the college yard unless it was raining, snowing, or hailing, or unless he was on horseback or unless his hands were full. He could not laugh in his senior's face, talk saucily to a senior, throw anything across the college yard, or mingo (urinate) against the college wall. Presumably when he was a sophomore, he would not be so curbed.

James Otis, Jr., however, was not the kind to be easily humbled. He was, as he once said, "naturally and constitutionally inclined to social pleasures" and he spent his first year away from home following his inclinations. Word of his gay behavior and cavalier attitude toward his studies may or may not have reached Barnstable; there were, besides his roommate, Lothrop Russell, six Cape boys in his class. His own letters home were concerned mainly with money. "I have all so sent you recepte for all the money that I have paid away," he wrote his father on September 5, 1740. "I have got Aunt Russels c[h]ocolate and have been in every shop in Boston to get her bowls . . . If I cant get them I shall be glad to keep the money if you are willing if not I will return it."

James's life at college would not always be as lighthearted. Two weeks after he wrote home about Aunt Russell's chocolate, George

Whitefield, the most prominent figure in the revival movement that came to be known as the Great Awakening, arrived in Boston and threw all into confusion. Twenty-six years old, passionate, popular, eloquent, Whitefield whirled through New England, churning up emotions, breaking up congregations, and leaving in his wake crowds of panting converts on the one hand and knots of troubled skeptics on the other. In Plymouth, for instance, a group of citizens, disturbed by the "enthusiasms" they had witnessed, met to consider whether a sudden and short distress followed by a sudden joy was true proof of repentance. In Barnstable, the congregation supported Jonathan Russell against a handful of "New Lights" who charged him with hypocrisy because he *read* his sermons. How could God speak through a man who was reading? they asked.

But at Harvard University, students were carried away by George Whitefield's emotional gymnastics, and among them was James Otis, Jr. It was as if a finger had been laid on that secret place in him where his demons dwelled, and, in an effort to assuage them, he joined in the orgy of prayer and psalm-singing that was sweeping New England. Moreover, the experience apparently showed him his duty, for when he got up off his knees, he went to his desk. The Barnstable Otises, who would have disapproved of Whitefield's excesses, had him to thank for turning Jemmy into a student.

Young Samuel Adams was also a student at Harvard during the Whitefield convulsions, but if he did not carry on as so many of his contemporaries did, it was not because he was unimpressed. Samuel Adams was simply not a man to be acted upon as much as he was himself an actor. Besides, he felt no need for conversion. Three years ahead of James Otis in college, Samuel Adams was a blue-eyed, straight-walking, mild-mannered young man who knew his own mind as precisely as if it had been a pocket watch. He welcomed Whitefield, for Whitefield was in the tradition of the thundering Puritan churchmen of the early days and Samuel was not only in love with the past, he was fiercely committed to the idea that Massachusetts should return to the piety of its forefathers and to that early independence it had enjoyed before England began to take the New World seriously. But swooning after itinerant preachers was not Samuel's style; he was a political activist and during his college years he was more exercised by a scheme to change the power structure of Massachusetts than he was by the Great Awakening.

Samuel Adams had been brought up on practical politics at his father's house, a gathering place for popular leaders who were resentful of the aristocratic merchants of the colony and their control of money and government. Like many people in Massachusetts in 1740 and 1741, Samuel put his hope in the Land Bank, an inflationary project to float paper money and the popular party's answer to the problem of currency shortage. The Land Bank backers had no reason to think that their venture was illegal; a similar scheme had been approved for New Hampshire in 1734. Nevertheless, in 1741 Parliament suddenly outlawed the Land Bank by applying and making retroactive an act that Massachusetts considered irrelevant. The action was an arbitrary way to dispose of a project, no matter how unsound, and no one resented it more than young Samuel Adams, who was said to have set his course for life on the day that the Land Bank failed.

That money and religion, ever the twin concerns of the American people, flared up into public issues while Samuel Adams and Jemmy Otis were in college undoubtedly played as large a part in their education as the classically oriented curriculum in which they were immersed. There is no record whether these two young men exchanged views on the issues or if they even knew each other at the time, but they were both present at the Harvard commencement in 1743 — Jemmy to receive his bachelor's degree, Samuel to receive his master's. Samuel, already experimenting with the idea of civil disobedience, delivered a commencement address in which he contended that it was not unlawful "to resist the Supreme Magistrate, if the Commonwealth cannot be otherwise preserved." As for Jemmy, he gave the traditional party that members of the graduating class gave to their visitors (presumably a modest one since his father had warned him not "to make a Great commencement"), and then he went home for two years, to read in preparation for his second degree.

Four years had made a difference, Jemmy would find, in the family at Barnstable. Joseph, seventeen now, was working on the ledgers in the family store and old enough to get in trouble occasionally. Isaac Hinckley, the next-door neighbor of the Otises, took Joseph to court this year for allegedly getting the Hinckleys' Negro servant girl pregnant. The rest of the children were less troublesome. Mercy was fifteen now, old enough to share Jemmy's literary interests while he was home; Mary was thirteen, Hannah nine, Elizabeth four, and there was a new boy, three-year-old Samuel Allyne. Two more babies had been buried; another was expected. But the younger generation, including Jemmy, was, after all, still in the wings; it was James Otis, Sr., who was onstage.

Actually, he was ready for a larger stage. Over the last years James Otis had all but exhausted the local possibilities available to him. Few cases were tried in the Barnstable court now in which he did not represent a client on one side or the other; he served on committees, was elected selectman in 1744, and rode circuit to expand his already extensive practice. Of course, he was looking toward the General Court and had every reason to expect the citizens of his district to elect him as their representative. His politics were, for the most part, their politics; in the matter of the Land Bank, for instance, the province's most controversial issue in recent years, James Otis, Sr., like most Cape Codders, had stood firmly against it, which as it happened made sense from every point of view. Unlike Samuel Adams, James Otis was not against the aristocracy; on the contrary, he wanted to join it and, as so often happens, a war helped him realize his ambitions.

In 1744, France declared war on England and although neither country showed any inclination to fight on American soil, Americans became alarmed and the pace of politics quickened. The man to take the most immediate advantage of the situation was Governor

William Shirley of Massachusetts, who rather fancied himself in a military role. His attention was focused on Louisbourg, a Gibraltar-like stronghold on Cape Breton Island which belonged to the French. Its stone walls thirty feet high, Louisbourg rose up out of the sea, one of the most formidable fortresses of the world, threatening not only the trade routes between England and America but the New England fishing business as well. In addition, Louisbourg, being French, was of course Catholic, a bastion of "popery," New Englanders called it, right at their own back door and one which, Governor Shirley decided, might by bold measures and considerable luck be removed. Like his predecessors, Shirley had found his position as governor difficult, but now he saw a chance to please the king who kept him in office, to serve the province which paid him his salary, and to become, perhaps, a hero in the bargain. Accordingly, in January 1745, he proposed to the General Court that Massachusetts should storm Louisbourg — with the help of Commodore Warren's West India fleet, he hoped, but with no guarantee that Commodore Warren either would or could get there in time. If Massachusetts waited for a guarantee, Shirley pointed out, spring would come and go, France would send reinforcements, and the opportunity would be lost.

James Otis, Sr., was not able to vote for or against the Louisbourg expedition — his election to the Massachusetts House of Representatives did not come until four months after the decision had been made — but he would have supported Shirley. Once Otis had captured the votes in his own district, it was important for him to win the favor of the governor, for governors gave out war contracts, they made appointments, and in general they helped or hindered a man on his way up the political ladder. Besides, James Otis, as he would prove later, was as eager as Shirley to fight the French and was willing to work hard to do it.

Thomas Hutchinson, on the other hand, a member of the House of Representatives (except for a brief interval) since 1737, was able to vote on the Louisbourg question and he voted against it. Perhaps it is well to become acquainted with Thomas Hutchinson at this particular point of his career, not only because he is to figure so prominently in the drama ahead but because his attitude toward the Louisbourg expedition revealed so much of himself. He was a conservative man. He had been for hard currency in the Land Bank controversy and had made enemies accordingly (Samuel Adams included), but on the whole the people of Massachusetts respected his conservatism and gave him credit for his knowledge of fiscal affairs. Indeed, they took pride in him — one of their own, they felt, from a family that went all the way back to the famous Anne Hutchinson. Behind his back they might call him Tommy-Skin-and-Bones or the Tall Man; they might smile at the Hutchinson nose, although perhaps his was not quite as large as that of another Hutchinson, whose arrival in Boston Harbor had once inspired someone to write:

> *When Hutchinson came the people arose*
> *To clear a place to land his nose.*

Yet he was a patrician, all six feet of him, a true gentleman, the people said, born and bred among them, one who could stand up with England's finest.

There is little known about Thomas Hutchinson's childhood, but what stories there are seem peculiarly relevant, as if they had survived deliberately to point the way to Thomas Hutchinson, the man. In the first place, he had listened to his father. When Thomas, Sr., said that the most important thing in life was to obey one's conscience, Thomas, Jr., took it to heart. Indeed, he nourished his conscience so well that by middle age it was a formidable part of him. If he suffered sometimes in consequence, he could feel justified; his father had warned him, "If you serve your Country faithfully, you will be reproached & reviled for doing it."

In addition, Thomas Hutchinson had always liked life as it was. In his father's big, comfortable mansion at the north end of town, he had no reason either to question his manner of living or want to change it. When he felt the urge for larger experiences, he did what Mercy Otis and so many of his generation did: he read history. He started the habit early and reported later that as a child his favorite story had been the death of Charles I. There were not many people in New England who had tears to waste on the Stuart kings, but Thomas apparently never failed to be moved, particularly by the grisly execution scene. Later Hutchinson himself was to write history for the same disarmingly simple reasons that he read it. "We are fond of prolonging our lives to the utmost length," he said. "Going back to so familiar an acquaintance with those who have lived before us approaches the nearest to it of anything we are capable of."

At the present time, 1745, Thomas Hutchinson was thirty-two years old and divided his time between the family house in Boston which his father had left him six years before and a new home in the country. Eight miles south of Boston, this new home at Milton Hill was an extension, a fulfillment of himself, the way great homes were to certain eighteenth-century gentlemen. Much later and in less happy circumstances, he described Milton Hill to King George III: "A pleasant situation, and many gentlemen from abroad say it has the finest prospects from it they ever saw." It was fine no matter which way he looked. On one side were the Blue Hills; on the other, the Neponset River and beyond that — all of Boston Harbor from the wharves to the outer light. Later Thomas would plant a long double row of buttonwood trees on the hill and he would order three larch trees "about as large as a small walking stick & 6 or 7 feet high," a half-dozen mulberries, and pears — the "red-buttoned" kind.

The gods had been lavish in their gifts to Thomas Hutchinson. It was true that they had taken away two young Thomases at birth but they had finally let one stay, and they had taken away two Williams. Still, in 1745 there were three children on Milton Hill: Thomas, who was five, Elisha, who was two, and Sarah, not quite a year old. And there was Thomas Hutchinson's wife, Margaret, the dearest, most prized gift of all. He had married her when she was sixteen and he was twenty-two and every year since he had given a party on May 16, their wedding anniversary, to celebrate his good fortune and what he called the happiest day of his life.

An ambitious man, Thomas Hutchinson understood as well as James Otis the importance of getting along with governors, yet Hutchinson had a powerful sense of his own rightness and a finicky need to stick to orders. So when it came to the Louisbourg question, he was appalled at Shirley's romantic notion that he could launch an attack without even knowing if he would be supported or England would approve. The plan, he said, was "like selling the skin of a bear before catching him," and Thomas Hutchinson was careful about his bears.

In the end, Governor Shirley had his way. An army of three thousand was mustered at Boston, a navy was assembled (exclusive of transports) of three frigates, a snow, a brigantine, and eight sloops. On March 28, one of the coldest days of the year, after being blessed by George Whitefield, the little fleet set sail for its Louisbourg adventure. For Mercy Otis and the friends who would join together to wage another war in later days, the Louisbourg expedition was one of the most memorable events of their youth. Mercy, sixteen years old in the spring of 1745, may well have been in the group at the Barnstable waterfront watching John Gorham's squadron of whaleboats leave for Boston. John Adams, ten years old, spent the spring listening to soldier stories at the supper table. John Hancock, eight years old, living in his uncle's grand fifty-two-windowed house, watched soldiers drilling on Boston Common. And like everyone else, young and old, they all waited for news to come back from Louisbourg. Jemmy Otis, who had moved to Boston and was reading law with the famous Jeremiah Gridley, wrote home: "As for my Writing . . . the news all I can Say is that I had no account when I wrote neither have we any since but what are in print."

The news came on July 3 at one in the morning. Louisbourg had been taken. By daybreak all the bells in Boston were ringing; by nightfall Governor Shirley had been thoroughly toasted throughout the town. Jonathan Edwards said that God had baffled the enemy; Thomas Prince at the Old South Church said He was taking care of His chosen people. Some of the skeptics, however, still called the whole venture a wild-goose chase, justified only because "we got the goose." As for Thomas Hutchinson, he warned posterity not to depend on special interventions of Providence just because their ancestors had experienced them. Still the fact remained, lucky or not, that Commodore Warren's fleet had arrived in time and New England men had taken the famous French garrison and were now in command. There was not a man in New England who did not feel stronger for it.

Nor was there a man in New England who was not outraged three years later. In working out the peace negotiations between the two countries, England returned Louisbourg to France. It was as if the war had never been. It took a while for New Englanders to get used to the shock. They thrashed out the news in taverns, in kitchens, and in the pulpit. How *could* England? they asked. Didn't England understand what the capture of Louisbourg had meant to them? The next question followed quickly: How could anyone in America ever be sure again what England would do?

· · ·

For James Otis the year 1745 had been a year of personal victories. Not only had he been elected to the General Court, he had been made a colonel of the militia and had become a friend of Governor Shirley's and was soon to be known as one of Shirley's henchmen with patronage of his own to distribute on a local level. He was on his way up. The next step, he hoped, would be the Council (equivalent to an upper house), but he had his sights even higher. What he really coveted above all else was an appointment to the bench of the Superior Court. Benjamin Lynde, a justice of the court who had sworn Otis in as a lawyer fourteen years ago, had died this year, leaving a vacancy, but of course it was too early for Colonel Otis to look for such an honor. Someday, however, there would be another vacancy and he would be ready for it.

III

---◆◆◆---

THE WINTER of 1754 was remarkable for its warmth. John Adams and John Hancock, both students at Harvard, would have had a hard time finding enough snow in Harvard Yard to make a respectable snowball, had they been so inclined. There was not enough snow to whiten the dunes at Barnstable and barely enough to dust the new grave at Milton Hill. Margaret Hutchinson, beloved wife of Thomas, had died the spring before, a month after giving birth to her namesake.

All during January, February, and March the roads stayed clear, which meant, among other things, that it was a good winter for courting. Joseph Otis was courting Rebecca Sturgis that winter and James Warren of Plymouth was courting Mercy. James and Mercy had known each other for years, possibly since childhood, and even shared the same great-great-grandfather, that spirited dueler of the *Mayflower,* Edward Dotey. There are many ways they may have met — perhaps in Barnstable where James's grandmother lived after marrying her second husband, perhaps in Plymouth where there were still Allyne relatives, perhaps through the two fathers who had been doing business together for twenty years, but most certainly through Mercy's brother Jemmy, who had been in Harvard at the same time as James Warren, and if they had not met before, surely they did during those years 1748 to 1750, when Jemmy practiced law in Plymouth before moving permanently to Boston. Still, Mercy was twenty-six and James Warren was twenty-eight before they were finally married. It was in November 1754 that Mercy packed up her belongings and went with James to his father's house on Eel River, three miles south of Plymouth. With her, she had her wedding dress of watered silk (which she later cut up into christening gowns), the fancy card-table cover she had spent all summer embroidering, and Ann, her favorite servant girl, from her father's house.

Clifford Farms, the Warren estate on Eel River, had been in the family since the days of the first Richard Warren of the *Mayflower*. He had received it as his share of the community property when it was divided up, along with a black smooth-horned heifer and two she-goats. There were four hundred acres of land that rolled back through the hills (the "Mountains of Eel River," Mercy liked to call them), with fields for rye near the house, orchards on the slopes, pastures for sheep in the distance. The house itself was, like the Otis home, gambrel roofed but it was smaller, with a single room on either side of the front door and a staircase between. Here, tucked behind the shoulder of a small hill, between the ocean and the marshes, Mercy and James set about the business of marriage.

If he had not known it before, James learned now what it was to live with an Otis, for Mercy, in spite of the iron hand with which she tried to rule herself, was as emotional and moody as the rest of her family — only she took out her dark moods in worry, sleepless nights, and bouts of poor health. Yet James was always supporting, always loving. "He is blessed," he wrote to her, "that is connected with you and more especially when your spirits are in proper key." And in her turn Mercy said, "Were you to look in on me and in your way [say] 'Come up spirits,' and then paint some agreeable images as usual I know nothing would have so ready a tendency to restore health."

Mercy could scarcely have found a husband more unlike her brother Jemmy. In the inner circle of Boston lawyers now, Jemmy was both the hope and the despair of his colleagues. He was brilliant, he was violent, he was admired, he was feared, he disdained meanness, he stooped to the basest insults; he rode life as he would have a horse, whipping it, reining it in, abandoning it, leaping on its back again to drive it frothing ahead of everyone else. James Warren, on the other hand, was a prudent man with an informal, unassuming way, and for all his youth, he was an Old Colonist down to the bone. He had the Old Colonists' pride in first families, their loyalty to what they called "first principles," and something of their isolationist set of mind — a brand of independence rooted in their separatist religion (far more egalitarian than that of their theocratically inclined neighbors in the Bay Colony) and nourished by their political position in the province. The Old Colonists had not wanted to be annexed to the more aristocratic Massachusetts Bay and, although this was past history (1692) when James Warren was born, the psychological effects lingered, perhaps undefined, into the next generations, touching the character of some men more than others and surely the character of James Warren more than most. He was a stubborn man — indeed, no less stubborn than Thomas Hutchinson. "His attachments are strong," Mercy said, "and when he likes or dislikes either men or measures, the shaking of a leaf will not alter his opinion."

Mercy was, of course, an Old Colonist herself, but, more philosophically inclined than James, she had elevated the Old Colonists' thinking and set it into the eighteenth-century framework where, in fact, it fit very well. In the same way she had taken old-fashioned feminine virtues and given them intellectual substance. Well-trained in household management when she went to Eel River, Mercy found it not only satisfying to perform her duties because it was the virtuous thing to do, but also stimulating to reduce her day to routine — a victory of reason over time was the way she looked at it. Later, when she had nieces to advise, she told them that if a woman organized her work efficiently, she could perform her household duties first and still have time for what Mercy considered her greatest pleasure, "the book and the pen." During her first year of marriage, however, Mercy had her sister-in-law Sally to share the routine with. Since her mother's death in 1737, Sally had been mistress of the house, taking charge as soon as she was old enough. At the same time, James had been and still was his father's right-hand man, both on the farm and in his merchant business, buying and selling, shipping, and sometimes performing favors for and sometimes asking favors of the Otises. "Your Lemons & wine have not gone to Barnstable," he wrote to the Colonel. "I have secured them Both in my Cellar . . . I hope you won't forget me about a Negro fellow if you can hear of one to be sold."

Evening was the time at Eel River that Mercy cherished most — when the chores were done and James came home with news from town and perhaps mail from Barnstable or Boston. Perhaps there would be a visitor with him. The most frequent guest that year was William Sever of Kingston, who was courting Sally, and he was always a welcome addition to a party. He was a tall, dignified, considerate man, who in twenty years would be reminding everyone of George Washington, both in looks and character. The talk would be political talk, the kind Mercy was used to, the kind she liked best.

France. That is what they would be talking about. France was causing trouble again, threatening the edges of the English colonies in Pennsylvania, Virginia, Maine. During the summer a convention of the colonies had met in Albany to consider a military union but nothing had come of it. Thomas Hutchinson had represented Massachusetts. Since Margaret's death, he had immersed himself in public life; it was the only way he knew how to handle his grief. Indeed, he kept himself so busy that, as preparation for war took up more and more of the governor's time, Hutchinson became known as "Shirley's Prime Minister."

The first winter and spring of Mercy's marriage were the last of the so-called "good old days before the French and Indian War." The marsh grasses were turning green and the iris was coming into bloom on the banks of Eel River as General Braddock, the newly arrived commander in chief of British forces, began planning strategy with William Shirley, second in command. The orchards blossomed and dropped their blossoms on Clifford Farms, and as the days lengthened an army pulled itself together. It was June and strawberry time when General Braddock started his march to Fort Duquesne in western Pennsylvania and William Shirley set out for Lake Ontario.

Two months later the news reached Boston that Braddock's army had been defeated and all but destroyed. Major Thomas Gage narrowly escaped with a wound in the belly, a graze over an eyebrow, and some shots in his coat. General Braddock's aide-de-camp, George Washington, had four bullets through his coat and two horses shot from under him. Braddock's secretary, William Shirley, Jr., had been shot in the head and killed. And General Braddock himself, after surviving five horses, had fallen, fatally wounded.

It was not a propitious beginning to a war nor was the news over the next months any more heartening. But wars have a way of going underground over the winter: armies hibernate, and nature itself becomes the enemy. This year nature took Massachusetts by surprise with an earthquake. It came on at four o'clock in the morning of November 18 like the noise of coaches rattling, one observer reported, and continued for about four minutes, knocking down chimneys and walls in the coastal areas and stopping clocks in Salem. In Plymouth, where the Warrens were getting ready for Sally's wedding, a spring was moved from one side of the road to the other. In Boston, Thomas Hancock, uncle of John and proud master of one of the most luxurious homes in the city, looked around at the damage and sighed with relief. "Thank God," he said, "I had no hurt done to my house nor anything in it." John Adams, teaching school now in Worcester, was home in Braintree at the time. "The house seemed to rock and reel and crack as if it would fall in ruins about us," he wrote in his diary.

An earthquake was a challenge to eighteenth-century philosophy. On the face of it, it was both unreasonable and arbitrary and if there was one thing that Americans could not stand, it was arbitrariness, whether it was in nature or government or religion. As a result, all over the province people rushed into print or the pulpit to offer their explanations. For over a year there was a newspaper controversy between Thomas Prince of the Old South Church, who suggested that earthquakes were caused by lightning attracted into the earth, particularly by lightning rods (a new-fangled invention), and John Winthrop, professor at Harvard and one of the first experimental scientists in the country, who was infuriated by such nonsense. Earthquakes, he said, were forces of nature like rain and snow and he proceeded to collect information about this one which became the subject of one of his most famous lectures.

Most of the clergy managed to reconcile the autocratic Puritan God with the enlightened God of reason by saying that earthquakes were God's punishment for sin, God's warning to the impenitent. "Since the earthquake," John Winthrop wrote, "our pulpits have generally rung with terror." George Whitefield, who was in Plymouth that month preaching five sermons within three days, undoubtedly capitalized on it, although he was forty-one years old now and somewhat mellowed. Five years before he had publicly apologized for having used too much wildfire in his zeal.

If the people of Massachusetts, however, were looking for a sin to account for the earthquake, they had a fresh one on their doorstep — though there is no evidence that they made the association. They had just evicted from their homes in Nova Scotia two thousand French Canadians who had sworn to be neutral but had refused on religious grounds to pledge allegiance to England. James Warren's cousin, Colonel John Winslow (remembered for his horsemanship and his skinny legs) had been in charge of the expedition that brought back from Nova Scotia shiploads of miserable prisoners to be distributed over the province. Seventy-six arrived in Plymouth about the time of the earthquake.

The earthquake of 1755 was, if not a punishment, at least a physical manifestation of an upheaval in Massachusetts that would in the next few years upend the fortunes of some men and magnify those of others. Mercy Warren was four months pregnant and taking care of her sick father-in-law in May 1757, when the news reached Plymouth that William Shirley had been replaced as governor by Thomas Pownall, an ambitious man who was said to have talked his way into the job. At Eel River the news would certainly have occasioned much supper-table talk, for a new governor threatened the future of the Otis men. Colonel Otis had built up large stocks of credit with Shirley's administration and his family had prospered. Joseph was excise collector in Barnstable and a captain in the militia. James, Jr., was a justice of the peace for Suffolk County, and James Warren was a major in the militia. Most important, however, Colonel Otis had received Governor Shirley's promise to support him for the Council when the war was over and his promise of a seat on the Superior Court at the next vacancy — promises which now, of course, would have to be rewon from the new governor.

The thing to do, Colonel Otis decided, was to run for the Council in the current election before Thomas Pownall arrived. The timing was good from another angle as well. The Colonel's brother John, seventy years old and in poor health, who had served on the Council for seven years, would be unable to serve this year and James could run in his place. Although James did not have his brother's education, he was more aggressive and had worked harder to reach his place in politics than his brother had. In any case James felt assured that the General Court, if for no other reason, would elect him simply because it was a common courtesy to allow a man in politics to succeed his brother.

The Council, the closest thing that Massachusetts could manage to correspond to the House of Lords, was the elite body of the General Court in the sense that it was designed to serve the governor in a close advisory capacity and was elected not by the public but by a joint vote of the new House and the old Council. No one in the Otis family had any doubt but that the Colonel would be elected, but on Wednesday, May 25, when the votes were tabulated, Colonel Otis was, as the saying went, "left out." He had not even polled sufficient votes in the House where he had for over a decade been a representative. He could not understand it; he was angry and in the way of the Otis men — none of whom could tolerate much self-blame — he needed someone to be angry at. It was not enough to say, as Joseph had once said, "The world Is filled with fools and madmen"; Colonel Otis wanted to know which fools or madmen had worked against him and he wanted to know why. For the rest of the Otises, it was almost as if someone had suggested there was a flaw in the family itself and no one would be as sensitive to the defeat as James Otis, Jr.

Mercy worried about her father, but she had other worries as well. Her father-in-law died in July, leaving James his estate, including the house on North Street recently bought from John Winslow, who had moved to grander quarters in Marshfield after his Acadian expedition. Now with Sally married and her father gone, there was no one left at Clifford Farms and no reason why James and Mercy could not move into town if they wished. They decided to move immediately so that they would be settled when the baby arrived in October.

The new house was larger than the one at Eel River, yet it was modest in comparison with the elegant house at the opposite end of North Street which belonged to Edward Winslow, another of James's cousins. But Mercy made no comparisons. She was proud of the Winslow name but she had no desire to compete with the cousins, most of whom she considered frivolous and worldly. She was happy with her own little garden and her own house set snugly on the corner of Main Street, the thoroughfare between Boston and the Cape. She could sit on the wide window seat in the front room and watch for visitors who might be expected — her father, perhaps, or her brother Samuel Allyne, who was at Harvard and often passed through, or Jemmy — married now to the wealthy and proper Ruth Cunningham of Boston.

The first week of August, Mercy and James were in the midst of moving when Thomas Pownall arrived in Boston — a short, pudgy, sociable bachelor, more liberal and nationally minded, John Adams said later, than any governor Massachusetts had ever had. Yet he was never fully supported by the people. Some could not forgive him for deliberately working to unseat William Shirley; some objected to his informal manners which they thought inappropriate to a governor. (He often conducted business in a plain short frock without a ruffled shirt and with no sword at his side.) Some were so tired of English bungling of the war (particularly after the fall of Fort William Henry only seventy miles from the Massachusetts border), so tired of the arrogance of British army officers who treated provincials with contempt, so tired of the new commander in chief who wanted to quarter his troops in Boston, that they found it easy to take exception to an English governor on almost any grounds, even if only because he gave overly elaborate parties.

But Thomas Pownall did make loyal friends and the Otises were among them. He appointed James Otis, Jr., acting advocate general of the Vice Admiralty Court, promised the Colonel the next vacancy on the Superior Court, and early in his administration began sending orders for war supplies to the Barnstable Otises. Indeed, he had been in Boston only three weeks when he ordered "one hundred Whaleboats with suitable Oars" for the army at Lake George. The order came while the Colonel was still smarting from the news he had received from his friend David Gorham, justice of the peace in Barnstable. In a conversation with Gorham "about the Publick affairs" on August 15, 1757, Colonel Otis at last found out why he had not been elected to the Council. Thomas Hutchinson and Andrew Oliver had worked against him.

Colonel Otis went home after the conversation and wrote it all down on a torn-off piece of paper and preserved it. On one side of the paper in the Colonel's thin, tight, crabbed writing are the words: "Wt David Gorham told Me." On the other side he reported the conversation.

Hutchinson and Oliver, he wrote, "had a Bad Opinion of my Conduct and . . . Mr. Hutchinson had Said that I never did Carry things while in the Court By any merit But only By Doing Little

Low Dirty things for Governour Shirley such as a Person of ~~merit~~ worth [sic] Refused to medle with and that Shirley made use of me only as a Tool . . ."

It was a bitter blow to the Colonel, who in his years with Shirley had built up in his mind an image of himself that he had been rather proud of, but if he was hurt, he was also angry, particularly at Thomas Hutchinson, sitting so prettily on top of Milton Hill and choosing so carefully what work he "would medle with." How could a province fight a war, Colonel Otis might well have asked, if everyone was bent on keeping his hands clean? When the Colonel had a muster roll to fill, he filled it even if he had to go against the law and conscript Quakers, even if he had to make promises to volunteers that he might not be able to fulfill. He could not understand why the Council had such a tender regard for Quakers' conscience or later why men he had conscripted walked home from Lake George because they did not have all the articles they had been promised. Some even refused to fight because, they said, their blankets were so bad that they must have been sent by Colonel Otis himself who "was an Old Pirate and a Cursed old Rogue." But if Colonel Otis used every means to further the war effort, he also used the war to improve his own position. During the next three years he extended his trade as he supplied the army and padded his accounts until they were no longer acceptable at headquarters. When he tried again for a seat on the Council, he was once more defeated — this time by his own townsmen, who claimed he already had too much power.

. . .

The French and Indian War ended, in effect, in September 1760 when Canada surrendered to the British at Montreal. Mercy and James Warren had added two sons to their family during the war: James, Jr., born while the French were threatening the coastline of Massachusetts, and Winslow, born in the lucky spring of 1759, marked so auspiciously by the appearance of a comet trailing a long tail across the Boston sky. With the fighting over, the Otises and the Warrens looked forward to sitting down, as New Englanders were so fond of saying, each under his own "vines" where none could make them afraid. But Colonel Otis, in spite of previous disappointments, expected rewards under his vines and, indeed, he had immediate reason to hope that one of his long-cherished ambitions might at last be satisfied. Two days after Boston celebrated the Montreal victory, Chief Justice Stephen Sewall died of the flux, leaving a vacancy on the bench of the Superior Court, the vacancy that Colonel Otis had been waiting for all these years, the post that had been promised him first by Governor Shirley and then by Governor Pownall.

Only the month before, however, Pownall had been replaced as governor by Francis Bernard, a forty-eight-year-old man with eight children and little money who was said to have been attracted to Massachusetts because it was a lucrative spot for a governor. (Legally the governor received one third from the sale of all goods declared contraband.) Beyond this, no one knew much about Bernard, and as usual it was Jemmy's job to make friends. Accordingly, he went to Bernard and told of Shirley's and Pownall's promises, asking not that his father be made Chief Justice but only that he be appointed in the place of Benjamin Lynde, Jr., the first surviving judge who would be expected to move up the line. Then Jemmy called on Thomas Hutchinson, with whom he was still on good terms, superficially at least, and who as lieutenant governor was closest to Bernard. "Before the Chief Justice was buried," Thomas Hutchinson said, "Mr. Otis came to me with a letter from his father desiring me to use my influence with the governor."

Bernard had many callers. Peter Oliver pointed out later that while Colonel Otis had wide influence, it was largely with country jurors — "drovers, horse jockies & other lower classes in life." Two of the surviving judges said that integrity was essential in the Superior Court and they did not want Otis on the bench. Besides, the other judges with one exception were Harvard graduates and Otis would not be suitable. Jeremiah Gridley, the leading lawyer in Boston, urged that Hutchinson be appointed the new Chief Justice.

"Mr. Otis, the son, declared that neither he nor his father would give up pretensions to *anyone,*" Hutchinson reported.

Especially, Jemmy would have added, to Hutchinson, who had no more legal training than the Colonel (and less legal experience) and who, if he accepted, would have high positions in both the legislative and judicial branches of the government, which was certainly improper.

As the month went on, Jemmy became louder and angrier. It was intolerable to him that his father, disappointed twice about the Council, would have to give up a lifetime ambition because he, James, Jr., whose responsibility it was to manage the appointment, had failed in his mission. If Hutchinson took the job, Jemmy swore he would be revenged. He "would set the Province in flames," he cried, "if he perished in the fire."

In November, Thomas Hutchinson, restive after three comparatively inactive years as lieutenant governor, accepted the appointment as Chief Justice, warning Bernard, however, that there would be trouble from the Otises. No one who heard Jemmy make his threats ever forgot them. From time to time in the next decade as the province smoldered, people would remember and point at Jemmy. "From so small a spark," Hutchinson said, "a great fire seems to have been kindled."

Yet the fact was that the fire was being laid when Bernard took office and James Otis was simply thrown on center stage where his own conflicts became hopelessly entangled with the conflicts of the province at large. This was a new era, now that the French and Indian War was at an end — "a new scene," as Thomas Hutchinson phrased it, which (although Americans did not know it yet) already had a new director. George II had died in October and had been succeeded by his grandson, twenty-two-year-old George III. A newspaper account of the event arrived in Boston on December 27 and although Thomas Hutchinson, a stickler for the letter of the law, thought the province should wait for an official notice before acknowledging the new king, George III was proclaimed king by the government of Massachusetts on December 30, 1760. On the same day, Thomas Hutchinson took office as Chief Justice of the Superior Court.

Act One

IV

IT WAS almost immediately apparent that there would be no going back to the "good old days before the French and Indian War," no sitting easy under vines. The last battlefield had scarcely been cleared before rumors began drifting across the Atlantic that England was going to tighten its rein on the colonies. America was growing at a rate dangerous to British interest, a British customs authority reported. The power of the assemblies would have to be reduced. The king should pay the governor's salary and appoint his own council. Taxes — yes, taxes too were hinted at although England knew how jealously the colonies guarded the right to control their money. Even as good a friend as Thomas Pownall admitted that practices had grown up in the colonies that would make it hard in the future for England to keep control. "Rumors were everywhere spread," John Adams said, "that the English would now newmodel the colonies."

Even the rumors were hard to bear. America was feeling big after the war — tasting success, exulting in her strength, reaching out, ready to go ahead — and was as sensitive as an adolescent to the "no" words that England was bandying about so freely: *restraint, restriction, enforcement, abridgment.* Some of the words were already being applied in Boston. *Subjection* was one. In his opening speech as governor, Francis Bernard, with the tactlessness that was to mark his career in America, reminded the legislature of the blessings they derived from their subjection to England. When the Council bristled and acknowledged their *relation* to the mother country, they were not, as Thomas Hutchinson implied, being merely perverse; they were, consciously or not, selecting the words they would stand by and those they would reject once and for all.

Enforcement was another word that Massachusetts challenged, especially as it applied to the duty on West Indian molasses. Up to this time merchants had skated around the word rather successfully, evading, eluding, dissembling, and bribing customs officials, but it was soon evident that they would have to meet the word head-on. The customs officers, in order to carry out their new, more stringent instructions, were going to resort to writs of assistance, general search warrants which would enable them to enter any house or ship, to break down doors and open trunks or boxes as they looked for smuggled goods.

Such was the mood of "the new scene." The first action began one cold February day in 1761 in the Council chamber of the Town House where the five judges of the Superior Court were seated with Thomas Hutchinson in their midst. The judges were impressive in new scarlet robes adopted for the occasion, large cambric bands, and oversized judicial wigs. Behind them and towering over them were two full-length, larger-than-life portraits of James II and Charles II in complete royal regalia. These were another innovation. Soon after his arrival in the province, Governor Bernard had unearthed the portraits from a storage room where Governor Pownall had put them in deference to the provincial distaste for Stuart kings. There was, however, no such delicacy in Francis Bernard's make-up. He had the portraits cleaned, framed in gold, and hung in the Council chamber — a deliberate reminder of the glory and power of the British Empire, a reminder which would at no time be more important than it was on this day.

Today the legality of the writs of assistance was being tested. Taking advantage of the fact that the old writs had expired with the death of George II, a group of merchants had signed a petition claiming that the Massachusetts courts did not have the power of the Court of Exchequer, which handled writs in England, and therefore could not legally grant writs to the customs officers who had applied for them. But in effect the merchants were saying two things: first, that they would not tolerate an arbitrary invasion of private property, and second, that they would not and could not comply with the Molasses Act of 1733. They had given up trying to convince the Board of Trade in England that sixpence duty on every gallon of molasses was prohibitive. A penny or a halfpenny was the most they could afford but the Board of Trade was immovable. They knew that molasses was essential to the New England economy, but they never seemed able to grasp the fact that every penny made in the colonies was spent on goods in England and if New England merchants were put out of business, England would suffer accordingly.

The people of Massachusetts had devious means of getting their way. Indeed, if Governor Bernard had assembled his props and his portraits for the writs trial in an effort to intimidate the merchants, he was only using their own tactics; the merchants were masters at intimidation. Today they sat in the Council chamber, sixty-three merchants who had signed the petition — some of the most prominent men in Boston, who, if they did not control the assembly, had at least a mighty influence in it. And, of course, as everyone knew, the assembly paid the judges their salaries. The trial was a warning, but the fact that it turned out also to be a landmark in Massachusetts history was due entirely to the counsel for the merchants, the younger James Otis, who that day began his short, tortuous career as a hero of the people.

James Otis talked steadily for four hours. He had given up his post in the Admiralty Court in order to take this case; he had waited through the lengthy arguments of the other two counselors: Jeremiah Gridley, who spoke for the crown — a "lordly man," according to John Adams, "with a majestic manner"; and Oxenbridge Thatcher, who along with Otis represented the merchants and who might at times seem "queer and affected" to John Adams yet was admired for his staunch patriotism and his "musical eloquence." Today these two were surely at their lordly and musical best. Gridley

talked long and learnedly about the statutes of the twelfth and four-
teenth of Charles II, the sixth of Anne, the seventh and eighth of
William III, and Thatcher responded with equal learning. But at
two o'clock in the afternoon, when they were done, the basic question at the root of all the argument still lay unanswered or at least
not answered to the satisfaction of the merchants: Could Massachusetts refuse the writs of assistance without denying the sovereign
power of Parliament?

James Otis, Jr., stood up. A huge, powerful, intense man, he
faced the new Chief Justice, Thomas Hutchinson; he faced Charles
II and James II in their gold frames and he began:

"This writ is against the fundamental principles of English law."

It was as if all his life James Otis had been waiting for this issue,
as if he had been storing up his own passionate need for freedom in
order to release it at this moment, as if he had been saving all John
Locke's self-evident truths, all his natural rights, for this very argument.

"I oppose the kind of power," he cried, "the exercise of which, in
former periods of English history, cost one king of England his head,
and another his throne . . . The freedom of one's house is an essential branch of English liberty. A man's house is his castle; and
while he is quiet, he is as well guarded as his prince."

When he talked about liberty James Otis, who had been said to
look like George Whitefield, even sounded like him and, like many
Americans for whom the effects of the revival had long since worn
off, he would find that the quest for liberty could be as soul-shaking
as the quest for the kingdom of heaven and that a flesh-and-blood
tyrant could be as formidable an adversary as the devil himself.

"Let the consequences be what they will," he thundered, "I am
determined to proceed, and to the call of my country am ready to
sacrifice estate, ease, health, applause, and even life." As for Jeremiah Gridley's statutes, they were, he said, "enacted in the zenith of
arbitrary power," and of course for Americans anything arbitrary
was automatically damned. English liberty, James Otis contended,

was ultimately based on a grand and unwritten superstructure of reason and on a constitution, both of which were against this writ.

"Even if the writ could be elsewhere found," he said, "it would be illegal. No act of Parliament can establish such a writ. Though it should be made in the very words of the petition, it would be void; for every act against the constitution is void."

Here was the answer the merchants had been waiting for. It was, moreover, a direct refutation to what Governor Bernard had said only the month before: "Every act repugnant to an act of parliament extending to the plantations, is *ipso facto* null and void." The people's only security in the past had been tied up in their charter, a document almost as precious to the province as the Bible itself, but limited in scope and far from inviolable. It had been taken away once and even now, according to the persistent rumors, was being threatened. But here was James Otis saying that over and above charter rights the people had natural rights and constitutional rights, even if unwritten, and when Parliament denied these, Parliament was wrong. Although most of the people were well acquainted with John Locke's principles, they had never heard them applied officially and in such a practical way to their own specific needs. Nor had they since the early days of George Whitefield been exposed to such flaming oratory. It was a heady experience.

And it was an experience from which the two central figures James Otis and Thomas Hutchinson would emerge, whether they liked it or not or whether they even recognized it, cast by the public in new roles. James Otis, suddenly the center of adulation, of course liked it. Not until much later did he realize that his freedom might be jeopardized by the rigid part he was expected to play. Thomas Hutchinson, on the other hand, had no idea of the role he was stepping into.

For three days Hutchinson sat through the writs trial in his scarlet robe and white wig, occupying the chair that he knew James Otis thought belonged to his father and attributing all the young man's fiery opposition to his desire for revenge. He was partly right.

James Otis, Jr., was not a forgiving man, but at the same time Hutchinson underestimated, as he did again and again, the real thrust of the colonies toward autonomy. He assumed that all reasonable men, although they might be diverted by a firebrand like Otis, would in the long run think as Hutchinson himself did. He could not conceive that he could be wrong, not because he had a glorified picture of himself but simply because he had a neat, mathematical mind. Once he accepted a basic assumption, it became a fixed and elementary principle that must, he felt, appear as obvious to every thinking man as it did to him. Thomas Hutchinson's basic principle was that one served his province best when he obeyed his king first. Unpopular he might be as a result, but not wrong. Nor could he possibly be considered any less dedicated to the province. His deep devotion to Massachusetts seemed so self-evident, he should never, he felt, be required even to vouch for it.

He was not, however, above passing a problem on to someone else if he could do so with a clear conscience. At the end of the writs trial, his decision, with the concurrence of the other judges, was to refer the case to England. Everyone knew, of course, that England would support the writs and so it did. The word came back nine months later, but Thomas Hutchinson was the one who was held responsible.

Of the three men prominent in this cast of characters — John Adams, Samuel Adams, and John Hancock — only John Adams was present at the writs trial. He was twenty-six years old now, wearing the black gown of a barrister for the first time and eager to get ahead in the world. In the last month he had written two essays obviously meant for newspapers but not completed or not completed to his satisfaction for they were not published. In the first, a discourse on the evils of licentious houses, he assumed the pose of an elder statesman. "I am an old Man," he began, "seventy odd . . ." In the second, he represented himself as a wise uncle offering advice to his nieces on manners, morals, and love. Love was on John Adams' mind. He might chide himself for his weakness but he was not averse to gallanting the girls and he admitted he did not "wholly disapprove of Bundling."

At the same time as Adams was making these literary experiments, he was writing to Peter Chardin, a young lawyer whom he admired because his thoughts were "not employed on Songs and Girls, nor his Time, on flutes, fiddles, Concerts and Card Tables." Adams proposed that these two, like Tully and Atticus, exchange observations on court cases they attended — in secret, of course, lest they be thought silly, lest anyone say that, far from Tully and Atticus, the correspondence was that of a "Pigs turd to a Pine Apple." Perhaps it was this prospective correspondence that prompted John Adams to take with him to the writs trial a bottle of ink, his pen, and paper.

But he did not use his pen and ink as much as he had intended. "I was much more attentive to the Information and Eloquence of the Speakers," he recalled later, "than to my minutes, and too much allarmed at the prospect that was opened before me . . . The Views of the English Government towards the Collonies and the Views of the Collonies towards the English Government . . . were now by the imprudence of Administration, brought to a Collision." It was a chilling vision. England, he saw, "would never give up its pretensions. The Americans devoutly attached to their Liberties, would never submit . . . A Contest appeared to me to be opened, to which I could foresee no End, and which would render my Life a Burden . . . There was no Alternative left, but to take the Side, which appeared to be just, to march intrepidly forward." And so when John Adams left the writs trial, he too had a new role, a self-imposed one as yet but one which he accurately foresaw as having no end.

John Hancock would surely have been at the writs trial, sitting with the merchants who had signed the petition, had he been in the country at the time, but he was in England, learning the English end of his uncle's business. In August Thomas Hancock had lent John his pocket watch; he had filled him with advice and walked down the long wharf with him to say good-bye. John had sailed on the same ship with the Hancocks' good friend Thomas Pownall and had arrived in London just a few weeks before George II died and the city went into mourning — a dull time, John wrote home. "All Plays are stopped, and no diversions are going forward; [so] that I am at a loss to know how to dispose of myself."

Uncle Thomas was at no loss in telling John what to do. "Be frugal of expenses," he wrote, "do honor to your country, and furnish your mind with all wise improvements." As an afterthought he added: "Keep the pickpockets from my watch."

For John Hancock, who had always been a fashion leader, frugality was the hardest admonition to obey. In his Harvard days he had been famous for his handsome scarlet coat and he could scarcely be expected not to indulge himself in London. But the word got back home and provoked Uncle Thomas to repeat his injunctions.

John's reply, written in January, arrived during the writs trial. "You mention a circumstance in regard to my dress," he said. "I hope it does not arise from your hearing I was too extravagant that way." Still, John did not know exactly what his uncle had heard so he had to be careful. "At the same time," he admitted, "I am not remarkable for the plainness of my dress. Upon proper occasions I dress as genteel as anyone and can't say I am without lace." He summed up his lifelong problem neatly: "I find money, some way or other, goes very fast." At the time of the writs trial John Hancock was faraway indeed.

The only reason that Samuel Adams was not at the trial was because he was neither a member of the bar nor a merchant petitioner and the general public was not admitted. He was in the wings, however, waiting for James Otis. He had waited out a long war for such a day and such a man and he was eager to get back to his crusade. The same evils, after all, that had been rife in the Land Bank days were not only still present but flourishing: England was even more imperious than it had been, Thomas Hutchinson was more powerful, and the good old New England virtues of the early settlers were as remote as ever.

Samuel Adams might appear an unlikely person to take on the reformation of a province. Not only did he not look the part in his careless dress, his record since leaving college was hardly one to inspire confidence. Absorbed in politics, he had shown little interest in making a living; he had failed in business, mismanaged his father's estate, and was working now (rather indifferently, it seemed) as a tax collector. He was, however, a born reformer and, while it was not obvious what he was doing, he was at the moment deeply involved backstage. To the casual observer Samuel Adams looked like the inveterate loafer he was said to be, walking around Boston with his Newfoundland dog, Queue, never too busy for a word here, a word there, a visit to a tavern, a chat on the docks. His words, however, were well chosen. Day and night Samuel Adams on his rounds was fanning dissatisfaction, sympathizing with hardships, pointing out dangers, reviving grudges, sharpening dislikes, planting fears, interpreting events, deploring the times, building up egos, preaching natural rights: in short, he was orchestrating the emotions of the city in preparation for revolution — softly, subtly, patiently, and cunningly. "To my certain knowledge," John Adams said, "he made it his constant rule to watch the rise of every brilliant genius . . . to court his friendship, to cultivate his natural feelings in favor of his native country, to warn him against the hostile designs of Great Britain." There had never, of course, been as brilliant a genius as James Otis, Jr. When he walked out of the Council chamber at the end of the writs trial, Samuel Adams knew he had a star.

Three months later James Otis, Jr., was elected a representative from Boston to the General Court. In Plymouth Mercy Warren basked in the glory reflected from her brother. An avid reader of history, she had always had a tendency to think of provincial politics in literary terms. Though it was admittedly an insignificant chapter in the story of the world, once Jemmy became a hero, Mercy's version of Massachusetts history blossomed. She was now on the stage where all past freedom-loving civilizations were seeking vindication, where all future freedom-loving generations were being born. For Mercy, enamored of the classical period as were all eighteenth-century intellectuals, Massachusetts became the new Rome. Samuel Adams had long ago likened the purity of seventeenth-century ideals in Massachusetts to that of the early Roman Empire and it seemed to Mercy that the province was even now reenacting Roman history, but she hoped toward a happier conclusion. Massachusetts, in resisting British corruption, Mercy reasoned, was in reality saving the British Empire and Jemmy Otis was saving Massachusetts. In a few years Mercy would be casting Jemmy as Brutus in her new Rome and Thomas Hutchinson would, of course, become Julius Caesar.

Meanwhile, however, there were other names for Jemmy. His own party often referred to him as Furio; Thomas Hutchinson and his friends called him James Bluster, Esq., or The Grand Incendiary, and when James was elected to the assembly, one of these friends predicted: "Out of this election will arise a damned faction, which will shake this province to its foundation." And indeed no sooner had Jemmy taken his seat than he began hitting out in all directions, most particularly in the direction of Thomas Hutchinson. He attacked Hutchinson for holding office in both the legislative and judicial branches of government; he led the assembly in a move that reduced the salaries of the justices of the Superior Court; he tried to have the justices excluded from meetings of the General Court; he succeeded in getting the province agent, a friend of Hutchinson, dismissed; he opposed Hutchinson, the province's foremost financial expert, on a currency question. "I know it is the maxim of some," he sneered in the *Boston Gazette,* "that the common people in this town and country live too well; however . . . I do not think they live half well enough."

The province rang with James Otis' eloquence and logic and also with his sarcasm, extravagances, and crudities; within the same paragraph he could be a philosopher, a gentleman, a savage, a savior, and a cutthroat. In Plymouth Mercy, eagerly reading every report from Boston, thrilled to Jemmy's eloquence, defended his extravagances, probably delighted in his sarcasm, but at the same time she was afraid for her brother. His erratic behavior, which had been harmless enough in private life, was amplified on the public stage. Abandoning himself to his new role, he displayed his great talents but also exposed his terrible weaknesses. His wife, Ruth, conservative and aristocratic, found his performance increasingly embarrassing; Colonel Otis, that astute politician who was in fact voting with Hutchinson more often than with Jemmy, grumbled at his son's lack of moderation. Jemmy was not supposed to be alienating the government; he was supposed to be capturing it. The theory was that the Otis faction would discredit the Hutchinson faction with the new governor and in turn win the governor's support, including his approval if and when Colonel Otis was ever elected to the Council.

The Colonel hoped to be elected in May 1762, the year following Jemmy's election to the assembly. In April he was in Boston on family business — buying salt for a herring expedition to Penobscot, writing Joseph to "Despatch the fishermen & whalemen as soon as Possible," and undoubtedly keeping a sharp eye on Jemmy. Recently he and Jemmy had worked together, persuading the assembly to grant Mount Desert Island in Maine to the governor as a gift from the province. It was a shrewd move and as a result Governor Bernard seemed well disposed toward the Otises, but before the election, the Colonel knew, Jemmy could in an impulsive and indiscreet moment say something that would destroy the good will so carefully nurtured.

While in Boston, the Colonel may have stayed with his youngest son, Samuel, who had opened a shop and was acting as agent for the family business — although at the moment he seemed more interested in girls than in trade. What made girls behave as they did? Samuel had apparently given the question considerable thought before he reported his findings to his brother Joseph. Curiosity, he said, was their prime motivation. "Curiosity makes them in love with all the lads they meet — their sweet mouths water to know all abt them; which when they have happily experienced, Curiosity sets them agigg after something else." Samuel, however, confessed to one curiosity of his own: "That is to see a young girls brains anatomized." But, after all, he concluded magnanimously, "They are the best bedfellows in the world, so God bless them."

While Samuel was speculating on girls' brains, James Warren was inventing a contraption for sowing seeds, which he eventually admitted did not run well. At the same time Mercy was approaching the end of her third pregnancy. On April 16, Colonel Otis wrote to Joseph: "I hear Sister Warren is Well a Bed with another Son." This son was Charles, born six weeks before the election in which his grandfather was running for the Council.

On May 30, Colonel Otis wrote to Joseph again. There was good news. "I had 112 votes for the Board [Council] the Largest number Perhaps that any Person that was new almost Ever had so I hope that Matter is now Settled to your Mind." What was more, Governor Bernard gave his approval, signifying (so Jemmy thought) an amenability to the Otises that was encouraging. With the Colonel now on the Council and Jemmy in the House, with the family business prospering (voyages to Penobscot for fish, Antigua for salt, the West Indies for molasses, the southern colonies for rice), the fortunes of the Otis family had never been higher; their future had never appeared more bright. Appropriately, Mrs. Otis was in Boston to share the moment of her husband's success, and, for the several months that the court was in session, she stayed with him, enjoying the social season as wife of the new Council member, mother of the celebrated James.

At this felicitous point in the family career, James and Mercy Warren had their portraits painted. John Singleton Copley, who was just coming into fashion as a portraitist of Boston society, represented the Warrens with a dignity and grace that must have pleased Mercy, sensitive as she was to the impression she made on others. James is the country gentleman in Copley's portrait; cane in hand, he looks as if he had just come in from a slow walk over his estate and approved what he saw. Mercy, who once spoke of her style of living as one of "decent elegance devoid of show," wears a rich blue satin gown with sleeves of point lace. She appears first and last the lady, which is as she herself would have wanted it and as her hands are posed so artfully to intimate, yet in the thirty-four-year-old Mercy Copley insinuates Mercy, the young girl, too — petite, plain, serious, lively, tense. One sees the girl in the erect (and somehow vulnerable) way she holds her neck and in her stance. Mercy is barely standing still; surely she will be off again in a moment, walking quickly, lightly, purposively, her skirts rustling. And there are suggestions of the elder Otises in the portrait as well: Mercy has their pride, their conviction, and like them, one feels, she faced life braced for trouble.

In this decade, the trouble as well as the glory centered on Jemmy, who could not, hard as he tried, play his father's quiet, crafty game of power politics and at the same time take the part of the hero to the common man in Samuel Adams' game of demagoguery — a part which temperamentally Jemmy found irresistible and which, moreover, allowed him to exercise his considerable gifts as orator and philosopher. But with his father safely on the Council, Jemmy let himself go.

The only instance of injustice or autocracy that he could find to exploit was by itself insignificant. Nevertheless, when Governor Bernard reported in September that over the summer he had authorized a ship to be outfitted and sent to guard fishing boats supposedly in danger from a French privateer, Jemmy raised the cry that the action was arbitrary. The total expense had been under one hundred pounds; the Council had concurred in the governor's action, which had been taken when the House was not in session and at the request of the fishing towns, but for James Otis, the constitution was threatened. "The most darling privilege" of the House, the right of originating taxes, had in effect been violated, he said, and forthwith he wrote *A Vindication of the Conduct of the House of Representatives*, in which he defined a concept of government based on the natural rights of the people. "Kings," he said, "were (and plantation Governor's should be) made for the good of the people, and not the people for them." He claimed that the House of Representatives had the same relationship with the governor as the House of Commons had with the king and if anyone levied taxes without the consent of Parliament, he would be a tyrant. Jemmy, moreover, had specific words for Bernard. The governor should "take the advice of the general assembly" on all occasions if he wanted to succeed and renounce that of the "half a dozen or half a score" men opposed to the best interests of the province — meaning of course the Hutchinson clique. As for himself, Jemmy said (with more significance than perhaps he realized), he had never opposed the governor in anything "but what he would have opposed his own Father in."

The general principles of the *Vindication* were received enthusiastically by the province, remembered diligently, and in the next fifteen years put to use again and again in Massachusetts' contest with British authority. At a later date John Adams claimed that neither the Declaration of Independence nor any of Thomas Paine's writings said anything that James Otis, Jr., had not already said in his *Vindication*. Still, there were some even in the popular party and especially in the fishing towns who said that Otis was running wild again. The governor's action had not merited such a storm. As for the governor, he was not a man, it turned out, who could be bullied into making an alliance or taking advice. If Jemmy was disappointed that he did not make "a convert of the governor," he should not have been surprised. In October he admitted in a letter to the London agent: "We are now convinced that he [the governor] is gone."

The governor, who had tried to keep peace with all parties, quite understandably decided that it was not possible to work with young James Otis. His turn toward the Hutchinson party, however, was only one facet in the changing structure of Massachusetts politics. Under the pressure of threatening rumors from England, abetted by that master of propaganda, Samuel Adams, the people were gradually regrouping themselves according to issues, and just as in England, where the same liberal-conservative struggle was taking place, the names of Whig and Tory were being revived from the days of the Glorious Revolution. But Colonel Otis, concerned as he might be about issues, was neither a reformer nor a theorist; he was simply an old-time politician, a compromiser who realized the dangers of letting "the zeal pot boil over," as he was so fond of saying. He had climbed the political ladder carefully — exchanging favors, making deals, cultivating friends — and now, just as he had reached an upper rung, here was his son shaking the ladder. The Colonel could only have found it hard to have Jemmy lash out as he did while he himself was trying to consolidate his position with the Council and the governor. But it was equally hard on Jemmy. Every time he let himself go as spokesman for Samuel Adams' party, he found he was imperiling the career of his father. No matter how they disagreed, the two Otises could never be disassociated in the public mind. The father was like the son, the people said, only not as outspoken.

Colonel Otis was not the kind of man who would have submitted to being a martyr to any cause quietly, not even Jemmy's. Whatever scenes took place backstage must have contributed to Jemmy's mounting distress and accounted for his sudden reversals. In January 1763, obviously trying to make amends with his father, Jemmy convinced Hutchinson that he was, after all, "a clever fellow" and "on the right scent now," but in February he turned again, raving so violently that the Colonel went to Hutchinson and apologized for his son's behavior. Jemmy was now attacking not only Hutchinson and Bernard but also customs house officers, gentlemen of the army, and on one occasion the bar itself, when, according to John Adams, it was proposing some "unexceptionable Regulations" to systemize its procedure.

"With a whiff of Otis' pestilential Breath," John said, "was the whole system blown away . . . Such Tergiversation, such Trimming, such Behaviour."

A month later Samuel Otis wrote Joseph that Jemmy had been "attacked the other day by some *Yanky* officers but they dare not strike him tho they threaten'd it as had they done it it would have caused them a drubbing from the people of the town."

Indeed, Jemmy Otis' conduct was so outrageous that people in both England and America were calling him mad, but this was, Jemmy contended, only another effort "to ruin his reputation and deprive his wife and children of their daily bread" and to get, he added, "the guardianship of his person."

"I am not mad," he ranted in the *Boston Gazette,* "but speak the words of truth and when I have cleared the stage of the little dirty rubbish . . . it will be found that I can also speak those of soberness."

Desperately Jemmy asked, not only in private but in public:

What can a virtuous man do? If he Pities the People and Calamities, he shall be called Seditious; if he recommends any public Good, he shall be called Preaching Fool; if he should live soberly and virtuously himself, they will think him fit only to be sent to a Cloister; if he does not flatter the Prince and Superiors, *he will be thought to envy their prosperity; if he presumes to advise his Prince to pursue his true interest, he will be esteemed a formidable Enemy to the whole Court who will unite to destroy him.*

Samuel Otis was, perhaps, the only one in the family who did not get exercised by Jemmy's theatrics. In the midst of all the fireworks he advised Joseph to "act as the Dutchmen have done all the War — look on and laugh, however if it comes to loggerheads," he said, "I shall by all means stand by Esq. Bluster as he is an excellent fellow and ought not to be forsaken."

Not even Samuel, however, would have found it easy to look on and laugh when the results of the annual election were announced several months later. Hutchinson and Bernard's party, strengthened by their coalition, won a dramatic victory and set about immediately to put young James Otis in his place. They dismissed the House chaplain because he was supposed to be a friend of Otis'; they refused to let the publishers of the *Boston Gazette* print the House journal because James Otis' slanders had appeared in their paper;

most devastating of all, they tried to remove Colonel Otis from the Council and, indeed, might have succeeded, had not the Colonel's good friend Harrison Gray, treasurer of the province, come to his rescue.

As always, Jemmy found the pain he brought to his friends, and especially his father, unendurable. He was not, he wrote once with a gibe at Hutchinson, one of those men whose motto was "I am sure I am right." On the contrary, as soon as he saw he had caused grief, he was sure he was wrong. He would often say at these times that he did not know the wickedness of his own heart and then try to undo the damage he had done, invariably going too far in the process. And so after his father's seat on the Council had been threatened by Bernard, Jemmy in a fit of remorse made a speech resigning from the House. The next day he was back. He asked to be reseated. When the request had been rather reluctantly granted, he announced that he had a motion to make. Then with a characteristic flash of wit, Jemmy proposed that Governor Bernard's salary be paid. The legislators, friends and enemies alike, roared with laughter. What could they do with a man like that? Infuriating as he was at times, at other times Jemmy Otis' warmth and humor were irresistible.

But if Jemmy found it difficult to thread his way emotionally through provincial politics, he found it doubly difficult when England appeared onstage. Boston was in the midst of a smallbox epidemic and the General Court was sitting in Cambridge when word arrived that within a few months Parliament would surely pass a program of colonial taxation. George Grenville, the new prime minister (a financial expert, a pedant, and a notorious bore), would propose it; Parliament, wrestling with war debts and mounting colonial expenses, would accept it; and the king would approve it. And so it happened. In March 1764, Parliament passed the Sugar Act, which the colonies resented not simply because of its taxes (on coffee, indigo, wine, calico, linen, sugar, molasses, and other West Indian products) but most especially because it was a tax designed to raise revenue rather than simply to control trade. Moreover, the Sugar Act was accompanied by the announcement that a Stamp Act would follow the next year with duties on newspapers, almanacs, pamphlets, and all legal documents. This would be the first direct tax on the colonies — the first step to slavery, Americans claimed, for if people could not control their own pocketbooks, what freedom was there? "O, poor New England," George Whitefield moaned. "Your golden days are at an end."

When they heard the official news, Thomas Hutchinson and Jemmy Otis both went to their desks. Thomas Hutchinson, acting in characteristic fashion, wrote a letter to the province's agent about the proposed measure but asked that his name be kept secret. In his quiet, reasonable way, he marshaled his arguments against taxation but he did not want to be publicly represented as opposing an act of Parliament. In his position, he felt, it would not be fitting nor was it necessary. The people of Massachusetts, understanding his love for the province, would know he was against taxation in any case. And why should he unduly antagonize British authority when he could remain anonymous?

Jemmy Otis, who had spent his life trying to satisfy his desperate need to be loyal and his equally desperate need to be free, found himself now even more thoroughly entangled in his conflict. In his *Rights of the British Colonies Asserted and Proved,* he attempted to show that although Parliament was supreme, its power was yet circumscribed. Parliament could not tax unrepresented people, he wrote, any more than it could "make 2 and 2, 5; omnipotency cannot do it." This was the same kind of brave talk he had used in the writs trial, but now Parliament actually was adding two and two, and so Jemmy tried to excuse Parliament. It had been misled, he said; it had made a mistake and he had every confidence that the mistake would be corrected. Meanwhile it was the duty of the people to submit to whatever burdens Parliament pleased to impose. Jemmy was not unique in trying to reconcile these two opposing concepts: all over the colonies men were struggling with the same problem. Indeed, Mercy Warren wrote, "Independence was a plant of a later growth," and Jemmy kept protesting that British America would never be undutiful unless driven to it. Rebellion, he said (prophetically, as it turned out), would be a last resort, so dreadful even to contemplate that it would make "the wisest mad." At the moment he and Thomas Hutchinson were in rather close agreement. Although Jemmy, as always, showed his heart to the world and Hutchinson expressed himself prudently and privately, both admitted that once Parliament acted, there was nothing to do but obey.

But there were many other things to do, as it turned out. Merchants in Massachusetts signed an agreement refusing to import goods from England. Manufacturing was encouraged in the colonies. Shoes made in Lynn were "much easier," the *Boston Gazette* contended, than those made in London; cheese from the town of Weymouth was just as good as cheese from Gloucester, England. Secret organizations, the Sons of Liberty, sprouted up in the colonies as the time for the Stamp Act approached; liberty poles were erected, liberty trees consecrated. In Plymouth, James Warren was moderator of a meeting that instructed its representatives to resist the stamp tax. "This place, sir," the instructions read, "was at first the asylum of liberty and we hope will ever be preserved sacred to it."

Meanwhile, Thomas Hutchinson became more prudent and James Otis, Jr., more flamboyant. It was inevitable that the moderation in his *Rights of the British Colonies,* based as it had to be on ambiguous reasoning, would eventually break down, and it was not surprising that Jemmy flew to extremes when his *Rights* was criticized. From both sides of the Atlantic the criticism came: Otis was disloyal, it was reported in London; in New England Martin Howard, Jr., a defender of English policy, not only accused Otis of disloyalty but of inciting others to disloyalty.

Disloyal? Jemmy could no more bear to be charged with disloyalty to the parent state than he could bear to be charged with disloyalty to a parent. He had said that Parliament was supreme and now he rushed to his desk to say so again but in more extravagant, more abject terms. First came his *Vindication of the British Colonies*, then his *Brief Remarks on the Defence of the Halifax Libel*, in which he displayed what Governor Bernard called his "sackcloth and ashes attitude" and asked pardon "for the least iota that may have displeased his superiors." At the same time, he lashed out at Martin Howard, Jr., and his cohorts: "a little, dirty, drinking, drabbing, contaminated knot of thieves, beggars, and transports." James, Jr., wrote in high heat, angry not only at being accused of infidelity but at having his logic questioned by a man who, he said, had no head for argument. "It requires something more than a musical genius, or a catcher of butterflies, to reason clearly and conclusively on the origin and principles of government," James said, and lest he be misunderstood, he explicitly declared his belief in the "undoubted power and authority of Great Britain to tax her colonies" and maintained that representation of the colonies in Parliament was not a right that he had demanded but only an indulgence he had, with all humility, sought.

As a result of this cringing, bullying, and retracting, James Otis, Jr., was now, quite naturally, called disloyal not only by the prerogative side but also by his friends. "The rage against him," John Adams reported, "seemd without bounds." He was called a "reprobate, an apostate, and a traitor in every street in Boston." When his *Brief Remarks* was announced in the *Boston Gazette*, the editor added a note: "The gentleman . . . will be busy some time in drawing a piece he intends to call '*Tother Side of the Question*, another to be called *Both Sides of the Question* without any fee or ambidextral Reward." He was accused of having sold out to Hutchinson and Bernard and would most certainly have lost his seat in the House in the spring of 1765, had not an anonymous verse, "Jemmibullero," appeared in the *Boston Evening Post*, the prerogative paper, just prior to the election. One part ran as follows:

> *As Jemmy is an envious dog, and*
> *Jemmy is ambitious,*

And rage and slander, spite and
        dirt to Jemmy are delicious,
So Jemmy rail'd at upper folks
        while Jemmy's DAD was out,
But Jemmy's DAD has now a place
        so Jemmy's turn'd about.

Later this was thought to be the work of an angry customhouse officer, but in any case the Whig party could not claim that Jemmy had defected to the other side if the other side was attacking him. Moreover, Jemmy was now defending himself and reversing his position once more. He had always been true to his constituents, he insisted, but "the little chit chat of the coffee house and the jest cracked meerly for the pleasure of cracking it have been most gravely . . . magnified and worked up into infidility, treason, and rebellion." And in a dramatic appearance at a town meeting, he offered to take on George Grenville in single combat. Fortunately, he also had more productive ideas. He was making plans (reputedly at the Warrens' house in Plymouth) for an intercolonial congress to protest the Stamp Act. This congress actually convened the following October with James Otis, Jr., attending as a representative from Massachusetts. "Otis is now a quite different man," a New York delegate reported, "not riotous at all."

In Mercy's eyes, Jemmy was ever the hero, "his integrity unimpeached, his honor unblemished," and when he was vilified, she elevated him to martyrdom. She would hardly, in any case, have expected better treatment from the public. She had lived long enough with her father and close enough to the political arena to observe at first hand the capriciousness of popular opinion. As a result, there was a streak of bitterness in Mercy which was reinforced as she watched the painful career of her brother. Throughout her life she repeatedly remarked on the ingratitude of the public and the fickleness of human nature. "I should not be surprised," she once wrote her husband, "to see the most distinguished defenders of the rights of the people . . . become the objects of popular disgust without their ever departing from the paths of integrity . . . This opinion of mankind you have often heard me express."

Mercy did admit that Jemmy was "susceptible of quick feelings and warm passions" and that sometimes his "ebullitions of zeal . . . betrayed him into unguarded epithets," but beyond this she would not go in criticism. He was always the complete patriot. If he vacillated, he was simply stating his opinions fearlessly; if he leaned too far toward the British side, he was only trying to be a moderating influence. And indeed James Otis was so changeable, so many-sided, that there was truth to what Mercy said. It was one of the many paradoxes of this violent man's career that he could, in fact, be a moderating force at times. If in the early part of the decade he set himself to arouse the province, later (between sporadic outbursts) he set himself to pacify it. He dared not leave town, he told his sister in the spring of 1766, as he was needed to keep things from "running to some irregularity or imprudence." Moreover, he was effective. Not only James Warren claimed that the good conduct of Boston in one of its trying periods was due in great part to the "Singular Wisdom, Integrity, Intrepidity, & Goodness of my Friend and Brother," but John Dickinson of Pennsylvania, a patriot renowned throughout the colonies, also gave Jemmy credit for "composing the Minds" of his fellow citizens.

But although James Otis may have deplored violence, wittingly or not he prepared the way for one of Boston's worst riots. On the floor of the House of Representatives he contended that Hutchinson and Bernard had actually participated in forming the Stamp Act; he claimed that he could point to the room where the project had been conceived. At the same time Samuel Adams spread similar stories about town, and the Sons of Liberty, led by what was known as the Loyal Nine (a group of local artisans), made plans to insure that no stamps would be distributed.

The summer of 1765 was hot and dry. On the surface life went on as usual in Boston: Samuel Otis advertised that he had cod and mackerel hooks as well as "ticklingburgs" and "oznabrigs" for sale; James Otis, Jr., and his wife partied on one occasion at the famous Coffee House and on another at the Turk's Head where they dined on "barbikue." Thomas Hutchinson went back and forth to Milton and snatched what time he could to work on the second volume of his history of Massachusetts (the first volume had come out earlier in the year).

On August 16, Samuel Otis wrote to Joseph: "As to News, there was a Mob Night before last which demolished the new erected Stamp office & drove the Stamp officer [Andrew Oliver] from his house to the Street."

What Samuel did not mention was that on the next night, August 15, the same mob went to Hutchinson's house. Perhaps Samuel did not consider that this was news since no violence was committed. The people wanted only to hear Thomas Hutchinson talk. They had much to hold against him; only the night before he had brought the sheriff and tried to break up their activity, but still, Thomas Hutchinson was in spite of everything one of their own. He had been born and bred among them. Could he really have endorsed the Stamp Act? The people called to him from the street. They asked him to come to the balcony and tell them, once and for all, that he had never written to England to support the act.

But Thomas Hutchinson stayed behind the windows and the doors he had barred. "This was an indignity," he said later, "to which he would not submit; and, therefore, he made no answer." A neighbor dispersed the mob by telling them Hutchinson had gone to Milton and, indeed, he did go as soon as it was safe.

On August 26, Hutchinson drove back to the city. He had been told by his friends that the mob wanted nothing more of him and that he had, in fact, "become rather popular." He would have believed this. It would have seemed eminently logical that the people, given time to reflect, would have realized that a man of stature could not put himself at the beck and call of a night mob. And so, reassured, Thomas Hutchinson, dressed informally for the hot weather in a thin camlet robe, sat down for supper with his children around him: Thomas, Jr., who was twenty-four now; Elisha, twenty-one; Sally, who at twenty had just become engaged to Peter Oliver; and the younger children — Billy, thirteen, and Peggy, eleven.

The Hutchinsons were at their meal when a neighbor ran in with the news that the mob was out again. Thomas Hutchinson prepared to do what he had done before. He sent his children to a neighbor's and began to shut up the house with the intention of staying inside, but Sally would not have it. She had gone with the others but now she ran back. She would not leave, she said, if her father did not go with her.

"I couldn't stand against this," Thomas Hutchinson said, and so he too left. It was just as well. This was not the same mob that had visited him previously. The Loyal Nine were neither sponsoring nor controlling this group, which came armed with axes and warmed with liquor consumed along the way.

While Thomas Hutchinson ran through back yards in his camlet robe, the mob broke down his front door and poured into his house. "Some ran immediately as high as the top of the house, others filled the rooms below and cellars, and others remained without the house to be employed there." They cut up his fine Turkey rug, demolished his walnut and mahogany furniture as well as a "rich India cabinet very little used with 3 stands of wax-work in glasses," cut open his feather mattresses, stole all the clothing in the house (including his new suit with "french grey button holes wrought with gold"), scattered the manuscript of his history in the street, smashed his delft china and his blue and white tea set and "teapot with silver nose," destroyed his family portraits, carried off a cellarful of wine, broke the blade and hilt of his silver hilted sword, took the gold head off his cane, leveled every tree to the ground, and even tore off the wainscot and beat down the wall partitions. At four in the morning they were taking the slate from the roof. By that time, Hutchinson said, "one of the best finished houses in the Province had nothing remaining but the bare walls and floors."

Later in the morning, when the mob had dispersed, a neighbor gathered the sheets of the manuscript from the street and Thomas Hutchinson did what he would have done on any normal day. Court was in session and he went to court — "his look big with the greatest anxiety," one observer reported, "clothed in a manner which would have excited compassion from the hardest heart . . . with tears starting from his eyes." And reduced to such circumstances, Thomas Hutchinson finally said what the people had been asking him to say.

I call God to witness [he told the court] . . . I say, I call My Maker to witness — that I never, in New England or Old, in Great Britain or America, neither directly or indirectly was aiding, assisting, or supporting — in the least promoting or encouraging — what is commonly called the Stamp Act; but on the contrary, did all in my power, and strove as much as in me lay to prevent it . . . I pray God give us better hearts!

Even Samuel Adams was alarmed at the extent of the violence and made sure there were no more such outbreaks. When the Stamp Act officially took effect, the province, instead of erupting further, came to a standstill. The probate office was shut as well as the customs house and the courts — a situation that was endurable only because it was believed to be temporary.

In January Jemmy Otis wrote his father that he had been assured by an old acquaintance who had just arrived from England that "The Stamp Act will certainly be repealed . . . a good graceful retreat is all they want."

In May the word arrived on John Hancock's brig *Harrison* that the Stamp Act had indeed been repealed. "The Province was in a Rapture," John Adams wrote, but unfortunately he himself was out of sorts. His town had not recognized him at the election, his wife and baby had whooping cough, and, while the rest of the province was celebrating the repeal, he was riding circuit and not having any fun at all.

John had every reason to be grumpy about missing the festivity in Boston; it was a spectacular affair, starting off with bells ringing, guns firing, and drums beating at one o'clock on the morning of May 19 and working up in the evening to an elaborate pyrotechnical exhibit on the Common where a pyramid of lamps had been raised four stories high and where as a grand finale sixteen dozen firework serpents were set off simultaneously. John Hancock rolled a pipe of Madeira outside his front door facing the Common; James Otis, Jr., held open house all night; Governor Bernard entertained the Council and then he walked about on the Common, mingling with the crowds. From all accounts, John Adams must have been the only man in the country who by morning was not, as the saying went, "over the bay." One merchant drank fifteen toasts which were, he said, "suited to the Occasion." In Falmouth, Maine, a Harvard classmate of James Otis' gave a party and set before each man a glass and two bottles of Madeira. "Before the Bottles wher out," a guest reported, "we were, what you might call happy — for my part I Could hardly Stirr the next day and in fact have not got over it Yet."

In the overflowing of convivial spirits, the people of Massachusetts may have thought they could work together now and look forward to good times, but the Stamp Act had left its mark. Jemmy Otis' conflicts had been exacerbated. Thomas Hutchinson had been so deeply hurt that while, on the one hand, he would not move from the country ("Old trees don't thrive when transplanted," he said), on the other hand, he began looking to England for a firmer stand as the only solution to the colonial problem. And Francis Bernard, who had come to the province with the hope of establishing an administration with the people's support, had been like many a royal governor before him so demoralized that he could not take advantage of the spirit of reconciliation that prevailed. Instead, as the popular party swept into power, he embarked upon a course of wholesale negativing. First, he would not accept James Otis, Jr., as the speaker of the House; next, in retaliation for the fact that his friends (including Hutchinson) had been left out of the Council, he disallowed six new councilmen. Colonel Otis, who had never aligned himself consistently with any party, was among them.

The following year the Colonel was vetoed again. As always, he looked for the reason and, when he found it, he wrote to Joseph. It was Jemmy who was in his way. Bernard had told several members of the Council that "the father's principles and the son's principles were both alike, but the father was not so open."

"So . . . now," the Colonel concluded bitterly, "he [the governor] is become a searcher of hearts."

V

WHILE THE PEOPLE of Massachusetts abused Thomas Hutchinson, hung effigies, set off firecrackers, and talked politics, they had, of course, their private lives to lead as well. Regardless of what happened, John Rowe, the gentleman who drank fifteen toasts when the Stamp Act was repealed, would go fishing. He might miss church because his barber did not come to shave him or because his new shoes pinched, but only the outbreak of actual warfare in the province could keep him, spring and summer, from going to Salem for pickerel and perch, to Plymouth for trout.

And, politics or not, people had sometimes to contend with trouble beyond their own making. There was a summer, for instance, when it didn't rain enough in Massachusetts, a winter when not only the pumps in Boston but the harbor froze, a spring when the province was invaded by black caterpillars that marched from the northeast to the southwest, devouring everything in their path. An August rain one year fell on three hundred and fifty Sons of Liberty, dampening everything but their spirits as they picnicked in an open field in Dorchester; a high tide took off a meadow from the Otis farm. And in the middle of one green and leafy May, Plymouth was staggered by a full-fledged, twelve-hour-long snowstorm.

For Mercy Warren, the storm, like all extraordinary or violent displays of nature, would have seemed like a visitation of God, an all-powerful God who could both make a season and break it. On the occasion of another storm, Mercy, who had been writing poetry from time to time ever since she had been married, wrote a poem which she called: "Lines Written after a very severe Tempest which cleared up extremely pleasant."

> *When rolling thunders shake the skies*
> *And lightnings fly from pole to pole,*
> *When threatening whirlwinds rend the air,*
> *What terrors seize th' affrighted soul!*
>
> *Happy the calm and tranquil breast,*
> *That with a steady equal mind*
> *Can view those flying shafts of death*
> *With heart and will at once resigned!*

It is significant that Mercy wrote her lines after the tempest had cleared up "pleasant"; she could never have done it while the shafts were still flying. Unlike her brother Jemmy, who was stimulated by storms and said that when he died he would like to be struck by lightning, Mercy, although a strong-willed person, was also a fearful one, subject to many terrors which she tried to believe were due to the weakness of her sex rather than to the weakness of her faith. Mercy's God was no less demanding than her country, but while the one required resignation, the other required rebellion. So Mercy spent her life fiercely resisting tyranny in the temporal world and desperately struggling for sublimation in the spiritual one. "My Soul and body are ill suited for companions," she would say as she tried to talk herself into a tranquillity that was not native to her. When, for instance, after a death in the family she wrote in fashionably pious language that she desired "to adore the Hand that hath smitten" her, she was not just trying to impress her reader. Surely she was also attempting to convince herself and her God that she, who had such a strong will, had surrendered it — that she, who had such a faint heart, was unafraid. Such sublimation was particularly difficult in the presence of death and, of course, especially necessary, for every death was attended by the unspoken question: Will you be ready?

There were four deaths in Mercy's family in the 1760s. Her sister, Mary Gray, two years younger than Mercy, died one Saturday noon in 1763 "very suddenly," according to the newspaper; in 1767 Mercy's mother died in Boston during a December snowstorm. But perhaps most heartbreaking of all was the death of Abigail, or Nabby — twenty-eight years old, the youngest of Colonel Otis' children, the favorite aunt of little Charles Warren, and perhaps the fiancée of John Avery, leading member of Boston's Loyal Nine. In 1765 Nabby paid a prolonged visit to her brother Samuel and his new wife, Elizabeth (daughter of Harrison Gray), and in May Samuel wrote back to Barnstable:

"I think it proper to inform father & Mother & the famili that young John Avery is Courting Nabby. He has proposed matters to me but [I] referd him to father — He is a good lad in point of disposition, but know nothing of his Circumstances."

Ten months later Nabby died in Barnstable and in a few weeks she was followed by Rebecca, wife of Joseph Otis. "I am heartily grieved for brother and his children," Jemmy wrote Mercy. "Their loss can never be made up. I am more and more convinced of the vanity of things under the sun. Hope we shall all be prepared for a better state."

The immediate state of the small circle of Mercy and James Warren's own family, however, was quite satisfactory. James was now a representative from Plymouth to the General Court; Mercy, a week before her thirty-eighth birthday, gave birth to George, the last of her five sons. On the domestic level, these were happy times with much of Mercy's and James's attention and pleasure centering on the children: James, Jr., the oldest, serious and often melancholy; Winslow, the charmer who even at an early age showed a desire for the "pretty things" ("The trumpet satisfied his wishes and made him for a while Happy," his father once reported); Charles, perhaps the most compliant; gay Harry, later remembered for his social qualities and his gentlemanly deportment; and George, invariably described as grave and solemn. As they grew up, Mercy frequently protested to George, the jealous one, that she had no favorites, but no matter how she denied it, she could never quite hide the fact that Winslow, the most elusive, the most frivolous, the least likely by Puritan standards, was the most beloved — Winslow, who became the handsome, dashing, fashionable one, disposed to selfishness, affectionate and indifferent as it pleased him, dependent and independent as it suited. While her brother James was Mercy's hero, and her husband, James, her enduring comfort and her stay, Winslow was the one who could with the least effort make her the most happy. And it was for Winslow that Mercy shed the most tears, lost the most sleep, and made the most excuses.

In raising her children, Mercy had little use, she said, for "the Irksome Methods of Severity." Instead she put her faith, as one would expect her to, "in the Force of Reason" and the "obligations of Duty," which meant that Mercy talked a lot. Indeed, to prepare her sons for the world and to protect them against it, Mercy fed them words of advice, words of warning; she clothed them in words, armored them with words, and when they left home, she followed them with words. She was simultaneously friendly, dutiful, and worried and perhaps not too oppressive; this was what sons expected of parents in this talkative, moralizing century and this was what sons undoubtedly learned early, as they ever have, to resist. And in spite of the talk, Mercy and James created an informal and easy atmosphere in the home. The children looked forward to trips to Barnstable; at home they fished, gardened, read (the boys always liked books, Mercy said), followed the activity on the docks, hunted when they were old enough, were entertained and perhaps treated by their many visiting aunts and uncles. Moreover, the boys had Ann, the faithful and loving housekeeper who had come to Plymouth with Mercy when she was married and who shared now in the care of the family.

Mercy's own life, while centered on the children, was not bound by them. Like most of their friends in the coastal towns, Mercy and James were surprisingly mobile; leaving the boys in Ann's care, they frequently visited both in Boston and Barnstable, sometimes together when the occasion permitted, sometimes separately in which case there were always letters to bridge the space between them.

"The Days are so tedious," James wrote to Mercy in Barnstable, "& everything Appears so different without you."

Another time it was James who was away and Mercy who wrote: "My Dearest Friend — What, a Letter Every day! Yes. Why not. I wish for one, and why not forward one to a person who Loves them as well as myself?"

Friends were essential to Mercy's life. Returning from a trip to Boston, she could complain about the noisy city and laud the solitary pleasures, but when Mercy's life was at its best, it was far from solitary. In addition to the friends and relatives who were constantly stopping off at Plymouth, there was James's cousin, Penny Winslow, who would come up from her big house on the corner of North Street and keep Mercy company overnight when James was away. ("A Whig & a Tory Lodging in the same bed," Mercy laughingly reported to James.) And across the street was Ellen Lothrop, wife of a Plymouth doctor and Mercy's dearest friend. Scarcely a day passed when these two did not see each other. They would run back and forth, sharing the little fortunes and misfortunes of domestic life, sitting down by a fireside to talk, to sew together; it was a warm, unassuming, and gay companionship.

Mercy's most long-standing friend, however, was Hannah Winthrop, wife of the famous Harvard professor and sister of Jemmy's classmate Sam Fayerweather. Hannah lived in Cambridge and although she and Mercy visited from time to time, their friendship was for the most part pursued through a correspondence which they both enjoyed, surely not so much for what they said but for the way they inspired each other to new circumlocutions and embellishments of speech. They not only followed all the conventions of the "epistulary" style, they improved on them. Their husbands were their "ribs," their "other selves"; their children were their "olive branches," their "twigs," and Hannah in a burst of glory once referred to James Warren, Jr., as Mercy's "little loadstone," but still Hannah never felt that she was Mercy's equal.

"If you should find me sublime," Hannah wrote, "remember I catch it from you." It was one of her simpler sentences.

But of all the people that came to the Warrens' house during these years, no one was more welcome than John Adams and later his wife, Abigail. The friendship developed slowly while John Adams was riding circuit and visiting Plymouth, a town which at this time he heartily disliked.

"Tomorrow morning I embark for Plymouth," he wrote Abigail in 1764, "with a (fowl) disordered Stomach, a pale Face, an Aching Head and an Anxious Heart. And What Company Shall I find there? Why a Number of bawling Lawyers, drunken Squires, and impertinent and stingy Clients."

Nevertheless, in 1767 John Adams in a better humor and with evident enjoyment wrote that he had dined with the Warrens on a Sunday and attended church with them.

A few years later he told Abigail that "in Coll. Warren and his Lady I find Friends," and within a short time the Adamses and the Warrens were visiting back and forth and writing regularly. Indeed, the close relationship between these two couples became one of the most important parts of their lives. Nor was this surprising; they complemented each other in a rather rare way.

John Adams, warm and witty as he was, did not often give himself unreservedly to a friendship. "I have a dread of Contempt," he once wrote, "a quick sense of Neglect, a strong Desire of Distinction," all of which would, and often did, come between him and other people. He was forever suspecting that he appeared ridiculous. What he wanted to see, he said, when he looked in the mirror was the noble face of a Roman senator; what he did see was a short, plump, round-faced man who surely must make other men laugh. What could he do to make a good impression? When he consciously tried, he caught himself in affectations that even he found absurd. And when he was thirty-seven, he said of himself in disgust, "My boyish Habits and Airs are not yet worn off."

But with James Warren, John felt at ease. They shared the same political philosophy, the same religious outlook, the same enthusiasm for farming, but most important to a man like John Adams, who longed for distinction, James Warren was not competitive. Although James was deeply involved in politics, he had no political ambitions; he was primarily a simple man, not the kind that one would try to impress or outdo — the ideal friend for John Adams at this point in his life, just as John Adams with his utter honesty and his sharp insights was the ideal friend for the less imaginative James. Moreover, they were both at their best with intimate friends rather than with groups of people.

Between John and Mercy, there was also a special relationship. Both quick-witted, they bantered back and forth, teased, made bargains, and when they were all together in the Warrens' parlor, they "drew characters," as they called it: they described and did takeoffs on people they knew. But perhaps most satisfying for two people who thrived on praise, they loved to compliment each other.

"Madam," John Adams wrote, "I never attempt to write you but my Pen conscious of its Inferiority falls out of my Hand."

"You was not made," Mercy wrote John, "for the purpose of Resting in the cool sequestered shade of life. It is yours to tread the bold and craggy path of politics."

Abigail became a friend only after the other three had known each other for some years and her first letters showed a deference to Mercy both because Mercy was sixteen years older and because Mercy had achieved a reputation in the province as a lady of learning. There was always a rapport between these two and as they became more intimate, there was an obvious delight that they had found each other — two intellectual women with so much to talk about. They discussed education; Abigail wanted Mercy's sentiments and Mercy replied that in her opinion the first and most important principle to teach children was an "invariable Attachment to truth." They compared views on Molière. Abigail said she had tried to like him but couldn't. Satire apparently made her uncomfortable; Mercy, on the other hand, who liked nothing better than to expose vice as cuttingly as she could, pointed out that ridicule could reform. They shared domestic news: husbands who were away from home, children who were sick, sewing supplies to trade. And conforming to the fashion of the day, they gave each other classical names. Abigail became Portia; Mercy was Marcia, a name she liked so much that it became within the family almost an endearment.

"I could spare a yard of very good Irish Linnen," Marcia wrote Portia.

Portia needed "Garlick thread . . . If you should know of any, be so good as to let me know."

Politics, however, was their most absorbing interest, a subject generally considered inappropriate and improper for ladies to discuss, especially in mixed company. Even John Adams, who had a great respect for his wife's political judgment and enjoyed her "saucy" observations, expected her to save her comments until they were alone or at least alone with family or close friends. But between Mercy and Abigail there were no inhibitions and a letter was seldom sent off without, as Mercy said, "a little seasoning" of a political nature.

The political seasoning of their letters would become stronger and sharper as time went on, but in 1766, after the repeal of the stamp tax, Mercy and Abigail, like most people in Massachusetts, hoped for a respite from politics, a time when they might at last be able to retire under their vines. On the whole, they were rather optimistic about England. There was on the record, of course, the Declaratory Act, passed at the time of the repeal, which upheld Parliament's right to tax the colonies; but surely, the people reasoned, Parliament had learned a lesson and had passed the Declaratory Act only as a graceful way out of an embarrassing situation. The main stumbling block politically was within the province itself: Governor Francis Bernard. He was "still keeping up the same game," Colonel Otis reported, "constantly writing hom against the country and endeavouring by all ways to keep us uneasy."

He was, indeed, writing home. With the popular party in power,

Bernard said that he had no more influence than a doorkeeper nor would he have, he believed, until the government was reorganized. He had been saying this for years. In 1764, he had outlined ninety-seven specific recommendations for reorganizing the colonies, including one for establishing an independent upper house or Council which he proposed should be drawn from an American nobility appointed by the king for life. As long as the Council was elected by the House, he said, the government was "like an open pleasure Boat, fit only for calm Seas and favourable Gales." And since he had no talent for smoothing troubled waters, he could only toss and turn in the present situation, complain, scold, and oppose the local government, and at election time use what John Adams called his "mighty Negative."

It was in such an atmosphere that Charles Townshend, England's Chancellor of the Exchequer, decided to settle the affairs of the empire. "Champagne Charley" he was called because of his famous speech in the House of Commons when he had appeared half-drunk with a patch over one eye and for most of one night had entertained that august body with the wit, humor, charm, mimicry, and dramatics that he used so often and so well to entertain guests at his own table. Charles Townshend craved the center of the stage and it was almost as a performer, even as a sleight-of-hand artist, that in the early part of 1767 he turned his attention to America, a big problem for which, characteristically, he found a quick and easy solution: taxation. Inoffensive taxation, he claimed, because it would be "external," laid on glass, lead, paint, and tea, rather than "internal" like the stamp tax to which the colonists had objected. The tax, moreover, would resolve all those internal difficulties that Francis Bernard was forever complaining about. Part of the money raised by the tax would be used to pay the salaries of the governor and the judges and so make them free agents, independent of the people; part would be used to support a standing army in America which would be used, if the colonies were recalcitrant, to keep them in order. And then to make sure that the duties would be collected, the

Townshend Acts authorized writs of assistance, provided for the
establishment of new vice admiralty courts, and proposed the appointment of five commissioners of customs to be stationed in Boston. All this was in one neat, foolproof package and Parliament
accepted it.

No one in Boston was more affected by the Townshend Acts than
James Otis, Jr., hero of Mercy Warren's private drama, and Thomas
Hutchinson, villain — these two men who were so far apart in their
life styles yet, strangely enough, were not so far apart in their political thought as they imagined. Both were for British liberty — Otis
stressing liberty while admitting British authority, Hutchinson
stressing authority with the hope that it would be generous enough
to allow liberty. "An ingenuous writer," Hutchinson once wrote,
"who would keep the mean between subjection on the one hand and
absolute independence on the other would do great service." Unfortunately, neither Hutchinson nor Otis could fill this need. Partly this
was due to the roles in which the public had cast them, and partly it
was due to their own temperaments. No matter what he said,
Hutchinson sounded too aloof to convince the people that he was
interested in their liberty. And no matter how strongly Otis declared
his allegiance to Parliament, he was too intemperate to sound sincere. With each new crisis, these two men, pushed by public pressure, reached for appropriate resources and too often all they found
were their old humors, their old habitudes, and so inevitably
Thomas Hutchinson became tighter and colder as time went on and
James Otis built up the fires around him.

Thomas Hutchinson was fifty-six years old now, an age when he
should have reached the peak of his accomplishments, when he
should have been enjoying the rewards of his public service. But
instead, he said, "I am a mere cypher and deprived of what used to
be the lieutenant governor's right to a seat in the Council. The year
has passed without the least notice taken of it." In an agony of frus-
tration, he took to writing more and more letters, just as Francis
Bernard was doing. One of the letters in the fall of 1767 was to his

London tailor. Thomas Hutchinson was meticulous about ordering his clothes, specifying such details as the kind of buttonholes he wished (he liked frogs on a coat but only if they were in style); this year he told his tailor that his waistcoat should be trimmed "according to the fashion for old men."

James Otis, Jr., was also writing letters. In the early part of 1768, in conjunction with Samuel Adams, he wrote what came to be known as the Circular Letter sent from the House of Representatives to the other colonies, stating Massachusetts' response to the Townshend Acts. It was a legitimate letter, Otis felt (not suggesting any specific action), and it was a respectful letter, ending with a firm expression of confidence in the king. Moreover, it should not have been a surprising letter; the political theory contained in it was the same as he had been preaching for years. The letter admitted that Parliament was the supreme legislative power but said that Parliament itself derived its power from a constitution based on natural rights, including the right of a man to call his property his own, to be taken from him only with his consent. The revenue act was therefore an infringement on this right and was unconstitutional.

The letter, moderate as it might have seemed to Jemmy Otis, aroused different reactions. John Adams did not think it was strong enough: it should have declared that Parliament had no authority in America whatsoever. On the other hand, some members of the House thought it was too strong and when it was finally passed, the Tories claimed, it was "by surprise in a thin House." But of course the main question remained: What would the king think of it?

The king, as it turned out, did not care for it at all. Lord Hillsborough, the new secretary of state for North America, informed the people of Massachusetts that the king considered the letter a "seditious paper" and advised other colonies to treat it "with the contempt it deserves." In His Majesty's name Lord Hillsborough required the Massachusetts House of Representatives to "rescind the resolution that had given birth to the circular letter . . . and to declare their disapprobation of that rash and hasty proceeding." If the assembly should refuse, Governor Bernard was told to dissolve it.

The enormity of the word *required* was enough in itself to rouse the province, sensitive as it was to the sound of autocracy. And then *rescind.* Here was a new negative to add to the others, and if the house refused it, there was yet the most arbitrary word of all: the House would be *dissolved* and could not meet again without express permission from Parliament for a year or until May 1769. Hillsborough's order, even the terseness of it, was clearly insulting to a people brought up to believe in the right of free speech and the right of free petition.

In the House of Representatives James Otis, Jr., rose to his feet. He had led the campaign for order and moderation for months. He who found it so difficult to talk softly had warned the populace against provoking tumults and disorders, but now he was angry. He had not only the province's anger to voice but his own, not only the suggestion of disloyalty to combat but the implication that a letter written by him was, as a literary product, less than elegant. "A rash and hasty proceeding" indeed! What about Lord Hillsborough's performance? James asked. *His* letter was no better than a schoolboy's. What was more, all the ministers that the king assigned to North America were nothing more than boys. Warmed up, Jemmy took a deep breath and let his vocabulary roll. Parliament, he cried, was a "parcel of Button-makers, Pin-makers, Horse Jockeys, Gamesters, Pensioners, Pimps, and Whore Masters." Then after praising Oliver Cromwell and applauding the era in which Charles I was murdered, he came to the word *rescind.* Parliament had better rescind *its* order, he concluded, or be lost forever.

There were other speeches, perhaps not as colorful as Jemmy's but they put off the vote until at last Governor Bernard, adopting phrases as arrogant as any of Lord Hillsborough's, said he would regard a further delay as an *"oppugnation to his Majesty's authority"* made by *"an expiring faction"* of the province. That *"expiring faction"* (which included such fine Massachusetts names as Adams, Warren, Hancock, Otis, Cushing, Bowdoin) still would not vote, however, until it had pointed out in rather forceful terms that it was "the best blood of the colony who opposed the ministerial measures, men of reputation, fortune and rank, equal to any who enjoyed the smiles of the government."

Then only was the vote taken to rescind or not to rescind — a grave decision since a refusal to rescind would be the province's first open, direct, and absolute rejection of an act of Parliament. The gallery (a recent innovation by James Otis, Jr.) was filled with the radical wing of the popular party whose very presence may well have contributed to the outcome. Ninety-two members of the House voted against rescinding; seventeen voted for rescinding, and Governor Bernard, after lecturing like an "angry pedagogue" (according to Mercy), dissolved the General Court. The people, however, did not need lecturing; they knew exactly what they were doing. Indeed, so important did they consider the vote that the numbers 92 and 17 took on a special significance. For years "92" was a password in Massachusetts, a magical number, the subject for innumerable toasts, while "17" was synonymous with infamy. Later looking back on this period, Thomas Hutchinson said that the war could be dated from this vote.

Mercy Warren dated the war from the day the troops arrived, which was not surprising; most New Englanders felt that free government was doomed when a standing army was introduced. "The experience of all ages," Mercy wrote, ". . . [shows] that a standing army is the most ready engine in the hand of despotism." In the early part of September the governor acknowledged that troops were on their way; at the end of the month Samuel Otis wrote to Joseph that "we expect them [the troops] in town every moment and I suppose they will spend the winter here."

On October 1, he wrote again: "The fleet is come up and a number of transports. The two regiments are to take possession on this day . . . and I imagine camp in the Common . . . I know not but that my house will be full before night."

October 1 was one of those black days in the life of a people, a

day cut out from the calendar, forever separate from all other days, a
day that would be remembered in every painful detail. Twelve ships
of war, their cannon loaded, were anchored around the town that
morning in position for a blockade. At noon two regiments, a detachment from another, and a train of artillery with two pieces of
cannon landed on Long Wharf. The people watched. They stood, as
Mercy said, in "sullen silence" while the soldiers marched up King
Street — one thousand redcoats in full regalia with bayonets fixed,
drums beating, fifes playing, colors flying as if they were occupying
an enemy town. When they reached the Common, they stopped, reformed, and then staged a smart, full-scale drill to show Boston
what British troops were made of.

If it was hard to watch the troops arrive, it was equally hard to
live with them. Samuel Adams did not like being stopped and challenged by soldiers, although apparently this could happen to anyone,
any time and any place. "To be called to account by a common
soldier . . ." he said, "is a badge of slavery." John Adams complained of not being able to sleep in the mornings. Early every day
he was roused by the "Spirit Stirring Drum, and the Earpiercing fife"
as a regiment exercised directly in front of his house in Brattle
Square.

Thomas Hutchinson, on the other hand, never slept better, he
said. The very presence of the troops would have helped to restore
not so much his sense of safety but, what was more important to
him, his sense of order. It was very necessary for him to believe that
he was a right-thinking man in a basically right-thinking world, but
before the troops came there had been times when it had seemed to
him that either his brain was "turned inside out or all the brains of
most people" about him were turned so.

Actually, however, as he would soon find out, the troops created
more problems than they solved, if they solved any. They certainly
could not stop Samuel Adams from writing his inflammatory pieces
or from calling town meetings; they could neither keep merchants
from signing a nonimportation agreement nor guarantee safety to

merchants (such as Hutchinson's own sons) who might not want to sign; they had no effect at all on the election the following May when the Whigs scored an overwhelming victory. Indeed, the military authority was stated in such a singular way that the troops could not have been called out to stop a riot, had one developed, without official sanction of the Boston civil courts. The following summer they could not, nor did they try to, curb the town's exuberance, disrespectful as it was, when Francis Bernard (now Sir Francis) sailed for England, presumably recalled for consultation. The troops just stood by and watched while the flag of St. George was raised to the top of the Liberty Tree, while bells were rung, cannon fired from Hancock's wharf, and bonfires built on the top of Fort Hill.

Thomas Hutchinson became the acting governor, but, although he realized that the troops were ineffective, he was convinced that they were a symbol of an authority that the province would have to accept if there was ever to be peace. Hutchinson came to such conclusions reluctantly, he claimed; indeed, he never thought of the "measures necessary for the peace and good order of the colonies," he wrote his friend Thomas Whately in England, "without pain." He was in a particularly forthright mood the January day in 1769 when he wrote this letter, one of many to Whately, whom he later cautioned "to keep secret everything I write untill we are in a more settled state." Although he did not spell out what measures he thought necessary to secure a proper "dependance" of a colony upon the parent state, he did say that something more than declaratory acts was needed. It was just not possible, he believed, to create a government so perfect that people in a colony three thousand miles away could enjoy all the privileges of the people in the parent state and the sooner Americans recognized this, the better it would be for them. "There must be," he concluded, "an Abridgment of what are called English Liberties."

A firm policy would, of course, have been the only congenial one in any case for Thomas Hutchinson with his logical mind and com-

manding conscience. He sincerely believed that if he, who knew
what was right, could be strong enough and if England could be
equally resolute, the people would come around, just as wrong-
thinking people in previous periods had come around to admitting
their errors — as in the days of his persecuted ancestress, Anne
Hutchinson, for instance, or in the days of the witch trials when the
public had temporarily gone mad, as it was apparently wont to do
from time to time. At the moment, however, with the people in
power, there seemed to be little that Thomas Hutchinson could be
firm about, though he had no doubt that he would be firm in every
instance where it was possible to take any stand at all. It would not
have occurred to him that he might ever disappoint himself. Yet
once he did.

It happened in January 1770, when the year-long nonimportation
agreement, which Hutchinson's sons, Elisha and Thomas, Jr., had
signed, ran out. They had never wanted to sign it; they had only
recently set up as partners and just prior to the signing they had
received their first big order, a ton of bohea tea and naturally
enough, when the agreement expired, they lost no time in applying
for a key to the warehouse where the tea was stored. They were
denied the key. They would have to wait, they were told, until their
competitors could order and receive goods; otherwise it would not
be fair or in keeping with the spirit of the agreement.

But the Hutchinson boys had been pushed far enough. They
broke into the warehouse and removed the tea to a secret place and
began selling it. Nor would they return the tea when they were
asked. It was Thomas Hutchinson who relented one night after
being visited by an angry contingent of merchants and townsmen,
threatening the safety of his sons. He stood on the steps of his house
that just five years before had been invaded by a mob and for a time
he argued, but it did no good. His children were his vulnerable
point and at last he surrendered: he agreed to advise his sons to
restore the tea. Afterward he hated himself for it. He "felt more
trouble and distress from this error," he said, than he had from the

destruction of his house and property in the Stamp Act riot. Years later, while writing the history of this period, he still cringed at the memory but was too honest to erase it. The experience, however, had one lasting effect: it served to harden his already strong will.

Jemmy Otis was, of course, more accustomed to self-recrimination. For that brief period when he was working to restrain his party, his family (particularly his father and perhaps also his wife) were encouraged to believe that Jemmy had at last found a reasonable plateau from which he could operate, a position he could support steadily without feeling obliged to leap to the right or left to prove his point. His extravagant behavior in the past, hard as it had been on his father, had been equally hard on his wife, Ruth, a proper aristocrat and a high Tory. She would have found it difficult, of course, in these times to have been married to a Whig in any case, but if he had only been a quieter, more gentlemanly Whig, it would have been easier. As it was, she was appalled at the vulgarity he displayed when he was excited; she was embarrassed by the lowlier members of the Whig party he sometimes consorted with (and whom she refused to entertain); she was worried about her young son James, exposed to his father's language and influenced by his politics. (Little James once told Hannah Winthrop that his mama would be a finer lady "if she was a Daughter of Liberty"). Nevertheless, Jemmy in his serene moments always professed an affection for his "Ruthie"; it was only when he was upset that he admitted the pressure he was under at home from her "Curtain Lectures," and only when he was out of control that he abused Ruthie, railing against her as he did against his father, his brothers, and the rest of his family, whose hold over him he could neither escape nor forgive.

The arrival of the troops made any kind of harmony for James Otis, Jr., more difficult than ever. The very sight of the redcoats made him feel more loyal, more angry, and even more fearful of an ultimate separation from the mother country which, above all else, he dreaded. "The present measures," he said, "can have no Tendency but to hasten on with great rapidity events which every good and

honest man would wish delayed for ages, if possible, prevented forever." He was infuriated, not that England could be so tyrannical
but that she could be so obtuse; not that she should try to bind her
colonies to her but that she should unwittingly be cutting the cord
that bound them. And doubly infuriating was the fact that his anger
was misunderstood. British Tories were forever calling him disloyal.
Just as Thomas Hutchinson, no matter what he did, expected his
love of Massachusetts to be recognized by the province, so James
Otis, Jr., the number-one spokesman for the Whig party, the master
of invective, expected his attachment to England to be universally
acknowledged.

Certainly he considered he was behaving as a gracious and loyal
English gentleman when he sent a dinner invitation to General
Thomas Gage at the time that the general was in Boston to see to his
troops. The Otises were accustomed to entertaining visiting officials,
to dining with the highest Boston society, Tories and Whigs alike,
and had no reason to expect anything but courtesy in reply. The
rejection, when it came, was curt and pointed; there was no doubt
that the general *would* not, rather than *could* not, dine with the
Otises. It was a bitter blow to Jemmy, especially humiliating because it was a rebuff not only to him but, through him, to his Tory
wife. Misunderstood again, he became more belligerent, more sensitive, more often depressed, and, as the year went on, he took to dram
drinking.

Then in August 1769, his loyalty was challenged even more
bluntly. A copy of a letter arrived in Boston written some months
before by the commissioners of customs to one of the ministers in
England. In the letter James Otis, Jr., was accused of being an
enemy to the "rights of the crown and disaffected to his Majesty."
Eager as always to discredit the commissioners with the public, Samuel Adams had the letter printed in the *Boston Gazette*.

The charge of disloyalty was more than Jemmy could honorably
endure. On September 1, he and Samuel Adams had a conference
with each of the commissioners; on September 2, Otis went alone at

six o'clock in the morning to the British Coffee House to meet the commissioners again. "The Cause, and End of these Conferences," John Adams reported, "are Subjects of much Speculation."

On Sunday, September 3, Jemmy was showing the effects of the strain. "Otis talks all," John Adams said. "He grows the most talkative Man alive . . . he grows narrative, like an Old Man."

On Monday, September 4, Otis had his say in the *Boston Gazette*. He called John Robinson, the commissioner whom he had singled out for his wrath, a "superlative blockhead." If he could get no other satisfaction, Otis said, he claimed "a natural right" to break Robinson's head. Perhaps it was the same day that, having heard that Robinson had bought a cane, Jemmy went into the same store and asked for "the fellow to it." That evening John Adams complained that Otis monopolized the conversation at the "Clubb" in a most unpleasant way, showing "no Politeness nor Delicacy, no learning nor Ingenuity, no Taste or Sense."

On Tuesday, September 5, Jemmy was through with talk. Waving his stick, he entered the British Coffee House where Robinson was and demanded "a gentleman's satisfaction." Whatever satisfaction he meant, it was obvious as he rounded the table toward Robinson, he intended it to take place then and there. Robinson, so the story went, grabbed for Otis' nose — whether to stop him or to lead him on is not clear (tweaking a man's nose in colonial days was equivalent to throwing down the gauntlet); in any case, Otis raised his cane which struck Robinson. Later Samuel Adams, embroidering the event for his own purposes, claimed that a number of friends provided Robinson with a sword and joined in the attack, crying, "Knock him down . . . Kill him, kill him!" At the very least, the two men clubbed each other and when James Otis, Jr., came out of the fight, he had a deep cut on his forehead, which according to Dr. Thomas Young (a Whig), who attended him, was not serious. Later generations blamed Otis' mental disorders on this blow but at the time people generally considered the fight just another episode in the wild career of Jemmy Otis.

When she first heard the news, Mercy in typical fashion let her imagination run rampant. "I saw you fallen," she wrote. ". . . I saw your wife a widow, your children orphans . . . your country in tears." She was soon reassured about his condition, however, and then she worried about his future: what would Jemmy do next? She begged him never "to give or receive a challenge" and never to let anything or anyone "ruffle or discompose him." Dueling, she said, was against "the law of reason and the laws of God as well as man," but James was not a man whom a younger sister could easily lecture. "You will excuse the freedom of my pen," she concluded, "when you consider it is held by one who has your welfare more at heart, after a very few exceptions, than that of any other person in the world."

Mercy need not have worried about a duel. At the moment James Otis, Jr., did not have the heart to fight anyone. He was filled with remorse — not for the Robinson affair but for all his past sins. It was his usual pattern — an aggressive step forward followed by retreat and self-recrimination — but the aftermath of guilt this time was total. Thomas Hutchinson had once said Jemmy Otis was capable of committing suicide and blaming it on someone else; now he blamed himself for everything. The widening gulf between England and America, the inevitable dissolution, was, he believed, all his own doing. In November 1769, he wrote in despair: "I have done more mischief to my country than can be repaired. I meant well but am convinced I was mistaken." On another occasion he "wondered what our parsons meant by thanking God for their existence; [I] never did, never would nor never could." He cursed the day he was born and drank in his misery.

In January 1770, while Thomas Hutchinson was berating himself for surrendering to his night callers, James Otis, Jr., was rambling and wandering "like a Ship without an Helm . . . I fear he is not in his perfect Mind," John Adams said. "The Nervous, Concise, and pithy were his Character, till lately . . . Now the verbose, roundabout, and rambling, and long winded."

On February 26, Adams noted that Otis had been "raving Mad" all afternoon — "raving vs. Father, Wife, Brother, Sister, Friend." Actually James Otis' behavior reflected not only his own deepening sickness but also the growing tension of Boston at the end of its second winter of living with troops. Violence about him always aggravated Jemmy's own feelings of violence, his anger at himself, his family, his friends, his God — even more so now that he was convinced that nothing but ultimate violence lay ahead. Surely it was no coincidence that Jemmy Otis was "raving Mad" on the same day that Boston buried its first casualty in the patriot cause, a twelve-year-old German boy killed by the bullet of Ebenezer Richardson, a former customs officer who had shot out of his window into a crowd of boys harassing a Tory neighbor. The Whigs turned the funeral into a mammoth public and patriotic event with a procession of five hundred children who marched before and behind the bier. "This shewes," John Adams said, "that there are many more Lives to spend if wanted in the Service of their Country."

Within a week three more were dead on a Boston street and two lay dying. The so-called Boston Massacre on the night of March 5, starting with snowballs thrown at a sentinel and ending with shots fired into a savage mob, was a crisis not only for the city but for its leaders. For James Otis, Jr., it was plainly too much. He who had so effectively both roused and restrained Boston was too deeply engulfed in private distress to take any part at all. A few days after the Massacre, he was found in another mad spell breaking the windows of the Town House. Six weeks later, on the same day that Ebenezer Richardson was convicted of murder, he spent the afternoon shooting out of his window as Richardson had done.

For Samuel Adams the Massacre was not so much a tragedy as it was a necessary evil, possibly one which he helped to provoke. The notices that appeared shortly before March 5 warning the town of a military attack and signed by British soldiers were the work not of the British, it was thought later, but of a Whig element trying to stir up trouble. Certainly the Massacre served Adams' purpose in dem-

onstrating the danger in allowing the troops to remain, and certainly
Adams capitalized on the event and perpetuated its memory.

For Thomas Hutchinson, on the other hand, the Massacre was a
test. No matter what happened, he had determined to be firm and
indeed he had been, steadily refusing to move the troops, even
through the last weekend before the incident, when the pressures had
been heavy and rumors and threats had left little doubt but that a
clash was imminent. Yet when the clash came, Thomas Hutchinson
rose to the occasion, not by refusing the town anything, not by remembering his principles or by following his conscience or by thinking either of the king or himself. Surely, when he stepped out on the
balcony of the Town House that snowy night of the Massacre and
faced the milling, angry, frightened people, many of whom blamed
him for the impasse they were in, his thoughts were for the people;
surely, when he spoke, his voice must have carried both his genuine
concern and his natural authority, for the people listened. Some
were undoubtedly the same people who had torn his house apart a
few years before, many had opposed and abused him, yet they listened. As unpopular as he had been from time to time, Thomas
Hutchinson had not completely lost his hold over the people; when
he promised them justice, they were reassured; when he told them to
go home, most of them did.

Yet the next day, when the question of removing the troops had
to be faced again, Hutchinson was back defending his policy, up-
holding his authority, resisting Samuel Adams, and refusing to surrender. When he finally conceded, it was, according to Hutchinson's
own account, not his decision but that of the commanding officer
who ordered the two regiments out of the city, one on March 10, one
on March 11 — a move, Hutchinson believed, that encouraged the
people to feel they could be free of all exterior power if they were
only persistent enough, a move which compelled Thomas Hutchinson to be more persistent than ever.

But if the issue over the troops was lost, Hutchinson soon had
another to take its place: the meeting place of the assembly. Should

the assembly sit in Boston where it normally sat and insisted it should sit, or in Cambridge, away from Boston's inflammatory atmosphere, where Hutchinson convened it, on the specific instructions of the king, or so he said. This new controversy was obviously going to be a bitter and prolonged one and although Hutchinson set himself stubbornly to match wills with Samuel Adams, he was tired and discouraged. He thought longingly of the days when he had been Chief Justice, a position he had truly enjoyed; and when he was notified in April that he had been appointed governor in Bernard's place, he begged to be excused. He did not think he had the firmness of body or mind equal to the opposition ahead, he said.

It was not until eight months later, in January 1771, that Thomas Hutchinson reconsidered his decision. He had not wrung from the assembly a declaration of submission, but still the assembly had agreed to meet in Cambridge. The Townshend duties had been removed now (all but the tea duty) and the town was quieter than it had been in seven years. Indeed, it was quiet enough so that even Jemmy Otis had regained some of his composure, and it was harmonious enough so that on the queen's birthday (January 18) the town celebrated the new spirit of peace and friendship. There was dancing and music for the occasion, Boston's merchant-fisherman, Mr. Rowe, reported, but "very Bad Wine and Punch." Thomas Hutchinson, convinced that the opposition was broken and the worst was over, wrote to England accepting the post as governor of Massachusetts.

The ordination was held in the spring and celebrated throughout the province. In the midst of the festivities, ex-Governor Shirley, retired and living in Roxbury for the last three years, died. His body lay in state in Boston for a week and was visited by members of the legislature, officials, and friends — among them Colonel Otis, sixty-nine years old now and weighted with memories. For him, the occasion was another link gone to the "good old days before the French and Indian War" when politics were simpler, or so it seemed, and governors more compatible. Yet, compatible or not, governors were

to be worked with, and within a few days Colonel Otis was calling
on Thomas Hutchinson to pay his compliments and extend his con-
gratulations.

In Plymouth James and Mercy Warren were thoroughly disgusted with the fuss and parade of the ordination and with the success of the Tories. "Oh the Transitory & fleeting nature of all
worldly Enjoyments," James wrote to Joseph Otis. "There seems to
be no great happiness here but what the Tories have in Possession . . . How long this is to last God only knows . . .

"The Wheel goes round," he concluded, "& I hope the axletrees
are well greasd, to make use of a homely Metaphor."

VI

ON SOME DAYS Thomas Hutchinson really believed that he might succeed as governor where so many others had failed. The province seemed at rest, he wrote optimistically to England; only in Boston was there opposition and this too had weakened. The faction was dying, he reported.

But on other days the peace that he described seemed to be only a sullen discontent that could flare up at any moment, and often did, into the old defiance. Only Parliament could establish a lasting peace, he believed, and then only if it took such measures as to make Americans admit, once and for all, Parliament's supremacy. Specifically, in letters to England he recommended that Parliament should punish anyone who denied its authority, that Parliament should curb town meetings, that salaries of provincial judges should be paid by England. But such changes should be gradual, he said, and it would be best if he were "not suspected by the people here of having suggested any alterations."

Meanwhile the Whigs were responding to the lull in the "cold war" in various ways. Some were wavering — John Hancock among them. He was sick of being called Samuel Adams' tool and sick of hearing it said that he was cultivated for his money. But when Hancock complained of being criticized, Samuel Adams only snapped at him.

"You say you have been spoken ill of," Adams once said. "What then? Can you think that, while you are a good man . . . *all* will speak well of you?"

Hancock, of course, would have liked nothing better. He adored being in the center of the stage, moderating town meetings, making dramatic announcements (it was he who announced the removal of the troops to a crowd of 4000), and presenting Boston with spectacular gifts — a concert hall on one occasion, a bandstand, a fire engine. And so in a period of general amnesty when Hutchinson appointed him colonel of the cadets, Hancock responded with friendship and was soon, as Hutchinson said, forming "a new set of acquaintance."

John Adams was simply angry. In April 1771, he had renounced politics and moved from Boston to Braintree, determined to divide his time between law and husbandry and to "meddle not with public affairs." But the spirit of unity and reconciliation, the expressions of harmony between the governor and the House were as hard for John Adams to bear as dissension had ever been. "How easily the People change," he grumbled. Had they forgotten how Hutchinson came to be governor? Had they forgotten how Hutchinson had supported Bernard, the army, the navy, the commissioners of customs, and "Every other Thing we complain of"?

John Adams' irritation spilled over into his diary again and again, although he insisted he was simply an observer — uninvolved, disengaged, a private man who had lent himself to public affairs when the need was great. But never again. From now on he would avoid politics, political clubs, town meetings; he would spend his evenings in his office or with his family. Resolutions like these were a recurring thread throughout his life. John Adams renounced politics as some men renounce drink — by fits and starts and never with any lasting success. Even now as he was jotting down a recipe for manure, he was also developing thoughts on the science of government, the balance of power, the nature of liberty. He was translating his political experience into a broad philosophical base upon which he would build and from which he would work for the rest of his life.

James Warren was also distressed at the "Languor and feebleness" of the country, but, unlike John Adams, he was no philosopher. His political experience was less a source for creating the future than it was a means of confirming the past. Government was for him a matter of simple, long-established morality; politics was the clear-cut business of opposing tyranny and when politics became complicated and devious, when there were reverses, when there was apathy or variance within the ranks, James Warren, like an Old Testament Jeremiah, cried doom. The Old Colony towns were dead, dead, dead, he said. Liberty was vanquished; nothing but a miracle would revive it now.

Samuel Adams was no philosopher either, but he was a born revolutionist — single-minded and practical. His emotions were less a personal matter than they were a political resource to be used as he used people and events, manipulating them toward an objective. And despair, even if justified, served no purpose. "When you *once* spoke the Language of Despair," he wrote to James Warren, "allow me to tell you, it gave me offence." Hate, resentment, perseverance: these were the emotions to cultivate. "Nil desperandum," he told his downhearted friends. "Where there is a Spark of patriotick fire, *we* will enkindle it." And so he did.

Mercy Warren undoubtedly reacted with the same despair as her husband did. Their response to public events was so similar that instead of providing a counter each for the other and so broadening their joint outlook, each tended to underline the other's thoughts. At the moment, however, Mercy had private as well as public worries: her brother James was going on "in his old way," according to Samuel Otis; her son James was entering Harvard — the first of her sons to leave home, the first to step into the giddy world beyond her reach.

"If you escape uncontaminated," she wrote, "it must be . . . by learning early to discriminate between the unoffending mirth of the generous and open hearted and the designed flighty vagaries of the virulent and narrow minded man." It was so easy to be misled, Mercy said, and she used the word *easy* again and again. It was so easy to "glide into paths of folly," so easy to be led "into mazes of error." And, she reminded James, just as her father had once reminded her brother James: he was the eldest son and the honor of the whole family depended upon his example. Hannah Winthrop reported from Cambridge that James "and his little chambermate" were happily placed and she would keep an eye on them, but still Mercy wrote, "I tremble for my children."

If Mercy was overly apprehensive about what the world might do to her sons, it may have been partly because she saw what the world had done to her brother. Through 1771 and 1772 Jemmy was in and out of retirement, steady enough at times to take on new clients in Boston and to be elected to the General Court, disturbed enough at other times for John Adams to predict trouble. "He trembles. His Nerves are irritable. He cannot bear Fatigue." In the controversy over where the assembly would meet, he was well enough to join Hancock and Cushing in support of Hutchinson. The governor, he cried with a flash of his old oratory, could carry the assembly to the Housatonic if he saw fit. Yet two months later, Jemmy was wild again, cursing the servants at a bar meeting for not putting enough candles on the table. *Four* candles were needed, he shouted. *He* could still afford four candles for his own table at home. Every table should have four candles. Another time he ordered a servant to bring his horse to the door and hold him by the head for an hour before he was ready to mount. His passions were "all roiled," John Adams said. "He runs into one Door and out another, and Window, & & &."

The revival of the John Robinson case undoubtedly contributed to this new attack of madness. Two years before, following the Coffee House brawl, Otis had filed suit against Robinson, claiming three thousand pounds in damages. The suit, continued from session to session, finally came to court in July 1771, just prior to the wild outbursts that John Adams described. Otis was awarded two thousand pounds but this did not satisfy his honor; he appealed the case (Robinson did also), but in the meantime he lost whatever tenuous hold he had on his mind.

"I fear he is as bad as ever," Samuel Otis reported to Joseph, adding, however, that "This is a matter I intend to be by no means busy about." At the moment Samuel was feeling unappreciated, having "but little approbation from the famili," he said, "for doing my utmost to support a falling friend." Yet Samuel always did support James. "Let's take heed," he said, "lest we fall."

In November at the request of his family, James was declared non compos mentis and on December 3 he was driven away in a chaise, bound hand and foot.

Hannah Winthrop, who must have been present at the legal proceedings, wrote Mercy a note of sympathy. "With grief did I behold the afflicted countenance of his [James Otis'] venerable father, obliged to engage in the arduous business and to restrain the overflowings of parental affection . . . O how inestimable the blessing of reason! Do we sufficiently attend to it?" As a further consolation, she recommended Pope's "The Dying Christian to His Soul."

There was a strong feeling throughout the family that Jemmy's trouble stemmed in part at least from his loss or lack of faith, for Jemmy's relation with God was as ambivalent as it was with any father figure; his religion was as conflicted as his politics. He was not alone, of course, in finding it difficult to reconcile traditional seventeenth-century Christianity with eighteenth-century rationalism; some of his contemporaries (particularly in Europe) had rejected Christianity altogether, some had rejected God as well, some had worked out a compromise in deism, some had used reason to serve religion and adapted religion to reason, some had remained skeptical, and finally some had simply compartmentalized religion, defending it against all change.

James Otis, Jr., in typical fashion tried all positions. In his troubled periods he would throw himself on the mercy of God in one moment and in the next behave like an infidel. In his sane periods he attended the Old South Church with his wife although he never joined it, perhaps because the church was so notably conservative, perhaps because having been so swayed by emotional appeals during the Great Awakening, he was wary of himself and loath to make commitments. In any case, Jemmy battled his conflicts instead of submitting them to God as his family wished him to do. "I doubt not," Mercy once wrote him, "but all such as put their trust in the supreme Governor of the universe, and look to him alone for help in affliction, will sooner or later be relieved from whatever distresses they may feel."

In April Jemmy was back in Boston and Samuel was able to say that he had "behaved well the last 40 hours and am in hopes it will continue for life tho I am afraid it will not. I have gotten so far as to deliver his books and papers & shall get his Guardianship taken off in a day or two if he continues to behave well."

Samuel's fears were well founded. In August the Robinson case which had been appealed came up again. And again it was, along with other pressures, too much for James. "In one of those intervals of beclouded reason," Mercy said, "he forgave the murderous band," asking only for a written apology plus the actual medical and legal expenses. This was granted but unfortunately it did nothing to restore Jemmy's equilibrium. During the summer and fall he had a number of what his contemporaries called his "mad frieks," many of which took place in his own home. Colonel Otis witnessed one of these scenes, a particularly distressing one apparently in which Jemmy treated everyone in the family "cruelly." When the Colonel returned to Barnstable, he was so upset that he determined to speak out, in spite of the fact that he knew this would aggravate Jemmy further. "I must let you know my mind in the matter," he said, "for I am loath to bring old Eli's curse on me or mine That when his sons made themselves vile he restrained them not."

It is a bitter letter, yet the picture of the father writing it is no less bitter than the picture of the son reading it. "It is amaseing to me," Colonel Otis wrote, "that a man of your Learning Sense and understanding should throw yourself away & by that means ruin your family & children give your nearast and dearest Relations especially an old Father so much uneasiness and endeavour to bring his gray

hairs with sorrow to the Grave: you certainly know better and therefore don't give away to the Temptations of the Evil one by your
prophane language & in the hearing of your children O consider
what a dreadful example you set them . . . you are continually
profaneing his Great & Dreadful name in their hearing, they have
learnt it of you especially your son & who will be undone to all
intents and purposes if you continue the way you are in with him
and don't put him to School and sett him a better example."

Pity and guilt were ever the way to reach the secret springs of
Jemmy's remorse and the Colonel did not hesitate to use them. He
was cut to the heart, he said, "especially when I considered the care
& pains & costs I have been at to educate my first born the beginning of my Strength and what a fine prospect I had of his being
usefull to me himself family & the World and to have my hopes
thus blasted by his Perverseness of Spirit is too hard to bear." He
advised Jemmy to "Sett up the Worship of God in your family pray
with & for them (instead of curseing and swearing at them)" or else
he would be ruined, "not only in this world but in the world to
come."

Jemmy took little part in public affairs now; he did preside over a
town meeting in November but not effectively. He left Boston soon,
apparently unable to live in peace with anyone in his family, either
in Boston or Barnstable. Over the next three years he was intermittently under the care of Captain Daniel Souther of Hull, where he
calmed down sufficiently so that on winter evenings he was able to
conduct the local school. And when he couldn't sleep at night, he
walked the beach, a lumbering, lonely figure at the water's edge,
stooping for beach stones which he used later to pave the captain's
yard.

. . .

But by this time the mood in Massachusetts had changed. Parliament had acted again. In October 1772, the rumor reached Boston
that England was going to take the support of justices of the Supe-

rior Court out of the hands of the province and instead pay the justices a fixed salary out of the customhouse revenue, a measure which
Thomas Hutchinson had long been promoting. As former Chief
Justice, Hutchinson was particularly sensitive to the position of the
justices; not only were they subject to intimidation by the people,
they were scandalously underpaid by them. There would, of course,
be a clamor about the change, Hutchinson said, but it could not be
helped. The people would have to get used to it, just as they were
(or seemed to be) getting used to the fact that his salary as governor
was now being paid by the crown. Just as they had finally come
around with concessions (ambiguous as they might be) so that he
had felt free to move the assembly back to Boston. Thomas Hutchinson braced himself for whatever lay ahead and resolved to be adamant.

And adamant he was. In November when a town meeting asked
him what his instructions had been, Hutchinson refused to say. It
would be improper, he contended. His instructions were confidential
and the town meeting that had asked for them was not even war-
rantable. Then Hutchinson was asked to convene the assembly so
that the matter of the justices could be considered; again he refused.
He had already set a later date for the assembly, he said; it was not
the people's prerogative but the governor's to say when the assembly
should meet.

Here, indeed, were sparks for Samuel Adams and he lost no time
in "enkindling" them. In Boston, a town meeting adopted a set of
resolutions listing all the instances when Parliament had infringed
on the people's rights — the whole of it "calculated," Hutchinson
said, "to strike the colonists with a sense of their just claims to independence." And then, since Hutchinson would not convene the assembly and there could be no discussion through regular channels,
Samuel Adams acted on an idea (reputedly suggested by James
Warren) that the Whigs should form channels of their own: committees of correspondence throughout the province whose purpose it
would be to arouse the countryside and to return to Boston expres-

sions of support — evidence, contrary to the Tories' claim, that opposition was not confined to Boston but came from rural Massachusetts as well. At first some Whigs (Hancock, for instance) were cautious about identifying themselves with the committees of correspondence, but they were soon swept up by the enthusiastic response of the province.

The so-called lull in Massachusetts was over. John Adams was one of many who frankly wished for war; indeed, according to Peter Oliver, the sentiment was "90 to 1 to fight Great Britain." Throughout the province the reaction was so immediate, so intense, so unreasonable from the Tory point of view that Thomas Hutchinson found it difficult to sit by and wait for the clamor to subside, as he had originally intended to do. He had to act. Didn't the people realize, he asked, that Britain's power was "sufficient to crush us at one stroke"? Didn't they know that they could not "presume upon such unexampled, incredible contingencies as favoured us in our rash, though successful, expedition to Louisburgh"? Hutchinson was so absolutely convinced that he was right, he felt both contempt and compassion for his adversaries — his own countrymen embarking on what seemed to him a suicidal course. Surely he had to try to talk them out of it. Surely they could not resist the truth if it were properly presented. Moreover, if he did not speak, he might be accused of conniving with proceedings that should be exposed. And so in January 1773, although he had always avoided open argument on constitutional questions, Thomas Hutchinson opened the new session of the General Court with an invitation to debate, or as he put it:

"I endeavoured to show them what their constitution was, and called them to join with me in supporting it or to show me where I was erroneous."

For two months the argument went back and forth. The governor, far from admitting he was erroneous, insisted that it was impossible for there to be two independent legislatures in the same state. ("It is essential to the being of government that a power should always exist which no other power within such government can have the right to withstand or control.") The opposition countered that if "supreme" authority meant unlimited authority, the governor was offering them only a choice between slavery and independence; even supreme power had to be defined and fixed.

But even after the argument had been going on for several weeks, even after the opposition had shown its strength, Thomas Hutchinson did not realize the tactical blunder he had made. Not only was he giving the Whigs an unprecedented opportunity to state their case but he was actually illustrating to many of them the inevitability of independence. As Mercy Warren said, he "gave a fair opening to the friends of their country which they did not neglect" and in the end he "fanned rather than checked the *amor patriae* characteristic of the times." Yet during the debate, Hutchinson wrote blandly to a friend: "I send you my speech, their reply, and my answer, which may be some little amusement to you, though I need to apologize for laboring to prove points so evident; the prejudices people were under made it necessary."

Meanwhile John Adams, along with other Whig leaders, stood "amazed at the Governor, for forcing on this Controversy" and predicted that his "Ruin and Destruction must spring out of it, either from the Ministry and Parliament on one Hand or from his Countrymen on the other." And, indeed, within a few months enough Tory disapproval had been expressed on both sides of the ocean so that Hutchinson was writing the Earl of Dartmouth, the colonial secretary, in quite a different vein. "It gives me pain," he confessed, "that any step which I have taken in the most sincere intention to promote his Majesty's service should be judged to have a contrary effect."

Yet he still felt blameless and blameless he would always feel, although more and more often his actions were having "a contrary effect" and his words were being misinterpreted. Hardly had the excitement of the debate subsided than another opportunity to discredit Hutchinson fell, again quite fortuitously, into the laps of the

Whigs. Again it was Hutchinson's own words that rebounded, this time words that had been written in private to his friend Thomas Whately one January night four years before. "Keep secret everything I write," Hutchinson had said to his friend, but Thomas Whately was dead now, Hutchinson's letters (along with letters from Andrew Oliver and others) had been passed on to Whately's brother, and through some mysterious agent to Benjamin Franklin, who in turn sent them to Thomas Cushing, Speaker of the House, with the injunction that they should be read only by a certain few Whig leaders and that under no circumstances should copies of the letters or any part of the letters be made public.

John Adams read them on March 22, loosed a string of appropriate epithets in his diary, but could not see that public use could be made of letters so bound in secrecy. They were, however, so provocative, so pertinent, so obviously the perfect tool for damning the Tory clique and particularly Hutchinson that even the most honorable Whigs could scarcely resist dropping a hint here and there and letting a friend or two in on the secret. The more the Whigs read the letters, the more they repeated certain phrases and the more convinced they became that a deliberate conspiracy existed among the letter writers to subvert the liberties of the people. Certainly they suspected collusion between Andrew Oliver, Hutchinson's brother-in-law, and Hutchinson himself. They had for a long time felt threatened by the growing domination of the governor's family: Andrew Oliver was the lieutenant governor, Peter Oliver (Andrew's brother) was Chief Justice, and Hutchinson had a brother, Foster, who also held a prominent position. But it was Hutchinson's own letter that the Whigs found most offensive, particularly that portion in which he doubted that a colony three thousand miles away could enjoy all the same liberties as the parent state and in which he stated: "There must be an Abridgment of what are called English Liberties."

A month after he had first read the letters, John Adams was still fulminating. "Bone of our Bone," he railed in his diary, "born and educated among us!" On the same day Adams reported that he had told two of his friends about the letters and had let his aunt into the secret.

Hutchinson heard rumors that the Whigs had a story that would amaze the province if it could be told, but he did not concern himself with it. He operated on the theory that there was enough trouble for him to deal with from day to day without borrowing trouble or promises of trouble from the future. Besides, during some of the time these rumors were circulating, Hutchinson was not in town but in Hartford, Connecticut, heading a delegation to negotiate a boundary dispute with New York. This was the kind of mission at which Hutchinson was particularly skilled and he welcomed the opportunity to perform a service for the province which the people could not suspect and for which they could only be grateful. And indeed the boundary was settled more favorably to Massachusetts than was expected and not even John Hancock, a member of the delegation, could deny that this was largely the governor's doing. Hutchinson was pleased and, as he later recorded, "he flattered himself that he should be cordially received on his return to the province."

In view of his cheerful expectations, however, Hutchinson's homecoming seems especially bitter. The assembly, bent on destroying Hutchinson, could scarcely have been very cordial, yet they did not question his negotiations nor, in fact, did they require him to lay the settlement before the House; instead he was instructed to send it directly to London. "No instance of the like confidence placed by a Massachusetts assembly in their governor" could be found in history, Hutchinson wrote later, as if even on the eve of his downfall he was trying to rescue crumbs of success, some last vestige of the people's esteem.

On May 31, John Hancock, assuming the role that he liked best, announced to the assembly that portentous news would be revealed within forty-eight hours. And on June 2, Samuel Adams read excerpts from the famous letters to a packed House and crowded gallery. As for that injunction of secrecy, Samuel Adams had probably never been troubled by it. As early as 1770 he had tried to acquire some of Hutchinson's English correspondence and now that he had a few letters, he had only to find a device to enable him to publish them and still maintain a semblance of honor. Nor would he find this difficult. For Samuel Adams, the ends he served not only justified the means he used, but he seemed to feel that justification was impertinent. Certainly the story that John Hancock told the assembly was transparent almost to the point of insolence: Hancock claimed that some sheets of paper had been thrust into his hands while he was walking through the Common one day and upon examination he had found they were duplicates of the letters then being discussed. He proposed to submit them to the assembly and if, indeed, they were the same, there would no longer be any reason to prevent the letters from being printed for the public. Copies could be made of the copy and no promises broken. In this way the letters were actually published along with a set of resolutions claiming that the letters were insidious, misrepresentative, written with the intent to alienate the affections of the king, and requesting that both the governor and the lieutenant governor be removed from office.

Hutchinson did not publicly fight the resolutions; it would not have been, as he wrote a Harvard classmate, "in character." Instead he said he would simply wait until truth prevailed and take comfort, as he had done so often, in the thought that "The deception cannot last longer than it did in the time of the witchcraft." In private he complained, however, and of course he was justified in saying that statements from the letters were read out of context and otherwise misrepresented, that he had no knowledge of the letters written by the others, and that there was no conspiracy in the country.

Yet when he protested that he had said nothing in the letters that he had not also said publicly, surely he knew that it was one thing, as a servant of the king, to publicly support England's unpopular measures and it was another to support them voluntarily behind the backs of the public and in the process to refer to the people as "enemies of government," and "friends of anarchy." And surely he would remember other more recent and, from the Whig point of view, more incriminating letters which Massachusetts never saw and which suggested far more specific restrictions and changes.

Yet just as Jemmy Otis had felt wounded when his loyalty to England was questioned, so Hutchinson was defensive about his loyalty to the province. By October he had persuaded himself that when he had mentioned an abridgment of liberties, he had in reality only been thinking about representation of the colonies in Parliament, which he considered impractical. "The Council say," he wrote a friend, ". . . that I have declared there must be an abridgment of English liberties. They might have just as well charged David with saying, 'There is no God.'" Thomas Hutchinson was clearly feeling the strain of his office.

As for the Whigs, they had never been more alive, more united, more devoted to each other and to their cause. The *amor patriae* that Mercy Warren spoke of as being characteristic of the times — aroused by the issue of the judges' salary, spread by the committees of correspondence, strengthened by the open debate on the constitution, and inflamed by the exposure of the letters — was truly a new and different kind of patriotic experience. The people were no longer simply joining forces to resist a specific measure or save a special liberty; they were saving Liberty itself. They had found large areas of agreement, large enough perhaps to comprise a nation; now they were trying on a new identity: the American identity. What would it feel like to be, first and last, Americans? For Puritans particularly, the idea was full of promise. Having missed out on the opportunity to establish a new country geographically, they might have the opportunity to establish it politically, to complete the work of their highly romanticized ancestors. Then free at last of corrupting European ties and influence, they would surely, like their ancestors, achieve righteousness, Godliness, and brotherhood — all of which they would need in abundance if they were to form a republic of their own. A republic, they recognized, required more virtue than a more autocratic form of government — less self-interest, more self-discipline — but if at times the people worried that they might not measure up, at other times they told themselves that once they had their republic, they would be transformed. If a republican government required virtue, it would also inspire virtue.

Already they felt quite virtuous and a great deal more brotherly than usual. The shadows of war were close enough so that all their finer instincts had been animated, yet not so close that those instincts had been tested. It was a moment in history when peace and war were balanced, when one could talk bravely about sacrifice and still avoid thinking about husbands and sons, when one could decide what form government should not take and yet not be required to define too specifically what form it should take. It was, in short, a period of such idealism among the Whigs, such community of spirit, that afterward Mercy Warren and her friends would look back on it as the good old days before the Revolutionary War, just as their fathers had looked back on the days before the French and Indian War.

John Adams could not resist the spirit of the times. "I was born for Business," he decided abruptly, and entered the lists again. He ran for a seat in the House in the spring election, was duly elected, and quickly negatived; but he was in no mood for retirement. The private life which he had been celebrating only a few months before could no longer compete with the mounting excitement of public affairs. "I have never known a Period," he said, "in which the Seeds of great Events have been so plentifully sown." He spoke with the obvious relish of one who enjoyed sowing.

As for Samuel Adams, he was ready for great events. That winter he had his house "new covered and glased" and his rooms refurnished, papered, and painted. There was momentous business being transacted in that house these days; important men were coming and going, yet perhaps nothing was more significant than what Samuel Adams was doing alone at his desk. It was here that he was advancing the idea that Parliament had no authority whatsoever over the colonies, that each colonial legislature was its own parliament, subject only to the king. When Samuel Adams spoke of the Parliament at Westminster now, he called it specifically the "British Parliament" to distinguish it from the American legislatures, and when he mentioned the Massachusetts House of Representatives, he referred to it grandly as "his majesty's commons." The people, experimenting with the sound of a new America, took up the phrases. Hannah Winthrop, writing to Mercy Warren in April 1773, spoke with possessive pride of "our house of Commons." Benjamin Church, one of the inner circle of Whig leaders, said liberty was "the happiness of living under laws of our own making."

For Mercy Warren the period was especially exciting. At the age of forty-five, she had the heady experience of discovering potentials within herself that she had scarcely explored. Up to now Mercy had, in line with her literary interests, experimented with genteel verse, conducted a wide and often florid correspondence, read avidly, and talked as much as it was becoming, but this was all in the female tradition. She admitted that at times she regretted she was not a man, for then she believed she would be free of the conflict between body and soul. Occasionally she chafed at what she called "the bounds, The narrow bounds" of female life, but Mercy was no pace setter, no feminist. She admired the old-fashioned, retiring virtues in a woman (even if she confessed to being deficient in them): the modesty, "gentleness, charity, and piety that adorned the female of earlier times." Then all at once she found that perhaps she could be suitably modest and at the same time enter the male world of politics that had always attracted her. It was John Adams who encouraged her to apply her literary talents to the patriots' cause and who reassured her that she was not being unseemly. James Warren would also have backed her up, but Mercy did not completely trust his judgment; he was her husband and prejudiced (although she liked to hear him say — and he often did — that she had a woman's temperament and a man's mind which was exactly the way Mercy liked to look at herself). Abigail Adams was another staunch supporter but Mercy said that Abigail would be partial to her because she was a woman. What Mercy craved was the approval of John Adams; indeed, her confidence in her new role depended on it.

In the spring of 1773 Mercy's first dramatic and political work, a satire, appeared in the *Boston Gazette,* probably intended as part of the anniversary observation of the Massacre. She called it *The Adulateur,* set it in the fictional country of Upper Servia, and peopled it with Boston's leading political figures disguised as Roman citizens. Thomas Hutchinson was the archvillain, Rapatio — ambitious, self-seeking, power-hungry, planning a massacre in retaliation for the destruction of his house. ("Hell! what a night was this — and do they think/ I'll e'er *forget* such treatment! No.") The hero, Brutus, was of course James Otis, Jr., the perfect patriot-philosopher, soldier, martyr, talking reason at times, breathing fire at other times, and intermittently weeping for his country. ("Long have I wept in secret — nay, could weep/ 'Till tears were chang'd to blood.") *The Adulateur* was, as a takeoff on Shakespeare, uninspired — neither subtle nor witty; yet as verse, it was competent enough, equal to anything of its kind being published in America, and as a piece of rousing propaganda, a call to arms, it served its purpose admirably. In the bargain, it would have amused the Whigs. They would have enjoyed reading about togaed Tories (whom they all recognized) with names like Dupe, Meagre, Gripeall, Hazelrod, boasting of deeds that would make even "Nero weep."

Satire was uniquely suited to this moment of history and it was also suited to Mercy's pen. She was an Otis, and like the Otises, she was a fighter; all she had needed was a weapon and an audience and now she had them. There was no question that she had an enemy; once she had established Rapatio as her stand-in for Thomas Hutchinson, she went after him as one who had long overdue grudges to settle. One play was not enough nor one punishment sufficient. On May 24, 1773, she brought him out again in the *Boston Gazette* and this time she stood him on the scaffold.

> "I fall *unpitied* [*he said*], *not one weeping Eye*
> *Shall wail my Fate or heave a Tender Sigh."*

This play was *The Defeat* and in it she introduced her friends: James Warren as Rusticus, John Adams as Hortensius, Samuel

Adams as Cassius. But Mercy Warren had a literary problem. She could hardly hang Rapatio in one drama and expect him to be around to play the villain in her next, and yet she could never bear to let him survive. Apparently this did not worry her. In July, after the Hutchinson letters had appeared, she revived Rapatio for Part Two of *The Defeat,* stood him on his feet for a few pages, and then annihilated him again. At the end he might well ask:

"Is the Game up? Can I deceive no more?"

Mercy obviously reveled in her battles; yet, like her brother James, sometimes after a round she gave way to doubts — never that she might be wrong but that she might appear unwomanly. Was it appropriate for a woman to write satire at all? she asked. She did not question that satire by its very nature had to be bold nor did she suggest that she felt any feminine delicacy in approaching it. If blood had to be spilled in print, she was more than ready to spill it, to pave the street with human skulls, if need be. Actually she seemed to dote on gory descriptions of battle: soldiers belched slaughter in her plays, daggers sweated blood, men emptied their veins; the implication seemed to be that the bloodier one was, the more patriotic one would be. And it was as a patriot that Mercy wished primarily to be known; her literary ambitions were secondary and she had no desire at all to be called a feminist. She liked to think of her writing, as she later expressed it, "as the amusement of solitude, at a period when every active member of society was engaged, either in the field, or the cabinet, to resist the strong hand of foreign domination." The question was: Would others approve? Was she, by writing satire, exposing herself to criticism?

Once in a doubtful mood she wrote to John Adams. "Though . . . a Little personal Acrimony Might be justifiable in your sex," she said, "must not the female Character suffer. (And will she not be suspected as deficient in the most amiable part thereof . . .) if she indulges her pen to paint in the darkest shades, even those whose Vice and Venality have rendered contemptible."

"I should think myself very happy," John Adams replied gallantly, "if I could remove a Scruple from a Mind, which is so amiable that it ought not to have one upon it . . . The faithfull Historian delineates Characters truly, let the Censure fall where it will. The public is so interested in public Characters, that they have a Right to know them, and it becomes the Duty of every good Citizen who happens to be acquainted with them to communicate his Knowledge."

This was surely reassurance enough, but John went further, addressing himself specifically to Mrs. Warren's talent.

"Of all the Genius's which have yet arisen in America," he wrote, "there has been none, Superior, to one, which now shines, in this happy, exquisite Faculty . . . I know of none, ancient or modern, which has reached the tender the pathetic, the keen and severe, and at the same time, the Soft, the Sweet, the amiable and the pure in greater Perfection."

With such encouragement, Mercy must, at least for the moment, have felt capable of writing anything. That the doubts returned, however, from time to time is not surprising; Mercy, who did not approve of audacity in a woman, was in a sense being quite audacious. Few women were writing anything in America, let alone satire, and in England the only woman writer whom Mercy admired or whose approval she would have sought was that champion of liberty, Catherine Macaulay, customarily referred to as "the celebrated Mrs. Macaulay," who was practicing what Mercy considered the most noble of all art forms, the writing of history. Indeed, not only was she writing the history of England, but in the best Puritan tradition she was grounding it in morality, extolling the virtues of liberty-loving, republican-minded men wherever she found them and, as John Adams said, stripping off the "Gilden and false Lustre from the worthless Princes and Nobles." John called her "one of the brightest ornaments not only of her Sex but of her Age and Country"; as such a paragon, she must have been an inspiration to Mercy Warren who, of course, was also eager to ornament but not betray her sex.

American Whigs adored Mrs. Macaulay, corresponded with her,

visited her in England, and speculated about her endlessly. What was she like? Abigail asked her cousin Isaac Smith in London. "One of my own Sex so eminent in a tract so uncommon naturally raises my curiosity." There were various reports about Mrs. Macaulay, depending largely on whether the reporter was a Whig or a Tory, but all would have agreed that Mrs. Macaulay, although not handsome, played her role with considerable flair. She was said to receive visitors in exotic foreign costumes, to appear on formal occasions with the longest train in the room, and in later life to use mud baths for her complexion. In England, James Boswell, a Tory and always glad to make fun of her, drew her in caricature:

> Like a Dutch vrouw, all shapeless, pale, and fat,
> That hugs and slabbers her ungainly brat,
> Our Cath'rine sits sublime o'er steaming tea,
> And takes her dear Republic on her knee:
> Sings it all songs that ever yet were sung,
> And licks it fondly with her length of tongue.

Isaac Smith was kinder. He wrote John Adams: "She is not so much distinguished in company by the beauties of her person, as the accomplishments of her mind."

In June 1773, Mercy Warren, emboldened perhaps by her own recent literary success and encouraged by John Adams, wrote to Catherine Macaulay. She had no need to introduce herself; Mrs. Macaulay had been a long-time admirer of James Otis and had once sent him a copy of her history. Mercy's letter, written at the height of the excitement over the Hutchinson letters, was the beginning of a friendship between these two like-minded women, although at the time Mercy said that "conscious inferiority checks the ambitious hope of a long correspondence." Yet they did write back and forth for many years and, if Mercy ever needed courage, surely she must have found it in the example of Catherine Macaulay; a tougher, more independent and opinionated woman did not exist in the eighteenth century.

Mercy's first letter to Catherine Macaulay was primarily a solicitation for friendship, but it also posed a question that must have troubled any Whig who had the least memory of loyalty stirring within him: What had happened to England? Mercy, of course, couched the question in far more elevated terms: "Has the genius of Liberty . . . forsaken that devoted Island?" she asked. "What fatal infatuation has seized the parent state?" The time, however, was already passing when Whigs concerned themselves with such speculation. Even now as Mercy was writing, the parent state had passed a new measure for the colonies that would, in fact, be fatal.

The Tea Act of 1773 was proposed by Lord North, who had been the prime minister for three years. A lazy, good-natured, honest, loyal, and unselfish man, he was free of vices but devoid of strengths and utterly unsuited to the business of leading, let alone saving, an empire. Nor apparently did he look the part. His protruding eyes, thick lips, and bloated cheeks gave him the air, Horace Walpole said, of a "blind trumpeter." He did not even enjoy his role and kept it only because he was too loyal and too passive to resist the king's entreaties.

At the moment, however, Lord North was happy. The Tea Act was the kind of legislation he could endorse with a whole heart; it should please everyone. Certainly it would please the East India Tea Company, which was on the verge of bankruptcy with its warehouses full of tea that Americans would not buy. The colonists were retaliating against the high cost of tea — due to Charles Townshend's three-pence tax per pound on tea sold to the colonies and to Britain's stipulation that the East India Tea Company land American-bound tea in England first, pay an importation duty, and auction it to the highest bidder.

Now under the new act, the company would no longer have to stop in England; instead it would be allowed to consign the tea to a small group of its own agents and export it directly to America, thus avoiding both the middleman fee and the importation duty. This would reduce the price of the tea from twenty shillings a pound to ten shillings, making it cheaper than tea sold in England and cheaper than tea smuggled from Holland, which, Lord North reasoned, should certainly please Americans. And, of course, the king and Parliament would also be pleased because Lord North had maintained the right of taxation. Mr. Townshend's three-pence tea tax was still in effect and it would be collected in America.

It apparently did not occur to Lord North that America, able now to buy tea at a substantial saving, would not be happy. Yet to the Whigs, of course, the Tea Act was a trick. If Americans accepted the tea, they would be recognizing England's right to tax them and they would also be supporting a monopolistic practice that discriminated against the majority of merchants in favor of those few consignees of the East India Company, the real beneficiaries of the act. As it happened, two of the five consignees in Boston were Thomas and Elisha Hutchinson, sons of the governor, another was Richard Clarke, a nephew; and Thomas Hutchinson himself owned stock in the company.

Long before the tea reached Boston, it was apparent that this was an issue which might actually start hostilities. Indeed, it was said that by the time the first ship, the *Dartmouth,* arrived on November 28 there was not a pistol that could be bought in the town.

On December 5 Abigail Adams, recovering from a long illness and able to leave her bedroom for only part of every day, sat down to write her friend Mercy Warren.

"The Tea that bainfull weed is arrived," she said. "Great and I hope Effectual opposition had been made to the landing of it . . . The flame is kindled and like Lightning it catches from Soul to Soul . . . My Heart beats at every Whistle I hear, and I dare not openly express half my fears."

But the story of Boston's tea belongs not to the Whigs as much as it belongs to Thomas Hutchinson. It is the story of the last stand of a governor, the last stand of a certain kind of aristocrat; for although Hutchinson believed in self-government, he looked back wistfully to the early days in the province when the people voluntarily elected

men from the first families to govern them, and, although he had
once taken considerable pleasure in the popularity that attended him
when he moderated town meetings, now he looked on town meetings, at least as they were currently being conducted, as invitations to
mob rule. He worried about "levelling" tendencies in the government and what he called "creeping statesmen," and when he took his
stand on Boston's tea, he was not only supporting the king, he was
defending a way of life. And saving his country, or so he believed.

No one doubted but that Thomas Hutchinson would be firm —
least of all, Thomas Hutchinson himself, who still smarted from the
memory of that one time three years before when he had given in to
the Whigs and when his sons, then as now, had been in difficulty
because of tea consignments. The circumstances, although more serious now, were similar enough to have freshened Thomas Hutchinson's sense of guilt about the previous affair and to have stiffened his
resolve for this one. Yet firm and duty-bound as he was, he was a
reluctant fighter. Up to the last minute he hoped that the ships
would anchor above Castle William so that if it was decided they
should return to London without unloading, they could do so without involving him and without requiring a customs permit. Once
they had tied up at the docks, this would be impossible. But they did
tie up. There were other goods on board — most of New England's
supplies for the winter, as it happened, including perhaps Hutchinson's own order: a scarlet suit, a cloth frock with waistcoat and
breeches "not a pure white but next to it," a surtout of light shag or
beaver, and a velvet cape to give (as he told his tailor) "a little life"
to the outfit.

At the moment, however, Hutchinson was not interested in scarlet suits and velvet capes and the people were not interested in sacri-
ficing their goods just to make the return of the tea easy for the
governor. What the people wanted was for the consignees to resign
their commissions and send the tea back. But Hutchinson's sons
would not do it. When they were asked to come to the Liberty Tree
at a certain time, they did not appear. When representatives from

the town called on them in Boston, they found that the sons had
gone to Milton; when the representatives went to Milton, they were
told that the sons had left for Boston. Under pressure the consignees
wrote one letter claiming that they could not resign because they did
not know the particulars of their commissions. Later they wrote another letter saying that there were now legal contingencies that put
it out of their power to comply with the request of the town.

These answers were voted unsatisfactory by a town meeting and
in a last attempt at mediation John Singleton Copley offered to go to
Castle William (where the consignees had taken refuge) and bring
them back to the meeting if in turn the people would guarantee
their safety. But even Copley, a relative of the Clarkes and a Tory
himself, was unsuccessful. The consignees refused to move. And
without their resignation the tea could not be shipped back unless
the customhouse cleared it and the customhouse would not clear it
unless the taxes were paid. What was more, a ship had only twenty
days of grace; after that, a customs officer could legally seize the
cargo.

Meanwhile Thomas Hutchinson had tried to dissolve the town
meetings; he had refused to allow any vessel to leave the harbor
without his permission; he had ordered the cannon at Castle William to be charged and he had arranged for two government ships to
guard the channels to prevent the tea ships from slipping out to sea.
Then on Thursday, December 16, one day before the twenty days
were up, Thomas Hutchinson retired to his home in Milton, hoping
perhaps to avoid a last-minute delegation but knowing that he alone
still had it in his power to override the customs officer and to issue a
pass to the tea ships, even if it was irregular. But, of course, it was
too late. He and his sons and the customs officer had all gone too far
to retreat — not that he would want to in any case. He had always
believed that the Whigs would back down in a final confrontation if
the government were only strong enough; how could they help it?
God ruled Thomas Hutchinson's world even above Parliament, and
a man who did his duty had every right to expect God's will (and

his own) to be done. "I know," he wrote once, "that the great Governor of the world always does right"; he was equally confident in the governor of Massachusetts. Yet simply because Hutchinson did not question his duty did not make that duty any more palatable. It could not have been easy for him to give that final no to his countrymen when they arrived at Milton Hill late in the afternoon — a delegation sent by the people who awaited, seven thousand strong, in the Old South Church to see if he would change his mind.

When it was all over, when Hutchinson's no had been relayed, when the tea had been finally dumped in the harbor, when it had drifted out to sea and had been washed like seaweed back on the shores around Boston, Thomas Hutchinson spoke about "the forlorn state" he was in. To an old friend he wrote: "Nobody suspected they would suffer the tea to be destroyed, there being so many men of property active at these meetings."

Yet Thomas Hutchinson's life was built so solidly on a single premise, the power of Britain seemed to him so absolutely irresistible, that even after he had proved himself wrong in this instance, he continued to believe that the trouble in Massachusetts was due to a few seditious leaders. All would be well again if only England would play a strong hand and impose upon the colonies a sense of parliamentary authority. No matter how united, how determined, how successful the Whigs demonstrated themselves to be during the next months, no matter how much he and his family suffered as a result, Thomas Hutchinson never gauged the depth of the province's drive toward autonomy — not even after the Whigs tried to impeach the Chief Justice, Peter Oliver, not even after the shameful funeral of his brother, Andrew Oliver, who was cheered by irreverent Whigs into his grave, not even after Hutchinson's son Elisha and his wife had been forced to flee Plymouth (his wife's home) in the midst of a January snowstorm, and not even after he himself had been hung in effigy. Hutchinson bore it all, even his moods of depression, with stoicism and dignity, convinced that since it was a just world, he would finally be vindicated.

He was also sustained by the knowledge that he would shortly be

going to England. At the beginning of 1774 he had been notified
that he had been granted a leave but his departure was delayed, first
by the illness and then by the death of the lieutenant governor, Andrew Oliver. Meanwhile he looked forward to being in London,
where he could answer in person the allegations the Whigs had
been making against him and where he hoped to have a direct
hand in shaping a successful colonial policy. It was May, however, before England informed him that a successor, General
Thomas Gage, had been appointed to take his place while he was
away. The news arrived along with the announcement that as a
punishment for the tea incident Boston Harbor would be closed as
of June 1 and would stay closed until obedience was paid to the
English government.

As it happened, Thomas Hutchinson left Boston the very day that
the port was closed — indeed, while the bells of the city were tolling
to mark the unhappy event. He did not expect to be gone long. He
left his home in Milton in care of his son Thomas, Jr., and although
he had planned to leave his seventeen-year-old daughter Peggy and
his son Elisha behind also, he had finally succumbed to their entreaties and allowed them to go with him. Peggy had written her sister-
in-law Polly: "You may not know how to pity me, who have been
running from a mob ever since the year sixty-five; but soon do I
hope be out of their reach, as I am now pretty certain papa will not
go without me. We had a little contest, but you know the women
always gain their point." Billy, the governor's youngest son, who
never seemed able to latch on to any kind of satisfactory employ-
ment, was already in England, where the governor hoped to establish profitable connections for him.

Thomas Hutchinson was in good spirits the day he left town.
Milton Hill never looked better than it did in June, the meadows
newly green, the fruit trees in bloom or ready to burst into bloom;
and to make the day seem even more agreeable, Hutchinson carried
with him a letter of appreciation that he had just received, signed by
one hundred and twenty men — an indication perhaps of even
larger numbers of quiet and reasonable men who still held him in

esteem. And so as he walked for the last time between the two rows of buttonwood trees he had planted, he was filled with love for his land and his people and possibly also with dreams that in England he could serve his country in its political conflict as successfully as he had served it in its boundary and currency disputes. Thomas Hutchinson walked slowly down the hill to his carriage that waited for him at the bottom, taking time to savor the texture of the New England spring and to greet his neighbors as they came out to the road to bid him good-bye. He would be back soon, he told them; he would be back soon.

The next day the province received the worst news of all, but by this time Thomas Hutchinson was at sea beyond the reach of an angry populace. The announcement of Parliament's so-called Intolerable or Coercive Acts reached Boston on June 2. The first act, which came to be known as the "Murder Bill," stipulated that disturbers of the king's peace would be transported out of the province for trial, either to England or a place designated by the governor. Further acts provided that the governor should appoint his Council instead of having it elected by the House; elected juries were to be replaced by juries appointed by the sheriff, who in turn would hold his post at the discretion of the governor; town meetings, except for annual elections, could be held only if the governor gave his permission in writing; troops could be quartered wherever the governor wished to quarter them. The Massachusetts charter, which the people had clung to as they clung to their Bibles, was at last broken, pending only the final signature of the king.

• • •

"The ball of empire rolled westward," Mercy Warren wrote later. ". . . The painful period hastened on, when the connexion which nature and interest had long maintained between Great Britain and the colonies must be broken off; the sword drawn, and the scabbard thrown down the gulf of time."

Act Two

VII

"WE ARE ALL upon our oars in expectation of War," Samuel Otis wrote Joseph in February 1774. By summer Boston was an armed camp. The Common, where townspeople were accustomed to put their cows to graze, was occupied by four regiments, three companies of artillery, and twenty-two pieces of cannon. The docks, normally the heart of Boston's life, were deserted except for knots of sullen seamen who gathered from time to time to stare beyond closed warehouses to a harbor stripped of everything but bare masts and British warships. "It is now a very gloomy place, the Streets almost empty," the wife of one of the commissioners reported.

From a Tory point of view, Boston must have seemed particularly gloomy, for like Thomas Hutchinson, the Tories had generally believed that Boston would be cowed by severe measures and a show of force and, if it were not, it would surely be abandoned by the other colonies and even by the rest of the province. Instead, it was the Tories who were giving ground. Soon after Hutchinson left, many of those who had signed the address of appreciation to the governor found it expedient to confess that they had signed "inadvertently" and to publish their retractions. As for the other colonies, they not only supported Boston in its continued refusal to pay for the tea, they agreed to meet in the fall at a continental congress to consider further measures to protect their liberties. Meanwhile the whole country united to help Boston in its beleaguered state. In every issue the *Boston Gazette* reported new donations to the town: a gift of wheat from Quebec, a drove of sheep from "Our brethern at

Scituate," 1200 bushels of rye and 50 barrels of flour from Monmouth County, New Jersey, 900 bushels of grain from Hartford, Connecticut, rice from South Carolina.

The news that the king had signed the Coercive Acts arrived during the first week in August, along with the list of thirty-six men who had been appointed to serve as "mandamus councilors" in the General Court of Massachusetts. Mercy Warren heard the news on her return to Plymouth after a visit to Barnstable and recognized it immediately as another step, perhaps an irrevocable one, toward war. "I think the appointment of the new counsel," she wrote Abigail Adams, "is the last comic scene we shall see Exhibite'd in the state Farce which has for several years been playing off. I fear the Tragic part of the Drama will hastely Ensue."

It was inevitable, perhaps, that Americans should think of themselves now, as Mercy did, in ever more dramatic terms — a unique people moving to the center of a stage to fulfill their special destiny. The more seriously American liberties were threatened, the more clear it became to Americans that theirs was the Promised Land, the last hope of civilization, the one place uncontaminated by history, where it might yet be possible to establish a virtuous society. Virtue for the eighteenth-century American was equated not only with freedom but with simplicity; it was founded on nature and natural law; its progenitors were the classical heroes; its source was a God who, if inscrutable, was reasonable; it flourished best in a rural atmosphere; it was most liable to corruption if exposed to luxury; and it was doomed to destruction if subjected to power, that allconsuming, least resistible evil against which the people of Massachusetts were even now taking steps so extreme, so independent that, from the point of view of the ministry, they could only be considered treasonous. After the Coercive Acts became official, Massachusetts set up its own provincial government, closed the courts rather than imply submission to parliamentary acts, substituted a provincial treasurer for Harrison Gray, who represented the crown, stopped mentioning the king in prayers, began arming and training what it

called its "minutemen," and in one county convention after another
expressed determination to resist arbitrary changes in government,
even to the point of fighting if necessary.

Every town had its confrontations. Timothy Ruggles, newly appointed mandamus councilor from Hardwick, was persuaded to resign from office after his horse had been painted and its tail and
mane cut off; Peter Oliver was persuaded after an unpleasant visit
from some Sons of Liberty; Timothy Paine of Worcester, after he
had been forced to walk through the center of town with his hat off
(always a disgrace). It took less to subdue George Watson of
Plymouth. On the Sunday after he had been sworn in as councilor,
he went to church dressed in the scarlet coat he customarily wore,
but when he took his seat, one by one his friends and neighbors in
the congregation rose, put on their hats, and left. As they passed his
pew, he bent his bald head over his cane and determined then and
there to retire from public life.

In Barnstable, Colonel Otis, Chief Justice of the Inferior Court,
was persuaded against opening the court for its September session,
although this was an argument not between Whigs and Tories but
primarily between moderate and radical Whigs who for the next
years were to keep this town in a constant ferment. Colonel Otis, a
moderate who as always sought a broad political base, was not surprised by the army of twelve hundred citizens that marched from
Sandwich to Barnstable in double file and "at the beat of a drum."
Joseph Otis was a member of this citizen army and the Colonel,
standing before his house, watched the army on its way to town.
Indeed, he acknowledged their greeting, for the "whole people
raised their hats . . . as they passed," it was reported later, and the
Colonel was not one to alienate "the whole people" or, as they also
referred to themselves, "The Body of the People" — a phrase much
used now, reflecting the fact that after years of opposition to their
rulers, the people had come to think of themselves in corporate
terms and with a common and somehow infallible will. The
Colonel respected this will, and although in the matter of the courts

he refused the people initially, he did this largely as a matter of form and probably as a concession to more conservative members on the court. In any case, his reputation as a Whig suffered not at all. The next day, the people marched in formal procession, accompanied by music, to ask his assurance that he would attend the next (and, as it turned out, the last) session of the General Court. When he agreed, "the whole body with their heads uncovered . . . gave three cheers in token of their satisfaction."

Many Whigs found it difficult to follow the province down a path which had clearly turned from mere opposition toward outright re-bellion. Edward Bacon, Colonel Otis' cousin and long-time rival, opposed every step of the provincial government vociferously. Sam Fayerweather, brother of Hannah Winthrop and minister at St. Paul's, could not bear to leave the king's name out of his prayers and so stopped officiating. Hannah Lincoln, a friend of Mercy Warren's, was so resentful about what the radical Whigs were doing that she sat down and wrote Mercy. Hannah had not corresponded with her before, but it is not surprising that in her present mood she should address Mercy who was, perhaps like no other woman in Massachu-setts, at the center of the radical movement and well known for her strong, outspoken views. Why, Hannah asked, did the Whigs insist upon inviting more trouble?

"You seem inclined to censure the spirit of independence," Mercy replied. "I wish you would for a few moments contemplate the nature of man." Mercy had always found it invigorating to enlighten her friends and, indeed, no one articulated more staunchly and with fewer deviations the basic truths accepted by the New England in-tellectual, Puritan-oriented Whigs of her generation. All men, she said, were endowed by nature with the same spirit of independence. What was astonishing was that in spite of this common endowment, "the greater part of the species in all ages of the world should be-come the willing dupes of a few." Some government by mutual consent was of course necessary, but the least government, the better, and although Mercy admitted that Whigs had sometimes committed "irregularities," this was "productive of less evil than an abject submission to corrupt and venal governors."

Mercy's own spirit of independence flamed through her correspondence, but she too was afraid. Sometimes she worried that the patriots would not be equal to the days ahead, sometimes that she herself would not be equal to them — that "the woman in her," as she often expressed it, would get the upper hand. And, indeed, "the woman in her" was a force to be reckoned with, especially at night when, unable to sleep, she did most of her worrying. She was concerned about her husband, particularly when it was rumored that Gage, under the authority of the Coercive Acts, would arrest the leading Whig radicals and send them to England to be tried for treason. Samuel Adams and John Hancock, who would be the first on Gage's "wanted" list, were, along with John Adams, in Philadelphia attending the Continental Congress. But there were many in that inner circle of rebels: Joseph Warren, the attractive young doctor who was more or less in charge of Boston activities during Samuel Adams' absence, Benjamin Church, James Warren, and others. And if James were actually taken from her, Mercy asked herself, what would she do then? She could scarcely imagine living without him. Would it be best to take her own life in the manner of Portia, Brutus' wife, who had swallowed hot coals at her husband's death? No, she finally decided; it would be cowardly not to finish her "part in the Drama of Life." Besides, there were her sons to think of, although in her nighttime fantasies she foresaw dire consequences for them, too. Only James, Jr., at seventeen was old enough to fight; George and Henry were eight and ten years old respectively, but Mercy saw all five forced to "Buckle on the Harness." "No one," she concluded, "has at stake a larger share of Domestic Felicity than myself."

Yet fearful as she might be, Mercy was obviously stimulated by the times. She was writing. A year before, just prior to the Tea Party, she had written a poem for John Adams which had been inspired by a discussion between the two couples on that much-

debated question of the day: Was mankind motivated only by
self-love? Although Mercy was forever bemoaning the selfishness
inherent in man, she rejected the more formal and, indeed, more cyni-
cal expression set forth in such works as Hobbes's *Leviathan* and
Mandeville's *Fable of the Bees,* which claimed that self-love was the
only impetus to human behavior and only a strong monarchy could
control a society composed of self-centered men.

> *If such is Life, And Fancy throw the Bowl,*
> *If appetite and caprice Rule the Whole,*
>
> . . . .
>
> *Then I must Wish to bid the World Farewell,*
> *Turn Anchorit and choose some Lonely Cell*
> *Beneath some peaceful Hermitage Reclin'd*
> *To Weep the Misery of all Mankind.*

Shortly after the Tea Party, she wrote at John Adams' request a
mock heroic celebration of the event in which she depicted a group
of sea nymphs delighted at suddenly finding "a profusion of Deli-
cious teas" in the water — "Choice Sochong, and the imperial Leaf."
Later in "A Political Reverie" she implored "each languid soul" to
rise

> *Till every bosom feels a noble flame*
> *And emulates a Locke or Sydney's name.*

Now in the fall of 1774 she was working on what she would later
consider her most important dramatic work, *The Group,* a satire
about the mandamus councilors, whom Mercy showed surrounded
by "a court of sycophants, hungry harpies, and unprincipled danglers
. . . hovering over the stage in the shape of locusts." Since Hutchinson was in England, Mercy could not have included Rapatio in her
cast much as she might have liked to, but she saw to it that her
"group" acknowledged him as their master when they spoke of their
sins. And Mercy's villains were disarmingly open about their sins.

If their minds were venomous, they said so; if they were greedy or
power hungry, they advertised it. They saw themselves exactly as
the Whigs saw them, and indeed, what made them seem so evil
(and at home in satire) was the fact that they pursued evil so deliberately, even in the books they read. With considerable care Mercy
selected what she thought would be appropriate books for a Tory
library and placed them in a cabinet in the corner of her set:
Hobbes's *Leviathan,* Hutchinson's *History,* Mandeville's *Fable of the
Bees, Hoyle on Whist, Lives of the Stuarts, Statutes of Henry the
Eighth, Statutes of William the Conqueror,* and *Acts of Parliament
for 1774.*

Mercy obviously found it satisfying to dispose of her enemies so
neatly on paper; in real life it was not so easy. The Tories were
writing too. The *Massachusetts Gazette,* the Tory newspaper, was
filled with attacks on the Continental Congress, with prophecies that
the rebels would be destroyed by the British and damned by God,
and with exhaustive essays on the Tory position, most notably by
someone who signed himself *Massachusettensis.* Actually, Daniel
Leonard of Taunton, the foppish Beau Trumps of Mercy's "group,"
was Massachusettensis, but the Whigs did not know this yet and
Mercy referred to him only as "that state Crokedile." Harrison Gray,
Samuel Otis' Tory father-in-law and long-time friend of the Otises
and Warrens, was also attacking the Whigs, first publicly in a
pamphlet, *The Two Congresses Cut* (which the Whigs called *The
Gray Maggot*), and then privately in a letter to James Warren in
which he talked darkly of treason and ruin and confronted Warren
with a demand for instant satisfaction of an old debt.

"I am very sensible that I owe you money," James Warren replied, "and that every Man has a right to Call for his Debts; but
then I think every man should give a little warning." He could not
pay the money at present, James said, and wondered at the extraordinary nature of Harrison Gray's letter. "If you expect . . . to Intimidate or drive me from the Paths I have walked . . . you have
mistaken your Man. I have long since fortified myself against either

Allurements, or Threats. I am now perfectly satisfied with the part I have taken in Government both from its rectitude and the prospect of Success attending it."

Most immediately aggravating to the Warrens, however, were the Tories in Plymouth, particularly the Winslow family, James's cousins. "Little" Ned Winslow, as the Warrens persisted in calling him as much for his officiousness as his youth, had been a thorn in the side of Whigs ever since his graduation from Harvard in 1765. He had opposed the formation of the committees of correspondence, had tried to block the embargo on tea, and had protested the Tea Party. Moreover, he had been one of those who had refused to allow the public to take any part in planning the celebration of Forefathers' Day, the anniversary of the landing of the *Mayflower*, which was Plymouth's most gala day of the year. This was a private affair, Winslow said, the exclusive business of the Old Colony Club and its twelve members (all *Mayflower* descendants) who had first started observing the day five years before.

Now, however, it was 1774 and high time to take Forefathers' Day out of Tory hands, at least so reasoned James Warren and the few Whig members of the Tory-dominated club. Accordingly, they did not consult the club; they simply went to work on a program which would, it was hoped, set the town afire with patriotic zeal. They planned to move the rock on which the Pilgrims were supposed to have first stepped and give it a more noble setting. As it was now, only a portion of the rock could be seen and not even this would be there if anyone had ever been able to move it. It had been tried once, not with any thought of preserving it but simply because it was in the way of a wharf that was being built. The wharf had eventually been built around it. Now the bottom of the rock was submerged in the sand beneath the wharf and the top poked through the plankings, hardly a dignified situation for an historic landmark, but then no one had realized its history until a few years before when a ninety-five-year-old elder of the church, after considerable prodding, had recalled the story. In any case, whether or not the

Plymouth rock had served the Pilgrims' cause, James Warren and his friends determined that it would serve theirs.

On the morning of December 22 they went to the waterfront with twenty yoke of oxen, a supply of large screws and chain, and a contingent of the strongest and burliest members of the Sons of Liberty. The whole town turned out, if not all out of a sense of patriotism, then out of a sense of curiosity, and surely no one was more curious than Ned Winslow, who could have watched the scene (and probably preferred to) from the window of his house overlooking the harbor. From there he would not have been able to follow the struggle in detail but he would have seen the straining oxen; he would have heard the cheers when the rock was finally secured.

It was not a complete triumph. While the rock was being mounted on its carriage, a crack, which no one had noticed, deepened. The rock split in two and the lower portion fell back into the sand. Still, the Whigs had the top half which weighed several tons and ignoring the scattered rumblings that the broken rock was a portent of a broken empire, they formed a grand procession to escort the rock to its place of consecration at the foot of the liberty pole. The schoolchildren of the town marched first; then came the oxen, the rock, and the leading citizens, and finally a cart which was drawn by six young boys (surely including at least one of the Warrens) and which carried a miniature reproduction of the *Mayflower*. John Cotton, a local minister, gave an address, a volley of small arms was fired, and the rock, which may have borne the footprints of the first settlers and certainly bore the footprints of everyone since who had walked down that busy wharf, became exactly what the Warrens had hoped it would become: a symbol of liberty.

But if the Whigs had their day, less than a month later the Tories had theirs. They had convinced General Gage that they needed protection from their rebel neighbors, and so on one cold January day several British vessels anchored outside the harbor and the "Queen's Guards" marched down from Boston to make their headquarters in Marshfield on the edge of Plymouth. Mercy Warren called the movement "Ridiculous"; Ned Winslow entertained the officers; and Marshfield's town clerk, described as "not a robust man," simply pulled the skirts down around the bed of his spare room. Under this bed was stored a large part of the town's powder supply which the Whigs had managed to hide just before the troops arrived.

Actually, the presence of the troops was more a vexation than a threat. The Whigs resented being wakened at night by the cry of the sentry; they disliked seeing redcoats on their streets and once they broke the sword of one whom they considered arrogant. But on the whole they tried to ignore what was, after all, a relatively small detachment of about one hundred men.

The Whigs had far more serious threats to worry about. In February after hearing that the king and Parliament had renewed their pledge to exert authority over America, Abigail Adams wrote Mercy: "The die is cast . . . Infatuated Britain! poor distressed America. Heaven only knows what is next to take place but it seems to me the Sword is now our only . . . alternative." And, indeed, on several occasions in the next weeks the sword was almost drawn: once when a regiment of British regulars was narrowly diverted from capturing a cannon at Salem, again at the service to commemorate the Boston Massacre which was attended not only by Whigs but by a large number of redcoats, obviously looking for trouble and probably hoping for evidence that would justify a wholesale arrest of Whig leaders. The fact that trouble did not develop was due partly to Joseph Warren, the orator (dressed in a toga), who studiously avoided using the words *bloody massacre*, and partly to luck. According to one tradition, at the first insult a British soldier was supposed to throw an egg as a signal for his fellow soldiers to advance, but the soldier had slipped and dropped the egg on the way to the meeting. Furthermore, the meeting came to a premature end when a cry of "Fie! Fie!" in the audience was mistaken for "Fire! Fire!"

Everyone agreed, however, that there would have been war long before this if it had not been winter and if it had not been for what seemed a peculiar reluctance on the part of General Gage. All winter General Gage and Samuel Adams, these two men who were said by their contemporaries to look so much alike, had walked softly around each other, neither one willing to back down from the war that seemed inevitable, neither willing to be the first to strike. General Gage had insisted that he needed reinforcements, but spring was coming and General Gage, reinforcements or not, was expected to act.

Spring came suddenly in 1775, a whole month earlier than usual — a fine spring with prospects of plenty and, as one newspaper reported, "a good fall of lambs." It was as if nature were hurrying not only to create life but to make it memorable. Watching spring move into her little garden at the back of the house, Mercy was filled with apprehensions especially because James, as a member of the provincial congress at Concord, was away. She was always more prone to her spells of despondency when James was gone. Yet she tried not to worry him. "My spirits have done tolerably well," she reported in March, but, as she went on with her letter, it was evident that she was in fact distressed. She had had a dream the night before just before dawn, she confessed, and had awakened trembling, suddenly overwhelmed by the full impact of what lay ahead for the country, overwhelmed by the fact that there were now no alternatives, "no passing or retreating," no avoiding the bloodshed that would engulf a whole generation, perhaps her own family first of all. In one breath she maintained that she had no doubt of "the final success of so righteous a Cause"; in the next she asked what chance they had, "Naked & undisciplined as we are without resources or allies." Indeed, it was a measure of her despair that she who had so disdained compromise could now wish so wistfully for an honorable way to be "reconciled to old friends."

On the first of April James Warren was again in Concord, worried that he had not heard from Mercy on this trip but planning that she should join him for a few days. He had even reserved a room for her but on the second of April he canceled the reservation. News had arrived that made war seem imminent: both houses of Parliament, in spite of repeated overtures from America, in spite of pleas in America's behalf by such prominent British leaders as Lord Chatham and Edmund Burke, declared New England in a state of rebellion, denied New England fishermen the use of the Newfoundland fishing grounds, voted to reinforce General Gage's army and send three top generals to Boston (Howe, Clinton, and Burgoyne).

On April 6 James Warren wrote to Mercy, knowing that she would have heard the news and anxious as to how she was taking it. "I seem to want nothing to keep up my Spirits," he said, ". . . but seeing you in Spirits, and knowing that they flow from the heart. How shall I support myself if you suffer these Misfortunes to prey on your tender frame . . . This state of things will last but a little while. I believe we shall have many chearful rides together yet." The town of Concord, he went on to report, was full of cannon and people were beginning to move out of Boston; but at the moment he was concerned not with public affairs but with Mercy. "I long to see you. I long to sit with you under our Vines etc. and have none make us afraid. Do you know that I have not heard from you since I left you."

The next day, before sending the letter, he added a postscript. Perhaps they should prepare themselves, he said, in case they were forced to leave home. Plymouth was generally considered to be a vulnerable point, not only because it was open to navy attack but because of the army unit in Marshfield and the large number of Tories who were rumored to have made plans to take the town. "I begin to think of the Trunks which may be ready against I come home," James wrote, "we perhaps may be forced to move; if we are let us strive to submit . . . with Christian resignation and phylosophick Dignity. God has given you great abilities; you have improved them in great Acquirements . . . For all these I esteem I love you in a degree that I can't express. They are all now to be called into action for the good of mankind . . . Don't let the fluttering of your Heart interrupt your Health or disturb your repose.

Believe me I am continually Anxious about you. Ride when the weather is good and don't work or read too much at other times. I must bid you adieu. God Almighty bless you. No letter yet. What can it mean? Is she not well? She can't forget me or have any Objections to writing."

By Saturday, April 15, the Whigs had gathered enough evidence to feel sure that Gage was planning a move, probably on Concord. The provincial congress adjourned; some of the members were to return home to alert the militia, some were to go to neighboring colonies to ask for help. James Warren, on the way to Rhode Island, stopped at Plymouth and persuaded Mercy to go along. They had always enjoyed traveling together and the luxury of having long stretches of uninterrupted time to talk; on this occasion they not only had news to exchange, they had plans to make. Their route took them inland through Taunton, which seemed the most convenient place to move in case they had to evacuate Plymouth. They had friends in Taunton and probably it was through them that they were able now to locate a house and make tentative arrangements for it.

They had been in Providence only a few hours when they heard that a battle had taken place at Lexington. Express riders, thundering across the colonies, spread the news as well as rumors of atrocities that grew more barbarous with every telling. James met hastily with Rhode Island leaders; then he and Mercy left for home, "full of the most painful apprehensions," as Mercy said later, hardly able to cover the ground fast enough. At home they found the boys safe and the town deep in military preparations. The crews of the sixty vessels anchored in the harbor had already scrambled ashore to join the contingent of Plymouth men marching north. James Warren stayed home a few days to make sure the town was in no immediate danger and then he left for Watertown, the new headquarters for the provincial congress.

Actually faced with a military crisis, Mercy rose above that troublesome "woman in her" and took command like a general — planning, packing, arranging household details in case of emergency, and at the same time dispensing cheer to the troops. One moment she announced that God had proved He was on the American side; the next she repeated a horrendous tale about a British soldier who cut a woman "in pieces in her bed with her new born infant by her side." She sent fifteen-year-old Winslow to Watertown and Cambridge to deliver some letters. "He has so great a desire to see the American army," she explained. Then she wrote a bracing letter to her father: "I beg you would not suffer your spirits to be depressed by the aspect of public affairs. The clouds which now gather round us will scatter." With luck, the Colonel had time to read the letter; he was busy these days with his own rallying efforts. Immediately after the Battle of Lexington, he had entertained forty-four men at breakfast at his house and forty-three men at dinner the same night at a total cost (including toddy for the gentlemen and hay for the horses) of twenty-three pounds, ten shillings, and six pence.

The Warrens did not move to Taunton. Boston was surrounded now by the New England militia — farmers, fishermen, tradesmen, boys, veterans — coming and going "in such a shifting, fluctuating state," James Warren said, "as not to be capable of a perfect regulation" but strong enough, it was hoped, to keep the British in town at least until their reinforcements arrived. The trouble was in regulating this army, supplying it, supporting it, officering it without a "fixt settled Government." James Warren longed for a Washington or a Charles Lee to head the army; he wished that a grand constitution could be formed "with the same ease [as] we could build a Bird Cage" but this was a "Business of such a nature, so important . . ." he said, "That I am afraid to meddle." When a few days later he was proposed as the president of the provincial congress, he declined, suggesting that Joseph Warren take the position instead.

Meanwhile Mercy was hearing about the adventures of those who had been closer to the battlefield. Samuel Adams and John Hancock had spent part of the night hiding in a swamp; Mercy's nephew, nine-year-old Harrison Gray Otis (son of Samuel), had stood at his window watching the redcoats march past; Abigail Adams had thrown her house open to soldiers and refugees; Hannah and John Winthrop, fleeing from Cambridge, had found "the roads filled with frighted women and children, some in carts with their tallest furniture, others on foot fleeing into the woods." On passing the battlefield at Menotomy, they had met a man with a cart looking for the body of his son and picking up his neighbors who had fallen. Joseph Warren took part in the fighting and had his ear grazed by a bullet and a curl from his wig carried off.

"Little" Ned Winslow was also at the scene. He showed the British army the way to Lexington and Concord and had his horse shot from under him.

Property suffered as well as the people. Lexington residents claimed that the British stole everything, from aprons, handkerchiefs, moose skins, and beaver hats to windowpanes and horses, with looking glasses and clocks being the most popular items. On the other hand, Thomas Hutchinson's house in Milton fell to the Whigs in the aftermath of the battle. There was no plundering of the Milton house; a town committee removed the furniture carefully piece by piece to safety — the red morocco-bottom chairs from the dining room, the silver epergne, the bronze busts of Shakespeare and Milton that had stood on each side of the parlor fireplace, the damask window squabs, the hair settees. Later everything was sold and the money used to pay bounties to American soldiers. There was only one item that the committee overlooked: an old trunk filled with papers hidden in a corner of the garret. Yet this too was soon found. A few days after the battle a Mr. Samuel Henshaw, "desirous of seeing how the house looked when stript of all the furniture," discovered the trunk and inside it the copies of letters written by Thomas Hutchinson in 1771 at the time he was convening the General Court in Cambridge, supposedly under the specific instructions of the king. An examination of the letters, however, showed that those instructions had not been so specific after all. The letters were passed to the army, then to the provincial congress in Watertown, and then to newspapers. The *Essex Gazette* in Salem announced that they "would astonish everyone, who has not before been thoroughly sensible of the evil Designs of that Man against the Liberties of this Country."

Yet the people did not need old evidence from 1771 to convince them of Hutchinson's evil designs; they were constantly being supplied with new reports from England. "Hutcheson I hear flatters the ministry with assurances that you will soon be tired of the Contest, and Submit," Catherine Macaulay wrote Mercy, "& he is supposed to be well acquainted with your temper & meaness of Spirit. He is to have 2000 £ a Year (I suppose out of the American Revenue) and has taken a House in Golden Square. In these times it seems it is more profitable to betray than to serve the Interest of one's Country."

·   ·   ·

The Hutchinsons did, indeed, seem to be leading a gay life in London. Peggy had been presented at court, which she claimed was "next to being married"; Elisha had worn his ruffles and his wedding suit to the theater; they had all attended the king's levees and responded to the king's endless inquiries about the New England climate. Thomas Hutchinson had been to Bath to take the waters, had visited Sir Francis Bernard at Aylesbury, and had spent weekends with Lord Dartmouth and Lord Gage (who looked twenty years younger than his brother in America, but then everyone in England, according to Elisha, bore his age better). In the evenings Hutchinson played cards at a shilling a corner, entertained American Tory friends, wrote letters, or worked on the third volume of his history of Massachusetts.

One Saturday evening in October 1774 Richard Clarke (one of the tea consignees) dined with the Hutchinsons. "We had a dispute after dinner," Peggy reported to her sister-in-law Polly in Plymouth,

[about] which was the best country — New England, or Old? Papa, your husband, and myself, were for the former: Mr. C. and Billy for the latter. I own I still feel a partiality for my

native country. Papa could not help expressing his in very
strong terms. Mr. C. said he never should lose the idea of the
last winter: that the injuries he then received were too strongly
impressed upon his mind ever to be erased. I told him I was
surprised to find his affections so alienated from his country
. . . and as to the climate, surely, said I, we have the ad-
vantage. They would neither of them allow it, but said the
extremes of cold and heat were enough to ruin people's con-
stitutions. I, in return, had no mercy upon this, but exclaimed
against it as cold, damp, dirty, and altogether disagreeable, and
declared that I could not take a breath of air, but it gave me a
cold and cough . . . and that if I lived here fifty years, I never
should be reconciled to the climate, or to living in London
. . . We carried on till it was time for them to go to the Play:
and I believe Mr. C. was glad to get off with a whole skin.
How happy should I be to see that country restored to a state
of peace and quiet! not so much for my own sake as papa's,
who I think will be happier there.

Actually, Thomas Hutchinson was miserable away from New
England. He was not only a man with a strong sense of home,
rooted in history, bound to the soil, he was a man with an inordi-
nately strong sense of order. To him it was essential to feel the fixed
shape of a society securely around him — specifically Massachusetts
society, so happily structured in the relationship of one part to another: England to America, the government to the common man,
and himself firmly stationed at the juncture of the parts. He could
not conceive of such a society collapsing — in the distant future,
perhaps, when America had outgrown the colonial relationship, but
not now, not in his lifetime, not while he was onstage. "I will not
permit myself to believe that it's possible," he wrote his brother
Foster, "we should hazard actual hostilities, from a country so dis-
proportioned in power. God, I trust, will open the eyes of the blind
before it comes to that."

Along with his singleness of mind, Thomas Hutchinson possessed a temperance of spirit, a combination of qualities that had often stood him in good stead but had also often confused him. He wanted to be an agent in the restoration of peace and did, in fact, suggest revoking the tea tax; but he could no more serve both countries than James Otis had been able to. He could not urge England to use force and at the same time inspire England to show generosity. He could not be a friend to America and refuse to see the American point of view. Most important, he could not break a lifelong habit of trying to please the ministry. In the matter of the Coercive Acts, for instance, he wrote to Boston: "I am not only free from any share in these three Acts of P., but I am also willing to own that they are so severe that if I had been upon the spot, I would have done what I could, at least to have moderated them: and as to the first of them, I have all encouragement possible to hope and believe, that my being here will be the means by which the T[own] of B[oston] will be relieved from the distress the Act brings upon it." Yet some of the measures Hutchinson himself had recommended years ago; moreover, when he had had a chance to express himself he had not used it. In his first interview with the king, Hutchinson was asked what the people of Boston thought of the acts and he said only that he had left before the acts arrived. That the first act (shutting the port) was severe, he did not "presume to say." The result was that, whatever Hutchinson may have said, the king reported to Lord North: "I have seen Mr. Hutchinson . . . and am now well convinced they will soon submit. He owns the Boston Port Bill has been the only wise and effectual method."

It would have made little difference what Hutchinson advised. The king was determined to wring obedience out of the colonies and make an example of America lest other members of the empire also take advantage of him. As for Lord North, he was like a physician, Elisha said, who having administered the medicine calmly awaited the operation. Thomas Hutchinson never had the influence with the court that he expected or wanted to have; the story of his years in London is less a political story than it is a personal one —

the story of a lonely man. "New England," he said, "is wrote upon my heart in as strong characters as Calais was upon Q. Mary's." And every month he was growing more homesick.

In August he began thinking about the cranberries that would be ripening in the fields near the river. He wrote to Thomas asking for "six or eight bushels, but let somebody be employed to get the largest and fairest, and when they are come to their colour, and not too ripe." He wanted the dimensions of the parlor floor in Boston, and recalling a large cheese that had been in the house, he decided that he would like that too.

In November during the time that Thomas, Jr., was hiding out in Boston because a liberty pole was being erected near the house at Milton, Thomas Hutchinson was worrying because the newspapers in America were still abusing him. "I hope none of my friends will suffer any Part of my letters to go into the Papers," he said, and then he added: "Peggy thinks if we had the Coffee pot & plate we might change them for more fashionable Articles."

In February he hoped that before the next winter he would be able to go back to Boston. "If there is a prospect of my being serviceable," he said, "I would return in my publick character, which I have no doubt I may do if I chuse it." Meanwhile he asked Thomas, Jr., to have a new tomb built at Milton and instructed him to move the remains of his wife and leave space for him.

In March Hutchinson was thinking about his garden again. He sent Thomas, Jr., a parcel of gooseberry cuttings to be set out and reminded him to graft the heads of the pear trees which had been grafted the year before and failed. "And the trees will bear to have some of the old boughs taken off."

In May the three new generals — Burgoyne, Clinton, and Howe ("the three bow-wows," Americans called them) — arrived in Boston. At the same time Thomas Hutchinson was sending to the museum at Harvard "a fish converted into chalk, which I bro't from under a chalk cliff in Sussex, and was perfect, but by handling, the tail is broke off." But he was depressed; time was slipping by far too quickly. "I see my contemporaries dying away so fast," he wrote, "that I am more anxious than ever to hasten home, lest I should die here, which I dread above all things."

Four days later, on May 29, the first report of the Battle of Lexington arrived in London. It was a Whig report and as such Hutchinson was inclined to discount it, yet he had to admit when Gage's report arrived it was not much different. The Americans had not only fought, they had apparently fought well, and Hutchinson was forced to confess that he had guessed wrong. Yet when he was blamed for the fact that England had not sent stronger forces, he felt it was unfair. "There never was a more unjust charge," he told his son Thomas.

Still, the Battle of Lexington was in Thomas Hutchinson's view a temporary setback. This was the season for Americans to plant Indian corn, he pointed out, and just as he had once refused to believe that merchants would sacrifice their property, now he could not believe that farmers would jeopardize theirs. Far more disturbing to him was news that came two weeks later. Dr. Quincy, a Tory refugee who had just arrived in England, took breakfast with the Hutchinsons on June 26, "the most distressing" day for Thomas Hutchinson since he had been in England.

"My house at Milton [is] in possession of the rabble," Hutchinson wrote, "all my letters, books, papers, & taken and carried away, and the publication of some of them already begun." There was nothing new in them, he insisted, nothing not consistent with loyalty to the king. As for the statement that he had not had specific instructions to hold the General Court in Cambridge, he had never said he had had *specific* instructions, but only "such instruction as made it necessary." He considered the fact that Bernard had advised him to do this was justification enough. But Hutchinson found it unpleasant to have to defend himself. And to have everything of a private nature exposed to the public was "a cruelty hard to bear."

．　．　．

While Thomas Hutchinson was recording his distresses in London, the people in Massachusetts were recovering from their second engagement with the British army. They had known, of course, that sooner or later the British would try to push out of Boston.

"Necessity will oblige Gage to take some desperate steps," Abigail Adams wrote in June. "We are told for Truth, that he is now Eight thousand strong. We live in continual expectation of allarms. Courage I know we have in abundance, conduct I hope we shall not want, but powder — where shall we get a sufficient supply?"

Ammunition was a major concern of the Massachusetts patriots in the months following the Battle of Lexington. They rejoiced over every cannon that was cast, counted up every barrel of powder, reported on recipes for making saltpeter (mold from under the stables could be boiled, John Adams said), and all the time they took care to conceal the critical state of the magazines. In Plymouth it was voted that anyone who fired at a bird should have his gun taken from him, and James Warren, who had a knack for making homely comparisons, said he longed for powder more "than turtles or pine apples."

In Philadelphia John Adams worried too. He was a voracious worrier; nothing was too large for him to grapple with — provinces, nations, empires; nothing was too small to receive his attention. He would be seized by a sudden thought and fire it off staccatolike to Massachusetts. He worried about night attacks on the American army and warned James Warren that Burgoyne was fond of surprises. He worried about disease and dashed off a reminder that cleanliness was a cardinal virtue among soldiers. "They should be encouraged to go into Water frequently, to keep their Linen washed and their Beds clean." He wanted to make sure that the Braintree company was being exercised, that the Braintree minister was opposing tyranny on Sunday mornings as passionately as he ought, that his clerks were minding their books, that his friends were writing to him, that his children were learning how to draw "Plans of Cities, Provinces, Kingdoms, and Countries — especially America," that his wife, on the one hand, was not being upset by hysterical neighbors and that, on the other hand, she was taking proper precautions. "In case of real Danger . . ." he told her, "fly to the Woods with our Children."

Yet it was not only the patriots who feared the next engagement. Both Thomas Hutchinson, Jr., and Peter Oliver, Jr., who like so many Tories had sought safety in Boston, felt the desperation of their position and were not a little annoyed at the insensibility of family and friends in London. To Thomas Hutchinson, Jr., it must, in fact, have been maddening to receive gooseberry cuttings in the wake of one battle and on the eve of another. "Everything that has hapned," he wrote Elisha, "has afforded matter of triumph to the people, and I believe them to be ripe for any undertaking: they appear to be desperate and determined throughout the continent."

Young Peter Oliver, whose house in Middleborough had been burned and whose farm was being worked by the rebels, wrote in considerable heat to Elisha: "We are besieged this moment with 10 or 15000 men, from Roxbury to Cambridge . . . We are every hour expecting an attack by land or water. All marketing from the country stopt ever since the Battle. Fire and slaughter hourly threatened . . . You seem in England to be entirely ignorant of the temper of our people . . . By the time this reaches you havvock will begin, and whether we shall ever see one another in this world, I am not clear in . . . O tempora! O mores!"

Peter's father was equally bitter. "You who riot in pleasure in London," he wrote Elisha, "know nothing of the distress in Boston: you can regale upon delicacies, whilst we are in the rotations of salt beef and salt pork one day, and the next, chewing upon salt pork and salt beef. The very rats are grown so familiar that they ask you to eat them. G. Britain hath no idea of our situation." The Tories knew, of course, that reinforcements were on the way but they were not at all sure that reinforcements would settle matters.

Mercy Warren, on the other hand, was horrified at the very thought of reinforcements — "Irish and British cut throats," she called them, "Ready to Come out and Execute the most infernal plans." Indeed, whenever she mentioned reinforcements she was so agitated, James chided her for sounding like a "Modern Soldier." James was a colonel in the militia now and after telling Mercy a story about a colonel in Boston who was supposed to have quieted the panic of a superior officer, he advised her gently: "Let your Colonel's remonstrances etc. have a Similar Effect." Mercy would have smiled; she was very dependent on her colonel.

But at least the patriots had one advantage, or so they believed. Surely in the long run God would support them if they showed they were worthy. Accordingly, the clergy exhorted the people to rush to God's side, to forsake their old immoral society and establish a new, virtuous one; at the same time, the clergy urged God to come over to them. In Plymouth a minister dropped the whole matter of reinforcements in the Almighty's hands. "If more soldiers are on their way hither," the minister cried, "sink them, O Lord, to the bottom of the sea."

By the middle of June it was everywhere said that troops of light horse would scour the country within a week, but Mercy, although apprehensive, was not, she assured James, "under the pressure of a sudden panic" as he might well have expected. Instead, perhaps because she wanted to see her father before the light horse descended, perhaps because her son Henry had not been well and fresh air was supposed to induce health, perhaps simply because June days were too scarce to be squandered, she set out with her boys for a quick visit to Barnstable. Colonel Otis was seventy-three now and although he still seemed active, Mercy had become solicitous, casting him in the role of a Roman patriarch, making rhetoric about his gray hairs (which presumably were under his wig most of the time), and grieving that he could not decline in peace. But if not in peace, he was at least declining in company. The Otis house was full. After the Battle of Lexington, Samuel left Boston and was now in Barnstable with his wife, two sons — young Harrison Gray and Sam — and two babies. Mercy's sister Hannah was of course always there, and if Joseph's family was not in the house, they were running in and out: two grown daughters, Rebecca and Elizabeth, from his first marriage and Maria, his second wife, and her brood of small children.

Joseph would not be home. He was a new representative to the provincial congress and would be in Watertown. And there was Jemmy. There was no way to know whether Jemmy would be there or not. He was living in Barnstable these days, sometimes quite peacefully, going to church with the family, conversing with visitors in the Otis house. After the Battle of Lexington, he had even participated in the brief march of the Barnstable company before it had been recalled. But he was erratic, subject to his old spells, likely to disappear suddenly, driven to unknown destinations by unknown demons. He had been reported wandering around the army camps outside Boston — drunk, disheveled, a general nuisance, and the butt of jokes.

As it happened, Jemmy was not home this time, but Mercy and the boys visited with the rest of the family and, on June 16, the day after their return to Plymouth, Mercy sat down to write James about it. Her sister Hannah and her twenty-one-year-old niece, Rebecca, had decided to accompany her on her return, she said, as far as Sandwich, but since it was such a beautiful day and they were having such a good time, they had come farther and farther until at last they had traveled all the way to Plymouth and there they had spent the night. And what had they done in Plymouth? They had regaled themselves on strawberries. Mercy took great pride in her strawberries; it was a high point for the Warren family every year when her strawberries ripened. This year, she said, they were the finest she had ever seen, but even as she wrote she slipped into lonesomeness for her "Beloved Husband," not present to share in the feast and stationed in a "place where I am Greatly Apprehensive of personal Danger to him."

She concluded, however, on a firm note: "Don't write anything for the sake of keeping up my spirits, but Let me know Exactly how persent appearances are in your Eye . . . Your family are all well except Henry & I think he is Better for his journey."

June 16 was a busy day for James Warren. The provincial congress had before it a recent proclamation by General Gage, listing the crimes of an "infatuated multitude" yet offering pardon to all who should lay down their arms "excepting only from the benefit of such pardon, SAMUEL ADAMS and JOHN HANCOCK." Now the congress was drawing up an answer which in turn would list the grievances of the people and offer pardon to all offenders to liberty, excepting only General Gage, a customs official, those mandamus councilors who had not resigned, and "all the natives of North America . . . who went out with the regular troops on the nineteenth of April last."

On the same day, the provincial congress was making arrangements for degrees to be conferred on Harvard graduates and for books to be removed from the Harvard library to safety; it granted a number of commissions, approved an expense account, empowered officers to draw on the commissary for "spiritous liquors" for such soldiers as might be "particularly circumstanced," and finally, "as we have reason to fear that unless we become a penitent and reformed people, we shall feel still severer tokens of the divine displeasure," it drew up a resolution to discourage profanations of the Sabbath. But if James Warren had been writing to Mercy a true account of all that happened that day, he would also have had to have told her that General Gage was known to be planning an attack on Dorchester and Charlestown on June 18, that the Massachusetts Committee of Safety had resolved to fortify and defend Bunker Hill, and that this very night the army would proceed under cover of darkness to build their entrenchments.

But James Warren did not write to Mercy that day nor yet the next. By the time he did write to her on June 18 the battle was over: the Americans had defended their hill against two assaults and had abandoned it on the third when they had run out of ammunition. They had now retired to their lines in Cambridge and the British, who had "nothing to boast of but the possession of the Ground," were picking up their dead (1000 casualties including 92 officers).

"It is impossible to describe the Confusion in this place," James wrote Mercy. "Women and Children flying into the Country, armed Men Going to the field, and wounded Men returning from there fill the Streets . . . Your Brother [Joseph] borrowed a Gun, etc. and went among the flying Bullets at Charlestown returned last Evening 10 o'clock."

James Winthrop (son of Hannah and librarian at Harvard) had been hit on the hand by a musketball. And Dr. Joseph Warren, president of the provincial congress, had been killed.

As he wrote, James Warren was sitting at a committee meeting, stealing time "to add Sentences separately," he said. "I need not say that I long to see you, perhaps never more in my life. I shall try hard for it this week. I hope your Strawberries are well taken care of and that you have fine feasting on them . . . Your Brother Jem dined with us yesterday, behaved well till dinner, was almost done and then in the old way got up went off where I know not; has been about at Cambridge and Roxbury several days. Adieu."

The next day James Warren was elected president of the provincial congress to replace Joseph Warren, and two weeks later he was officiating at the ceremonies to welcome to Cambridge the new commander in chief of the American army, General George Washington.

VIII

THE PATRIOT LEADERS were assuming new roles and accommodating to them in various ways. John Hancock at thirty-eight suddenly married, and Samuel Adams at fifty-three learned to ride a horse — two of the most unlikely things that could ever have happened, according to John Adams. For years John Adams had been trying to get his cousin Samuel on a horse and in September on the way to Philadelphia he tried again. All renowned statesmen, including Cecil and Sully, had been horsemen, John pointed out, and he did not wish Americans to be inferior in the least way. As John talked, Samuel must have been reminded of his awkward situation a few months before at Lexington when, unable to mount a horse, he had been obliged to call for John Hancock's chaise to make his escape from the British. Obviously he could not be an embarrassment to his country, so with a boost from John and the help of two servants, Samuel managed to get astride a horse and even to stay there. The next day, fortified by a makeshift pair of flannel-lined drawers, he rode into Philadelphia, the very picture of a noble statesman arriving for his congress.

As for John Hancock, it was appropriate that he settle down now; he was president of the Second Continental Congress, chosen to replace Peyton Randolph who had been called home to Virginia — chosen on the spur of the moment, according to Mercy Warren who disapproved of the whole proceeding. A Mr. Harrison of Virginia, apparently in high humor, had nominated Hancock. The congress would show England what they thought of her, Harrison declared;

they would select a man from Massachusetts, a man whom General Gage had specifically excluded from his pardon. Accordingly Hancock was taken by the arms and placed in the presidential chair in a manner, Mercy felt, that displayed "rather too much levity for the times, or for the dignity of the office." Mr. Hancock, however, took the office seriously enough. Once in the chair he became so attached to it, he did not even offer to relinquish it when Mr. Randolph returned. Mercy, who had always found John Hancock's vanity hard to bear, compared him now to a celebrated pope who "after putting on the triple crown . . . often felt his own pulse, to see if he was the same identical person he was a few years before."

John Adams' role was played behind the scenes at the Second Continental Congress, trying to encourage the timid members to move forward, trying to restrain the overly bold. The progress of America, he said, was "like a Coach and six — the swiftest Horses must be slackened and the slowest quickened, that all may keep an even Pace." For a man like John Adams, however, this was frustrating business. He could see America's course so clearly, he had for so long accepted the necessity for revolution, and he was so impressed by the need to accomplish a thousand important things at once — to organize a government, make a constitution, fortify the continent, raise a navy, arrest the Tories, establish a treasury, open up trade. Yet he must agree to petitions for peace, endure endless long-winded debates on trifling matters, and deal with men whose interests and views ran at cross-purposes: army officers who quibbled over rank, leaders like John Dickinson of Pennsylvania who were unable to face the idea of separation from Britain, and men in his own Massachusetts delegation whose narrow outlook John Adams found especially infuriating. There was Thomas Cushing, for instance, who James Warren said had been in the clouds for the past seven years and was evidently still there in June 1775 when he suggested that the army be discharged lest the country be involved in debt; and Robert Treat Paine, notoriously stingy, who proposed that the army be clothed from private donations. It required, John

Adams said, "all the Philosophy I am Master of, and more than all"
to maintain his composure under such conditions.

Besides, it was a thankless job that John Adams was doing. The
soldier in the field, he said, received more applause than he did and
he sometimes envied the soldier. When James Warren wrote that
they should both be "content without a slice from the great pudding
now on the table," John Adams tried to feel content; but sometimes,
in spite of himself, he was hungry for that pudding. Certainly he
was on the day that General Washington left Philadelphia to assume command in Cambridge. John had, himself, nominated
Washington for his post, a diplomatic maneuver of the highest consequence, and now as he watched Washington mounted grandly on
his horse, surrounded by generals, attended by the militia and a
troop of light horse, accompanied by fifers and drummers, honored
by Congress, John Adams could only feel sorry for himself. "I, poor
Creature," he wrote Abigail, "worn out with scribbling, for my
Bread and my Liberty, low in Spirits and weak in Health, must leave
others to wear the Lawrells which I have sown; others, to eat the
Bread, which I have earned."

To Abigail and to James Warren, John Adams confided his true
feelings and reeled off his grievances — a practice which was of
benefit to all parties concerned as long as it was confined to those
parties. Occasionally, however, letters fell into the wrong hands. So
in the summer of 1775, John Adams' already complicated life was
further complicated when a young lawyer, delivering letters to Abigail and to James Warren, was captured by the British while cross-
ing Narragansett Bay on a ferry. Apparently the lawyer might have
thrown the letters overboard but did not think to; in any case the
British took them, published them, and even paraphrased the one to
James Warren, calling it an epistle from "John the round Head to
James the prolocuter of the Rump parliment," and beginning, "Dear
Devil."

What the British thought of the letters, however, was no more
important than what the Americans thought, and Americans had no

trouble identifying the men whom John Adams wrote about. When he spoke of a "certain great Fortune and piddling Genius, whose Fame has been trumpeted so loudly," everyone knew who was meant, including John Dickinson, who would not speak to Adams for months. And when Adams said in reference to the behavior of his compatriots: "The Fidgets, the Whims, the Caprice, the Vanity, the Superstition, the Irritability of some of us, is enough to ———" Thomas Cushing and Robert Treat Paine were correct to take it personally.

There were many currents of ill feeling which ran through the Massachusetts delegation. Robert Treat Paine, obsessed with the idea of rank, had always been jealous of Adams, his junior and ranked behind him in order of alumni in the Harvard catalogue; later he would refuse an appointment to the Superior Court because Adams was Chief Justice. Thomas Cushing resented the pressure that both Adamses used on other members of the delegation when the members did not, as Cushing remarked sarcastically, "pay an implicit Obedience to their Sovereign Dictates." As for John Hancock, he had wanted to be commander in chief of the American army and could not forgive John Adams for nominating Washington nor Samuel Adams for seconding the nomination. Although Samuel had been Hancock's close friend, there was a rift between them now that lasted for years.

It is little wonder that Abigail Adams, surveying the American scene, felt discouraged about human nature. "I am more and more convinced," she said, "that Man is a dangerous creature, and that power whether vested in many or a few is ever grasping, and like the grave cries give, give." This was not, of course, a new sentiment for this revolutionary generation; it had been drummed into them by their clergy and demonstrated by an imposed government. But now the people were themselves proving the truth of it. "The great fish swallow up the small," Abigail wrote, "and he who is most strenuous for the Rights of the people, when vested with power, is as eager after the perogatives of Government." Mercy Warren, speaking in the same key, said that she was persuaded that there was a basic "propensity in human nature to tyrannize over their fellow men."

The Massachusetts patriots had been familiar enough with each other's weaknesses but it was troubling to see those weaknesses, thrust onto a larger stage, appear suddenly to expand so that at every turn someone's vanity, someone's jealousy, someone's obstinacy, someone's acquisitiveness impeded action and obstructed the view. Yet these were but the side effects of exposure to power. What was really terrifying to contemplate was a man's complete capitulation, and, at the time they were writing, Abigail and Mercy had just such an example before them. Like everyone else in Massachusetts, they were trying to recover from the shock at finding that Dr. Benjamin Church from their own inner circle was a spy for the British — a man who had once worked with James Otis, Jr., and Samuel Adams to discredit Bernard and Hutchinson, a member of the Committee of Correspondence and the Committee of Safety, orator at one of the Boston Massacre anniversaries, a member of the House of Representatives, and most recently appointed the surgeon general of the Continental army. Notoriously unfaithful to his wife, Dr. Church was discovered through a letter to the enemy which he had entrusted to his mistress (an "infamous hussey," according to James Warren).

"Good God!" John Adams exclaimed on hearing the news. "What shall We say of human Nature? What shall We say of American Patriots?"

Samuel Adams, however, thought they should not have been surprised; the conduct of Church only verified what Puritans had always believed: private and public vice as well as private and public virtue were closely related. Once Benjamin Church had betrayed his wife, it was but a step to betray his country.

The worry that lay behind the questions about human nature was, of course, that Americans might not after all, even if given a chance, be able to establish a Godly society. What kind of a government could they invent that would protect man from himself? Would people, averse to change as they were, be willing to adopt new patterns? Would they submit to government at all? Ever since the Continental Congress had first convened, there had been talk about forming a confederation of the colonies and making a constitution; but what kind of a constitution? Mercy begged John Adams and the gentlemen in Philadelphia to take care; a constitution should be constructed "with such symmetry of Features, such Vigour of Nerves, and such strength of sinew, that it may never be in the power of Ambition or Tyranny to shake the durable Fabrick."

The Continental Congress, however, was not ready to discuss formal articles of confederation, yet there had to be government of some sort within the colonies and in no place was it more urgent than Massachusetts, where war was being waged. The provincial congress had no legal foundation; it was simply a group of men who had been elected to the assembly when the province was still acknowledging royal jurisdiction. There had been no election since. The members operated without a council, without a governor, and without courts. Accordingly, the province requested the Continental Congress to authorize the establishment of a civil government and to recommend the form it should take. And in June 1775, the Continental Congress, still in a conservative frame of mind, complied. Massachusetts was to return to its old charter; it was to hold a new election for representatives who in turn would elect a council to "exercise the powers of Government until a Governor, of his Majesty's appointment, will consent to govern the colony according to its charter."

Although this was admittedly a temporary expedient, there were objections. Some felt that the people should elect a governor immediately; some wanted the people rather than the council to select the judges and the county officials; others felt that if the supreme power of the government resided in the body of the people (as everyone agreed), it should be administered by the people in a single assembly rather than in a government made up of two or three branches. James Warren said simply, "I can't . . . say that I admire the form of government prescribed." And as time went on, as quarrels between the two houses multiplied (endless arguments, for instance, about who should appoint field officers for the militia), as the council, supposedly the aristocratic branch, became more insistent on its prerogatives, James liked the form even less. "I am sick of our constitution," he exploded one day to John Adams. "I hate the name of our charter, which fascinates and shackles us. I hate the monarchical part of our government, and certainly you would more than ever, if you knew our present monarchs . . . They have a whirl in their brains, imagine themselves kings, and have assumed every air and pomp of royalty but the crown and scepter." And when in the midst of such controversy a rising young star in Philadelphia, Thomas Paine, wrote a pamphlet called *Common Sense,* James Warren, like many of the Massachusetts patriots, not only welcomed the author's arguments for independence but was intrigued by his vision of a free America governed simply and loosely by the people in a system of single assemblies — a notion that John Adams declared was crude, ignorant, and as dangerous as all the Tory writings put together.

But this was a subject that the patriots could not argue yet; they had too many other immediate concerns. James Warren had been elected speaker of the Massachusetts House in the new elections and had also been appointed paymaster of the army. He was as busy, he said, "as you ever saw pismires on a mole hill" — far too busy to travel to Plymouth as frequently as he would have liked or even to keep up with his daily letters to Mercy, although his affection for her, he said, continued to be "as great as ever any man had for a beloved wife and is one of the predominant passions of my soul." Absence from home was probably harder on him than it was on John Adams, who, for all his grumbling, was thoroughly caught up in the ideas the country was grappling with. Unlike John, James Warren was less motivated by a spirit that rose to meet the times than he was by a conscience that pointed out his duty. Politics brought him little pleasure. Although he had no personal ambition and seemed aware of his limitations, he was at the same time easily slighted so that while he was denied the rewards of public life, he remained subject to its pains. Perhaps in consequence as politics became more complicated, he drew closer to Mercy, becoming in his way as dependent on her as she was on him. "It is enough for me to get into foolish habits of keeping awake," Mercy scolded. ". . . Let me hear in your next that you are less anxious and sleep better."

Fortunately, Mercy was able to visit Watertown frequently during the fall, winter, and spring of 1775 and 1776. The Massachusetts legislature had rented a house in which the council met and in which one bedroom was reserved for James Warren and the other bedrooms used by a succession of legislators, visitors, and wives. "Every body either eats, drinks or sleeps in this house," James Warren said, and here it was that Mercy, when she could, presided as hostess and met many of the leading personages of the day. "I want to know all that passes," Abigail wrote, and John Adams, equally curious, struck a bargain with Mercy. He would "draw the Character" of every new person he met in Philadelphia on condition that Mercy would do the same. Afterward, Mercy accused him of not living up to his end of the bargain, while she had for months been drawing "characters" for the benefit of the Adamses: Franklin (a "venerable person" who combined a philosophic character with affability and politeness); Washington ("the most amiable and accomplished gentleman, both in person, mind, and manners, that I have met with"); General Charles Lee (plain "to a degree of ugliness, careless, even to unpoliteness — his garb ordinary, his voice rough, his manners rather morose — yet sensible"); General Gates ("a brave soldier, a high republican . . . an honest man, of unaffected manners, and easy deportment"). As for the ladies, there were Mrs. Washington, who Mercy decided had all the proper attributes to qualify her as wife of the general, and Mrs. Putnam, wife of the popular General Israel Putnam who was supposed to have dropped his plow when he heard about the Battle of Lexington, unhitched his horse, and ridden straight to Boston. Mrs. Putnam, Mercy said, was "what is Commonly called a very Good kind of Woman."

With her keen sense of history and with the recognition she had received for her literary efforts, it was not surprising that Mercy should think now of writing a history of the struggle with Britain which, as a sister, daughter, wife, and friend of revolutionary leaders, she had had such a unique opportunity of observing and which she was watching now at such close range. It was a bold step, for although she had the example of Catherine Macaulay to follow and although she contended she was not one who believed "all political attentions lay out of the road of female life," she was still as sensitive as ever to any suggestion that she was improper or unfeminine. Only recently, when John Adams, on vacation in Braintree, had written her a letter that deliberately avoided all mention of politics and war, Mercy had felt rebuked. Was he hinting that in the future she should not approach "anything so far beyond the line of my sex?" No, no, John reassured her. Far from being unfit for politics, she and Abigail had "a Share and no Small one neither, in the Conduct of our American Affairs."

In any case, while she was in Watertown Mercy spoke of working on her "Book." Here in her room above the chamber where the Council met, Mercy, not knowing where or how her record would end, set down in a long, marble-colored notebook her "introductory Observations."

"History," she said, "the deposite of crimes, and the record of everything disgraceful or honorary to mankind, requires a just knowledge of character, to investigate the sources of action." Mercy never doubted that she had such a knowledge or that the future of the struggle she was reporting would revolve around the same principle that had always been at the core of history. However the present conflict resolved itself, it would be the story of man's conscience and man's reason pitted against the corrupting drive for power and wealth. Her story would be a moral one, its theme fixed, and when she felt that she needed further justification for writing it, she said she was writing to instruct the young, which was certainly in the province of a woman and certainly very much on her mind since her younger sons were reaching an age where their consciences would be tested.

Mercy was at a rare peak in her life. Stimulated by being at the center of the political stage, hopeful (as well as fearful) for her country, excited by the vision of her "Book," and zealous for the future of her sons, she was at the point where none of her ambitions had been either realized or defeated, yet all seemed promising, all possibly even at the brink of fulfillment. But nothing was as important to her as her sons, who had received the full thrust of her moral convictions and the full fervor of her soul. She had such high aspirations, she said, that if disappointed, the shock would be "in proportion to the height I have soared." Yet she had no reason to feel anything but pride. Hannah Winthrop was always complimenting her on her "well-regulated" family and had only recently remarked on the "pleasing prospect" she had of being repaid for all her love and instructions. And so as Mercy wrote to James from Plymouth, her pride in the boys spilled out. She described how the younger ones had greeted her on her return from Watertown — laughing, running to meet her, rushing to pick the choicest flowers in the fall garden and pouring "the yellow produce" into her lap before she could even change from her riding clothes. Not until the next day did they report any trouble during her absence; then "each one had his little grievances to repeat, as important to them as the laying of an unconstitutional tax to the patriot." Winslow, she said, was "half affronted" at her staying away so long and tried to hide his pleasure in seeing her.

Often Mercy wrote to James in the evening while the boys studied: Winslow, handsome and charming, seated "in your armed chair before the fire engaged with Plutarch's Lives"; Charles on the other side of the table studying English history; Henry reading about Telemachus; and George standing at Mercy's elbow with a message for his father that he had caught two snowbirds. As Mercy looked around the circle of her sons, however, her eyes invariably came back to Winslow.

"Every laudable principle I discover in my Winslow makes me happy," she confided to her husband. "He is a promising youth indeed."

Mercy's fall and winter were punctuated by news of action on various fronts: General Gage had been replaced as commander in chief by General Howe in October 1775; the British had burned Falmouth, Maine; Newport had been fired on; America's General Montgomery had been killed in an assault on Quebec — much of it bad news. But the big news, the final decision as to who would possess Boston, lay ahead, as everyone knew, in the spring. Anticipating spring, Mercy went one winter day to the old house on Eel River, where she felt she always worked best, and wrote a poem for James. "To Fidelio," she called it.

> *Yet gentle hope! come, spread thy silken wing*
> *And waft me forward to revolving spring,*
> *Or ere the vernal equinox returns*
> *At worst, before the summer solstice burns*
> *May peace again erect her cheerful stand*
> *Disperse the ills which hover o'er the land.*
>
> *Long life I ask and blessings to descend*
> *And crown the efforts of my constant friend;*
> *My early wish and evening prayer the same,*
> *That virtue, health, and peace, and honest fame*
> *May hover o'er thee till time's latest hour . . .*

February slipped into March, and when the confrontation came it was not really a confrontation at all. Working secretly at night, the Americans erected a battery at Dorchester Heights and on the morning of March 5 they awaited an attack which they assumed would be of the proportion of the Bunker Hill battle the year before. As it happened, however, just as General Howe's troops were embarking from Castle William, a violent storm came up which prevented their departure. By the time the storm was over at the end of the next day, General Howe had changed his mind about fighting; instead, he began preparations to evacuate Boston — a turn of events which the patriots, quick to recognize the hand of God, viewed as a clear demonstration not only of His partisanship but more particularly of the divine nature of the American cause. Two weeks later, standing on a hill near Braintree with Abigail Adams and James, Mercy watched the last of the British ships leave Boston, sail upon sail — some with troops which the patriots would learn later were on their way to New York, some with Tory refugees (over a thousand) on the way to Halifax or London. Among them were Harrison Gray, Daniel Leonard, the Olivers, and Hutchinson's brother and his sons.

The town of Boston was back in the hands of the patriots — at least in the hands of those who had smallpox. There was an epidemic in town and those who had not had the disease were advised not to enter. Mercy and Martha Washington, riding in Thomas Hutchinson's coach which had been confiscated for General Washington's use, went together to see the deserted lines of the enemy and the ruins of Charlestown, which the British had burned after taking Bunker Hill. Although the ladies did not go on to Boston, like everyone else they undoubtedly talked about what the British had done there. They knew, for instance, that the fruit trees were gone. They had been cut down, just as fences had been pulled up and many of the buildings demolished to supply the British with firewood. There were other changes: Fanueil Hall had been turned into a theater; the West Church had had its steeple removed; the Old North Church had been razed; the Old South had been converted into a riding school for the Seventeenth Dragoons. The floor had been covered with dirt and straw and all the pews had been removed but one which served as a pigsty. Some private homes, such as John Hancock's which had been occupied by General Clinton, had fared well (only one backgammon table was unaccounted for). Abigail Adams had been told that their Boston house, used by a British army doctor, was in good condition although dirty. But some homes had been roughly treated and many had been plundered. General Burgoyne was said to have cut raw meat on Mrs. Samuel Quincy's good mahogany tables and to have exposed her damask curtains to the rain. And "Silver-tongued" Sam Cooper of the Brattle Street Church came home to find most of his furniture stolen, although he promptly replaced it by going into the empty homes of Tory refugees and helping himself. (Later he was required to pay the state for the goods.)

Everyone was pleased, however, to find that the bells were still in town. No matter how poorly the churches had been used, the bells that were the very sound of Boston's history, the bells that had rung for the capture of Louisbourg and tolled for the closing of the port, that had struck alarms, mourned the dead, greeted holidays, honored heroes, and marked the hours — the bells had for the most part survived.

John Adams and James Warren had little time to celebrate the evacuation of Boston; neither was even able to attend the belated funeral service for Joseph Warren, whose body had been found buried in Bunker Hill and removed to Boston. John Adams, his mind as usual running almost too fast for his pen, was worrying about the next phase of the war and about how his compatriots in Massachusetts were preparing for it. They should be fortifying Boston Harbor, he said, in case the British fleet returned. "Cannot Hulks be sunk?" he wrote James. "Cannot Booms be laid across? Nay, cannot the Channell be filled up or at least obstructed with stone? Cannot Fire be employed as a Defence?" And where were the Massachusetts troops that were supposed to have marched south to join the Continental army in the defense of New York? "For God's sake and the Land's sake," he barked, "send along your Troops . . . The Languor of New England surprises me."

There was a brittleness that occasionally crept into the letters between these two friends. Both men were tired and overworked; each felt the other did not write as often or as fully as he might and, while John was out of patience with Massachusetts for its many procrastinations ("If I was there," he said, "I should storm and Thunder, like Demosthenes, or scold like a Tooth drawer"), James complained that Massachusetts had been neglected by the Continental Congress, depleted by the army of tents, arms, men, ammunition, and cannon. "Is not Boston and this Colony of as much consequence as New York?" he asked on one occasion. On another he asked if Congress was expecting Massachusetts to defend itself with slings ("as David slew Goliah"). Their irritation was most often drawn, however, on the subject of independence, which of course they both wanted declared but which John Adams explained could not be forced. There were other steps that the Continental Congress was taking which were all in the right direction: it had opened up trade; it had authorized a navy. Yet in spite of his explanations, John was repeatedly pressed, sometimes by James Warren, sometimes by Abigail, sometimes by John Winthrop (a member of the council now), and other members of the legislature.

Finally one April day John Adams could contain his exasperation no longer. Specifically, he took offense at a rather innocent outburst by James Warren.

"I can't describe the sighing after independence; it is universal," James had written. "Nothing remains of that prudence, moderation or timidity with which we have so long been plagued and embarrassed."

"You say the Sigh's for Independence are universal," John snapped. "You say too what I can scarcely believe that *Moderation* and Timidity are at an End. How is this possible? Is Cunning at an End too . . . Is trimming at an End too? and Duplicity? and Hypocricy? . . . You deal in the Marvellous like a Traveller . . . Why don't your Honours of the General Court, if you are so unanimous in this, give positive Instructions to your own Delegates to promote Independency."

James held his ground. "We are certainly unanimously ripe here for the grand revolution," he replied, and although he could not report positive instructions from the General Court, he was able to say that as a first step they were ordering the towns to declare themselves.

Such exchanges between the two men, however, were only a ripple across their friendship. Although John may have acquired a continental point of view and been annoyed by what seemed to him a strain of naiveté in James Warren, the two were nevertheless devoted, trusted each other implicitly, spoke frankly, and did not allow their occasional vexations to take root. Indeed, in the crosscurrents of Massachusetts politics, they needed each other. Thomas Cushing, who had not been on good terms with Warren or Adams, became even more hostile when the General Court replaced him in Philadelphia with Elbridge Gerry of Marblehead, a more radically inclined delegate who was more to the taste of the two Adamses. Cushing blamed the Adams-Warren clique for influencing the General Court not only against him but against John Hancock, with the result that Hancock and Cushing drew together as the nucleus of a faction which would become increasingly powerful in Massachusetts. During the same period, James Warren alienated Robert Treat Paine by referring to him in uncomplimentary terms in a letter which Paine happened to see. These were but some of the personality conflicts in Massachusetts which may have been sublimated for the sake of the American cause but which could not be hidden: little resentments, bitternesses, prejudices, boiling and bubbling just under the surface of the political pot and making it impossible for a man in public life to take a step without in some way disturbing them.

Certainly when James Warren was appointed a justice of the Superior Court in the first week of May, he knew that, whether he accepted or rejected the appointment, he would be criticized. There was no particular honor connected with the appointment, or so James thought, since the post had already been rejected by at least three men (including Robert Treat Paine and James's own brother-in-law, William Sever of Kingston) and was offered to James only because no one from the bar could be found to accept it. James was embarrassed by the appointment; he had supposed, he said, "that many blockheads might be hit upon before it came to his turn," but he knew that if he refused, many of his friends would be displeased and among them John Adams, who was to be the new Chief Justice. Moreover, this refusal would follow on the heels of another refusal. James had just resigned his office as army paymaster rather than move with the army when it left Massachusetts. And since the court appointment with its circuit duties also required one to be away from home much of the time, he could be accused of putting personal considerations before public welfare, of taking only those assignments that did not unduly disrupt his private life.

On the other hand, Massachusetts lawyers (including John Adams) had for years been expounding on the importance of choosing Superior Court justices from the bar; indeed, had not the patriots said that Thomas Hutchinson was unqualified for this reason? And surely qualification was never more essential than now, when the courts, after being closed for so long, faced exceptional difficulties. James's inclinations were all to refuse; he would only "injure his country," he told John Adams, "and expose himself."

Yet he did not give his answer immediately. "I cant bear the Thought of your refusing," John Adams wrote, and Abigail pointed out that the office itself would suffer if "banded about from hand to hand."

Then suddenly private misfortune descended on the Warrens' "well-regulated" family and political thoughts were pushed aside. James Warren, Jr., who had been more or less at loose ends during the army's occupation of Cambridge when Harvard was closed, was one day, according to Abigail Adams, brought home "disordered in his mind."

The Warrens did not reveal the nature of the trouble; indeed, Abigail warned John not to mention it, as it was a "wound which cannot be touched." Mercy, writing at this time, said only that she was suffering from a prolonged nervous headache and "some Axiety of Another Nature." Apparently, however, James had a breakdown of sorts, perhaps a severe depression, complicated possibly by alcohol and quite likely aggravated by tension at home where the expectations for him were not only high but rigid. Hannah Winthrop had seen him several times during his "illness," presumably on trips to Cambridge, and although she seemed to have realized something was wrong, she did not apprehend his trouble would "rise high." In any case, whatever the trouble it was erratic; he was able to go back to Harvard when it reopened in July and everyone hoped, as Hannah Winthrop expressed it, that being with his contemporaries would have a "happy effect." Yet he continued to be a worry. He was "impaired in Health, impaird in Mind, impaird in Morrals," Abigail Adams wrote John, and Mercy, whose great concern had been to train her children "up in the way which they ought to go," was "beyond description almost Heart broken."

In the midst of this personal distress James Warren turned down the Superior Court appointment. Mercy had always been against his taking it and even had he been so inclined, James could not have opposed her now. Indeed, he would have liked to protect her from any further ordeals at the moment, but this was not possible. If Massachusetts was temporarily free of war, it was not free of pestilence. The smallpox epidemic which had been raging in Boston all spring was spreading outside the city, and although normally inoculation could take place only in specific hospitals where patients could be isolated from the rest of the community while they went through the three- or four-week ordeal of contracting the disease (presumably and with luck in a mild form), now, since there was no containing the disease, Boston was turned into a huge center for inoculation with fumigating posts at the edge of town where all who left had to undergo a "smoking." But within the city people at various stages of smallpox walked freely, attended church, and visited back and forth. Part of the cure was, in fact, to get all the air possible; patients were ordered to sleep with windows open, to walk, and when they could not walk to ride, and when they could do neither, they were to be led.

On July 12 Abigail Adams and her children were inoculated in Boston at the home of an uncle and aunt who had also invited other relatives and a number of Abigail's friends. Each patient was required to bring his own straw bed (which would later be destroyed), two sheets, and a counterpane, eighteen shillings a week for board, and a guinea for the doctor. Abigail also drove a cow into town. "God grant," she said, "that we may all go comfortably thro the Distemper, the phisick part is bad enough I know."

James and Mercy Warren were among those invited to join the group and at the last minute they decided to accept. General Court was in recess now, which made it a convenient time; James, Jr., was back at Harvard, and Mercy was anxious to get her own inoculation over so that she could put the boys in a hospital near Plymouth and take care of them there. Accordingly, on Saturday, July 13, they arrived, the first time either had been in Boston since the siege. It was a gloomy-looking town, James thought. "No Business, no Busy Faces but those of Physicians. Ruins of buildings, wharfs, etc., etc., wherever you go, and the streets covered with grass."

On the same day as the Warrens arrived in Boston, there also arrived a postrider with eight-day-old mail from Philadelphia. Abigail received a letter from John. "Yesterday," he wrote, "the greatest Question was decided, which ever was debated in America, and a greater perhaps, never was or will be decided among Men. A Resolution was passed . . . 'that these united Colonies are and of right ought to be free and independent States.'" And from Elbridge Gerry James Warren received a broadside copy of the Declaration of Independence.

The Massachusetts patriots had waited long for this day and if some of them were too sick to celebrate, they could at least, in the eighteenth-century way, wish each other joy on the occasion. They were now free men, they told each other — free but at the moment rather miserable. In the next six weeks the members of Abigail's household would all suffer in various degrees from sore eyes, lame arms, fever, weakness, headache, and nausea; Mercy would be more severely afflicted than the rest (one day she lay "in a State little better than nonexistance"), yet fortunately before the inoculation had time to take its full effect, Boston officially celebrated the Declaration and Abigail and her friends were able to participate. At noon on Thursday, July 18, they went "with the Multitude" to King Street to hear independence proclaimed from the State House balcony. At the conclusion, there was a grand national salute of thirteen guns, taken up by cannon and muskets throughout the city, taken up by the bells of Boston, taken up by the people themselves, sick and well together, cheering their country and huzzaing for freedom. That night the people built one of the largest bonfires in the history of the town; in it they burned, along with all the Tory signs they could find, the king's arms taken down from the cornice of the State House.

"Thus ends royall authority in this State," Abigail said, "and all the people shall say Amen."

IX

In 1775, soon after the Second Continental Congress had returned Massachusetts to its old charter form of government, Samuel Adams, in reply to James Warren's repeated criticisms of the government, asked what the people had expected. Surely, he said, the people did not "already hanker after the Onions and the Garlick!" Now that independence had been declared, however, the people had to decide specifically what kind of constitution they wanted, both for the country at large and for the individual states. They were no longer rebels, as Mercy Warren pointed out; they were "a distinct people" with new ground to tread, but still, whether they recognized it or not, they were not transformed into a nation. They were, as they had always been, first and foremost citizens of their individual states, not only from habit but from conviction. A large republic made up of many kinds of people could never succeed, they believed; a republic by its very nature had to be a small homogeneous unit. On this Americans were agreed: the states would be sovereign; the nation would be a confederation with no more power than was absolutely necessary — able to conduct foreign affairs but unable, for instance, to raise money. Indeed, so jealous were the states of their own rights, it was two years before the Articles of Confederation were completed and another two years before they were finally ratified.

Meanwhile, the states were working on their own constitutions and sometimes, small and homogeneous as they were, they were finding it difficult. One might expect Massachusetts, one of the most

homogeneous states with its population largely of English descent
and almost entirely of Protestant faith, to be the most efficient, particularly since it had always been one of the most articulate about
the nature of government. On the contrary, however, Massachusetts
was, as James Warren admitted, embarrassingly slow. Most people
in the state believed in what they called a "mixed government" as
opposed to a "pure" or simple government, the theory being that any
simple form contained in it the seeds of its own destruction: monarchy led to despotism, aristocracy to oligarchy, democracy to anarchy
or mob rule. Samuel Adams was said to favor a unicameral legislature but James Warren had come "to dread the consequences of the
levelling spirit" and had long since given up this idea. Like John
Adams, he was for a mixed government. The question was: How
should the mixture take place? How should the balance be effected?

James Warren was not at all sure. He was geared by nature to
think in terms of personalities rather than systems, tyrants rather
than tyranny; and although he could criticize what he called the
"monarchical" part of the General Court, when faced with con-
structing a government, he said frankly that he felt "very unequal to
[it]." His friends had stronger convictions. Samuel Adams could
not understand why people were so afraid of abusing freedom that
they argued against enjoying it, yet he was for unity in Massachusetts at all costs. John Adams believed that man was by nature so
self-seeking that he had to be controlled by a government of strong
checks and counterchecks. James Warren knew simply that he did
not trust men who put on airs and were obviously ambitious,
whether they were members of the aristocracy, whether they were
common men who in the vicissitudes of war were suddenly coming
up in the world, or whether they were from the democratically inclined western counties which had always claimed that they did not
have an equal part with the eastern establishment in running Massachusetts. Actually, what James Warren wanted was for the government to be safely in the hands of people like John Adams, Samuel
Adams, Elbridge Gerry, and himself — modest, unpretentious men

of the old families who venerated the Puritan past and the Puritan virtues. He wanted society to return to the way it used to be but without the Tories, the way it might have been in the days of the Old Colony.

One could hardly, however, expect a constitution to be clever enough to adapt itself to such a wish, but James Warren could at least vote for its being framed, not by a specially elected convention (which many towns insisted was the only proper way to form a compact of the government with the people) but instead by the General Court which promised, partly out of a desire to perpetuate itself, to be more conservative. Accordingly, the people were asked at their next election to vest their members with special powers for that purpose. But once James Warren joined the committee of the General Court to draw up the constitution, he appeared to be in no greater hurry than anyone else. Neither Warren nor the other members of the drafting committee could rise to the challenge of what they were doing; the final document, long delayed and uninspired, was, like most stereotyped constitutions before it, a series of loosely connected articles of a cut-and-dried, businesslike nature with no expression of underlying principles, no statement that showed concern for individual liberties, no recognition of the idea, so dear to the people of Massachusetts, that government was a compact, and indeed not even a careful definition of the responsibilities of each branch of the government. James Warren, who wished for higher property qualifications for voters and who had compromised on the question of representation between the east and west, wrote simply that he was afraid the constitution was not "marked with the wisdom of the Ages."

Long before the constitution was completed, however, James and his friends were worrying about who would be the first governor. The only executive the state had now (or would have until a new constitution was adopted) was the Council, acting in lieu of a governor and not very efficiently, Samuel Otis said. "At present if there is any [executive power], you would be puzzled to find it:

hence the chariot wheels drag so slowly." James Warren did not like dragging chariot wheels any better than his brother-in-law did but James was older, had lived longer under British rule, and, while Samuel looked forward to an executive getting things done, James could never rid himself of the specter of Thomas Hutchinson and was suspicious of anyone in power. Consequently, he was pleased when the new constitution, for all its shortcomings, at least denied the governor a veto.

But a constitution could not guarantee virtue in a governor nor in a people whose character, James and his friends believed, was largely determined by the quality of leadership. Even before independence had been declared, John Adams was describing what kind of governor Massachusetts should have: "the clearest and coolest Head and the firmest Steadyest Heart, the most immoveable Temper and the profoundest Judgment." He favored James Bowdoin or John Winthrop or preferably James Warren "provided an equal Number would agree to it" (the implication being that of the three, Warren was the most controversial, the least popular). But the man they were all afraid would win the governorship was the one who so obviously wanted it, John Hancock — "the Great Man," they called him now, as they made sarcastic reference to the pompous display he was putting on in Philadelphia as president of Congress.

"Is a certain elevated Citizen to put his Hand upon the Pummel of one Chair, and leap into another, at 370 Miles Distance?" John Adams asked James Warren.

In November 1777, when the new constitution was almost completed, the Great Man, with his eye on the governorship, took his leave of Philadelphia to go home and mend his fences. He could not, of course, do it simply. Being John Hancock, he had to deliver a parting speech about himself and his services which, in effect, all but required Congress to give him a vote of thanks. Congress complied but not the two Adamses; they opposed the resolution. "We have had two Presidents before," Samuel said, "Neither of whom made a parting Speech or receivd the Thanks of Congress." In the same way six months later at another farewell, James Warren took exception to Hancock's breaking precedent by shaking hands with the Speaker of the Massachusetts House while the House was in session. "The Great Man . . . went off," Warren reported, "with the Pomp and retinue of an Eastern Prince. I was not in the List of his Attendants . . . I suppose the Sin is unpardonable."

John Hancock could afford to go off for a while now. The constitution that was sent to the towns for their approval in March 1778 was overwhelmingly defeated so there would be no governor elected in the near future. Some towns rejected the constitution because the property qualification of voters was too high, others because it was too low; some claimed that the proposed representation would result in an unwieldy House, some said that legislative and executive powers were improperly vested in the same persons, and some pointed out, as they had before, that in order for a government to have the consent of the people, its constitution should be drawn by representatives specially chosen for that purpose by all adult males (rather than by those entitled to vote under the normally restricted franchise). Most towns were concerned that in one way or another their natural rights were being infringed. "Why Doe we wast our blood and Treasure to obtaine that which When obtained We are not fitt to Enjoy," the little town of Westminster wanted to know. "Why Were We uneasie under George?" Essex County, which made the most thoughtful and literate return, expressed (as did many towns) the desire for a bill of rights which would distinguish between a man's alienable rights (those which on a voluntary basis and for the good of the whole he could part with for an equivalent security of person or property) and his unalienable rights (those inherent rights of conscience for which there could be no equivalent in exchange). These unalienable rights, Plymouth said, "should be expressed in the fullest and most unequivocal terms."

The framers of the constitution had, of course, been handicapped, as Essex County recognized, by the fact that they were busy men, fighting a war at the same time. Massachusetts was not the scene of battle in 1777, but on one side a contingent of British occupied Newport, Rhode Island, and on another side a formidable army fought for upper New York State. In April Fort Ticonderoga was in danger and while John Adams in Philadelphia worried about Massachusetts meeting its commitments, James Warren worked on fulfilling those commitments and defending himself to John Adams.

"If Ticonderoga is not lost," John Adams fumed, "it will be because it is not attacked . . . In plain English, I beg to be Supported or recalled. The Torment of hearing eternally Reflections upon my constituents, that they are all dead, all turned Tories, that they are Small Beer . . . is what I will not endure."

"We have lately ordered 1,500 Militia from the County of Hampshire to Ticonderoga," Warren replied hastily, "one half of the County of Berkshire are gone to Albany . . . ; two thousand men are ordered . . . to reinforce the State of Rhode Island." Now, James asked, "Will the Southern Gentry give us credit, and call us good fellows?"

In July Fort Ticonderoga fell or, to be exact, it was evacuated and so suddenly that food, supplies, arms (70 cannon), and tents were left behind. Not even shortage of men (and James insisted Massachusetts was well represented) could explain such precipitous action, not even cowardice could account for it, Samuel Adams said; and in the end the people of Massachusetts, like everyone else, blamed the officers in command: Arthur St. Clair ("an officer always unfortunate," according to Mercy Warren) and General Schuyler, whom the Massachusetts delegation had never liked. But no matter where they laid the blame, Americans felt humiliated, perhaps never more so in their history. "How shall the disgrace be wiped away?" Abigail Adams wrote John. "How shall our lost Honour be returned?"

There was still, of course, the campaign to be conducted against what the two Adamses called "the Nest of Hornets on Rhode Island." The nest was admittedly a small one but dangerous because it offered a safe harbor to the British fleet and convenient entry to

New England. And in August when part of the fleet was sighted off the Massachusetts shore, it seemed imperative to wipe out the nest once and for all. Ten thousand men enlisted in the militia for one month, strictly as an emergency force and on the understanding that when the month was up, they would return to their harvest and other "business of the Season." Since the militia, once it was in the field, would be under the command of the Continental army, the Council presumably might have appointed one of its lower-ranking officers to be in charge, but instead the command was given to a major general, the only one available, as it happened, since John Hancock was back in Philadelphia and Massachusetts' other major general, Benjamin Lincoln, had recently been transferred to the Continental forces. James Warren was given the command.

When James had first been named a major general in the spring of 1776, Mercy had called the appointment "a Dagger in my Bosom." "How Earnestly did I Ever entreat my Dear Mr. Warren," she wrote, "not to accept of an Appointment which my Foreboding Heart Intimated would involve me in the Depths of Distress." When six months later James was asked to lead the Massachusetts contingent to New York, Mercy had become almost hysterical. "If you march to New York in your feeble state," she said, "I do not imagine you can have much expectation of returning . . . I must march with you . . . I hardly know what I write." She tried, as she always did, to talk herself into submission but admitted that "when Contrary to my Wishes, oh! how Involuntary the Resignation." As it turned out, James did not march to New York. Still weak as a result of his smallpox inoculation, he asked to be excused because of ill health.

There is some question why James Warren accepted the commission in the first place, unless he found it embarrassing to refuse at the same time as he was refusing the court appointment. He had recognized that "it may be hard work for some Persons in the Militia to serve under the Command of those who are not only Inferior in age but in rank," but he obviously had not anticipated how much he would personally resent the Continental troops, who he later claimed displayed the same contempt for the militia as the British regulars had once displayed for the provincials. On several occasions he had threatened to resign but at the time of the Rhode Island expedition he still had not done so. Indeed, he was prepared to fight, he said, and would have fought if the Council had worded its orders differently. James Warren was told to go to Rhode Island and receive his directions from General Spencer (a Continental officer) *"or such other officer as should be appointed to command there."* It was the careless disdain for his rank in the last part of his order that Warren found offensive. "If we have no right to appoint Major Generals we should not have done it," he said. "If we have they ought to have their rank . . . or at least the depreciation should have been settled prior to their appointment and . . . [before] they came within the splendid orb of a Continental Officer." Warren resigned his commission immediately on receiving his orders. "I have too much pride to submit to circumstances humiliateing and degradeing."

As it happened, James Warren's time was put to better use. He began work on what was, perhaps, the most arduous assignment of his career — an appointment to the newly created Navy Board for the Eastern Department. He had himself suggested that such a board was necessary, that Congress could not conduct its naval affairs efficiently from Philadelphia, but he had not wanted the appointment. He had enough responsibilities. Not only had he served as president of the Massachusetts Board of War, he had of course been working on the constitution, trying to fill military quotas, outfitting vessels, fulfilling regular duties for the General Court as well as for his town. (In 1777 he was chosen a fire warden, put on a committee to take care of Plymouth Beach, and asked to help procure a new schoolmaster for the grammar school.) He was in no mood in the middle of May to receive notice of another job. He had been in Boston all spring and what he wanted was to go home and set out a few trees and ramble again among "the herds at Eal-river." How could he commit himself to further duties in Boston?

Mercy thought that "after a ten years ineffectual struggle," he could with a clear conscience quit public life altogether. She was discouraged about the conduct of the war, afraid of an invasion, shocked by reports of British brutality in New Jersey, disgusted at what James called the recent "Inglorious affair at Danburry" in which the British had destroyed one of New England's most important arsenals. Indeed, Mercy was so despondent that she had abandoned work on her history. What incentive was there to write a story whose ending seemed doomed? How could she represent her countrymen as Roman heroes? The old prewar spirit had disappeared, manners had changed, and the people were defeating their own cause — some by their pusillanimity, she said, some by avarice. In addition, Mercy was peeved at her neighbors; none of them had had the "common civility" to call on her after a long absence in Boston visiting her husband.

On June 5 James Warren wrote to John Adams about the navy appointment. "I have taken such a lurch lately for a more private way of life," he admitted, "that I am undetermined what I shall do."

John Adams had also been sighing for private life. He suffered every day "for Want of my farm to ramble in" and at times he felt so confined, so indisposed, so frustrated, so angry that he called himself both a fool and a galley slave to work so hard. Writing to Abigail one day, he burst out in apostrophe to future Americans. "Posterity!" he cried. "You will never know, how much it cost the present Generation to preserve your Freedom! I hope you will make good Use of it. If you do not, I shall repent in Heaven." Nevertheless, John Adams remained steadily at his post and he expected James Warren to do the same. "You must not decline your Appointment to the Navy Board," he wrote.

In August James accepted the appointment in the same letter as he explained to John his resignation from the militia and his refusal to go to Rhode Island. If in the months ahead he sometimes regretted his Navy Board decision, he would never have been sorry about the Rhode Island one. The expedition came to nothing. The men arrived late and when they came, the boats were not ready; then by the time the boats were ready, the enemy had been reinforced, the commanding officers were in conflict with each other, and it was time for the Massachusetts men to go home. By the end of October, people no longer even talked about Rhode Island. There were other events to talk about. The British had taken possession of Philadelphia but even that was not a subject of conversation for long. Bad news could not compete with good news and there was good news now from the north.

On October 17 General Burgoyne and his army of more than five thousand surrendered at Saratoga to General Gates, commander of the American army in the northern department. The people of New England had not been so elated since the fall of Louisbourg thirty-two years before. Under ordinary circumstances they conserved their powder and their lead (Plymouth residents were asked to donate the lead from their window sashes to the war effort), but on the night that the news of Burgoyne's surrender arrived in Boston, cannonballs flew. At a victory celebration of the principal gentlemen of town, a cannon was discharged each time a toast was proposed. And there were many toasts. The gentlemen began drinking to the health of Generals Gates and Washington and became progressively expansive until at last they were drinking to the freedom of the whole world. But if people were impressed by the news, they were all but overwhelmed by the actual sight of the conquered army marching to Boston. "So many thousands . . ." Mercy said, "led captive through the wilderness, the plains, and the cities of the United States was a spectacle never before beheld by the inhabitants."

Hannah Winthrop was on hand for their arrival in Cambridge.

Last Thursday which was a very stormy day [*she wrote Mercy*] *a large Number of British Troops came softly thro the Town via Watertown to Prospect Hill. On Friday we heard the Hessians were to make a Procession in the same rout . . . To be sure the sight was truly astonishing. I never had the least Idea that the Creation produced such a sordid set of Creatures in human Figure, poor, dirty, emaciated men, great numbers of women who seemed to be the beasts of burden having a bushel basket on their backs by which they were bent double, the contents seemed to Pots and kettles, various sorts of Furniture, children peeping thro gridirons and other utensils. Some very young infants who were born on the road, the women barefoot clothed in dirty raggs. Such effluvia filld the air while they were passing had they not been smoking all the time, I should have been apprehensive of being contaminated by them. After a noble looking advanced Guard, Genl. J——y B——n headed this terrible group on horseback.*

In the rear, closing the cavalcade, Hannah wrote, were the Americans: "a fine Noble looking Guard of American Brawny, Victorious, Yeomanry who assisted in bringing these Sons of Slavery to Terms, Some of our Waggons drawn by fat oxen driven by joyous looking Yankees."

Here at last was material for the kind of history worth recording. Mercy recognized it and took hope. John Adams, writing from York, Pennsylvania, where the Continental Congress had been forced to move, said that the tide of war had been turned. And in France, the government, ever eager to defeat its traditional enemy, smelled victory in the air and allied itself with the American cause.

·   ·   ·

Winter came early that year with ice on the streets in October. Abigail Adams and Mercy settled down at their respective firesides with their winter needlework, handicapped though they were by the scarcity of goods and the rising prices. There was no cambric fit to use under nine pounds a yard, Mercy wrote, but she was able to secure some thread and sent ten skeins to Abigail until she could do better. The ladies worried about the cost of food (butter at three shillings, cheese two, corn not to be had at any price, rye sold only by barter, coffee at ten shillings per pound), they read newspapers for reports of the army camped at Valley Forge, they rejoiced when Benjamin Church was finally exiled, and all winter long they exchanged outraged letters about General Burgoyne and his troops, who were still in Boston waiting for the terms of surrender to be ratified in London. The British officers were treated far too well, the ladies thought. They were "rioting on the Fat of the Land," according to Hannah Winthrop, who had a close view in Cambridge; they were "Stalking at Large with the Self-importance of Lords of the Soil" — these same men who had so recently stabled their horses in the Old South Church and cut their meat on Mrs. Quincy's mahogany tables.

The ladies were also upset that winter over a story about Lord Lyttelton in England. It all had to do with a controversial statue of Catherine Macaulay which had recently been erected in a church vestry in London. The parishioners objected to the statue being there, but Mrs. Macaulay's female admirers objected to the inscription at the foot of the statue, reputedly taken from a letter by Lord Lyttelton in which, after a number of compliments, he said: "Once in every Age I could wish such a Woman to appear, as a proof that Genius is not confined to Sex; but at the same time — you will pardon me — We want no more than one Mrs. Macaulay."

"What must be that Genius," Abigail countered angrily, "which cannot do justice to one Lady, but at the expence of the Whole Sex?"

It is a tribute to Abigail that she could become so exercised about Lord Lyttelton on the day after she had said good-bye to John, surely one of the most difficult days of her life. John had been away most of three years, but the last separation had been the longest — eleven months — and during seven of those months she had been pregnant and had given birth to a stillborn daughter.

In May 1777 Abigail had written: "Tis four Months wanting 3 days since we parted, every day of the time I have mourned the absence of my Friend."

In June she wrote: "I want a companion a Nights, many of them are wakefull and Lonesome."

"Yesterday," she wrote in September, "compleated Eight months since you left me. When shall I see you."

John returned in November and took up his law practice, but scarcely had he settled down than Congress elected him to go to France on a joint commission with Benjamin Franklin and Arthur Lee. Abigail, unable to see how she could bear another separation so soon, at such a distance, and for so long a time, poured out her anguish to Mercy and asked Mercy what she would do in the same circumstances. Abigail thought that she could prevail upon John to stay, if she tried.

Mercy admitted her answer was "problematical." She had "too Great a Regard" for her character to think that she would urge her husband not to accept such an appointment, she said, yet she was too "suspicious" of her heart to give a positive yes. She was, of course, quite right to be suspicious, yet she did urge Abigail to consent.

John Adams and his oldest son, John Quincy (aged ten), sailed for France in the middle of February 1778. With the exception of a three-month interlude in 1779, John was gone ten years — too long, some said, to remain in touch with America; long enough, he believed, to become thoroughly acquainted with other governments, to observe their weaknesses and strengths and profit from the observation. He was a man open to experience and bound to be affected by it. In time he would find that some of the sentiments of his old friends seemed parochial; in time his friends would fear that his foreign service had given him exalted notions. Even now there were moments in 1778 when James Warren was afraid that John had moved beyond him. Once after a long interval without a letter, James announced: "I don't write to the Embassador, or make a distinction between the Embassador and the Delegate I write to my Friend and use no kind of ceremony, I leave that to the Great, and the Numerous Courtiers about you." But if their letters were not as frequent, they were as warm. They still mourned together the de-

pravity of man, they still traded insults about John Hancock, and
they still looked forward to the day when they could go back to
farming.

The Adamses and the Warrens were especially worried at the moment about virtue, the rock upon which their new republic was to be
built. Virtue had not increased with independence, as the leaders
had hoped. On the contrary, it had declined alarmingly and the old
prewar dream of establishing a new Rome on American soil seemed
more remote than ever. Currency had depreciated, class patterns
were changing, people were profiting from the war, speculating,
peculating, gaming, living high, dressing extravagantly, riding
around in chariots — "fellows who would have cleaned my shoes
five years ago," James Warren observed. Ladies were buying cambric no matter how much it cost and were decorating their hats lav-
ishly with flowers and white gauze, and, as one Boston merchant
noted, even hoop petticoats were "crawling in." Surveying the scene,
James Warren said he envied the Indians their simplicity and Mercy
wrote a brisk poem on the "Follies of the Day" in which she lined up
all the old, familiar, money-mad sinners and then introduced a new
breed that threatened the very basis of the Puritan dream: the skep-
tic brought up in "deistic schools" who disputed Newton, spurned
Locke, and thought it was "heroic to deny his God."

"Ah, Ninevah, Babylon, and Tyre, how are ye fallen," Hannah
Winthrop echoed. Then in a more practical vein she told Mercy:
"Your shoes are done. The shoemaker was as prudent as he could be
of trimmings"; but even so, the shoes were "tinctured with the pre-
vailing spirit of the times."

All anyone could hope was that manners and morals would improve when the war was over and the economy was stabilized; but
for this to happen, there needed to be vigorous and virtuous leaders.
And where were they? On the national scene people were even
finding fault with George Washington, the most noble republican of
all, according to Mercy. As for the state, it had not, in Mercy's opinion, had a hero since her brother Jemmy had played the part of

Brutus before the war, a part he would obviously not be playing again, although there were brief flurries of hope. In the spring of 1778 he was well enough to be elected moderator at a town meeting in Boston and well enough to be given a commission in Joseph Otis' brigade. But his recovery was, as usual, temporary. A few weeks later he was drinking his way down the road to the American camp at Newport, stopping at every tavern, and trying to find the money to pay his bills. He had long since given up supporting his family; his wife annually applied to the General Court for interest on a loan Jemmy had made to the province in 1774 and when Jemmy's son, an ensign in the navy now, had to borrow twenty pounds from the Massachusetts delegates at Philadelphia, he asked that the money be collected from his grandfather. In 1778 Jemmy was reduced to trading his law books for liquor.

Unfortunately the only popular leader that Massachusetts had was John Hancock and he had acquired a truly impressive following. Men needed an idol, James Warren said, and those who had once worshiped Hutchinson had now fallen under the spell of Hancock, who even his enemies admitted had a way with people, a flair for showmanship, and certainly a ready hand with money. But John Hancock as the leader for a new Rome? Mercy was indignant at the idea and tried to enlighten her friend Hannah Winthrop, who had always been rather close to the Hancock family and was apparently not aware of John's weaknesses. Actually, Mercy said, John Hancock was worse than Caesar, if such a thing was possible. He possessed all of Caesar's vices but none of his talents — none of the valor, the vigor, and the magnanimity that had accounted for Caesar's success. John Hancock was simply a man whose vanity had led him "to sacrifice the best interests of the country at the shrine of flattery."

But if Massachusetts society was to be afflicted with John Hancock and if it was to be characterized by all the deadly sins, at least it did not have to put up with the Tories, James Warren contended. Like his friends, he was appalled at the attitude of permissiveness in regard to the Tories that had sprung up among many so-called moderate Whigs, men who, James Warren claimed, had "hid in Holes and Corners" until the country was committed to independence and only then surfaced, affecting a condescending attitude toward Washington and the French and displaying a self-righteous generosity toward the Tories. Some of these genteel Whigs fraternized with General Burgoyne and his officers, some exchanged toasts on the king's birthday, some introduced a movement (which did not succeed) to bring a few select Tories, including Harrison Gray, back from England, and some simply performed favors for Tories in distress. In Plymouth one Whig arranged for Edward Winslow to receive money regularly from his son Ned, who was serving with the British army in Newport; another Whig contrived to have two casks of wine delivered to Winslow from a British ship forced by bad weather into Plymouth Harbor.

To the Adamses and Warrens it was inconceivable that in the midst of war Americans should tolerate men who had not only opposed their cause openly in the past but were in many cases still opposing it surreptitiously. "Can a man take Fire into his Bosom," Samuel Adams asked, "and not be burned?" The Tories were obviously acting as informers to the British army; they were manufacturing rumors designed to intimidate and divide the Americans, and they were behaving with an impudence unbecoming to a people about to be defeated. In Plymouth one Sunday the Tories even played a joke. They contrived to have an egg found in the roost of a Whig hen, an extraordinary egg which bore an inscription: "O America, Amerca! Howe shall be thy conqueror." With considerable excitement the egg was exhibited to a congregation assembling for church and it was generally agreed (with the Tories concurring) that since there was no other explanation, the prophecy must have been written by a supernatural hand. If there were some good Puritans like Mercy Warren who had no trouble distinguishing between God and the Tories, there were others who, having always acknowledged that God moved in a mysterious way, were hesitant to say that

He might not with perfect propriety speak, if He chose, through a Plymouth hen. In any case, the egg caused a sensation: the story was reported in newspapers all over New England and was satirized in rhyme by Mrs. Warren.

Obviously Tories capable of creating a prophetical egg were capable of operations of a far more dangerous nature. James Warren had tried time and again to secure legislation to suppress them, but either the towns would not support the measures or the Council defeated them. An act requiring Tories to take an oath of allegiance was one of the first measures suggested, the longest in passing, and in the end the least successful. The Tories, instead of refusing the oath and taking the consequences (banishment or prison), were disappointingly unprincipled; most of them, James Warren said, "swallowed it without difficulty." But if the Tories did not convict themselves, their townsmen did not convict them either. In an attempt to distinguish between the so-called "honest" (sincere but quiet and contrite) Tories and the dangerous ones, James Warren and his friends in the House proposed that each town draw up a list of suspected Tory offenders, question them, and then vote if their names should be submitted to the state for trial. In Plymouth five men, including Edward Winslow, were accused of "endeavouring since the 19th of April, 1775, to Counter Act the Struggles of this and the United States," but the evidence was slender, the accused were persuasive, and the charges were dropped.

In general, Tories were the victims of more persecution by the Whigs than they were the recipients of what James Warren called "false Lenity." For the Winslows, who suffered many personal insults, the year 1778 was difficult. The property of those Tories who had left the state was put up at public auction and the remaining Tories had to observe the clothes and the personal effects of their friends being paraded through the town by their enemies. ("Dear Mr. Hallowell's clothes," Sally Winslow reported, "pass the house every Sunday on the back of a nasty great cooper.") In February Edward Winslow was rounded up to take the oath of allegiance and at the end of May he was required at the age of sixty-four to turn out as a common soldier, hire a man to take his place, or go to jail. Since his house was already mortgaged and he had no income except what he received through Ned, it is possible that Whig friends came again to his rescue and helped him hire a replacement. It is possible, even probable, that Mercy lent him money on this occasion, perhaps for the sake of Penny Winslow and their past friendship, perhaps simply because Mercy, as strong as her convictions were, was less stubborn than her husband, more willing to allow a general principle to have a few exceptions. In any case, she did have money of her own and she did lend some to Edward once, perhaps more than once, making it clear that *she* was lending the money and not James, a distinction that James undoubtedly insisted upon and one that Edward Winslow undoubtedly resented. He had become increasingly bitter against James, who was behind every piece of anti-Tory legislation in the state; indeed, no matter what Mercy did, Edward Winslow would have welcomed an opportunity to strike back at James.

On June 1 Winslow had his chance. For seven years he had not, for obvious political reasons, attended a town meeting or participated in the election of the town's representatives to the General Court, but this year, Tory or not, he not only went to the annual meeting but he spoke out. Against James. "He was suffered yesterday in full meeting of the town," Mercy reported indignantly, "to stand up and cast the most illiberal reflections on a man whose primary object has been to rescue these people from the thraldom of a foreign yoke."

When it came to vote, Plymouth for the first time in years did not elect James Warren as a representative. Initially, James was more amused at Mercy's anger than he was angry himself. "I love you should feel some such passions," he wrote; "I believe they are Good for your Constitution." In comparison, he felt almost stoical, but had he been at the town meeting, he conceded, "that would have roused me to have given the old Scoundrel one Broadside at least for his Lying falsehood." What was harder to bear was that the General Court, which might have elected him to the Council, did not see fit to do so. James did not attribute his defeat entirely to the Tories. He blamed John Hancock, who wanted to get him "out of sight" and made political use of the fact that he had refused his court appointment; he blamed the general temper of the times ("The people feel themselves uneasy and don't know the reason"); and he blamed the new "moderate" class whose politics were so different from his own.

James Warren's political life, however, was far from over. He was reinstated by his town the following year, but he was known more and more, as he himself admitted, as "an old Fashioned Fellow" with a reputation (so exploited by his enemies) of refusing offices not agreeable to him. He felt the accusation was unfair. "You know I have been on Deck for twelve years," he wrote Samuel Adams, "and I believe you will not be able with all your discernment and Watchfulness to recollect an Instance of my flinching." Certainly he stuck doggedly to his Navy Board post in spite of the fact that on various occasions he found conditions so unbearable that he did not see how he could go on. He was a proud fellow, he said, and was constantly embarrassed both financially and professionally. On the one hand, his simple living expenses in Boston (without even a "Glass of Wine") exceeded his pay by $500, which he could ill afford; on the other hand, he had been given insufficient authority or money to carry out his duties effectively. In time Congress corrected both deficiencies and later supported him when the integrity of the Board was viciously impugned in an anonymous letter.

Yet James Warren's ardent prewar activities, his years of devoted service on the Navy Board and in the General Court were gradually (and artfully) replaced in the public mind by the record of his refusals, many of which represented not so much an evasion of duty as a conflict of duties. He was truly concerned about Mercy's emotional stability and when she went to pieces at the prospect of a long separation, he scarcely knew how to cope. This happened again in 1779.

After he had been reelected to the House, it appeared for a while that he would be chosen a delegate to the Continental Congress at Philadelphia. But again Mercy was upset. Indeed, she was as anxious about his possible appointment as she had been angry about his defeat in the House election the year before. But now instead of "loving" her passion James wished rather wistfully that her mind were as "Sluggish" as his own. How was it, he asked, "that a Mind, possessed of a Masculine Genius well stocked with Learning, fortified by Phylosophy and Religion, should be so easily Impressed by the adverse Circumstances . . . of this World?" But Mercy's imagination — brilliant and mischievous — was a constant mystery to him and if he stood in awe of its brilliance, he had long ago set himself the task of guarding her against its mischief. He had several reasons for refusing the Philadelphia assignment but chief among them, he told Mercy, was her "trembling Nerves."

Mercy, of course, had always lived on the brink of precipices, more often imagined than real, but she was finding the precipices higher now and the footing less sure. She was experiencing the irony of middle age. Just when the world she had tried so hard to mold seemed most critically in need of her, she had to relinquish her hold. The generations were slipping away on both sides. Her father had died in the winter of 1778 and of her five sons, three had left home and only two were left, as the saying went, "in the parlor." She tried to find the strength to let them all go, but it was doubly hard without James and would be insupportable, she thought, were he to assume still more duties away from home. Yet she felt guilty. "I am sometimes Ready to think you could serve the public as well & perhaps better, unincumbered by anxieties for me." And when her father died, she berated herself for indulging in grief; after all, he had done his work and was happy to be released. "Why was this such a painful Circumstance to me?" she asked, as if in grieving she was in effect questioning the will of God. As for her three oldest sons, her duties were ended, she told herself time and again; heaven alone could mature the seeds of morality she had planted, yet in actual practice, how could she leave the maturing entirely to heaven?

Of all the sons, James, Jr., resisted Mercy most successfully. In 1778 a lieutenant in the Marines, he obviously had recovered from whatever emotional disturbance he had suffered, yet he was aloof to his family, perhaps to protect himself from their ministrations, and in turn his family was sensitive about him. While his father secured an assignment for him on the *Alliance* which sailed to France at the end of the year and while he carried with him letters from both parents to John Adams, no letters survive between Mercy and James, Jr., and few references to James exist in Mercy's correspondence to other people, which seems strange, considering how prone Mercy was to dramatize danger, how eager to cast the men of her family in the role of heroes. Even when it became known that the *Alliance* was threatened with mutiny and was commanded, if not by a madman, by a "bewildered man — an embarrassed Mind" (so said John Adams), and even after the *Alliance* had returned from battle, Mercy did not talk about James except to say once to her husband that in her prayers a "Long absent son" was not "Lost or forgotten." And John Adams, writing from Paris about the *Alliance,* had only this comment: "Your son is on board, by this time inured . . . to War."

Meanwhile Charles Warren had entered Harvard, not only under the watchful eye of Hannah Winthrop but under her roof as well. Hannah's diary (a record of when the hogs were killed, when the horses were put out to pasture, how much butter was churned) contains regular notations of money received from General Warren for the boarding of "Mr. Charles." But Mercy need not have worried about Charles. His most serious offense at Harvard was abusing a volume of Shakespeare for which he was duly fined. Charles was not only good but, like Mercy, he enjoyed talking about being good. He assured his mother that he was praying for the fortitude to resist the innumerable temptations that confronted him daily and he told his father that, as far as amusements were concerned, he entered into them only deep enough to refresh his body "and believe me, Sir, no deeper than." For Mercy, such moral affirmations were of course good news, but not so much a reason for the subject to be closed as an indication that the subject was acceptable, that it could be pursued and expanded. All the lessons that Mercy longed to urge on her less receptive sons, she heaped upon Charles, the one who needed her instructions the least, the one who most wanted to please.

It was Winslow, however, who was the hero, taking the part that Jemmy Otis had once played — not in a state drama but in Mercy's own private drama. Winslow was gay, social, handsome, literary, ambitious, somewhat arrogant; but, unlike Jemmy, he was neither rocked by soul-shaking philosophies nor fired by public conscience. When his mother extolled the Puritan virtues of simplicity and moderation, Winslow asked bluntly what, in such a world, became of ambition? He chose not to go to college but instead entered directly into a commercial career, moving to Boston before he was twenty. Mercy's correspondence with him began in 1779, a significant year in many ways for Mercy and her friends. John Winthrop, Hannah's husband, died in 1779; John Adams came home from France and went back again, in the interim not only attending a new constitutional convention but writing most of a new constitution for Massachusetts; John Hancock made a flamboyant bid for military glory in a new campaign to Rhode Island but left prematurely or, as he put it, when he had exerted himself to the extent of his "slender constitution"; and in October the British fleet evacuated Rhode Island. But nothing that happened in this year or indeed in the next years affected Mercy as much as fresh news from Winslow. How was he? Where was he? What was he doing? What was he thinking? When would she see him? What was the state of his soul?

Mercy admitted that when she wrote to her sons, her "pen as it were mechanically glides into a moralizing strain," but with Winslow there was both an intensity and a restraint in her moralizing that there was not with Charles. On the one hand, she wanted desperately, passionately, to insure the future of this favorite son whose "taste for elegant amusements" was, as she said, "carried rather high"; on the other hand, she always had to ask herself: How far could she go with Winslow, how much would he tolerate? Sometimes she tried to take the curse off her preaching by injecting an apology; sometimes she delivered her message on a cushion of compliments; sometimes, particularly when the subject was too delicate to be touched, she used quotations to serve her purpose. Abbé Raynal, she pointed out, said that gaming was "attended with the most shameful and pernicious Consequences." But the day that Winslow wrote in praise of Lord Chesterfield's controversial *Letters to His Son* (which John Adams would not have in his library), Mercy took the bit in her teeth and ran for three pages.

"I have no Quarrel with the Graces," she said, ". . . But I Love better that frankness and sincerity which bespeaks a soul above dissimulation, that . . . Manly Fortitude that . . . Resists the temptations to Vice in the purlieus of the Brothel or the Antichamber of the Princess, in the arms of the . . . distempered prostitute, or Beneath the smiles of the painted Courtesin." In other words, Mercy was saying what Samuel Johnson put more succinctly: Chesterfield's *Letters* taught "the morals of a whore, and the manners of a dancing master."

In spite of Mercy's care, however, Winslow Warren was acquiring a questionable reputation. John Adams, en route to France in November 1779, heard that Winslow had made great profits not only by buying what he knew was wanted by the navy and selling to the Navy Board, but also by "purchasing Sailors Shares and by Gambling." While John admitted that there was no evidence of a fortune acquired and said that the rumor, if true at all, must have been greatly exaggerated, Mercy attributed the whole ugly story to the same malicious source that was trying to eliminate James Warren from the political scene and was also at work on the character of Samuel Adams. Mercy may have been right. Yet she continued to make veiled references to gaming whenever she saw the opportunity, she continued to warn Winslow to be careful in his selection of friends, and once she went so far as to say that when a youth emerged from an "accidental deviation" from virtue, it could serve as a "beacon" for the future.

In March 1780, Mercy, who had vice enough to worry about in Boston society, was suddenly informed that Winslow was going to Europe to seek business opportunities there. For three months she had been waiting for the visit he had promised her, but Winslow promised easily; he set the date repeatedly and repeatedly he did not keep it. Mercy had been tossed between expectation and disappointment, she said, until her mind was almost "unhinged," and of course now that she knew his plans the disappointment was harder than ever to endure.

"I know not what reasons our son may have to urge him abroad at this perilous time," Mercy wrote to James on March 12. ". . . My children leave me Early, & I seem to Grow useless to them."

On March 15 she wrote again: "No Winslow yet."

On March 26: "Do I raise my hopes too high . . . I begin to think Winslow does not intend to Come & see me or that something Extraordinary has taken place . . . I have been so many times disappointed that I feel sometimes as if I never was to see him more . . . What a trifle it appears to me for a Man to go from Boston to Plimouth! I would have rode it over twenty times since Last December to save one of my Family half the pain I have felt in a Week."

On April 2 Mercy wrote that she expected Winslow the next day "with Mr. Tillotson and Lady and others. I hope they will keep the appointment as you know the Difficulties of being prepared at all times to Entertain strangers."

At the same time James was writing Mercy from Boston: "I can't bear you should be disappointed, & yet you may be again Tomorrow. Winslow has just been in & doubts whether he can go there or not. he has some Business to do which will suffer if it can't be Done this evening."

Mercy had still one more disappointment, one more company dinner to prepare for which "no mortal" would show up. Winslow finally came to Plymouth in the middle of April, stayed for a few days, and promised to return for another visit in two weeks. "I dont Believe he will keep his word," Mercy said. "But I dont love to urge him Least he should not come so often."

He did not keep his word and when a month had gone by, Mercy, fearing she would not see him again, went to Boston for a last good-bye. She could scarcely have chosen a more dramatic day — May 19, famous in Massachusetts history as the mysterious Dark Day or Black Friday. The darkness began about ten o'clock in the morning; at half-past eleven, it was reported that "in a room with three windows, twenty-four panes each . . . large print could not be read by persons with good eyes." Hannah Winthrop burned candles for three hours in the afternoon while woodcocks whistled and frogs peeped as though it were night. Schools were dismissed, ministers held impromptu services, and according to one diarist, "fear seized on all except sailors." Some more scientifically minded attributed the darkness to smoke from a forest fire in the north but whatever the cause, Mercy, tense enough at parting with Winslow, found the atmosphere ominous.

The *Pallas,* on which Winslow had passage, did not actually sail for another two weeks, although it was uncertain from day to day just when it would leave. Meanwhile James Warren prepared letters and papers for Winslow to deliver to John Adams in Europe, including a copy of Massachusetts' new constitution which would be submitted to a ratifying convention in the middle of June. The constitution was essentially as John Adams had conceived it, prefaced by Adams' own preamble with its precise definition of government as a social compact ("by which the whole people covenants with each citizen, and each citizen covenants with the whole people") and followed by a detailed and eloquent declaration of rights. James Warren would have been pleased with that declaration; he would have been happy to have seen the powers of each branch of government so clearly defined; he might have approved the increase in property qualification for voters (higher than under the charter), and he might even have favored Samuel Adams' controversial Article III in the Declaration of Rights, which allowed the legislature the right to require towns to tax for church support. But James Warren, defer as he might to John Adams' system of checks and balances, would surely have been uneasy about the expanded powers of the executive. No governor in the United States would have as many appointive rights (plus the power of veto) as would be allowed the governor of Massachusetts under this new, basically more conservative constitution.

The *Pallas* sailed on June 3. Mercy did not see Winslow again but she had time to send him one final message. "You have surveyed the portrait of human nature in the historic page," she said, "you have now only to know yourself." To James she wrote: "Did he do Everything to your Wishes. had he everything he needed, and did he go off in Good Spirits?"

As it happened, the *Alliance* sailed from France with James Warren, Jr., on board a few weeks after the *Pallas* left Boston. Presumably under normal circumstances the two Warren boys might have passed at sea, but there was nothing normal about either of their crossings. Moreover, before Winslow kept his appointment with John Adams, several new pages had been added to the history of the United States: Charleston had fallen, General Arnold had defected, the Massachusetts constitution had been ratified (although many — especially in the west — were uneasy about it), and a new state government had been installed.

The faction that had been opposing James Warren and his friends emerged triumphant at the polls. Although James himself had been one of those in the contested election for lieutenant governor, he asked to have his name dropped, supposedly because of his duties on the Navy Board but actually because of his distaste for those in power. In any case, Thomas Cushing, Hancock's old ally, became the lieutenant governor. John Avery (who had once courted Abby Otis and was married now to Thomas Cushing's daughter) replaced Samuel Adams as secretary of the Commonwealth. And the new governor was John Hancock, inaugurated in a crimson velvet suit amid a round of assemblies, entertainments, and balls.

. . .

"If this Infant Common Wealth can thus stand in its pupilage," Mercy wrote John Adams, "will it not become the Wonder of the World."

X

---◦•◦---

THOMAS HUTCHINSON was spared the knowledge of John Hancock's election, but if he had heard it, he would not have been surprised. Too many unpredictable, unreasonable things had happened for him to wonder at one more. The events of the last years had not shaken his convictions but they had upset his sense of order. The revolution in America could no longer be brushed aside as a bit of temporary insanity like the witch trials; people were not coming back to their senses; Britain was not displaying dazzling power, and heaven was not elevating the righteous. A lesser man might have questioned his God in such reversals; a stronger man might have questioned himself. In a moment of dejection, Thomas Hutchinson said simply: "I see that the ways of Providence are mysterious, but I abhor the least thought that all is not perfectly right."

After Burgoyne had surrendered at Saratoga, Hutchinson, who had always dreaded the idea of dying in England, admitted, "Most of us expect to lay our bones here." Yet he continued to think like a homesick New Englander, rating English towns by the way they compared to towns in Massachusetts, referring to days of superior weather as "New England days." And he missed his work. Having immersed himself so completely in public affairs, he was lost without work and unlike many of his friends he was unable to take pleasure in the traditional English amusements. He did not care for racing (a picture of a horse race was as agreeable as the original, he said) nor could he understand why people were flocking to the theater to see David Garrick perform (when Hutchinson saw Farquhar's

Beaux' Stratagem, he said either Garrick was too old for the part or he was too old to see him); he did enjoy, however, talking with his old friends, visiting historical sites, and attending certain ceremonies (including the ceremony in which he was awarded an honorary degree at Oxford on the same day, as it happened, that America's independence was declared), but strangely enough nothing in London seemed to intrigue Thomas Hutchinson as much as the sight of two visiting elephants stabled behind Buckingham Palace. Like a small boy, he marveled at the way the elephants used their trunks, but this was one of the few flashes of enthusiasm Hutchinson displayed in his later years. He appeared an old man now and had become, according to John Adams, a ridiculous figure at court. Still intent on trying to justify his policies in Massachusetts, he attended the king's levees, watching for every opportunity to press his points. Courtiers laughed at his stiff manners, at his constant quoting of his brother Foster, at the awkward way he was forever fumbling in his pockets for some letter to read to the king, with whom he had long since lost favor.

Later, men who knew Thomas Hutchinson and saw his loneliness said that he "died of Milton Hill," but actually he died bit by bit of many tragedies. In 1777 his beloved daughter Peggy (so much like her mother), died at the age of twenty-three after an agonizing summer which Hutchinson reported in pathetic detail in his diary, making minute observations about her cough, hopefully recording every small improvement (once he was able to carry her on a pillow for a short ride on an easy horse), and sadly acknowledging subsequent setbacks. Then in February 1780, his son Billy died, also of consumption. A few months later Hutchinson, apparently afflicted in the same way, began making entries in his diary about his own health. "My shortness of breath does not mend," he wrote on May 12. On May 22: "A week passed and no abatement: last night almost sleepless." On June 2 it was apparent to everyone, including Thomas Hutchinson, that he could not live long. But it was a bitter time for a man who loved order to die. On that day a madman named Lord George Gordon instigated London's famous anti-Catholic riots which turned the city into a bedlam of death and destruction (450 killed or wounded) far exceeding in violence anything that had ever happened in prewar America. Yet Thomas Hutchinson's passion for order was his strength as well as his weakness. On the morning of June 3, in spite of the riots and in spite of the pitiful state of his health, he prepared to follow his daily routine. The end was near, he said, and he repeatedly interrupted his conversation to quote scripture and appeal to God; but it was his habit to take a daily drive and he called for his coach as usual. Just before leaving, he summoned his servant, Riley, and asked for a clean shirt. He must die clean, he explained; it was about all he could do now to set his house straight. So, attired neatly in a way that he had long ago decided was becoming to an elderly gentleman, Thomas Hutchinson walked to his coach and collapsed on the way. He died a few hours later, his son Elisha wrote, "with one or two gaspes," resigning his soul to God who gave it.

. . .

The news of the Gordon riots reached Boston on the frigate *Alliance* but, as it turned out, the news was scarcely less dramatic than the story of the *Alliance* itself and its forty days at sea. James Warren, Jr., was on board as one of the Marine officers and later gave his testimony about the trip and the behavior of Captain Pierre Landais, whose mind was obviously not just "embarrassed," as John Adams had said, but quite insane. Indeed, Captain Landais had already displayed this insanity in the engagement against the *Serapis* when he had vented his jealousy against his squadron commander, John Paul Jones, by hanging back from battle and firing deliberately (so it was claimed) on Jones's own *Bonhomme Richard.* For this Landais had been stripped of his command and ordered to America to stand court-martial. But Landais would not accept dismissal or brook opposition. He simply set sail without orders and without most of the supplies which he was supposed to deliver to the American army.

So began the *Alliance*'s mad voyage across the Atlantic. On the first day at sea, Landais threw Captain Parke of the Marine Corps into the brig for refusing to swear unqualified obedience to him and in rapid succession he put men in irons for not demonstrating sufficient respect. Once in a tantrum he suddenly ordered the ship's course to be reversed; once he threatened a distinguished passenger, Arthur Lee of Virginia, with a carving knife because Lee had helped himself first to roast pig at the wardroom table. Twice the crew mutinied and when Landais refused to allow them to fish off the Grand Banks of Newfoundland, they simply took control and fished. In the end the officers and passengers, led by Arthur Lee, forced Landais to give the command to a lieutenant who was under arrest. When the *Alliance* finally docked in Boston on August 19, Landais was dragged screaming and kicking ashore and that, of course, was the end of his service in the American navy.

Under such conditions it is not surprising that the paths of James Warren, Jr., and Winslow did not cross at sea, but they did in fact come closer than either knew. While the *Alliance* was fishing off the coast of Newfoundland, Winslow was actually in Newfoundland as a prisoner of war. Soon after leaving Boston, the *Pallas* had been captured and taken to St. John's, where for several months the passengers and crew were held, awaiting orders for their further disposition. Since Winslow was a civilian with no military or official status, he was in no danger in Newfoundland nor did he suppose he would have difficulties in England, were he to go there. American civilians lived as freely and easily in London as they had before the war, a great deal more easily than Tories did in America. In any case, the prisoners were treated kindly and the Newfoundland experience was for Winslow merely an interruption, and perhaps not an uninteresting one, to his European trip. His adventures lay ahead in England, where he landed on October 5, was questioned, and in short order set at liberty.

In typical style, Winslow found his way quickly into the social life of London and in the process teamed up with three other young

men: John Trumbull, son of the governor of Connecticut, who was
in London to study art; John Temple, son-in-law of James Bowdoin;
and John Tyler of Boston, who had come to London to settle a mercantile matter. Tyler and Warren became particular friends and obviously had much in common; Tyler, according to Trumbull, was a
"man of pleasure" and Winslow Warren was "a somewhat amphibious character, and withal young, handsome, and giddy." For six
weeks these two led a gay life together, rushing from one social
engagement to another, attending the theater, and quite possibly,
judging from later references, visiting the gaming tables as well.

Meanwhile James Warren wrote his son: "I pray God to protect
you from every evil, natural and moral"; and Mercy asked John
Adams to give Winslow some "philosophic Hints" when they met
on the continent, and some "Explicit opinions . . . both of Men,
and Manners."

Long before Winslow and John Adams could meet, however, the
news of Benedict Arnold's treason and Major André's execution
reached London (November 13) with implications for Winslow
and his friends that no one could have anticipated. All at once there
erupted in London a kind of spy fever. Loyalists had for a long time
been talking about the potential danger from rebel Americans and
they had pointed to the Tower where Henry Laurens, former president of the American Congress, was a prisoner. Mr. Laurens, on a
secret mission to negotiate a treaty with Holland, had been captured
at sea along with incriminating papers and on his arrival in England
(on the same ship with Winslow Warren) he had been arrested and
accused of treason. Londoners watching him take his daily walks on
the Tower platform found their imaginations excited; sometimes
they whispered that the Americans were behind the Gordon riots
but with the news of Arnold and André they began voicing their
suspicions more loudly. Americans who had previously been accepted in London society were suddenly regarded as possible spies.

On Saturday, November 18, John Trumbull was arrested and on
Sunday a warrant was issued for Tyler, accused of being in the serv-

ice of the American army. Winslow Warren was in Kensington that evening, having dinner with some young Loyalist refugees from Boston. Perhaps the Loyalists were unaware of Winslow's friendship with Tyler, perhaps they were simply indiscreet; in any case during the course of the conversation Winslow Warren learned that Tyler was being accused of treason and that police were even then stationed outside his lodgings. As soon as dinner was over, Winslow explained that he would not be able to linger over after-dinner wine as he had a previous engagement with some ladies on the east end of town. Excusing himself, he rushed to the place where he knew Tyler was dining and helped him make his escape to the continent.

Fortunately, Winslow's part in Tyler's escape was never discovered, but one wonders why Winslow continued to stay in London when the atmosphere was so suspicious. Perhaps there was a lady involved; Mercy's replies to Winslow's letters include a warning that he should "guard against the fascinating power of Beauty" and save himself for someone worthy. ("Virtue is melted away by Wine & Women.") Winslow's father, on the other hand, was more concerned with Winslow's money than with his women. "Why have you not told me in some of your Letters what Money you received at Newfoundland?" he wrote. ". . . Your Uncle Otis has brought me a charge for money paid you on his acct." As for his staying away from home so long, James supposed "it possible for a young fellow to make but little distinction between days & weeks when he has seated himself at the Court end of a Great City among the *Polite & Genteel.*"

But whatever Winslow was doing or not doing, he stayed in London too long. At the end of January his papers were taken from his room and at the same time he was put in prison while Lord Hillsborough, secretary of state for the colonies, reviewed his case. The papers, however (which included a group of Mercy's letters), revealed nothing incriminating either to him or his friends and after four days Hillsborough released him, following a long personal interview which Winslow described to his mother: "Lord Hillsbor-

ough asked me many questions about my situation and views, repri-
manded me for visiting Mr. Trumbull confined in Totill Fields,
Bridewell. His Lordship condescended to give me a great deal of
advice, saying he was prepossessed in my favour from my appearance. He and others to whom my papers were consigned, lavished
many praises on my mother's letters — said 'they would do honour
to the greatest writer that ever wrote,' and added, 'Mr. Warren, I
hope you will profit by her instructions and advice.' "

Winslow finally reached The Hague in May 1781 and met John
Adams, who was taking Henry Laurens' place in negotiating a treaty
with Holland. Mercy was, of course, eager to hear John's report on
Winslow but although John wrote often enough, he did not refer to
Winslow. Later she had a favorable account from John Temple
when he came to America, but even when Winslow wrote that he
had been with Adams for nine successive days in Paris, Adams made
no mention of it. Finally Mercy asked: "has any part of his Conduct
since in Europe rendered him *unworthy* that Mr. Adams had Never
once Named him in his long absence." Still John Adams did not
reply. Once in a rough draft in his Letter Book he wrote: "He has
been travelling from Place to Place; and altho' I have often en-
quired after him, I have seldom been able to hear of him. I have
heard nothing to his disadvantage, except a Shyness and Secrecy
. . . and a general Reputation which he brought with him from
Boston of loving Play." But when he copied the letter in the final
form that went to Mercy, this portion was struck out and John
Adams never made any comment on Winslow's deportment.

Mercy led a double life while Winslow was in Europe. In Plymouth she began a routine of requiring her sons to write a daily composition to give them an easy style. She superintended their garden-
ing efforts and helped them manage small commercial ventures of
their own. Abigail Adams sent George some black handkerchiefs
which she said he could sell for seventy-five cents each. At the same
time, although her eyes were troubling her, Mercy kept up her correspondence: with two of her nieces, Sally Sever and Elizabeth Brown

(daughter of James Otis); with Catherine Macaulay, the Adamses, and Hannah Winthrop. Once Hannah, struggling to overcome grief at her husband's death, asked Mercy if she did not think the sorrows of life were felt more keenly than the joys. Mercy, Puritan that she was, probably agreed, yet the truth about her emotional life in this period was that she felt both the sorrows and the joys but she felt them most keenly when they related to Winslow. Her most intense experiences came through the mail or were caused by the absence of it.

It was a happy day when Winslow let her share his adventures. "Three quarters of the Low Country," he wrote from Holland, "look like the Barnstable Great Marshes at high water — only the prospect is larger. You see the country round till it makes an horizon and ride on dykes like the mud that is thrown out of the ditches at the Great Marshes." She rejoiced when Winslow, adopting a moral tone, condemned Paris as a wicked city, when he wrote that the sight of the misery in Europe heightened his appreciation of America, when he announced that he was actually engaged in business. On one red-letter day that almost compensated for months of worry and disappointment, Mercy received a pamphlet which Winslow had translated especially for her benefit; on another she received an elegant dressing cape.

Yet Mercy never really knew what kind of life Winslow led in Europe, what his plans were, or when he would be home. "When shall I see my dear Winslow?" she wrote after two years. At the end of three years she wrote that at every dawn she inquired "if my Winslow is safe." When she heard that he was visiting Paris again, she tried to be casual. Was it business or pleasure, she asked, that prompted him to return? And when he reported that he was going to Italy, she inquired archly: "What judicious, Experienced, Virtuous Friend, have you Chosen for a Companion in this Dangerous rout?" She tried to put her advice on an adult basis; once she signed herself *Mama* and crossed it out and wrote *Mother,* but she was able to speak more freely and at the same time to appear more detached when she wrote in verse. In a poem entitled "To a Young Gentleman Residing in France" she compared all the "gaudy" scenes of the "airy chase" to the solid joys of the simple, virtuous life, frankly trying to make Winslow homesick for Plymouth. Yet Mercy knew him too well not to anticipate his reaction:

> *Methinks I hear the youthful bosom sigh*
> *And nature whisper fancy's fond reply:*
> *"These old ideas are quite out of date*
> *. . . . ."*

But in poetry, at least, Mercy could have the last word.

> *Not so, my son.*
> *. . . . .*

> *Economy to virtue close all'd*
> *A frugal pair, with wisdom by their side.*

Winslow had not been gone long from Boston when the Warrens had an opportunity to change not only their place of residence but perhaps to some degree their style of life. Many of the most elegant homes in the state were changing owners these days as the estates of absentee Loyalists were put up for sale at public auction, but surely no one would have anticipated that the Warrens might move into the residence of their old arch enemy, Thomas Hutchinson. The house at Milton Hill had been bought some years before by a Mr. Broome, who offered it now to James Warren at a price (£3000) that was reasonable considering the nature of the property, but somewhat exorbitant considering the nature of James Warren's resources. It was a temptation, a "sweet" place, James said. What should he do?

"Oh, my Dear Husband, what a Life of embarrassment perplexity & care is yours," Mercy wrote. "I love to Relieve to assist & advise you as far as I am able, but had I been with you the Last 10 days, I should have been entirely at a Loss . . . I beg you would not be anxious about paying for the place . . . I don't doubt we shall Get through that by and by." She knew no pleasanter spot, she said, but *"how Came Mr. Broome to part with a place he was so Excessively pleased with."*

James Warren had always thought of himself as a modest but frustrated husbandman, a term which in the eighteenth century embraced the concept of professional farmer, gentleman farmer, and experimental farmer: a man who lived a graceful life as lord of his estate, a virtuous life close to the soil, and a creative life, expanding the science of agriculture. From every point of view, Milton Hill was the ideal place for such a life. The house was elegant and comfortable — a long, low structure of English white oak with pitched roof and gabled ends and with walls a foot thick insulated with seaweed. The property was extensive, imaginatively developed, and close enough to Boston so that James could conveniently carry out his duties on the Navy Board and Mercy could enjoy a more stimulating social life, which James thought was good for her. Besides, James was fifty-five now, looking forward to peace and retirement from public life, and where else would he find finer vines to sit under? And there was still another argument in favor of the purchase: Winslow would be pleased with Milton Hill. He might even be persuaded to live there. The fact that Milton Hill was a luxurious setting and the purchase was hardly an exercise in the frugality the Warrens preached would not have occurred to them. Mercy defined luxury as an unbecoming display of wealth, an indulgence in new fashions and frills; her own style of life, on the contrary, was simple and appropriately elegant and, of course, virtuous. Furthermore, Mercy was her father's daughter: there was nothing wrong in getting ahead in the world if you were the one getting ahead; success was God's reward for good work when the success was yours.

The Warrens moved to Milton Hill on June 1, exactly seven years to the day that Thomas Hutchinson had left it. On June 3 James wrote to Winslow: "When you return [we] shall be happy to see you at our new habitation. This remove is thought by some an Extraordinary Step at our Time of Life . . . but if you have not altered your Mind is an Event that falls within your Taste." It was an expensive move, however, and "were I not pushed to pay for this Farm," he wrote, "I should forward you some Bills, but as matters are it is out of my power . . . You are to Consider I can sell nothing at Plymouth."

Winslow was still in Holland when his father wrote; Charles was at Cambridge in poor health and beginning to show symptoms of consumption; James, Jr., was at sea. James had signed up again on the *Alliance* when it was put under the command of John Barry, and in February he had sailed on a special mission to France. But even under Barry, the *Alliance* seemed destined for drama. It had left Boston with an inadequate crew ("not ten men, officers included, that could steer her," Barry said), encountered ice fields on the way, survived a threatened mutiny, and witnessed a duel between two of its distinguished passengers — Thomas Paine and the Viscount de Noailles (Lafayette's brother-in-law). Then at the end of March the *Alliance* set sail for its return trip but was so long at sea, people feared it was lost. On June 3, when James Warren wrote his son Winslow, the ship had still not been heard from. Worry about James, Jr., hung like a cloud over the Warrens as they made their move and their worry seemed justified. A privateer that the *Alliance* had captured soon after leaving France had arrived in Boston three weeks before, but still there was no news of the *Alliance*.

On June 4 the Warrens' furniture which they had sent by ship from Plymouth arrived at Milton. On June 9 the *Alliance* limped into Boston Harbor. One main yard was gone, the sails were perforated, the spars and and rigging were shattered, Captain Barry was wounded in the left shoulder, and at least four men had been killed in a frightful encounter with two English sloops. Lieutenant James Warren was carried to his parents' new home on Milton Hill with a shattered right knee. He was put to bed in the half-settled house and for several days suffered excruciating pain until the doctor finally had to advise amputation. James at first refused, but the pain was so severe and the entreaties of his family so strong that in the end he had to consent. According to Charles, he "bore the Stroke with a magnanimity & perseverance that did him honour both as a soldier & a man."

For Mercy, the first year at Milton Hill was crossed with anxiety for her sons. James, Jr., became dull and dispirited, reverting to his old depressions as he tried to adjust to his physical condition; Charles coughed, grew thin, then rallied but, as if he were preparing for the worst, began talking in an excessively religious vein. As for Winslow, he was obviously running into financial difficulties and attending to business in only the most halfhearted way. Yet in spite of her worries, Mercy enjoyed Milton Hill. She liked moving about in the elegant spaciousness of the new house. She wrote Winslow that she was setting aside an apartment for him that overlooked the garden and she asked him to buy a carpet for one of the parlors, fourteen feet by twenty, and charge it to her account. She liked walking down the tree-lined paths so carefully planned by Thomas Hutchinson; she liked standing at the front door and looking down at the harbor; she liked sitting in the green parlor at her writing table placed before the window that framed the western hills. And if sometimes she also enjoyed the dramatic irony in the fact that she had become the mistress of Rapatio's mansion, she did not mention it, although her friends did. It was not often, they said, that the seats of the wicked fell into the right hands. Mercy said only that her lot had "always fallen in pleasant places."

As the Warrens set up housekeeping, the prospect for peace began at last to look encouraging. All that was needed now, James said, was a loan from Europe; in September he wrote Winslow that "our affairs wear a pleasant aspect and afford a most agreeable prospect." In October Cornwallis surrendered at Yorktown and in June of the following year John Adams successfully concluded negotiations for a loan from Holland. Yet peace did not burst upon the country in a sudden brilliant explosion, the way the news of the capture of Louisbourg had broken or the fall of Saratoga. Peace came bit by bit, like a heavy fish that, once hooked, still had to be pulled in slowly, hand over hand; and although Americans celebrated at each stage of the journey, it was two years after Yorktown before they could raise the final flag of victory.

Meanwhile James Warren gradually became the complete farmer. In the spring of 1782 he resigned from the Navy Board and asked that the accounts be audited; he was a private man, he told John Adams, and looked forward to John's return to his own hill in Braintree. "I shall certainly take pleasure in roving with you among Partridges, Squirrels, etc., and will even venture upon an Emulation with you which shall make his Hill shine the brightest." He expected John, however, to bring back advice on the latest improvements in Europe in the science of husbandry. At the moment he was interested in fertilizer. "Do ascertain what Marle is," he asked. At the same time James was making his own contribution to science; to the newly incorporated Academy of Arts and Sciences in Boston, James, a charter member, presented a paper on the growth of vegetables — a significant if homely illustration that America was beginning to enjoy a few of the leisures of peace.

As for Mercy, now that a happy ending seemed assured to her story of the revolution, she took out her marble-colored notebooks and set to work in her parlor with renewed vigor. She was not alone in pursuing such a project; in this historically minded century, men on both sides of the Atlantic were beginning to describe, assess, and interpret the war years. John Adams, in one of his self-pitying moods when everyone but him seemed to be wearing laurels, wrote that his friend the Abbé Raynal was writing a history, giving John credit for much of the success of the revolution but also blaming him for some of the mistakes. But what of Mrs. Warren's work? he asked. "I dread her History, more than that of the Abby." Later he said he hoped Mercy would give his Dutch negotiations (which he took special pride in) sufficient place in her history.

Mercy's assurance about her writing had grown over the years;

she could now say quite firmly that, however subordinate women were to men, however retiring they should be, they were the intellectual equal of men and in the sight of God surely they were as important. Her work had become increasingly necessary to her; indeed, she felt possessive about it — it was the one part of her life that was wholly and peculiarly her own, the one area where she could exercise complete control. When her world seemed bound on a self-destructive and unreasonable course, Mercy resorted to paper and pen, taking comfort in creating her own order, wrestling with words, sentences, sequences until a pattern emerged which would seem to her as inevitable as truth itself. Yet Mercy remained sensitive about her writing and never more sensitive than with John Adams. When John said he dreaded her history, Mercy, who knew his gift for sarcasm like her own, was quick to imagine that he was making fun of her, perhaps humoring her, and that secretly he was thinking that a history written by a woman was nothing to take seriously, certainly nothing to dread.

"I assure you, Madam," John responded, "what I said about certain Annals was no Sarcasm. I have the utmost Veneration for them." But John, too, was sensitive and anxious to be represented in a fitting way in a history, no matter who wrote it; above all else, he did not want to be celebrated for his patience. "Of all Virtues or Qualities I hate most to be praised for my Patience," he said. "I had rather you should immortalize my Impudence."

Peace was a relief, but looking around at the state of Massachusetts in these transitional years, Mercy could see no hope that peace would usher in the golden age of republicanism. Indeed, if he had survived, Thomas Hutchinson, on the losing side of the revolution, would have been interested to know that his successors at Milton Hill, the victors, were often bitter. The Warrens' Puritan-minded world was hardly less shaken at the end of the war than Hutchinson's imperially minded world, and when Mercy reflected, as she sometimes did, that there were seasons in history when the human mind seemed particularly and inexplicably prone to error, she sounded like Thomas Hutchinson reverting to his witchcraft thesis. In her most sanguine moments Mercy talked about the challenge of the times — "What a field for genius," she said; but in discouraged moments it seemed to her that Americans had waded through rivers of blood only to have "a republican form of government with the principles of monarchy, the freedom of democracy, with the servility of despotism, the extravagance of nobility, with the poverty of peasantry."

Again Thomas Hutchinson would have been interested to know that in America's postwar convulsions he was at times actually missed. The most pressing problem of the country was economic and, as John Adams often remarked, the man who was needed was Hutchinson, whose financial talents even his enemies conceded. Wartime markets were shrinking, prices falling, land depreciating, debts mounting while the rich and the newly rich who had made fortunes in the war paraded their wealth and many who did not have fortunes borrowed in order to join the parade. The country was money-mad, and poor and rich alike complained of other people's spending, of their own hardships, and of the generally selfish and acquisitive climate of the times. James Warren, who like everyone was suffering from the revolution in currency, wrote to Winslow that, much as he enjoyed Milton Hill, he would enjoy it more if it were paid for. "You know I hate to be in debt," he said. "But as it is, I shall be pushed and straightened."

James would also have enjoyed Milton Hill more if his retirement had been respected, but the public was, as it so often is, voracious in demanding more of its servants than they have to give and then blaming them for what they are not. It is paradoxical that in his later years James Warren should have complained so often of feeling neglected when, in fact, all his life he suffered from attention he did not want, appointments that he felt ill equipped to handle, and demands that would take him into a larger sphere than he wished to move in. And in 1782, just as he had taken in his second harvest on Milton Hill, he was elected to represent Massachusetts in the Congress at Philadelphia, as uncongenial an assignment as he could have been given and one which he had even more reason now to refuse than he had had three years before. Having extended himself so far to purchase Milton Hill, he probably could not have afforded to leave it and Mercy, even if she had been inclined to accompany him, would have found it difficult to do so.

More important, however, were the political arguments against accepting the post. Old Colonist that he was at heart, James had become increasingly suspicious of the trend in the country to think in national terms. Now that the war was over, he felt, Congress should be slipping into a secondary role; the states should be assuming their own responsibilities, making their own decisions, returning to their own identities. That the states were not assuming their own responsibilities, particularly in the matter of the national debt, that they could not even agree as to how the debt should be apportioned, and that Congress, under the restrictions of the Articles of Confederation, could neither force the states to cooperate nor levy a direct tax on the country worried James Warren, of course, but he was no more ready than he had ever been to allow a government other than a state government to tax its citizens. He had not fought against the stamp tax and the tea tax for nothing; any plan of general taxation, he said, was "a Step which has been the Leading one to the ruin of so many Nations," including the ruin of Great Britain. As always, he thought in colonial terms, based his policy on his own well-worn experience, and stubbornly applied old maxims to new situations.

And as always when James Warren was suspicious of power, he focused his suspicion on specific people. Robert Morris, who had been created superintendent of finance in 1781 ("super Intendant," James called him), was one of those the Warrens thought of as a new enemy to the republican scheme; Benjamin Franklin had become another, the "Old Man" who had for so long dominated international politics and irritated John Adams. ("I never know when he speaks the Truth," John said. "How long will he live?" James asked.) But there was a new friend too: Arthur Lee of Virginia, whom the Warrens had met after his ill-fated voyage on the *Alliance,* a man of wide experience with the same political inclinations as the Warrens and with an obvious liking for them. (He had never met a lady, he said, whose conversation pleased him more than Mrs. Warren's.) Unfortunately, however, Arthur Lee had a jealous, quarrelsome, paranoiac disposition and he confirmed the Warrens' fears and deepened their distrust of the federal government.

Mercy and James found a variety of excuses, over and above personal ones, for keeping James at home. On the one hand, James argued that the only people who entered public life now were those who wanted to gratify their vanity; on the other hand, Mercy asked what a few uncorrupted men could do in a government dominated by the corrupt. (When writing to John Adams, however, about John's taking his place again in domestic politics, she was far more optimistic about what the "Example of one Good Man" could effect.) Actually, James Warren's embarrassment about the appointment sprang from the attitude of his friends. Even his son Charles, who was studying law in Worcester and at the moment in better health, thought his father should "exercise his patriotic feelings" and go where he would be most "extensively useful." And John Adams said flatly that "old Hands" were still needed and that it was too soon for Mr. Warren to retire. Still, James postponed making, or at least reporting, a decision. He could not attend Congress immediately because his election had been, as he said, unexpected and "out of Season," but when Congress convened again in the spring, James could no longer avoid mentioning the subject to John Adams. "If you ask why I dont go," he said crossly, "I will tell you because I have been Sick the whole Spring."

It was true that James was bothered at times by gout, which would trouble him increasingly in his later years, but perhaps he was not as incapacitated as he indicated to John Adams. In a letter to Winslow he said only that he had not been as well as usual; but then, most of the "old Hands" in the spring of 1783 were showing the effects of time and the strain of seven years of war. John Adams claimed that all the travel he had done by sea and land and the shock of various climates had affected his health and spirits; "I am no longer a Boy, nor a young Man," he said with an air of surprise at finding himself at a ripe forty-eight years. Samuel Adams, thirteen years older than John, had since the early years of the revolution been afflicted with palsy, but it was more severe now and, although his enthusiasm for work was not affected nor his involvement with public affairs, he did not cut as noble a figure on horseback as he once had riding into Philadelphia; moreover, he had difficulty writing his letters.

There was one patriot, however, who was in better health than he had been for years. James Otis, Jr., seemed at last to have found a measure of peace for himself. His father was dead now and George III had recognized America's independence; it was as if Jemmy's conflicts, along with the country's, were played out. For the last two years he had been staying in Andover with a Mr. Osgood and had evidently found the atmosphere of the home congenial and the friendship of Mr. Osgood both strengthening and quieting. Jemmy did as he liked without pressures or claims put on him, and as he lay in bed reading sometimes far into the day or as he puttered about outside finding small chores to do, the wildness gradually slipped out of him. One day after church he wrote on a scrap of paper: "I have this day attended divine service, and heard a sensible discourse, and thanks be to God I now enjoy the greatest of all blessings, mens sana in corpore sano."

He was not, of course, the same man as he had been before; he had grown fat, he was slower in movement as men often are who have suffered an emotional breakdown, and, instead of giving vent to passionate bursts of emotion, he was apt to be simply sad. Indeed, he had much to be sad about: his only son, James, had died in a British prison in 1777, his daughter Elizabeth had married a British officer, much against James's wishes, and was living in England, and of course Colonel Otis, the most powerful figure in James's life, was gone, leaving him, along with the memories, a silver-hilted sword and a silver-headed cane to distinguish him, the Colonel wrote in his will, as the eldest son. But Jemmy apparently could handle the memories now and in the opinion of his family he was able to return to normal life.

In the summer of 1782 Harrison Gray Otis, Samuel's son, who was a junior at Harvard, went to Andover in a gig to take James back to Boston. It was a pleasant ride of an hour or more, jogging up and down little hills and hummocks; and for Harrison it was a memorable ride, perhaps the longest time he had ever spent alone with this famous uncle who had already become a legend to the younger generation. Young Harrison recalled later the generosity his uncle had shown in offering to guide him when he was ready to pursue his legal studies. In Boston Jemmy took up residence with his wife and daughter Polly, but not as quietly, perhaps, as he would have liked. His return caused something of a sensation in town and the Otis home became "the resort of much company calling" — old friends and perhaps simply curious friends, but in any case, to the relief of his ever-watchful family, Jemmy retained his composure. His life as he described it in October to his brother Joseph sounded as normal, as calmly domestic as any man's. His sister Hannah had paid a visit, he said; Polly was sick; he had received the firewood but would need more to take him through the winter; and finally he would be glad of a few bunches of onions, a few beets and carrots, and two or three good cheeses.

The difficulty was that Boston society would not let him alone. Long after his return, people continued to call, to congratulate him, to reassure him, to watch him, to prod him into further activity. He had only been home a few weeks when he was persuaded to take a case in the Court of Common Pleas and again he was complimented and welcomed back into the fold: Massachusetts' own patriot displaying his old powers, it was said, but perhaps James himself knew better and suspected that behind his back his friends were whispering, as Harrison Gray Otis reported, that he was a "sun shorn of his beams." But still the final compliment was yet to be paid and the ultimate welcome to be extended. In the spring of 1783 as the country was celebrating the signing of a provisional peace treaty, John Hancock decided to give a party in honor of James Otis, Jr., the man who had first stood up to Great Britain and who, like a ghost risen from the dead, was back to share in the victory.

The gesture was, of course, typical of John Hancock who loved celebrations and, indeed, with the coming of peace, who of the "old Hands" had better reason to celebrate? Hancock had been reelected governor each year since the Massachusetts constitution had been adopted and as if that were not proof enough of his popularity, periodically he tested it further by threatening to resign, solely for the purpose, his enemies claimed, of hearing how indispensable he was. His vanity, or his insecurity — however one looked at it — was two-sided: on the one hand, he could not brook the slightest disparagement (when other names preceded his in the bill to incorporate the Academy of Arts and Sciences, he had insisted that the names be rearranged in alphabetical order); on the other hand, he had an overwhelming and childlike desire not only to be pampered but to please others, which may have saved him from being a despot but which earned him a new nickname with Mercy and her friends. They referred to him now as the "state baby." Yet in spite of the fact that Mercy said John Hancock had everything he wanted but a crown, he was, surely to even a prejudiced eye, a pathetic figure. At the age of forty-six he was stooped and crippled, in the advanced stages of gout. His infirmities, moreover, were reflected in his face; no matter how he acted, he looked like an old man, a living example of the motto on his family coat of arms: *Nul plaisir sans peine.*

But the party for James Otis was to be pure pleasure in the grand style that parties had been in the old days, in the spirit of 1773, for instance, when the patriots had not only been united but devoted — or perhaps like the night that they had all celebrated the revoking of the stamp tax and rolled the madeira out onto the Common. James Otis demurred about the party but John Hancock did not listen. There was a strong sentimental streak in Hancock; he was undoubtedly motivated by genuine warmth and, of course, since he

thrived on playing the benefactor, the idea of this party was too good
to give up. John could feel that he was giving James Otis back to
the city, that he was giving the city back to James Otis, and that he
was giving peace back to everyone. Harrison Gray Otis in referring
to the party used the word *forced*. Governor Hancock, he said,
"forced" James Otis "to dine with him at a large party." And up to
the last minute James resisted. On the evening of the party he lay in
bed, sad and thoughtful, postponing getting dressed, delaying his
departure.

But he did go. He drove in his carriage to the grand house on the
Common with its fifty-two windows lighted as they were always
lighted on special occasions. Inside the house, the party was waiting
for him, the guest of honor who had somehow miraculously returned from the grave in time for victory. Inside lay the past which
James Otis had so carefully put to rest and which was now brought
back by well-wishers, opened up, thrust upon him from all sides —
emotional mountains suddenly heaving up amid the noise and
laughter, abysses falling off from innocent conversations, explosions
and waves of remembering, blow after blow of remembering, all
leading back to the same well-known landscape that James had left
behind but could not escape, change, or return to, a time that was
never buried but eternally dead. James managed to get through dinner and the interminable toasts without betraying his emotions, but
immediately after dinner he was all at once overwhelmed by
memory. "There was a visible oscillation in his intellect," Harrison
Gray Otis said, but there was no frenzy. James's brother Samuel,
who had been observing him uneasily, suggested that they leave.
"He went like a lamb," Harrison noted — but not to his Boston
home. He was so severely disturbed that there was no question apparently as to his destination. Samuel drove him back to Andover.
The next day James took his letters and his papers which he had
stored in the Osgood home, all the records of his past, and he burned
them.

There were still days of quiet ahead, however. James trimmed the branches of the pine trees in front of the house; he stood on the hill, watching the young men work in Mr. Osgood's fields in the valley below; he even joked with Mr. Osgood, asking to be buried on the hillside so he could keep an eye on those young men. But there were not many days ahead. One Friday evening six weeks after Governor Hancock's party, there was a storm in Andover and James Otis, who had always exulted in storms, went to the front door to watch. This was not a severe storm; there was, in fact, only a single bolt of lightning, but it found James standing in the open doorway, leaning on the silver-headed cane his father had given him, and it killed him instantly.

He had always wanted to die in just this way, he had told Mercy, and his contemporaries agreed that it was the most fitting way. "Extraordinary in Death as in Life," John Adams said, and James's old friend and Harvard classmate, silver-tongued Sam Cooper, who was to die a few months later from overuse of Scotch snuff, wrote a verse (or at least the verse was attributed to him) which Mercy felt was the perfect obituary for her brother, placing him not only among the elect but giving him a more-than-mortal stature.

> *When God in anger saw the spot*
> *On earth to Otis given*
> *In thunder as from Sinai's mount,*
> *He snatch'd him back to heaven.*

Four months later the definitive Treaty of Paris was signed and peace, so often welcomed, was officially declared. Two of the original adversaries, of course, were gone — Thomas Hutchinson and James Otis — and another was showing symptoms of the mental illness that would in the end engulf him. George III had suffered recurring periods of derangement, especially during crises with America; now he was talking compulsively again. And in Massachusetts the people were regrouping, for if the war of independence was over, the revolution, as John Adams was continually pointing out, was not. Yet Americans hardly knew what they were regrouping for or what was expected of them. They could, as Mercy wrote, feel the "eyes of all Europe" on them, yet they felt themselves in such a state of infancy, she said, that "as a child just learning to walk, they were afraid of their own movements." Moreover, they were still "out of breath by their long struggle."

Act Three

XI

FOR THE NEXT ACT of the revolution, some of the characters were assigned new roles, some were sent offstage, and some walked on and off as they were called or as they were able, for this was, as the "old Hands" recognized, the last act for them. John Adams was elected a joint commissioner with Franklin and Jefferson to negotiate treaties of commerce abroad and he was joined at last by Abigail and young Abby. (He felt twenty years younger, he said, when he heard that they were coming.) Samuel Adams, the old populist, had become a dignified senator — indeed, none more dignified, for in his new Rome he was determined that all must appear noble. And John Hancock announced his retirement again, and again he reneged. "Alas," James Warren sighed, "his Fortitude did not . . . enable him to do this wise and prudent thing."

But if James was unhappy that one enemy continued to dominate the Massachusetts scene, he could be glad to be rid of another. Since there was no place for them in the new republic, the Winslow family sailed for Nova Scotia on August 30, 1783, seeking refuge by a strange quirk of fate on the same shores from which Edward Winslow's brother, General John, had evicted the Acadians a generation before. Behind them, the Winslows left for their creditors (the Warrens among them) the big house facing the harbor, which unfortunately brought only five hundred pounds, not enough to satisfy the many demands made on it or to include the demands of the Warrens. Still, according to rumor, there were additional assets: Mrs. Winslow was supposed to have entrusted certain valued objects to a lady in town in the hope of eventual restitution. Perhaps James Warren suspected that the lady had more than she actually had, perhaps his resentment was so high that it did not matter to him how small or how personal the objects might be, perhaps he was simply acting on principle, for, as it was becoming increasingly evident, principle was as powerful a factor in the life of James Warren as it ever had been in the life of Thomas Hutchinson. In any case James sent the sheriff to the lady's home with the demand that she either forfeit whatever Winslow property she had or take an oath that she had nothing. As it turned out, all she had was a single picture which had hung in the hall of the Winslow mansion and which she reluctantly turned over — the Winslow coat of arms embroidered by the two daughters, Sarah and Penny, who had hoped to hang it again one day in some other hall. Sarah, on hearing the news in Halifax, called James Warren the "compleatest Devil that ever was suffered to live," and said she had done with him; she would never again mention his name.

As peace was the signal for Edward Winslow to leave America, so the promise of peace was the signal for Winslow Warren to come home. In the spring of 1783, knowing that his father had been elected to Congress and assuming that he would be attending the spring session, Winslow decided to go to Philadelphia to seek a consular appointment in one of the European cities where he could at the same time continue his career in trade. Counting on his father's position to secure an appointment but without informing his family of his plans (he had not written home in four months), he boarded a vessel bound for Philadelphia and was, naturally enough, somewhat dismayed to find on his arrival that his father was not there and would not be coming.

Winslow's letter from Philadelphia reached the Warrens in the middle of May. Mercy was scarcely able to contain her excitement. "And is my son — my dear Winslow — again on the same continent with myself? How long is it to be before you design us a visit? I know not how to restrain my impatience to see you . . . I lay down my pen — I find myself too elate with expectation — I will not suppress it . . . Come on as soon as possible."

James was, if more restrained, equally pleased and, although he said his days of influence were over, he proceeded to list the men he would write to on Winslow's behalf: Elbridge Gerry, Benjamin Franklin, Arthur Lee, Benjamin Lincoln, and the members of the Massachusetts delegation (he could not ask favors of Mr. Morris, he said, "for reasons I will give you when you come here"). Yet there was an edge of impatience that crept into the letters, as it so often did in James's letters to this beloved but unreliable son. "I hope you will be able soon to discharge all your Debts in Europe," he said, and then more firmly: "Your Applications in future must be to true solid Business."

The moment of Mercy's unalloyed joy was short; indeed, she was seldom allowed to experience an emotion singly. It was as if her feelings traveled in schools and whenever one leaped to the surface, another and yet another was drawn along in its wake until all the water was disturbed. So it was now; a week after writing to Winslow, while she was still riding on the crest of her happiness, James Otis was killed by lightning. Puritan that she was, Mercy recognized the hand of God giving and taking, promising and denying, and in this dramatic demonstration returning her a dearly loved son while depriving her of a dearly loved brother. Mercy was not only impressed by the paradoxes of life, she was beginning to accept them. "It is the *world*," she said once, as if the very word was a synonym for contradiction. "I think we are obliged to live as if we expected to obtain salvation by our own works but to die convinced that it is impossible for man to merit anything from the hands of an all-perfect being."

Yet the living was no less easy for having come to terms with the difficulties. She was just more wary. Even in her first joy at hearing of Winslow's return she was erecting a shield against disappointment. "I would check the . . . hope," she said, "lest some intervening circumstance should interrupt or retard the happiness I expect."

A few weeks later a friend returning from Philadelphia mentioned that he had heard that Winslow might go back to Europe without first coming home at all. Mercy rushed to her writing table. "It cannot be — it must not be," she said breathlessly. "Come you must at all events before you leave America. I will not promise for my own fortitude if you fail." James had already written that he "most certainly and indispensably" expected Winslow home.

It was September before Winslow came, although Mercy had tried to lure him home sooner with descriptions of the cool northern climate as compared to the disagreeable heat of Philadelphia. Once he arrived, however, the long summer of waiting and watching was forgotten. The next months were, for the country at large as well as for the Warrens, a period of reprieve — not restful enough for people to sit under their vine trees but yet not turbulent enough to disclose the dimension of the gathering storm. For Mercy this was a happy time. Winslow was delighted with Milton Hill and, apparently in an amiable mood, he gave his mother the companionship she so much coveted. They talked books and politics and shared ideas for improving the house and grounds: Winslow described the kind of wallpaper the hall should have and he pointed out the spot where a group of trees should be planted back from the road. And if for any reason Mercy became downhearted, Winslow in his irresistible way teased her out of it. "Where now is your philosophy?" he would laugh.

In October James Warren worked among his potatoes and claimed he had no ambition beyond his composts. For the first time since they had moved the family was together and it seemed that Milton Hill might yet fulfill James Warren's dream — as a place where a man not only might invest his life but which he would be proud to relinquish to his sons. Charles was momentarily in better health; James, Jr., who suffered from alarming and "disagreeable spasms" when he was upset or overtired, was, as his father often described him, in "statu quo"; Henry and George were enjoying their last days of boyhood freedom. Within a year they would both

be away from home — Henry in Boston, George in Northampton.
Later James Warren would look back to this period and wish again
for "some of the scenes of last December," yet as in all families there
were crosscurrents of feeling running beneath the happy scenes.
George had always been somewhat jealous of Winslow: sometimes
he talked of following in Winslow's footsteps and going to Europe,
sometimes he simply accused his mother of loving Winslow more
than she loved him. Charles and Winslow had bickered in childhood (Mercy had made sure they had separate rooms during their
smallpox confinement) and the old antagonisms flared up again
from time to time. Only recently Charles, accused by Winslow of
troubling "great folks" with commissions for him in Europe, had
resorted to a sarcasm that in the midst of his usually pious rhetoric
came as a surprise. "No, Sir," he had written, "I should (with you)
think it great presumption indeed should I (the insignificant I) dare
approach even to think of the garment of the Great . . . I leave
such folks as these for Mr. W———n to deal with, who is possessed
of the graces of a Court, the *bon ton* of the City." And of course
beneath the crosscurrents, Mercy worried. An easy victim all her life
to imagined troubles, she had acquired a surprising stock of strength
to deal with the real troubles and it was real ones that Mercy would
be facing now.

The winter of 1784 was blanketed with snow — a "tight Winter," James Warren called it, and a cold one. No matter which way
the weather vane on the stable swung, the wind seemed to find its
way into the house on top of the hill. For Mercy, March was the
hardest month. Henry was not well and Charles had taken such an
alarming turn for the worse that not only the family despaired for
his life but Charles did as well. He felt, he said, as if he were standing "on the brink of eternity," and when he looked at life it appeared
to him a "bursting bubble." In the midst of this distress Winslow
announced that he was returning to Europe. He had become increasingly restless during the winter. His consular appointment, in spite
of James's insistent letters to Philadelphia, had not come through,

seemed unlikely to come through in the near future, and he decided to wait no longer. He would be in as good a position, or better, to receive such an appointment, he reasoned, if he were already established and conducting business at a foreign port. (Lisbon was his choice.) And in the meantime he would be working to pay off his European debts so that he could one day return to America in what his father called an "eligible manner." Accordingly, at the end of April, although at the time he was suffering from chills and fever, Winslow sailed for Europe.

"My dear Winslow," Mercy wrote on May 9, "Ten days have we watched the winds and the weather and so favorable have they been with us that we flatter ourselves you have made near half your passage. But the ideas of fever and ague will sometimes intrude on my mind."

There was no moralizing in the letter. As her sons had grown older, Mercy had become increasingly aware of the limited power of words over them, especially her words. "I have lived long enough," she said, "to be convinced that we must pass through the world ourselves in order to know it thoroughly. Neither the Page of History nor the . . . lessons of those who have gone before" could take the place of experience. Theoretically in the down-to-earth manner of the eighteenth century she had relied on experience to be the prime educator but preferably vicarious experience; it was in history, after all (or an edited version of it), that the moralizing eighteenth century found its morals and she had hoped that the lessons of man's total experience would protect the individual from pain. It was disappointing to find that this was not necessarily so; mankind profited "little by experience or the observations of others," she said, yet she was too confirmed a moralist, too avid an historian, too impassioned a teacher, too devoted to words, and in short too much a child of her own century to be quieted now. She was, however, less tense with her sons. When she felt advice was in order, she was inclined, like the oracle at Delphi, to depend on the watchwords *Know Thyself* and *Nothing in Excess*. But in this letter to

Winslow she confined herself to news. She talked about the coming election, using the code that she and Winslow had devised so that they could write freely about friends and enemies. (*B*, the initial letter for *baby*, for instance, was John Hancock.) As for the family, Mercy reported that James was busy planting chestnuts and elms, Charles was improved and able to walk through the house, and Henry was going to Halifax for his health.

Actually, there was more than Henry's health at stake in the Halifax trip. The Warrens had heard that Edward Winslow had just been given a pension of £120 and a grant of one thousand acres of land which should enable him, Mercy reasoned, to pay back that long outstanding debt. Certainly on the surface the Winslows seemed comfortable. Henry would have found them, by Sarah's own admission, "eligantly situated in a good house upon the Parade," a house large enough to accommodate sixteen at dinner with ease. Henry would also have found them inhospitable. Probably at no time would the Winslows have welcomed a Warren, but as it happened Henry arrived at the worst possible moment. Edward Winslow was so gravely ill that members of his family were taking turns watching at his bedside; three days later he died. Henry may have waited until the elaborate funeral was over to present his claim, yet he could not, or at least did not, wait long. Mercy reported on the outcome. "Ned behaved like a Brute," she wrote Winslow, "and so I have lost my money. & so the Tide sets yet." As for Henry's health, he was better.

· · ·

Spring gave way to summer, summer to fall; but although Milton Hill was one of the best places "on the celestial ball for real felicity," according to Mercy, one by one the boys left. James, Jr., was the last to go. He would have another year at home and then at the invitation of his cousin Polly (James Otis' daughter) and her new husband, Benjamin Lincoln, Jr., he would break his self-imposed seclusion, go to Hingham, and eventually teach school there. Meanwhile the others had gone and as the letters drifted back, not fast enough or often enough to suit Mercy, it was apparent that not one of the boys was happy. "Is it not singular," she said, "that three young gentlemen of the same family should be scattered wide in different parts of the world and not one of them pleased?" Perhaps they had been "too delicately educated," she suggested, perhaps too happy in the early part of their lives. In any case, Charles, who was in Haiti on his doctor's advice, reported that he ate an orange every morning, walked two miles before breakfast, was charmed with the climate, but disgusted with the people. In Northampton, George complained so much about the crudity and ignorance of the family he was living with that Mercy wrote Winslow that George sounded as if he were living among the Goths.

As for Winslow, he claimed that he did not like Europe any longer. He sent home blue wallpaper from London and a portrait of himself painted by Copley; he sent fresh grapes from Lisbon, but Lisbon, he said, was the vilest, dirtiest, ugliest, and most savage city he had ever seen, with little prospect for a stranger to find amusement. The women in the country were constrained, the men were jealous, and all were dominated by a superstitious and corrupt religion. Winslow described Portugal in vivid detail. "I love your letters," Mercy said, copying and preserving them as if she anticipated the day when he would be a public figure. Perhaps Winslow anticipated the day too; "I am going to work hard & Steady as possible," he promised. But all the time his debts were mounting, his enemies multiplying, his prospects for business dwindling; nor was this entirely his fault. Money was scarce and throughout New England merchants were failing, yet from month to month Winslow nursed the hope that he would redeem himself when his consulship was established. And from month to month James Warren wrote letters on Winslow's behalf. "I have a son, Mr. Winslow Warren," he would begin, and as time went on, as Congress deferred the assigning of consulships from one session to another, James's letters became more desperate. To John Adams, to Elbridge Gerry, to James Bowdoin, he referred to his own services to the country; if Winslow succeeded, he said, it would be the only reward he would ever ask. Still, in the winter of 1784–85 no one doubted that eventually Winslow would be appointed. He was the first on the list, Mercy said.

Henry was not one of the sons whom Mercy spoke of as being "scattered wide in different parts of the world." He was nearby in Boston and he was bored. Henry was being trained for a commercial career and had been promised the Plymouth house and business at his part of his father's estate to be shared with Charles when he was well. But this was in the future and he found the waiting difficult. Once in the middle of December Henry proposed to take "a Tour of pleasure to New York, Philadelphia, etc.," to relieve the monotony. He rode to Milton "in all the cold," James said, to ask permission and apparently he rode back from Milton in all the cold without it, for James simply laughed. "Don't you think . . . it would have been a Curious Voyage?" he asked George.

Sometimes the boys wondered if their parents were lonely with so many of them away and of course they often were, but they were seldom alone for long. Mercy entertained frequently, but of the many guests at Milton Hill in 1784 the most memorable was Catherine Macaulay Graham. In America to see how the republic was faring, Mrs. Graham drove to Milton before breakfast one clear November morning and stayed several days, long enough for these two distinguished ladies, so alike in thinking, so unlike in personality, to appraise each other thoroughly. (Indeed, if Mercy was less celebrated as a writer, it was partly because she was less flamboyant as a person.) Catherine was as usual dressed exotically, her face painted in the French fashion so that it looked, it was once said, "as rotten as an old Catherine pear," and she was accompanied by a new husband, William Graham, a man in his early twenties, thirty years Catherine's junior. The marriage had shocked more worldly people than Mercy on both sides of the Atlantic but Mercy was unmoved. Why should a woman not marry a younger man, she asked, if an older man could marry a girl of fifteen without being censored?

If Mercy were to find fault, it would be on other grounds. Catherine talked too much. She was brilliant, Mercy said, her manners were agreeable, but in both her writing and her conversation, she was tiresomely verbose. Catherine, in turn, found Mercy vivacious but opinionated; her "animated severity" was sometimes offensive. But the two women continued to be good friends; what they had in common far outweighed the differences. Most important, their response to the eighteenth century was the same: both were ardently Christian, avidly rational, militantly moral, and for the most part both approved and disapproved of the same authors and for the same reasons. Voltaire, who said Christianity was for chambermaids, was perhaps the first on their mutual blacklist; Edward Gibbon with his "sneers at religion" ran a close second. And when they surveyed the new republic from the vantage point of Milton Hill, Mercy and Catherine shared the same hopes and saw the same dangers.

The dangers were everywhere apparent. "Pure republicanism," Mercy once said, could only be "cherished by the philosopher in his closet" and certainly the republicanism that was on display now was far from pure: young people were defying their elders, soldiers were trying to be noblemen, farmers and judges were quarreling, merchants were running from sheriffs, common men and senators were finding fault with each other. Samuel Adams was particularly exercised by a group of young people who had formed a subscription club, the Sans Souci, for the purpose of dancing and card playing. The club met once every two weeks, adjourned promptly at midnight, and allowed no bets over twenty-five cents, yet for Samuel Adams this was profligacy, it was dissipation, it was a rejection of his dream of Boston as the Christian Sparta, and it was a threat to republicanism itself, for by definition a republic was virtuous and virtue was thrift. "Did we consult the history of Athens and Rome," he cried in the *Boston Gazette,* "we should find that so long as they continued their frugality . . . they shone with superlative glory." In the ensuing newspaper controversy, Harrison Gray Otis, a prominent member of the Sans Souci, was called an "arrogant stripling," Samuel Adams was called a "baleful comet," Mercy Warren was accused of writing a farce about the club (perhaps she had been contaminated by malicious forces on Milton Hill, it was suggested), and James Warren was called a "weak-nerv'd G-n-r-l."

Mercy did not enter the fray publicly, not even to deny authorship of the farce which she privately called a "little indigested farrago," or to reply to the insults which she recognized as coming from some pro-Hancock quarter, but she did use the occasion to point out to George the dangers of gaming on any scale at all. If little wagers gave pleasure, she argued, surely larger wagers would be soon found to give more pleasure and where would it end? Actually, the Sans Souci had a short and, except for the newspaper war, a rather dull life, but it was significant because it revealed the sudden gap between the generations. "Old republicans," proud of that title, all at once found themselves referred to as "rigid republicans," men of "contracted minds" who brooded over the virtues of ancient republics and contrived tiresome parallels where no parallels existed, men who erected barriers and issued prohibitions in an effort to control a society which they were too inhibited to enjoy. To the old republicans, this was heresy and, equally hard to bear, it was disrespect. Where would the young people be now, one old gentleman asked, if it had not been for a few men like Samuel Adams? Most of them, he declared, "instead of being Sans Souci would be Sans Six Sous." But young people were not impressed by this kind of talk or by this brand of republicanism. On the threshold of a new nation, they were finding the vocabulary of their fathers as constricting as their fathers had once found the vocabulary of Parliament.

Mercy worried more about the soldiers than she did about the young people. Specifically she was concerned about the Society of the Cincinnati, a fraternal organization created by officers who had fought in the war and who wanted to maintain their association. They adopted such elaborate trappings, however, and assumed such an aristocratic air that they were accused of wanting to create a military peerage, an American knighthood — dangerous both because it established artificial and unrepublican inequalities and because it was military in origin, "throwing an undue weight into the scale of the army," Mercy said. Moreover, they made membership in the organization hereditary, a provision so universally condemned that it was soon abandoned; but still the Warrens, along with many others, objected to the society. Every young man who had held office in the army for three years went about with the gold medal of the Cincinnati dangling from a buttonhole of his vest, Mercy complained, as if he were parading a superior brand of patriotism, almost as if he were expressing contempt for those "grown grey" in the service of their country — ambassadors from abroad, members of Congress and state legislatures, and others who had sacrificed as much or more and went about unrecognized and undecorated.

In the general atmosphere of recrimination in Massachusetts, however, the farmers were both the most criticized and the most critical. Burdened with debts they could not pay in the tight economy, pursued by creditors who could not wait, farmers in the western counties, many of them veterans, were forced with increasing frequency to give up their farms or their oxen or even, on occasion, to surrender themselves. And when they looked for someone to blame, they turned on the government in Boston. They had, after all, accepted the state constitution reluctantly, lived with it uneasily, and now they were convinced that the government by its very design was indifferent to them. The senate was aristocratic, they said, lawyers were extortionate, the courts were corrupted, the governor was overpaid, mercantile interests were favored over agricultural, and the state's economic system was dictated to support the eastern establishment. Besides, Boston was too far away to serve as a capital. Western towns often went unrepresented in the General Court simply because they were unable to find men willing to go so far and stay so long away from home. But if westerners found it difficult to participate in the government, they were, like all American revolutionaries, well trained in the tactics of working against the government; and so now, as in colonial days, they called county conventions, listed their grievances, and begged relief. They requested a suspension of court judgments against debtors, they clamored for paper money, and as part of a general reform they suggested that the senate be eliminated from the government.

The problem of the western farmer was one of the first tests for the new republic in Massachusetts and it was also the issue that first revealed the areas of difference that existed among the Massachusetts revolutionaries. United for so long in a common cause, equally committed to "first principles," they were hardly prepared for the fact that they might be divided when it came to founding the nation; but with the protest of the western farmers, each showed a slightly different stance toward the state. Samuel Adams, protective and possessive of the state, was furious. The farmers were unrepublican, he said, not only for complaining about debts which were inevitable in a postwar economy but especially for resorting to county conventions. Necessary as such conventions might be under a tyranny, in a republic any extralegal political organization could not be tolerated. Samuel Adams, the great incendiary, had turned into an uncompromising defender of law and order. So intent on presenting a noble image of America to the waiting and somewhat skeptical world, he would allow no detail of manners, morals, or simple routine to escape his scrutiny. He quibbled about senatorial rights and formalities; he even objected to spending money to plant oak trees on the Common. (The Common had done well for a hundred years without oak trees, he said.) It was as if Samuel Adams had come to the end of his script; he had finally defeated the villain of his story and now he not only expected everyone to live happily (modestly and virtuously) ever after, he was angry if they did not. So of course he was angry with the farmers.

John Adams was in London, serving as America's first minister to the British court, and he too was angry. Unlike Samuel Adams, however, John had never expected the revolution to end with the war; indeed, he had often said that the real revolution would only begin when the war was over and it was for this revolution — the building of an enduring government — that he had prepared. At first he could hardly credit the reports he received about the farmers in Massachusetts and he accused James Warren of taking a gloomy view and contributing to a breakdown in public confidence. Later, however, when he was convinced of the gravity of the situation, he saw that the real issue was not money or morals or national reputation, it was the state constitution and he flew to its defense. With a deep sense of urgency John Adams began writing his book, *A Defence of the Constitutions of Government of the United States of America,* in which he developed in detail his principles of a balanced bicameral government, including some sentiments which, he admitted, differed widely "from many of the best Characters, even from Mr. Adams and General Warren." At first James Warren did not seem to sense just how wide this difference was, perhaps because he often had difficulty making the leap between theory and practice. Yet John Adams said: "I think the first Magistrate must be sett up very high in real Power as well as in the opinion of the People."

James Warren took a lonely position in regard to the western farmers. He sympathized with them, although these were the same men whom the eastern establishment (and James Warren too) had generally regarded as dangerous and untutored levelers, but for James the issue was not John Adams' constitution nor Samuel Adams' fine American image, it was the original principle of republicanism. James Warren might not know how to implement these principles but he never lost sight of them. Indeed, he had committed himself unconditionally to what might be called the first American myth: a republic should be small, agrarian (the farmer in the generic sense was idealized, if not the western farmer), frugal, and always on the alert to suppress the first hint of tyranny; moreover, James was unwilling to tinker with the myth — not to strengthen the republic or to pacify it, for the myth was itself a formula for success. James Warren, Mercy once said, was "as resolute and as unchangeable as the father of Hannibal," and since a republic was made to serve the people, it should be responsive, James believed, when people were suffering as they were now.

It was not only the farmers who suffered. Merchants, shackled by British trade restrictions, were often equally hard pressed. So many of James and Mercy's friends went bankrupt during this period (on one occasion they took into their home the son and daughter of a friend who was hiding from creditors) that bankruptcy, Mercy said, was no longer a disgrace. But when the Otis family was threatened, bankruptcy was, if not a disgrace, a painful ordeal. Like so many merchants, Samuel Otis had overextended himself after the war, importing British goods on credit and in turn consigning them on credit to smaller merchants, particularly to his brother Joseph with whom he had a close and often exasperating business relationship. And like so many merchants in the spring of 1785, Joseph was at the end of his resources and his creditors at the end of their patience.

"Is there no possibility of selling part of the farm?" Samuel wrote on April 10.

On April 11: "If the Sheriff insists upon levying execution, I cannot advise you otherwise than I would conduct myself which is to shutt myself up and let them levy upon the Estate . . . I know of no resources under Heaven from whence to raise you the money."

On April 27: "I desire you would keep yourself from the officers, shutt yourself up . . . Keep the mortgage a profound secret . . . am so distressed I know not what course to take, in expectation of my own Creditors being upon my back."

Joseph refused to sell a part of the farm or to sue any of his neighbors who owed him money and he was afraid to let Samuel take his household effects for fear they would be lost to Samuel's creditors. On May 18 Harrison Gray Otis advised Joseph either to hold a room ready to lock himself in or to prepare for flight, yet within the next week the family, apparently as the result of a conference, was reversing its instructions. His advice to "shutt up," Samuel said, had been "in consequence of Mr. Warren's opinion, Much he has altered, and shutting up & going to Prison are so near akin I retract my opinion."

In the end Joseph disposed of most of his property, including the farm, store, and household effects, by secretly transferring them to members of the family, so that although he became insolvent his heirs were provided for. In September Samuel went bankrupt. "What a reverse," Mercy observed, "in one of the oldest & most Respectable Families in [the] Eastern states. Their struggles for a Revolution . . . laid the foundation of their Ruin."

James Warren, much as he might have liked to have helped his brothers-in-law, was also having difficulties. In order to keep the house at Milton Hill, he had for months been trying to sell other parts of his property — a lot on Milton Hill, part of the Plymouth estate, land that he owned in Maine — but nobody was purchasing land at the moment. Ironically, there was a prospective buyer for the house at Milton Hill. The eccentric Madame Haley, widow of a wealthy London merchant and sister of John Wilkes (radical English leader and long-time champion of American liberty), was living in Boston now and had her eye on Milton Hill, but the Warrens were determined not to sell to a "trembling widow" or anyone else if they could possibly avoid it. Yet in business everything went wrong. James would make arrangements for a vessel to go to Lisbon and the arrangements would fall through; he would receive a cargo of Portuguese wine from Winslow and not be able to sell it ("You will in future consider wines an indifferent article," he told Winslow); he would press suit for money owed him and the case would be held up in court. Winslow's consular appointment was delayed again and again, and, as if there was not enough trouble, Algerian pirates were all too frequently preventing goods from either reaching Lisbon or leaving it. "It is hard work," James Warren said, "to be always rowing against the Stream."

Moreover, the government did not help. "Our General Court sets often and long," James said, "do little and give no satisfaction to their Constituents. Paper Money, Tenders of Lands, etc., suspension of Law processes, and a variety of Expedients are proposed and nothing adopted . . . everything seems verging to confusion and anarchy and certainly great Wisdom and Address are necessary to prevent it." But there was no use looking to old friends for wisdom. Samuel Adams had become arbitrary and John Adams was too far away, James felt, to understand.

There was, however, one bright ray in the gloomy scene. John Hancock resigned as governor and this time he meant it. He blamed his gout, yet gout or not any man would have found it difficult to be a governor of Massachusetts in 1785 and, as Hancock knew, the next year would be more difficult. In deference to the people, he had postponed the collection of taxes this year, which meant, of course, that they would accumulate for the following year. And John Hancock, the expansive giver of gifts, the friend of the common man, did not want to be in the governor's chair then. He would have liked Thomas Cushing to succeed him, but actually he did not care who was elected, he said, as long as it was not the "man on Milton Hill." For a while Mercy thought James might be elected and, indeed, in one way they would have both welcomed it, for they were frustrated and hurt by the persistent and increasingly vitriolic reports that James Warren was a quitter, that he cared more for private comfort than for public good. Hancock and his group had capitalized especially on James's refusal to serve as lieutenant governor at the first election under the new constitution and, by reviving these attacks periodically, they successfully kept him out of office. Instead James Bowdoin was selected, although as Mercy pointed out he had also refused the post of lieutenant governor at the same election that James had refused.

James Warren was glad to see Bowdoin in office. No one, he said, could be a worse governor than the one they had had. But if the hard-pressed people of Massachusetts looked to the new administration for relief, they were disappointed. In his first months in office, Governor Bowdoin talked a great deal about frugality, issued a proclamation for the encouragement of piety, virtue, education, and manners, and ordered sheriffs, justices of the peace, and all courts to enforce laws against blasphemy, profane cursing and swearing, profanation of the Lord's Day, gaming, idleness, and drunkenness. But men who faced bankruptcy still faced bankruptcy and when they complained in the newspapers, they were frequently taken to task. They were told that they were downgrading the country; they were accused of wanting to get out of paying just debts; and, as for taxes, a writer in the *Independent Chronicle* said, "The distress of the people . . . arising from taxes are merely chimerical." The governor made no effort even to explain to the farmers the basic structure of the economy, yet there were men who by the nature of some of their complaints obviously did not understand and who, had they understood, might have been persuaded that at least there was no plot in Boston against them.

. . .

Mercy concentrated on her writing during this period, perhaps in the hope of augmenting the family income and certainly with the idea of publication, for although she had produced a respectable number of poems over the years, there were not enough to merit a book. Winslow urged her to return to play writing but, instead of limiting herself to topical and American subjects, he wanted her to choose tragic and classical themes for her dramas in the manner of Corneille or Racine. Mercy, who had seen the American Revolution as an act in history on the level of anything that had happened in the ancient world, was a bit defensive about her subject matter, yet she acceded to Winslow's wishes and wrote *The Sack of Rome* and *The Ladies of Castille,* which she designed for inclusion in her prospective book along with selections of her poetry. She let George see the plays first, although she may later have regretted doing this. George said that *The Sack of Rome* contained too many similes and moral observations and he objected to the title and many of the expressions in *The Ladies of Castille* as being not dignified enough for a tragedy. But then George was a hard critic. He did not hesitate to brand a poem of his mother's mediocre, to accuse her of redundancy, or to quarrel with her choice of words. But in spite of George, Mercy kept the title and began considering a dedication for her book. She would be inclined to dedicate it to George Washington, she wrote Winslow, except that "every Amateur in America Dedicates to him."

Mercy's ambition for her plays, however, ventured beyond publication. Like any playwright, she longed to have a play performed and, as she had so often in the past, she turned to John Adams for literary advice. Could *The Sack of Rome* be acted on the London stage?

John was gallant. "I should wish to see it acted on the Stage in London before crouded Audiences," he replied. "I should be proud to see it in print even if could not be acted." Yet, as John must have known, *The Sack of Rome*, for all its classical pretensions, was as transparently didactic as any of her earlier satires but, stripped of contemporary allusions, it was not as lively. In her plays, Mercy was still the propagandist; her characters were without tragic dimension, her story surely not sophisticated enough for the London stage; and her message, no matter in what century it was delivered, was as blatant as ever: liberty threatened, liberty lost, liberty married victoriously to virtue, liberty defeated by luxury — always liberty, and how could it be otherwise? Liberty was the political path that Mercy and her friends had traveled.

John showed Mercy's play to "several of the first tragical Writers" in England, but rather than repeat what they had said he simply enclosed their own evaluations. "In short," he concluded, "nothing American sells here . . . There is a universal desire and endeavour to forget America." But as for her history, "I hope you will continue [it], for there are few Persons possessed of more Facts, or who can record them in a more agreable manner."

So in the fall of 1785 Mercy was occupied with a variety of literary projects: "Dramatics to perfect — poetry to correct — letters to arrange and history to complete." She wrote feverishly, for no matter what her other motives she was writing, as she so often did, to take her mind off her worries. Winslow was sinking deep into debt and obviously accumulating enemies on both sides of the Atlantic ("Be guarded my Son," Mercy warned, ". . . there are many who lurk in secret to do mischief"); yet it was Charles she was more worried about at present. Even after a summer at home, his health had deteriorated, and now, with winter approaching, if there was to be any hope for his life at all, he had to escape the cold. Like the rest of the family, Charles must have realized how little hope there was, for rather than be among strangers as he had been in Haiti, he decided to go to Lisbon to be with Winslow. He left in September, accompanied by a servant and so weak that Mercy was afraid he would not even survive the voyage. Yet she would hope, she said, and take comfort in the knowledge that Winslow would be waiting to meet Charles and they would be together. Mercy and James followed Charles in their imaginations from day to day — watching the winds, praying for his life, calculating the distance he might have traveled, estimating his probable arrival — and on October 17 when James woke up, the journey presumably over, he addressed his absent son. "Well, Charles," he said, "how do you like Hispaniola?"

Having mentally landed Charles, Mercy and James began to calculate when they might hear from him. Not before December, they decided. Meanwhile the cold that Charles had dreaded crept slowly over Milton Hill: fields stiffened, leaves failed, nights prolonged, mornings broke sharp, and Mercy ordered a fire in her bedroom. She was sitting before the fire at "a lonely hour" one morning in December, thinking about her sons, when all at once she was startled by a familiar hallooing below the stairs. It was Winslow's voice. A moment later Winslow opened her door and stood before her, unexpected and unannounced. He had left Europe abruptly, it seemed, on hearing that no consul would be appointed for Lisbon (a consul general had been selected for a larger area instead). Perhaps he had also been forced to leave quickly in order to escape creditors, for Mercy said later that Winslow had stayed abroad longer than he should have for his own good. In any case, the fact remained that he left Spain shortly before Charles was due to arrive and Charles would be disappointed.

On December 29 the Warrens heard that Charles's ship had reached Cadiz and all were well on board. "God grant it may be true," Mercy said.

In January the Warrens received further news. Charles had died at St. Lucar on November 30. Mercy was visiting in Boston when she heard the news and could not go home until the next day to give way to her grief. What she found hardest to bear was that Charles had died among strangers. He had even been "attacked alone," Mercy was told, by a strange priest, wishing to convert him to Catholicism, but Charles had stood firm to the last and died in his own faith. Mercy took comfort in this story and wrote her sons that Charles was happier now; but for months she was haunted by what she called "tumultous" thoughts. How could she resign herself to the strangeness of Charles's death? "Strangers' tears," she lamented, strange hands, strange words, strange soil — strange, lonely, and faraway.

Yet life went on. In the first months of 1786 James Warren was occupied in settling the old accounts of the Navy Board; Henry Warren, who had left for Plymouth two days after hearing of Charles's death, was trying to establish himself in business. And Winslow, utterly enmeshed in a web of debts that spanned two continents, was trying either to avoid or to placate his creditors. Mercy and James held Congress partially responsible for Winslow's problems, claiming that he had stayed in Lisbon at considerable expense for twelve months on the strength of repeated assurances of a consulship which had of course never materialized. Three people in particular, it seemed, were causing Winslow trouble: John Codman, a merchant whom Mercy called a "wealthy, flagitious villain," and the two Van Staphorsts brothers, well-known bankers in Holland who had done considerable business with the United States government and to whom Winslow owed £570 — obviously the same creditors he was supposed to have paid off before returning to Massachusetts. The sequence of events suggests that Codman and the Van Staphorsts may have joined forces against Winslow, also that they may have found it difficult to take Winslow to court in Massachusetts where his father had so many friends.

But Winslow would not have expected trouble to follow him out of the state; indeed, in February when he set out on a trip to New York, he probably thought he was escaping his creditors for a while. At his father's request he was to deliver the navy accounts to Congress; he also carried with him a letter of greeting from his mother to the new wife of Elbridge Gerry. Perhaps he had business of his own, for he was away two weeks, making the customary overnight stops in Providence and New Haven on the way to New York and again on the way back. All went well until his return. He was in New Haven on March 1 when he was stopped by the sheriff with a writ demanding his appearance at court in April to answer to a claim of the Van Staphorsts.

John Chandler, the sheriff of New Haven, later recorded that he "attached the Body of the Within Named Winslow Warren and read the Same in his hearing and took great and Sufficient Bail for his appearance."

Only someone who knew that Winslow would be in New Haven on or about March 1 (who had, in fact, made it a point to know) could have arranged for the writ and its delivery, and Winslow apparently had no difficulty determining who it was. Back in Boston five days later, he retaliated on the floor of the Exchange, where the merchants of Boston were accustomed to gather each day at one o'clock. Henry Knox, one of America's most prestigious generals, was present at the Exchange that day.

"We had a caning match," he wrote afterward, "between Mr. John Codman and Mr. Winslow Warren . . . Warren attacked Mr. Codman with a very heavy cane without giving him the least precious notice. Mr. Codman was without a cane or anything to defend himself . . . he is much bruised."

For reasons that are not clear Winslow's case was postponed by the New Haven court from April to November. In the meantime, as he waited for his trial, the general tension of Massachusetts debtors, particularly of the western farmers, flared into open rebellion. James Warren blamed the General Court which "could not, or would not, see the general Uneasiness that threatened . . . but dosed themselves into an unusual Adjournment for six or seven months." His irritation at government indifference, his sympathy with anyone he felt to be imposed upon were characteristic of James Warren and now of course he had special reason to side with the aggrieved. Winslow was a debtor — a fact which was not lost on James's enemies.

But James did not support violence, and violence broke out in September. Determined that debtors' cases should not be tried until the General Court met again and could hopefully be persuaded to extend relief, an army of angry citizens led by a veteran, Daniel Shays, began forcibly to prevent the courts in the western counties from opening. "Three upper Counties . . . have refused submission to the Government established by the Constitution and Obedience to the Laws made under it," James Warren reported in October; "that is, they have violated their Compact and are in a State of Rebellion, while the three Eastern Counties are petitioning to be separated from us and formed into a new Government of their own Construction." In January Daniel Shays and his men attacked the arsenal at Springfield.

If some courts in Massachusetts were closed, however, this was not the case in Connecticut. In the midst of Shays's Rebellion (November 2), Winslow Warren's case came up in the circuit court of New Haven. Winslow claimed that a Connecticut court had no jurisdiction over him, nevertheless judgment was recovered against him and when he was unable to satisfy the claim he was taken to jail. He was not there long. According to the records, Winslow Warren "broke the gaol aforesaid and made a willful and tortuous escape from the custody of the sheriff." He quickly made his way back to Massachusetts where he was safe from Connecticut courts but not, as it turned out, from the malice of his enemies. The rumor circulated that Winslow was connected with Shays's insurgents and that his father secretly supported Shays too.

James was used to being misrepresented. He could not believe that anyone who knew his record could suppose that he would condone what was happening now. As for his sons — while he had one son who had happened into legal difficulties at an inauspicious time, he had another son who had actively opposed the rebels. Henry had joined the militia at the outset of the uprising and had been highly commended for his services. But James did not defend himself or his sons. Not only would it have been beneath his dignity, he had, as he readily admitted, no "Time serving Talents." Whether it was politically wise or not, James continued to criticize the government even when the climate of opinion was such that, according to a prominent Massachusetts lawyer (James Sullivan), any man who did not loudly acclaim the government at every turn was accused of rebellion. In the spring of 1787 after the rebellion had been quelled, James Warren complained that the General Court, finally awakened from its long sleep, was in a "peevish disposition," more interested in enforcing the law (even by such unconstitutional means as suspending the rule of habeas corpus) than in understanding the causes behind the rebellion, more concerned with punishing insurgents than with restoring harmony in the state. Completely disenchanted with the administration of James Bowdoin (although he could scarcely deny that Bowdoin had acted firmly and quickly in the emergency), he shared the opinion of many in the state that a less severe, more generous man was needed to bring the people together. And, of course, just such a man was available, waiting in the wings to be recalled. If James Warren did not actually support John Hancock for governor at the spring election, he admitted reluctantly that he did not "regret the change" as much as he once would have.

Old friends became enemies as a result of Shays's Rebellion; enemies became friends. It must have seemed extraordinary to James Warren to find himself on the one hand actually tolerating his old enemy John Hancock and on the other hand estranged from his old friend Samuel Adams, who had become so vindictive in his attitude toward the insurgents that he was, James said, "the most arbitrary and despotic Man in the Commonwealth." Equally strange to James would have been the shift in attitude toward him. While it seemed to him that he had merely pointed out dangers that could befall a state as a result of an unresponsive government (the very dangers that had, in fact, occurred), to many of James's old friends it seemed that he had behaved irresponsibly, not only because he had favored measures (paper money, for instance) that would have aggravated rather than improved the economic situation but also because such support may have encouraged the insurgents. It was, of course, only a step to the rumor that James and Winslow had both deliberately backed the rebellion.

But if James lost friends, he also made them. There were enough people in the town of Milton who appreciated his sympathy with the cause of the people to elect him a representative to the General Court in the spring of 1787; from there he was elected Speaker of the House. "The dread of reviving the Clamour of refusing everything," James wrote John Adams, ". . . has Induced me to accept." It would be two years before James Warren would learn that John Adams had also listened to rumors about James's position at the time of the rebellion. The rumors were undoubtedly exaggerated, John wrote Mercy in a letter that was to change the nature of their friendship, yet one thing was indubitable. "G[eneral] Warren did differ for a time from all his Friends and did countenance measures that appear to me, as they did to those Friends, extremely pernicious."

Shays's Rebellion was a watershed in the history of Massachusetts. While the Treaty of Paris ended the colonial status of the country, Shays's Rebellion forced the country to go beyond the colonial thinking upon which the national government was built. No one would deny, James Warren least of all, that under the Articles of Confederation Congress was operating inefficiently. Not only did

Congress not have the powers it needed to control commerce and to raise money, but what powers it did have it all too often dissipated because it could not manage to produce a quorum to act. James Warren's navy account which Winslow had delivered to Congress had never been passed because only seven states had been present at the time; with money matters unanimity was required. Indeed, so ineffective had Congress become that outside ways were sought to reach agreements between states. It was at such a meeting at Annapolis, in September 1786 during Shays's Rebellion, that a convention was proposed which would "enter so far into the general System of the foederal government, that to give it efficacy, and to obviate questions and doubts concerning its precise nature and limits." In February Congress, shaken by the anarchy in Massachusetts, assembled enough representatives to give its official sanction to such a convention to be called in Philadelphia in May 1787.

So began another realignment of forces in Massachusetts, as the people faced up again to the same questions they had wrestled with all their lives: How much freedom could people enjoy and still maintain order? How much power could a government exert and not infringe on individual liberty? The people argued and speculated through the hot summer of the convention (later to be called the Constitutional Convention) but they had no way of knowing what decisions were being made in Philadelphia, for the delegates had sworn to keep the proceedings secret. Mercy distrusted the secrecy. "It was thought by some . . ." she wrote later, "that the greatest happiness of the greatest number was not the principal object of their contemplations, when they ordered their doors to be locked, their members inhibited from all communications abroad, and when proposals were made that their journals should be burnt."

Mercy was, as usual, busy that summer. She attended her favorite niece, Sarah Russell (daughter of the Severs of Kingston), who was dying of consumption. She called on her brother Samuel's wife in Boston three days after she was delivered of a "fine little plump girl." She wrote letters on behalf of Winslow in an effort to persuade his creditors to accept equal payment on his debts. And one day in the early part of the summer Mercy had the pleasure of reading a long letter from Abigail Adams, the kind of letter they so enjoyed exchanging. There were reflections on Abigail's latest reading (Mrs. Montague's essays), the usual deprecation of manners and morals (London was a difficult place to cultivate friendship), a touch of what the two women had once called "political seasoning" (Abigail gently reproved Mercy for her despondency about America: "I have Faith that will remove Mountains," she said), a bit of scandal (the Prince of Wales's love life), and finally a personal note. Abigail had become a grandmother. Or as she put it: "I am — a grand — o no! that would be confessing myself old, which would be quite unfashionable and vulgar; but true it is, I have a fine grandson."

All summer the men in Philadelphia remained closeted together and Mercy worried about what they were doing to the country's freedom. In September — as it happened, on the day she turned sixty — Mercy expressed her fears to Catherine Macaulay Graham: "Our situation is truly delicate and critical. On the one hand we stand in need of a strong federal government founded on principles that will support the prosperity and union of the colonies. On the other we have struggled for liberty . . . and there are still many among us who revere her name too much to relinquish beyond a certain medium the rights of man for a dignity of government."

It was, of course, the advocates of a strong central government, soon to be known as the Federalists, that she feared: wealthy men eager to preserve their wealth and influence, members of the Cincinnati Society "panting for nobility," and ambitious young men (many of them at the convention) who saw that the more powerful and aristocratic the country was, the more opportunity they would have to attain honors and office. The higher the ladder, the higher they could climb. Mercy found it difficult to ascribe anything but selfish motives to the proponents of Federalism, just as the Federalists found it difficult to believe that the "antis" wanted anything more noble than to retain the local position and power they had enjoyed and to keep close control of their money and their fiscal policy. But as yet, of course, the strength of the two schools of thought had not been tested or even clearly articulated except by the constitution makers in Philadelphia. The sides had not been formed.

Once during the summer of silence Mercy wrote to her good friend Elbridge Gerry, a delegate to the convention and one of the few men there whose views she completely trusted.

"Does anything transpire from the conclave or is all yet locked up in silence and secrecy?" she wrote. "Be it so — yet some of us have lived long enough not to expect everything great, good, and excellent from so imperfect a creature as man . . . therefore [I] shall not be disappointed either at the mouse or the mountain that this long labour may produce."

At the end of September the signed draft of a new constitution arrived in Massachusetts. In spite of what she had said about maintaining her composure, Mercy would have been disturbed when she saw the name of Elbridge Gerry was missing from the signatures. Along with two delegates from Virginia, Gerry had declared that he could not in good conscience sign the document.

James Otis, Sr., and
Mary Allyn Otis, both by
John Singleton Copley

James Warren by John Singleton Copley

Mercy Otis Warren by John Singleton Copley

James and Mercy Warren's house at Eel River,
Plymouth, Massachusetts

Manikin in Mercy Warren's dress
poses beside Mercy's teapot and table
inlaid with embroidery that Mercy did
before she was married. Display at
Pilgrim Hall, Plymouth

James Otis, Jr., by Jonathan B. Blackburn

Thomas Hutchinson by Edward Truman

Abigail Adams by Mather Brown

John Adams by John Singleton Copley

Wharf at Plymouth. The photograph, taken before 1859,
shows base of rock embedded in wharf

The Edmund Fowle House, Watertown, Massachusetts, meeting
place of the Council of Provincial Congress, 1775–76, and
frequent residence of James and Mercy Warren.

Courtesy, the Museum of Fine Arts, Boston

Samuel Adams by John Singleton Copley

Winslow Warren
by John Singleton Copley

John Hancock

Elbridge Gerry

James Winthrop

Samuel Allyne Otis
and Harrison Gray Otis,
both by Gilbert Stuart

Thomas Hutchinson's country house at Milton, Massachusetts,
later owned by James and Mercy Warren

John Adams' study, showing the large chair in which he spent so
much time in his later years and in which he is said to have died

XII

———••———

REPUBLICANISM did not settle down easily in America; the republican idea, Americans would discover, was not conducive to the notion that people should sit long under their vines. Again and again new generations would be required to redefine republicanism (or democracy once the word lost its pejorative association) and each time the process would be an agony to the country. The period of the debate over the constitution was just such a time. Republicanism suddenly appeared to be a great wild thing bound on dragging the country either to chaos on the one hand or to tyranny on the other. Federalists were, of course, more afraid of the chaos; Anti-Federalists were more afraid of the tyranny that they said went hand in hand with bigness and power. They quoted history and cited examples of famous tyrants and fallen societies to prove their point. No one was more acutely aware of the past than Anti-Federalists; they spoke as if they themselves were standing knee-deep in the ruins of ancient civilizations and listening to the crash of empires. Indeed so attuned was Mercy Warren to the lessons of history, so committed to the idea that a republic should be small, manageable, and humble, that she looked with foreboding at the western territory and later observed that it would have been well if a "Chinese wall had been stretched along the Appalachian ridges."

Massachusetts was the first state to question the constitution seriously and Mercy Warren was one of the most serious questioners. She had not entered a political debate since before the war but now she marshalled her arguments, polished her rhetoric, and wrote what was to be one of the most protracted and vigorous of the Anti-Federalist documents, a nineteen-page pamphlet entitled *Observations on the New Constitution, and on the Federal and State Conventions. By a Columbian Patriot.* To the Federalists' contention that the country would collapse and the republican experiment would be ended if the constitution, imperfect as it might be, were not adopted, Mercy countered: If the constitution were adopted in its present form, would the country even be a republic? Specifically, Mercy's objections to the constitution were that it had no bill of rights, that trial by jury in civil causes was not secured, that the powers of the executive and the judiciary were not sufficiently separated, that there was not ample protection against a man staying in office for life (a six-year term for senators and a two-year term for representatives she considered dangerous), that the president had princely powers, and that there were no safeguards against a permanent standing army. For years the authorship of Mercy's pamphlet was mistakenly attributed to Elbridge Gerry, yet the style was pure Mercy at her elegant best — too elegant, as it turned out, for some readers. The Anti-Federalist committee in Albany, New York, which had received a number of copies for distribution complained that the expression in the pamphlet was "too sublime and florid for the common people in this part of the country" — which not only indicated that Mercy's style was becoming dated but also that the common people, that up-and-coming middle class of which the aristocratically inclined Federalists were so wary, were becoming a political factor of increasing importance.

While Mercy wrote her pamphlet, James sent off letters to the newspaper and the result was, of course, another period of political vituperation. The Warrens found themselves in the peculiar position of being accused on the one hand of aligning themselves with the radical, ignorant, democratic forces in the state and on the other hand of being conservative, old-fashioned, narrow-minded, provincial, bucking the wave of the future — all of which was confusing to two people who believed in the immutability of their principles.

The most devastating label of all, however, was "insurgent." Lumping all Anti-Federalists together as Shaysites or fellow travelers, the Federalists called their opponents the "insurgent party" — an effective device but hardly fair. The Anti-Federalists actually represented many different kinds of people and, as Mercy Warren was quick to point out, their arguments were "not the result of ignorance; they were made by men of the first abilities."

James Winthrop, for instance, Hannah's son and a former librarian at Harvard who had served as a volunteer in the army against the insurgents, was one of the leading Anti-Federalists. Samuel Adams was another. Rabid against the Shaysites for spoiling his picture of an ideal republic, he turned against the Federalists for the same reason. Certainly the grand scheme outlined in the constitution was a far cry from Samuel Adams' vision of a new Rome revolving around his beloved Boston, yet Samuel Adams was never as vocal an Anti-Federalist as either James Warren or Elbridge Gerry. During the debate he had been shocked to find that his prewar allies, indeed the very backbone of his republic — the mechanics, the tradesmen, the artisans of Boston (Paul Revere himself) — were for the most part in favor of ratifying the constitution. This had a sobering effect, for unlike James Warren Samuel Adams was, as ever, a practical politician.

Two of Massachusetts' most prominent old republicans did not participate in the preconvention wrangling. John Adams was still in England, "a very warm Federalist," according to Catherine Macaulay Graham. "You will not agree quite so well on public matters," she wrote Mercy, "as you did formerly." And John Hancock was indisposed. Like the eye at the center of the storm that raged around him, he stayed quiet. He simply did not know what to do. He sincerely believed in the prewar concept of government that the old republicans had shared and which the Anti-Federalists now embraced; had he not always championed the cause of the common people and in return been rewarded? But now the common people were on both sides of the issue; it was impossible to isolate them, impossible to defend them, impossible to appeal to them, and, most distressing of all for a man who liked to be a winner, it was impossible to predict on which side most of the people were. Accordingly, as time for the ratifying convention approached, John Hancock swathed himself in bandages and took to his bed. No one could deny that he was ravaged by gout, but as usual people observed how often his attacks occurred when it was most convenient for him.

The convention met on January 9, 1788, and from the outset it was apparent that Massachusetts was indeed taking the matter of the constitution seriously. In the dead of winter the representatives came — farmers from the west, merchants from the coast, seasoned politicians, landed aristocrats, veterans, debtors, old republicans, and excited young newcomers testing their political wings. They filled the taverns and rooming houses — one of the largest groups that had ever gathered for a meeting in Boston. But when they started to talk, their arguments sounded like echoes of the old arguments of Hutchinson's day. How could a sovereign power exist within another sovereign power? the Anti-Federalists asked. How could the people of Massachusetts allow a government so removed from their control levy a direct tax on them?

The Anti-Federalists outnumbered the Federalists at the convention but the Federalists had many advantages: they were better organized; they had waged a stronger as well as a more ruthless campaign; they had the benefit of a well-articulated philosophy expounded by their national leaders; they had more able men representing them at the convention. (Neither James Warren nor Elbridge Gerry had been elected as a representative.) Moreover, they had enormous conviction, enthusiasm, and drive — all positive elements, while the Anti-Federalists could only object and warn. If the constitution were rejected, the Anti-Federalists could neither guarantee that a new convention could draw up a better constitution nor could they suggest how the country would survive in the meantime. America, in a precarious position financially and under pressure from Europe, obviously could not debate forever. So the Federalists had a sense of urgency on their side too and they made the most of it. Still, they did not dare let the question come to a vote.

Instead, a delegation of Federalists went to the big house on Beacon Street to call on John Hancock who, gout or not, received them, probably in his wheelchair before the fire. There would have been an exchange of amenities over a tankard of punch or a bottle of madeira and then the Federalists would have broached their proposition: in return for his active support of the constitution, they promised to back him for the presidency of the United States if Virginia did not ratify (thus eliminating George Washington as a candidate); and if Virginia did ratify, they would back him for the vice presidency. They could go farther. They had in mind a series of amendments to accompany the ratification. These amendments would, in effect, be recommendations to the new government for incorporation into the constitution and should satisfy some of the objections the Anti-Federalists were raising.

John Hancock agreed. Accordingly on February 6, still swathed in bandages, he was carried into the convention (which he was supposed to have chaired) and he proposed the amendments. They were seconded by Samuel Adams, who had been convinced that a compromise was the only solution. Finally the vote was called and out of a total of 355 ayes and nays, the ayes won by a slender margin of 17 votes. The constitution had been ratified by Massachusetts. And so it was that John Hancock had again managed to serve his state, satisfy his vanity, and play the hero — all by simply sitting on the sidelines and waiting to be called. Nor should his contribution be underestimated. No one else in Massachusetts was in the position to have done what he did at that critical moment.

Mercy was somewhat appeased by the amendments, although they did not cover all her objections nor were they all incorporated into the constitution, but as a result of the recommendations of various states, a bill of rights was eventually included in the constitution and for this she was grateful.

At the moment, however, Mercy and James were tired. They had

had a hard, cold winter sitting on top of Milton Hill, the target of Federalist abuse, and some time during that winter they decided to give up the house on Milton Hill and move back to Plymouth. They had no immediate prospect for a buyer, but James's gout had become worse over the last year and he had found it increasingly difficult to keep up the farm. Moreover, it seemed pointless now. The house had been planned for Winslow but Winslow was living in Boston and traveling back and forth to Maine where the Warren boys owned property left them by their grandfather Otis. And of course, in debt as he was, Winslow could not in any case have held on to Milton Hill, had he fallen heir to it. As for the other boys, Henry was at the Eel River house in Plymouth, James, Jr., was still in Hingham, and George was not inclined toward farming. He had recently opened a law office in Milton but business was so poor, he may already have been entertaining the idea of moving to Maine (which he did shortly after his family left Milton).

Mercy was not unhappy about leaving Milton Hill. She had always found the house cold and drafty, and without Winslow her pleasure in it had dissipated. Besides, even on the best days at Milton, she had looked back at Plymouth with a certain degree of wistfulness. "I often . . . take a walk from room to room," she had once said, "peep through the Lattices that have lighted my Steps, revisit the little Alcove leading to the Garden and place myself in every happy Corner of a house where I have tasted so much real Felicity." Certainly if in retrospect it seemed to her that she had once found peace in Plymouth, she hoped to find it there again, particularly for the sake of James. He had grown bitter over what he called the "large share of malicious Slander" that had come his way; indeed during the constitutional controversy he had been called everything from a coward to a rogue, yet even now as he traveled back and forth between Milton and Plymouth, preparatory to moving, he exposed himself to still more slander by running for lieutenant governor. Perhaps he hoped to redeem his political reputation, for he was the recognized leader of the Anti-Federalists; per-

haps he simply would not have it said of him again that he refused
to run for office — but he also ran as a matter of stubborn principle.
The so-called "monarchical" forces were running strong in the state
and no matter what anyone said about James Warren's proclivity to
turn down uncongenial posts, he had never flinched from a direct
confrontation with Tories, whether they were the prewar variety or
the new Federalist kind. But the election did nothing to improve his
image or soothe his feelings. He did receive the hard-core Anti-
Federalists' support, but it was not the support of old friends ("You
are the only Confidential Friend I have," he wrote Elbridge Gerry)
and it did not carry the election. James lost to Benjamin Lincoln, a
popular figure who had led the Massachusetts militia in Shays's Rebellion.

Soon after the election twenty-year-old John Quincy Adams, a
Federalist like his father, called on the Warrens and had this to say
about the election:

> . . . stopp'd about half an hour at Genl. Warren's. He was
> gone to Plymouth, but Mrs. Warren was at home. The Genl's
> political character has undergone of late a great alteration.
> Among all those who were formerly his friends he is extremely
> unpopular; while the insurgent and Antifederal party (for it
> is but one) consider him in a manner as their head, and have
> given him at this election many votes for lieutenant governor.
> Mrs. Warren complained that he had been abused shamefully,
> and very undeservedly; but she thought me too federal to talk
> freely with me.

In June, as the Warrens were finally settling down in Plymouth,
John and Abigail Adams returned to Boston. Appropriately after
his ten-year absence, John was welcomed with ceremony: bells rang,
cannon boomed, crowds huzzaed, and Governor Hancock threw his
house open to them for as long as they wanted to stay. But for all
the attention, John Adams was ill at ease; the country had reserva-

tions about him and he knew it. On the one hand the Anti-Federalists accused him of being monarchical, of having his head turned by court life, of being unduly impressed by the English system and too often prejudiced in England's favor — in short, of having betrayed "first principles." On the other hand, the Federalists eyed him warily: Was he too independent to be trusted to carry out their ideas? Had he been out of the country too long to understand the subtleties of the political situation? And most important — how could he be fitted into the political structure without upsetting the places of other men?

Actually only time would reveal (even to John Adams) how independent he was. Although he classified himself now as a Federalist, he was not of the new breed; his thinking was firmly rooted in prewar concepts. As far as he was concerned, he had never deviated in his republicanism; in his system of checks and balances he had simply placed the chief executive in the key position, as an impartial head of state whose duty it was to stand between the aristocratic and democratic branches of government and throw his weight to whichever side it was necessary to maintain the balance. While James and Mercy Warren were afraid of an individual gaining too much power, John Adams was afraid of groups — perhaps the aristocratic element even more than the popular. It was not George III who had caused the trouble in England, he said, it was Parliament and so although he did not advocate monarchy and resented being called a monarchist, he did not believe that a monarch and a republic were mutually exclusive and he did not rule out that eventually one might become necessary in America. Adams was convinced that man by nature was a self-seeking, self-serving creature, but apparently he did not foresee that it might not always be in the interest of the president to maintain the delicate balance in government that he believed was necessary. And he did not understand that, unlike England, America would not be divided on class lines, nor indeed that the government rested on a different foundation. Since the government in America was completely new, the old social-contract theory was no longer relevant, according to many of the constitution makers. The government was wholly the creation of the people; it was not in a position to strike a bargain, to give up certain rights in return for other rights (which was why a bill of rights had not been thought necessary in the original constitution); the people retained all their liberties except those they specifically allocated to their government.

But as more states ratified and the constitution became binding, the question was not so much how the government should be run but who should run it. John Adams declared that he was through with public life and threw himself into a frenzy of farming — buying pigs and cows, clearing pastures, mending fences, supervising the reconstruction of the new house and barn they had moved into on their return from Europe. But he was peevish. He felt neglected, he told his daughter, "out of circulation"; yet when he was approached about being a state senator or taking a seat in Congress in order to build up a political following, he was insulted. He was willing to serve the public, he said, on "honorable principles, not mean ones." And obviously the most honorable way to serve the public at this moment was to serve it in the office of the president or the vice president. People in general agreed that since George Washington, who seemed to be the unanimous choice for president, came from the South, the vice president should be a New England man. Accordingly, two men watched the political maneuvering with particular interest: John Hancock on Beacon Hill and John Adams in Braintree.

And both were bitter about the outcome of the election. John Hancock, who had, of course, wanted the presidency even more than the vice presidency and who had never been considered seriously for either, was so angry at the Federalists that he made friends again with his old enemy Samuel Adams — thus, in effect, hoisting the flag of Anti-Federalism. (Adams welcomed the alliance, recognizing that in the new structure of government the Anti-Federalists would have to work together, and at the next state election, in which

Hancock was elected governor and Samuel Adams lieutenant governor, the two men appeared arm in arm in twin suits.) As for John Adams, he was the victor, the vice president–elect, but he too felt wronged. Behind the scenes Alexander Hamilton, the ambitious leader of the Federalist party who had reluctantly agreed to John Adams' candidacy, had persuaded electors in various states to divert a few votes from Adams to other candidates, ostensibly so that George Washington would be certain to win the presidency (the man who received the most votes automatically became the president) but actually so that John Adams would enter office in a politically weakened position. Adams did not know about the intrigue until later; at the moment he knew only that he had received thirty-four electoral votes in contrast to the sixty-nine votes that Washington had received. And so, despite his election, he was still in a petulant frame of mind, wondering if there was enough spirit in the country, he wrote Mercy Warren, even to insure that the laws would be obeyed.

John Adams and James Warren were too disappointed in each other to pretend to a friendship they no longer felt, but Mercy kept up the correspondence. And as she so often did, she took John's remark personally — a veiled slur at her political affiliations with the so-called lawless group in Massachusetts. "I am persuaded," she said stiffly, "that the new Government will operate very quietly unless the reins are held too taught."

. . .

The new government went into operation in New York in April 1789. Samuel Allyne Otis, who had been elected secretary to the Senate, held the crimson cushion on which the Bible rested when the oath of office was administered to George Washington. John Adams conducted Washington to the presidential chair but when it came to introducing the president, John in a flurry of embarrassment forgot part of his speech. Next to Washington, John Adams invariably appeared at his worst — shorter, plumper, more awkward; indeed all those pompous little mannerisms which Adams himself ab-

horred became especially prominent in the early days of his vice
presidency when he was so determined that the government should
start out on a proper footing and so convinced that no one knew
better than he what was proper.

If he was momentarily at a loss for words at the inauguration, he
was at no loss in the Senate chamber. Constantly overstepping his
prerogatives as presiding officer, he lectured the Senate like a school-
teacher, interrupted, explained, quoted from his experience abroad,
fussed over details, and argued incessantly for his favorite causes. In
particular, he was committed to the idea that a government, in order
to command respect both at home and abroad, had to adopt a certain
amount of pomp and pageantry and had to confer titles on its leaders. The president, he contended, should be called "His Most Benign
Highness" or at the very least "His Highness," but all John Adams
got for his concern was a nickname. The president, it was decided,
would be called "the president" and behind his back John Adams,
who wanted so much to cut a noble figure, was called "His Rotund-
ity." No matter how much he explained, he could not convince the
public that his insistence on ceremony sprang not from personal
vanity but from ten years' observation of the role that ceremony
played in the successful operation of government abroad. And he
could not accept the fact that the last ten years in America might
have afforded men as relevant an experience as his had been.

Mercy watched the proceedings in the new capital with interest,
misgiving, and a touch of scorn, yet she was careful not to reveal her
feelings to her Federalist friends, for whatever she thought of their
politics, she had no intention of alienating them now. Mercy was an
Otis: she had the Otis respect for political realities and the Otis habit
of looking at a new government with an eye for patronage. James
was through with asking favors; he would not again put himself in
the position of begging on Winslow's behalf or on behalf of anyone
else in the family, but Mercy's pride was like her father's: it did not
stand in the way of family interest. Accordingly, she resumed her
correspondence with Martha Washington. She wrote Henry Knox,

a close friend of Washington's and a member of his cabinet, to present the case of her son Henry, who wished to be appointed Collector of Customs for the port of Plymouth. In the same letter she spoke of Winslow, who had asked for an appointment in the army. This was not a request that Mercy relished; she could not bear to think of Winslow in the army, yet he was obviously still in trouble and the army might offer, if not a solution, an escape that he could not seem to manage in any other way. Only recently she had advised him: "Be assured that there are too many eyes on your movements for you to repair . . . any place without its being Generally known in what quarter you are within a very few days."

But there was one man, of course, who had the power, Mercy believed, not only to help Winslow but to reverse the political fortunes of the Warren family. Surely John Adams, in spite of recent differences, would recognize that the Warrens who had contributed so much to the cause of liberty deserved some consideration from the new government. Mercy found it difficult to defend her husband and her son to John Adams when she felt they needed no defense, to refute charges of insurgency, to play upon old friendship, yet she made a good case. Still, she could not avoid a certain imperiousness in her tone, nor hide the bitterness that ran between the lines. She did not ask for favors, she said; no one in her family was soliciting, but she knew that John Adams would not forget any one of them. She was "sure" of his patronage.

Mercy's letters brought her nothing but additional bitterness. In Plymouth a Federalist, William Watson, was appointed Collector of Customs — the most "contemptible character in the district," Mercy said, "a man totally unable from his ignorance to execute this or any other office of importance without the assistance and direction of another." Henry Knox wrote that no appointments were being made in the army at this time. And John Adams and Abigail were both offended by Mercy's aggressiveness (the very quality that Mercy had always been so fearful of betraying to John Adams). Abigail admitted to her sister that her feelings toward Mercy had changed and, indeed, that she knew no other lady "equally ambitious." John Adams replied: "In the first place, I have no patronage; in the next, neither your children nor my own would be sure of it if I had it." If she had any specific applications, he said, she should make them to the president. As for the Warren family's unpopularity, it was not his fault if he had listened "to the uninterrupted Ebulitions of the public wrath."

Mercy let the matter drop. There were other ways to restore one's reputation. She had looked forward to the publication of her books — largely to gratify her own literary aspirations — but with the rebuff by the Federalists, she had a new motive. Surely her poetry would remind the world of the major role the Warrens had played in the struggle for independence; possibly it would bring appreciation. Certainly for an American in the 1790s, reading Mercy's poems (most of them written in the 1770s) would be a nostalgic experience, a visit back to innocent days when the enemy was obviously the enemy, when patriots were united, when friends were heroes, when the future meant peace (after victory, of course), and peace suggested, at least for poetic purposes, an idyllic country peopled with happy farmers and virtuous statesmen. If Mercy did not apply to Washington for patronage, she did what she had once said she did not want to do: she dedicated her book of poems and plays to him.

Off and on during the summer of 1789 through the spring of 1790, Mercy worked at polishing and assembling her manuscripts. In July 1789 the French stormed the Bastille ("What an astonishing revolution!" Mercy wrote Henry Knox); in October President Washington visited Boston and Governor Hancock (who was supposed to escort him into the city) came down with an attack of gout; Benjamin Franklin died in April 1790; Hannah Winthrop, in May. As for the Warren family, James went to New York to try again to settle the Navy Board accounts which, although they had once been examined and passed, were now represented to the new treasury department as being unintelligible. Moreover, James had personal complaints to make to the government: he claimed that he had never been paid the increase in salary that had been promised him in 1778, the difference between £450 a year and £900. He may have once signed a settlement, he admitted, but if he had, it had been in the midst of clearing up other matters and done "inaccurately and without proper Attention"; but he received no satisfaction. Meanwhile young Henry Warren began courting a second cousin — a Winslow, in fact, one of the few Winslows who remained in Plymouth. Mary Winslow was the granddaughter of General John and the daughter of Pelham Winslow, who had been with the Loyalists in New York and had died there, embittered and drunk in a public house; she lived now in reduced circumstances with her sister and mother who supported them by operating a small shop.

In June Mercy was ready to submit her book to the printer; she received Washington's permission for the dedication — given, he said, because he was "duly sensible of the Merits of the respectable and amiable writer" — but all at once Mercy was afraid. A book was more permanent than anything she had attempted before; she was entering a new realm and, as a severe critic herself, she knew she would be judged in a new way. "As great an admirer as I am of good poetry," she had once said, "I think that which is not executed in a masterly manner is of all composition the least pleasing." But could she be sure that her manner was sufficiently masterly? How could she bear to let the book out of her hands?

Full of apprehension, Mercy left James, who was suffering from an attack of gout, and went to Boston to work with the printer. Apparently she stayed at least a week, but however long, it was a lonely time for James. They needed each other, these two, just as they always had — even more, perhaps, in the wake of the pain, the abuse, the disappointments, the broken friendships they had both endured. Indeed, as he thought of Mercy in Boston at this vulnerable moment in her career, James was filled with such tenderness that he wrote what could only be called a love letter. James was sixty-four years old now, his hand trembled with palsy, and he was

frustrated by his gout — "a dreadful thing indeed for a Farmer" —
but he wrote:

*I recd your letter by Harry on Sat . . . it told me that my
beloved had an agreeable journey and was very well after it.
That was a feast for a heart of sensibility. Tell me more such
good news in your next and make me more happy.*

*My foot grew better the day you left us . . . I tell you the
truth. I suppose you are busily Engaged in the Business of an
author of great abilities, Discernment & Judgment, yet Diffident and therefore hunting for Criticism & advise and correct-
ing . . . with a trembling breast. If you had half the good
opinion of yourself that I have of you, you certainly would not
feel half the anxiety you do now . . . Here the weather is fine
& all nature in bloom. I long to pluck a rose & gather a plate
of Strawberries for my little angel but the distance is too great
. . . Will you run over & take part of a fine piece of Beef &
Bacon & a most excellent Line of Veal no green pease but potatoes, sallad & Horse radish. if we had peas or rubies & dia-
monds we would give them to you. we have strawberries &
cream at your service . . . adieu, for why should I attempt to
Express the full of my affection for you.*

The finished book, *Poems, Dramatic and Miscellaneous* by Mrs.
M. Warren, was ready in September and Mercy promptly mailed
complimentary copies to friends — George Washington, John
Adams, Henry Knox, Elbridge Gerry, and to some government no-
tables (conspicuously not friends) like Alexander Hamilton, whom
Mercy characterized as a "young officer of foreign extraction." Their
acknowledgments came back over the next months, filled with
praise enough to reassure the most diffident author. "It is certain,"
Alexander Hamilton wrote, "that in the Ladies of Castille, the sex
will find a new occasion to triumph." Later she had what she called
an "elegant letter" of congratulation from one of England's most

renowned literary ladies, Lady Montagu, often called "queen of the bluestockings." But of course it was John Adams' reaction that Mercy was most anxious to receive; she had never been able to rest easy about a literary production until John had passed on it, yet she could not resist needling him even as she sent him a copy of her book. Often it seemed that Mercy was compelled to prod and pick at John as if she were trying to assure herself of a friendship which she was afraid was lost, was too proud to show her need for, and yet could not bear to part with.

> *Though the vice-president of the United States and his lady may have forgotten Mrs. Warren, yet her former friend, Mr. Adams, will accept a small volume from the hand of their sincere and very Humble servant*
>
> M. *Warren.*

In spite of the jibe, John rose to the occasion handsomely. "However foolishly some European Writers may have sported with American Reputation for Genius, Literature and Science," he replied, "I know not where they will find a female Poet of their own to prefer to the ingenious Author of these Compositions." As for the vice president and Mr. Adams, he said, they spoke in partnership.

Mercy should have been gratified and indeed she acknowledged that John's letter had been "in the stile of my old friend"; yet she could not let well enough alone. The letter had arrived unsealed. "Does not an unsealed letter from you, sir," she asked, "appear like a diminution of that confidential intercourse that long subsisted." And as she wrote, she thought of other diminutions. For over a year she had brooded about John's statement that it was not his fault if he had listened "to the uninterrupted Ebulitions of the public wrath" aimed at James Warren. Now she picked up the offensive phrase. At least she could never tax herself with a want of attention to "a friend I thought unimpressable by the *Ebullitions* of party or political malice."

John sighed. "A Civil war, Madam," he wrote, "is in my opinion a very serious thing." Although he could not forget the affection for old friends, he could not forget the politics of old friends either, particularly at such a critical time as Shays's Rebellion. And when those old friends continued to embrace principles which he could not approve, it was impossible that "there should be the same confidence between them" as there once was. When John Adams had finished, he reread what he had written. Perhaps more of the affection remained than he had suspected for he did not send the letter. Instead he took up a fresh sheet of paper and stated briefly that the unsealed letter was unintentional. It was the fault of a careless secretary.

But if Mercy was mollified by John's note and pleased by the Federalists' reception of her book, she was in no way softened in her attitude toward Federalist policy. Like other Anti-Federalists in Massachusetts, she regarded every step of the new government with suspicion. Hamilton's funding system she called "a monster . . . the parent of a national debt that would hang on the neck of America to the latest generations." She was dubious about the revenue system ("It ill becomes an infant republic to shackle its commerce, to check its manufactures, to damp the spirits of agriculture by imposts and excises") and she was critical of the style of life in the capital which, according to all reports, was high toned and courtly. (James Warren found it curious to see "a whole Country within the short period of ten years struggling with energy to get rid of Monarchy, and the same Country makeing every effort to fix another.") Indeed, so sensitive were some people to the idea of a strong centralized government that they even found the word *national* offensive; clergymen praying for the new government had to take care to say "federal" or perhaps "general" government.

Critical as they were, however, the Warrens claimed that they were able to watch the political scene with nothing more than curiosity and amusement; but if they were really so aloof, they did not remain so for long. With the establishment of the judicial system and the superstructure of courts, the long arm of the government reached directly into the Warren family, upsetting it perhaps as nothing had before. The United States Circuit Court opened in Boston in November 1790, and one of its first cases was *Nicholas and Jacob Van Staphorsts* vs. *Winslow Warren*. The old litigation had caught up with Winslow although he still tried to avoid it by insisting that there was no record of his case in the New Haven court. Yet, as he undoubtedly suspected, the records were complete, available, and irrefutable and all he was able to do was postpone judgment until the spring session.

Meanwhile he wrote again to Henry Knox, asking for a place in the army. There was reason to think the request might be granted. Indians had been fighting on the western border of the country, had recently delivered a rather crushing defeat to the United States forces, and now President Washington was calling for more troops. For Mercy the thought of such a venture, with or without Winslow, was odious. She had always believed that the Appalachian ridges were the natural boundary of the United States and that it was unbecoming for a new republic to lust after western territory, but of course with the possibility of Winslow's involvement she was, first and last, concerned with the danger. Yet she did not protest. "I dared not disclose the feelings of my soul," she confessed later, "for fear of the imputation of womanly weakness, maternal anxiety, and the creation of all apprehensions . . . that had only an imaginery existence but I ever thought reason pointed to evils that did not spring from female timidity."

Winslow's commission as second lieutenant arrived in March, but not his orders. He was still waiting for his orders as the circuit court met again and sentenced him to one month in prison, beginning immediately.

Mercy could not have been surprised, yet she had obviously been unable to prepare herself for the magnitude of the storm that engulfed her. She was like a bird buffeted; even the rhythm of her distress was like a bird's. She wanted to "fly to his assistance," she wrote Winslow. She could not command herself; she sank, she was lifted, she was tossed. What could she do? How could she be still? But in the midst of her pain, Mercy was also angry. The circuit court had gone against all the conventions of the state courts — indeed, Mercy contended, it had gone against the tenets of civilized society in its treatment of Winslow. Although confined, debtors normally were not subject to the same restrictions as prisoners committed for graver offenses, but Congress had as yet enacted no bankruptcy law (an unpardonable oversight, according to James); consequently, there was no distinction between debtors and felons and Winslow was treated like a common thief. Specifically, he was denied exercise and the liberty of the yard. If this seemed a minor miscarriage of justice, to Anti-Federalists it was an early symptom of tyranny, a foretaste of what they might expect from federal courts, and new evidence of the central government's indifference to states and individuals. "Shall the citizens of America," Mercy cried, "be subjected to the severities of the Divan or the usages of the Bastille?"

Actually, as Mercy and James both recognized, the discrimination against Winslow as a debtor was of more advantage to him than the liberty of the yard would have been, for now he was a martyr; Anti-Federalists rallied around his cause and even the General Court argued his case on the floor. (If a body of government just put in power was going on like this, one irate member contended, it was time for the people to rise up.) In Plymouth people were constantly calling on the Warrens out of sympathy or curiosity or perhaps both; in any case Mercy felt as if she were on public display. "I wish I could entirely seclude myself from company," she said, but, as it happened, on one occasion she even had to entertain members of the Supreme Court visiting Plymouth. "It was painful for me to go through the honors of the table," she confessed, when all she wanted was to be left alone, to secrete herself, to write to Winslow. She wrote often. "Can I do anything for you?" she would ask. "Let me know if you have a room to yourself, if it is airy and comfortable, in your depredation of exercise, you must be careful of your diet." And then: "What if I should send a few cakes . . . would you laugh?"

With all the attention that Winslow's case was receiving, it seemed quite likely that he might not have to serve his full term. This prospect, however, only presented new fears to Mercy. From prison to the western border to fight Indians — what consolation was there in that? "The idea of going into the army has been painful to me *indeed,*" she wrote, "but I hope for opportunities for conversing freely on that subject before you can go further." But Mercy never had that opportunity. Winslow was released about a week early but he wrote his mother that he would not be coming to Plymouth. He would leave directly to join the army. Perhaps it was on this condition that he had been released, for he implied that it would be "best" if he did not go home.

In any case, whatever his reasons Mercy had difficulty accepting them. "Why did you wish to hurry off so soon?" she cried. "Why, do I ask." Yet as she wrote, first one letter and then another on the same day, adding bits from hour to hour, she gradually became acquiescent, not from conviction but from exhaustion, "as a wayward child," she said, "is hushed into stillness from mere fatigue." She tried to comfort herself with his promise that he would write often ("You certainly *will not forget* it") and to look forward to his safe return, but this was not enough. If she could not see him, keep him with her, or follow him, she felt impelled to give more of herself than a letter could possibly contain; and so Mercy bequeathed to Winslow the copyright on her book of poems. She did not know if there was any value in the volume, she said, but there was "nothing else I can properly call my own." By the time she had finished the letter it was the next day; she had been refreshed by a few hours' sleep and was able to promise that she would be as cheerful as possible during his absence. Like a lesson learned by that wayward child she had spoken of, she repeated, "I shall not be afraid of evil tidings."

In the first weeks after Winslow's departure, Mercy was encour-

aged by a note from Henry Knox, assuring her that the western
forces under General St. Clair were so respectable that it was not
expected that they would even meet with hostile Indians. Although
Mercy could have had little faith in General St. Clair, who had once
abandoned Fort Ticonderoga to the enemy and was now known to
be broken in health, she tried valiantly to suppress her fears and to
pretend that Winslow's tour of duty was little more than a glorified
sightseeing expedition, a rare opportunity for a man who had examined civilization at its most sophisticated levels to observe it now at
its most primitive.

Winslow was obviously looking forward to the experience. He
had several letters of introduction to General St. Clair which should
put him in a favorable position, he said, and he believed he would
pass away "a year or two in the most agreable manner." Certainly
his first stopover in New York was agreeable. "You would be surprised & astonished," he wrote his mother, "to view the Superiority
of this City & its Inhabitants in Comparison to those of Boston. It is
a new world — there is Liberality — Politeness of European Towns
so much Cleverness Civility of good manners. I am disgusted with
Boston — I wish to God You could visit NYork."

A few days after writing this cheerful letter, Winslow joined his
regiment in Brunswick, New Jersey, for the long march across the
state of Pennsylvania. From the first, it was apparent that Winslow,
contrary to his expectations, was not going to be charmed either by
the wilderness or by army life. Indeed, he found nothing agreeable:
the woods were gloomy, the mountains were stony (on the seven-
mile march across Laurel Hill he had not once touched "the face
of the Earth" because of rocks and stones), the country was so
wretched that even the birds had deserted it, and little water was to
be found yet it was always damp ("notwithstanding we were under
tents — we would wring water from our blanketts in the morning"). As for the land on the western side of the mountains, it
could not be compared to the country on the Kennebec "in point
of fertility — Climate — wood — pleasantness of situation or any

other agreable thing." The people had no luxuries and nothing to drink but culled whiskey. "Tell our countrymen what fools they are," Winslow wrote, "to emigrate here."

But unpleasant as the situation might be it was not, Winslow insisted, dangerous. They were 600 strong in Pittsburg, 2300 more were waiting with St. Clair at Fort Washington, and when the army was collected there would be a total of perhaps 3600 — "sufficient, unquestionably, to Penetrate the Wilderness." Yet this was not completely reassuring to Mercy, for even as he wrote, Winslow said that savages were lined up on the other side of the Allegheny River, staring at their encampment. And only a few days before, Winslow had visited Braddock's Field ten miles from Pittsburg, the scene of General Braddock's terrible defeat by the Indians in 1755. "I viewed with different emotions, as you may well suppose, the whole ground," Winslow wrote. It was thirty-six years later, yet "the Bones of above 1100 men still lay above ground — & the trees are loaded with grape & musket shot." Winslow cut lead out of a few oak trees; he picked up a piece of a skull bone, a piece of a rib, and a piece of leather that had been part of a harness and he sent them home to Mercy to save as curiosities.

"We received yesterday," Mercy replied, "the reliques picked up on Braddock's field. My own sensations and reflections on the occasion I will not attempt to describe."

On August 29 Winslow wrote the last letter home that he would be able to write for some time. Within forty-eight hours his regiment would be starting the six-hundred-mile trip by boat down the Ohio River to Fort Washington, where they would pick up supplies and join General St. Clair. From there they would march to Miami village and then to Detroit "so that I shall soon be going nearer to you," he said. "If we should be Established in that Country & I suppose we shall — we shall have a regular convey over to Albany by the Lakes."

For the next two months the only news that Mercy had was an occasional item in the newspaper. The "little" western army was in

general health, she read (she resented the word *little*); the weather
was cold in Ohio; there were said to be 1500 warriors waiting in
Miami for the army. She continued to write to Winslow, not knowing if or where he would receive the letters but she had to try to
penetrate the forests that separated them. They were very real to
her, those forests, and as the weeks passed in silence they grew
thicker and darker. It came to the point where she could no longer
make small talk in her letters; the distance was too great, she said.
All she could do was to pray for Winslow — *"my* Winslow," she
called him. "I am often asked when I expect to see my Winslow.
What can I reply?"

In the middle of December 1791 Boston received the news that
General St. Clair had been defeated on November 4, his army
trapped and all but annihilated on a small hill overlooking the Wabash River. Everything, it seemed, had gone wrong for the army:
their supplies had not arrived on time, their ranks had been drasti-
cally reduced by deserting militiamen (a miserable lot of emigrants,
Winslow had written), and their commander, St. Clair, although
brave enough, was neither experienced nor adept in fighting Indians
and in addition was so sick and crippled that he had to be lifted onto
his horse. Like others, Abigail Adams wanted to know "Who &
who have been in fault," but in the end this did not matter. The fact
remained that along the Wabash, a hill was littered with the bodies
of scalped young men, just as Braddock's Field had been littered a
generation before. And among the dead was Winslow Warren.

On hearing the news, young Harrison Gray Otis responded as anyone would have who knew Mercy. "Good God," he cried, "what a
dismal Stroke for poor Aunt Warren, it will kill her I fear."

XIII

ALL HER LIFE Mercy had fought battles of will — her will against the Lord's, the Lord's will against hers; she had fought on both sides and, if sometimes she had struck a victory for the Lord, it was never completely decisive, never final, but then no battle had been as fierce as the one she engaged in after the death of Winslow. There were days when she was convinced that she would be destroyed by the battle (for months she did not leave the house); days when she thought she had won a round for the Lord and then suddenly she would see Winslow's face before her — smiling, teasing, *alive;* days when she could not tear her mind away from what she called those "forlorn" mountains of the west; and days when she hammered at time itself, longing to reverse it. Why had she not found some way to stop Winslow from going? she cried. Why had the family not united to prevent him? Sometimes in the name of the Lord she rebuked herself for fighting, but then she would come to her own defense: "We are not forbidden to *feel,*" she said. Sometimes she told herself the story of Xenophon, who when informed of his son's death on the battlefield did not interrupt what he was doing. "Alas, I knew he was mortal," he said, and went about his business. Mercy marveled that "cold philosophy" could produce such resignation and then she rejected that cold philosophy. Stoic insensibility, she said, was a vice not a virtue.

Yet in the end Mercy became resigned. That she struggled so long was a tribute to her vitality; that she finally submitted was a tribute to her religion. "May I ever remember," she wrote George,

"I have no right to call anything *my own.*" All she asked now was
to be firmly established on the path of duty until, as she said, "the
end of my walk."

Chief among her duties, after her duty to her family, was the
completion of her history. Self-imposed duty as it was, it was none-
theless compulsive, for in writing the history of her country Mercy
was giving shape to her own life as well (she often referred to her
history as an "Historical and Biographical Work") and rounding
out the lives of the three men who had been so important to her: her
brother James, who had led the fight for liberty and been consumed
by it; her husband, James, who had worked all his life for liberty
and so often been maligned; and her son Winslow, killed prematurely in the service of his country and who, perhaps more than
anyone else, had encouraged her to complete this history. Indeed, it
was one of his last wishes. "Revise & correct and make it perfect,"
he had said, "for which you ought to appropriate a number of hours
every day." Mercy had long ago finished the early sections and had
submitted them to James Winthrop, who had duly admired the style,
approved the organization, and commended the accuracy with one
slight exception: he had thought she was a bit too hard on Thomas
Hutchinson. Recently Mercy had been working on the war years
and reviewing the period with her friends Henry Knox and Benjamin Lincoln. Just prior to Winslow's arrest in the spring, she had
written to Elbridge Gerry for his assessment of some of the principal
characters. "Is Patrick Henry a good or a bad man?" she had asked.
What had become of Henry Laurens? What was the real character
of Robert Morris? Mercy's desk was filled with notes and notebooks
but at the moment she could not face them. She needed time to recover from her grief.

Fortunately during the next difficult years there were private sat-
isfactions within the Warren family which helped to restore Mercy's
spirit. James, in better health than he had been for several winters
("young, florid, and finely for a man of his years and sorrows," Mercy
said), had been appointed to the governor's advisory council, a mark

of respect which he must have appreciated in spite of the fact that he tended to disparage nonelective offices. It meant of course that he was away from home periodically, but he filled the absences with his affectionate letters. "I constantly contemplate you," he wrote, ". . . at one time as coming down with a Chearful & Enchanting smile to breakfast . . . then turning to literary pursuits and so on from one stage to another. As yet no Husband ever loved & respected a Wife more."

George was also in the government as a representative from Maine and, although away from home, he too was a source of comfort to Mercy. He wrote regularly, shared Mercy's literary interests, sent her as a lifetime loan the watch that Winslow had given him, and wrote to General Knox asking that Winslow's effects be returned to the family. (A small trunk finally arrived — unlocked and with only part of an old journal and a few papers inside.) Strangely enough, however, in trying to fill the gap that Winslow had left, George unwittingly brought out many of the same anxieties in his mother. In Mercy's letters there are refrains, although in a lower key, of the old worries over Winslow. George was extravagant. James and Mercy were astonished at the dimensions of the house that he built in Maine, at the "magnitude" of his projects, and at the amount of land that he continued to acquire. The hall in his home was so large, they suggested half-jokingly, they were afraid it might be appropriated as a dancing room. Was he overextending himself? Was he calculating accurately? "I cannot bear the thought of your being in debt to any man." And like Winslow (and perhaps more like his uncle Joseph Otis), George had a propensity for acquiring enemies. Indeed, he was continually in trouble — quarreling with the local minister ("Is it not best you should concede a little?" Mercy asked), antagonizing local politicians, and embroiling himself in controversies until Mercy cried out that she had "a thousand fears" for him.

It was Henry who brought his parents the greatest comfort: he presented them with a grandchild. Henry and Mary Winslow had been married in November, one week before Winslow's death (still another instance in Mercy's life of the Lord giving with one hand while taking with the other). Mercy seemed to have approved of Mary, or Polly (the eighteenth-century nickname for Mary), who was an amiable girl, according to other members of the family, and "the mistress of a good & affectionate heart," according to Mercy. Polly was probably not intellectually inclined and she may have been a mite sloppy, for Mercy counseled her against reading novels and warned her against becoming slipshod after she was married. "There is nothing," Mercy said, "more disgusting than the appearance of a slatternly woman." But whatever Polly's shortcomings, Mercy was ready to forgive her at the arrival eleven months later (on Mercy's birthday) of Marcia Otis Warren. Mercy was captivated by Marcia and particularly pleased that she had been given Mercy's own pet name, the one she had used in her early correspondence with Abigail Adams. "Marcia Otis is a very fine girl," Mercy wrote George, and ". . . she is not tongue-tied as that is not a deficiency incident to the family on either side." And in spite of her vow not to think in possessive terms, Mercy began referring to her granddaughter as "my little Marcia."

Mercy had recovered her interest in life. She was keeping abreast with her voluminous correspondence, accompanying James to Boston from time to time as he attended council meetings, advising George on household questions (sending him asparagus seeds, inquiring about his housekeeper), and except for an occasional complaint of lameness she seemed by the middle of the 1790s to be feeling well. Yet she could not bring herself to complete the history. The trouble now was not with herself but with the country. Under the leadership of the Federalists, the country was teetering on the brink of a foreign war and moving inexorably (so Mercy felt) toward monarchy. How could she tell the story of the republican experiment when she was not sure that the experiment would even survive the decade? She might, of course, have concluded her history with the Treaty of Paris, as John Adams said later she should have done, but she was a moralist and wanted to place the revolution in a moral perspective; she was a dramatist and wanted to reach a creditable conclusion. And in the present state of affairs Mercy could neither represent the revolution as successful nor could she yet admit to its failure. Besides, if Mercy terminated her story with the war, she would be leaving unsaid many of the things she was determined to say. She wanted to set the record straight, for instance, about her family's position in regard to Shays's Rebellion, the Constitution, and more recently the French Revolution, but Mercy did not have the heart to tackle these questions now. Just as she had abandoned her history in a discouraging period of the war, so now in a period of extreme dissension she put her history aside, refusing to bring it to a conclusion.

The divisions in the 1790s were perhaps particularly bitter because, although no one had expected the country to be without differences, few people had anticipated that with the Constitution universally accepted, the country would break so decidedly and with such animosity into two camps — in effect, Whig and Tory all over again, divided on many issues but basically on the old question of how far the people could be trusted to govern themselves. As the issues emerged, the people lined up either beside Hamilton (who believed in an energetic government supported by and supporting organized business, closely supervised by a strong executive, and in general controlled by those most qualified to govern) or beside Jefferson (who favored an agrarian republic, opposed a large national debt, and was committed to defending local rights and allowing power to rest in the hands of the people). The Hamiltonians were the Federalists; the Jeffersonians, many of them old Anti-Federalists, called themselves Republicans, and what they lacked in formal, conventional party structure they made up for in passion. Both parties upheld the Constitution. Indeed, because each felt the Constitution was safe only in its own hands, because each was convinced that the other was plotting to subvert the government, the two parties magnified their differences, polarized their positions, and turned on each other with a degree of hostility that has seldom been matched in the history of the country. Certainly Mercy Warren regarded the struggle between the parties as a mortal struggle for the survival of the republic. Far from thinking that the two-party system would be a permanent feature of American politics, she would not even dignify the parties with their familiar names. Like many others, she referred to the Federalists as Monarchists; after all, *federalism,* as it implied belief in a confederacy as opposed to belief in a central government, was what Mercy adovocated. The Republicans she described as simply those who "adhered to the principles of the revolution."

Nothing was more divisive than the French Revolution. In the beginning Americans generally had welcomed it; some were simply happy that their old ally was making its own declaration of independence and others had a more grandiose view and regarded the French Revolution as the second act in the divine drama of establishing God's will upon earth. Puritans had, of course, never doubted that the American Revolution was the first act and that America was still, as it had always been, "a city upon a hill," the chosen place of the Lord, the testing ground for an international utopia. They had been long accustomed to thinking in worldwide terms. In 1764 in one of his loyal moods, James Otis had said that his most ambitious wish was to see "Great Britain at the head of the world, and to see my King, under God, the father of mankind." Now, of course, Americans believed that God's ultimate plan was to rid the world of all kings and tyrants and make universal the liberty that had been initiated in America. Mercy remarked once to George on how fortunate they were to be living in a period when "we have such a clear revelation of the will of God"; but of course, as Mercy was the first to point out, God's will could not be realized without the help of man and to date man had scarcely shown himself to be ready, willing, or sufficiently enlightened to do his part, at least on any extended scale.

The French Revolution gave Americans a brief flurry of hope.

Perhaps more important psychologically, it restored their faith in the American Revolution and released them for a short time from the doubts, frustrations, and disappointments which were apparently the lot of practicing republicans. Indeed, Americans became intoxicated with the French Revolution and celebrated it with a gaiety and abandon that they had never been able to accord their own. In Boston people began addressing each other as "Citizen" and "Citizess"; they roared through the streets singing "Ça Ira"; they gave civic feasts, culminating in an unforgettable festival (January 1793) in which a one-thousand-pound ox labeled *Aristocracy* was roasted whole, dragged through the town on a cart drawn by fifteen horses, and then served to the public (along with two hogsheads of punch) on outdoor tables set up in State Street. At the same time more distinguished Francophiles held their own banquet in Fanueil Hall, presided over by the lieutenant governor, Citizen Samuel Adams.

The dream was short-lived. Within a few weeks after the famous ox feast, news reached America that the French Revolution had been taken over by mad extremists, the king had been beheaded, property destroyed, people killed, and atrocities committed, Mercy Warren said, that would "freeze the soul of humanity." Moreover, England and France were at war. For Americans who had never yet been able to avoid involvement in the quarrels between these two old enemies, this news had, of course, grave implications. Both American parties declared their determination to preserve neutrality, but psychologically they were never neutral and as time went on, they became increasingly partisan, increasingly emotional, and increasingly vicious — with the Federalists drawing toward England and the stable, steady world that England represented and the Republicans supporting France which, in spite of the atrocities, was committed to liberty. Americans were always inclined to view the question of authority in ultimate terms and so now Federalists saw the war as a conflict between anarchy and ordered government, while for Republicans it was a war between tyrants and the people. Like everyone else, Mercy deplored the bloodshed in France but she was impatient with those Americans who could not, as she said, "distinguish between principles and events," who could not see that the cause of liberation was more important than the means used to attain it. Yet Mercy, like most people in both parties, did not want war.

Still, a nation could not take unlimited abuse. Because of her command of the seas, England was the worst offender; she violated American neutrality with a flagrance that was hard even for Federalists to endure — impressing seamen, seizing shipping, and in general denying the freedom of the seas to America whenever she used that freedom to trade with France. With each transgression, Republicans became more attached to France, more incensed at Britain, and more militant. Writing from Philadelphia to Henry Warren, Samuel Allyne Otis, of the Federalist branch of the family, expressed his concern:

"How far our partialities to French madness may have tended to embroil us, is a subject on which you and I shall not agree, & therefore I am silent. I am persuaded we agree in deprecating a war."

In the spring of 1794 President Washington in one last attempt to save the peace sent John Jay, Chief Justice of the United States, to London to try to negotiate a treaty. Republicans disapproved of the mission. They did not think a treaty was desirable at this time; they believed that Jay was pro-British; they contended that it was improper for him as Chief Justice to act in a double capacity and embarrassing for the United States that a man in such a high office should, as Mercy said, "supplicate at the levee of a British minister." Nevertheless, there was nothing to do but to wait for the outcome.

In the interim, there was an insurrection at home and cause for further party conflict. The farmers of western Pennsylvania had long been unhappy about Alexander Hamilton's excise tax on whiskey, which they claimed was discriminatory and oppressive (they were in the habit of converting grain to whiskey so that they could move it more easily over the mountains); but the question that aroused the nation was not so much the justice of the law but the government's method of handling the farmers' rebellion. Washington, Hamilton, and the Federalists saw the uprising as a test of the government's ability to enforce its laws; accordingly, 15,000 troops were assembled, put under the command of Hamilton, and marched on the western counties. As it turned out, however, the insurgents had largely dispersed by the time the troops arrived and the government's show of force appeared so large and disproportionate that Republicans charged that the whole venture had been motivated not so much by a need to restore order (500 men could have done that, Mercy said) as by a desire to enhance the power of the president and, in Mercy's words, "to establish the basis of a standing army, and other projects approaching to despotic sway."

Such was the political climate in the spring of 1795 when John Jay returned to America with his treaty. There were concessions in the treaty but these seemed almost inconsequential beside the blatant fact that the treaty denied neutrals the right to trade with belligerent nations (even in those items which had generally been considered noncontraband) and forced the United States into a position that favored Great Britain. Even Federalists were disappointed. Republicans were outraged, but in spite of their opposition the treaty was ratified on June 24. Federalists said the choice was between the treaty and war and they chose the treaty; Republicans said that America had sold out to the British. What was the purpose, they asked, in winning independence if it was to be thrown away so cheaply? What was the purpose of befriending an old enemy (whose principles and policies were still inimical) and alienating an old friend? Clearly the treaty would anger France, and instead of preserving peace it would only endanger it. "Alas, humiliated America!" Mercy sighed.

Nothing that happened in postwar America caused such wide-scale disruption as the ratification of Jay's treaty. Rioting broke out in the major cities; stones were thrown at Hamilton when he tried to speak in favor of the treaty; John Jay was burned in effigy in so many towns, he said, that he could have found his way across the country by the light from the fires. James Warren and Samuel Adams denounced the treaty in such savage terms that John Adams accused them of being unconstitutional. Indeed, in Boston there was a week that reminded old-timers of the Hutchinson days. Mobs, contending that they had a natural right to riot, attacked the homes of prominent Federalists and were eventually stopped not by the governor but by an organization of concerned citizens. The governor was Samuel Adams, who had spent his life hating the British and could not stop now. When asked to stop the rioting, he affected surprise. It was only boys having "water melon frolicks," he said.

Republicans were, however, republicans too, and they knew well enough that the only way to change the government was to vote in a new administration. Although Washington did not formally announce his decision to retire until he delivered his farewell address in September 1796, there were rumors in the spring that he might retire and by summer both parties were discussing candidates. The Republicans put their hopes on Thomas Jefferson, and John Adams, who as vice president was the obvious choice of the Federalists, began in his usual fashion to deny that he had any further political ambitions and at the same time to gird himself for the storm. On one day he wrote Abigail that he would actually welcome defeat: "Then for frugality and independence —" he said, "poverty and patriotism — love and a carrot bed." On another day he winced at the very idea, imagining his feeling if he were forced to continue "a foolish, mortifying, humiliating, uncomfortable residence [as vice president in Philadelphia] for two tedious months after I shall be known to be skimmed."

John Adams was sixty-one years old now; he had lost most of his teeth and much of his hair but he could boast to Abigail that were he near, he could soon convince her that he was "not above forty." The young John was very much alive in the squat, bustling figure of the vice president; he was still subject to the same vanities as he had been in his youth, prone to the same despondencies, still introspective, witty, impetuous, impatient, restless, blunt, curious, skeptical (he found nothing more exasperating than another man's credulity). He was still inclined to worry about the impression he made, yet he was, as ever, incapable of compromising his beliefs for the sake of the popularity he would so have enjoyed. In his two terms as vice president he had learned to preside over the Senate with appropriate restraint, but he found this difficult, just as he found it difficult to sit still for long periods of time and listen to endless debates — a business, he said, which "is not very charming to a man accustomed to the conversation and amusemnts of Paris, of London, and The Hague."

Politically, it seemed to John that he had changed little. Just as in the days when he had argued with Mercy, he still believed, as he always would, that man was motivated by selfishness and that life was a "militant state on a militant planet." Contrary to the myth that seemed to be a built-in feature of American culture, he did not believe that Americans were morally superior to other people. Time had, if anything, deepened his distrust of humanity. Unlike the Federalists who had faith only in the so-called aristocracy, and unlike the Republicans who trusted "the people," John Adams trusted neither aristocrats nor common people and continued to think of them as distinct political groups with different interests. Once when he remarked that the people had a share in the sovereignty of the government, he was reminded by Samuel Adams that in a republic the *whole* sovereignty was supposed to reside in the people. Yet John insisted that it was not he but his Republican friends who had deserted their principles by confusing the doctrines of the American and French revolutions — by thinking, as the French did, that a simple government of one body was a superior government (a woman with one breast was *simple,* John snorted), by mistaking libertinism for liberty, by believing equality was natural and fraternity possible without legislation to check force by force. Yet despite differences, John Adams had supported his Republican cousin Samuel when he ran for governor though he supposed (and quite rightly) that Samuel would not support him for president. Samuel would not find him "supple enough to the French," John said.

Losing friends, however, was only one of the hardships John would have to bear if elected. He had no illusions about the office. Being the man that he was, he would feel a certain satisfaction in *being* president just as he would be indignant if he were not elected, but he did not look forward to the trials nor did he expect to enjoy the duties. "I hate speeches, messages, addresses . . . I hate levees and drawing rooms. I hate to speak to a thousand people to whom I have nothing to say," he wrote. As for Abigail, she dreaded becoming the First Lady and being "fastened up hand and foot and tongue to be shot at as our Quincy lads do at the poor geese and turkeys."

But during the summer of 1796, with the election still ahead, John and Abigail tried to put presidential thoughts out of their minds. In May they left Philadelphia for Quincy (part of Braintree had been renamed) where John resumed the life of a farmer, returning to his diary to record the long-neglected pleasures of his humble routine. He wrote out of pure joy so that he might stretch his days and linger over each small experience. He rose in time to enjoy the "earliest Birds," he wrote; he paid a visit to his new barn; he attended to the wind and responded to the weather ("a fine soft rain, in a clock calm"); he talked about black grass, clover, seaweed, and manure; he reeled off numbers — reveling, it seemed, in their precise and professional sound: 51 bushels of barley, 3 loads of salt hay, 12 hands at work, 6 hogsheads of lime, 2 barrels of cider. As the summer wore on and the bushels and the barrels accumulated, word came back to Quincy of preelection activities in New York, Philadelphia, Boston; but in John Adams' diary the important news was that caterpillars were in the corn, the hired man was drinking, John had stumbled over a wheelbarrow in the dark and hurt his shin. It was the most carefree summer he had ever spent, he said, but "Alas! What may happen to reverse all this?"

In August Abigail, accompanied by Mrs. Samuel Otis, journeyed to Plymouth to visit Mercy Warren for a few days. It had been twelve years since the two friends had seen each other, but if they felt some restraint in talking about politics, they felt no restraint in talking about grandchildren. Mercy had the pleasure of introducing

Marcia to Abigail, who was apparently charmed, for in future letters Abigail invariably referred to Mercy's granddaughter as "the Lovely Marcia." That there were future letters was an indication of the success of the visit. Writing to George, Mercy said that the visit "was unexpected — friendly, politic or accidental I know not, but she appeared very *clever*," by which Mercy meant, according to the eighteenth-century use of the word *clever*, that Abigail had been agreeable and good-natured.

John Adams delayed his return to Philadelphia until December, arriving just before the electors were to cast their ballots. In the next weeks, waiting for the votes to come in and anticipating the alternatives, he asked himself how he would conduct himself as president of the Senate if he were defeated. How could he bear to open the ballots and announce that Jefferson was president? In the event of his election, how would he perform at his inauguration? As it turned out, he need not have worried on either score. On February 8 he was able to announce to the Senate that John Adams, with 71 electoral votes, had been elected president and Thomas Jefferson, with 69 votes, had been elected vice president. (That the president and vice president were not of the same political party was due to both the unsatisfactory electoral system and the political maneuvering of Alexander Hamilton.) As for his inaugural performance, John Adams wrote Abigail that he had done well. Indeed, he said, in the opinion of most people his speech had been "the sublimest thing ever exhibited in America."

The French, however, were not pleased with the speech. Already provoked by Jay's treaty and now affronted that the Americans had elected a pro-British Federalist to be president, they claimed that the president's speech was unfriendly. In retaliation they ordered Charles Pinckney, the American minister, out of the country and at the same time began harassing American shipping and confiscating neutral cargos. Furthermore they announced that any impressed American seaman on a British vessel would be hanged when captured.

So began the new administration. In the key position, John Adams, who had used so much ink to define presidential power and had made ready to throw his weight to whatever side necessary to maintain the nation's equilibirum, tried to take command only to find that the power he wrote about was too often elusive or simply ineffective. On the one hand, much of the power of the party that had elected him lay in the hands of Alexander Hamilton, who used it offstage. On the other hand, John Adams' power, although not actually diminished, often *seemed* diminished by the stature of the man who had preceded him — "the Great Washington" who was already a legend and to Adams' never-ending irritation all but deified by the Federalists. Whatever routines or rituals Washington had inaugurated could not be violated without arousing indignation, Adams felt; whatever secretaries Washington had appointed to his cabinet were his legacy and under public protection. It would have been difficult, of course, for any man to have followed Washington in office but in addition it was an inauspicious time to be president. Not only was the country inflamed, it was so equally divided in its differences that no matter how he might shift his weight, John discovered, it was not enough to settle the nation. Nor, as it turned out, was he always judicious about where he took his stand.

Certainly the events of his administration, centered as they were around war with France, were formidable, yet the events alone were not responsible for the tensions. The "French madness" of the Republicans, which Samuel Otis had spoken of, was matched now, if not surpassed, by Federalist hysteria. Indeed, the French Revolution had an extraordinary effect on politics: those who had been Anti-Federalists during the debate over the Constitution, who had been represented as insular, negative, afraid of change, were suddenly the torchbearers, talking not so much about small republics as about world revolution, while those who had been the Constitution makers — creative, daring, forward-looking — were thrust by their fears and suspicions into an ever more conservative and defensive position.

Federalists saw enemies wherever they looked—not just in France, although of course that was the source of the danger, but at home as well. Every criticism of the government was regarded as a possible thread in a vast plot to break down America's strength from the inside. Republican editors (actually no more vicious than many Federalist editors) were believed to be taking orders from the French government; aliens were viewed with suspicion; disagreement was confused with disloyalty; and a person who expressed sympathy for France was automatically a Jacobin and suspected, if not of outright atheism, at least of religious infidelity. Harrison Gray Otis, one of the Federalists' most eloquent spokesmen, talked of "spies, emissaries, exclusive patriots" inciting slaves against their masters, the South against the North, the poor against the rich, the lawless element of society against the law-abiding. "I am ready to profess," he said, "my sincere persuasion that our difficulties with France are not to be imputed to any one man, but to a desperate and misguided party, existing in the bosom of our country, who are in league with other bad citizens resident in France, and with the French nation." So persuaded, the Federalists relied not on the three-man peace mission that was sent to France in 1797 but instead pressed for a larger army, new revenues, and a reinforced navy. And when the peace mission failed in 1798, the Federalists decided that not even armies and navies were adequate protection; they must, in effect, declare war on dissenters.

Hysteria found its way even into the home of the president. Like so many Federalists, Abigail Adams had come to view the European war as a holy war—the frail and righteous forces of Christianity pitted against the invading barbarians. She read and apparently took seriously a book by a Scottish scientist, John Robinson, who offered proof of an international conspiracy against all the religions and governments of Europe. She prayed, of course, that the Christian forces (led by England) would prevail without the help of the United States, but she was in no mood to tolerate Republican sympathy for France or Republican opposition to Federalists.

For public purposes, Abigail learned, as John had said she could, to keep quiet. "Fastened up hand and foot and tongue," she went through her duties as First Lady: giving dinners (often with thirty or forty guests), presiding at levees, receiving visitors ("rising up and sitting down" for hours at a time) but in the early morning between five and eight o'clock when she wrote her personal letters, she let her anger loose. Seldom was there a letter to her sister Mary Cranch that did not include at least one paragraph grumbling about the French, the Republicans, or about the man that Abigail had singled out as her number-one enemy — Benjamin Bache (grandson of Franklin, referred to by the Federalists as Lightning Rod, Jr.) who edited the most vicious of the Republican newspapers, the *Aurora*, and who was in the habit of referring to the president as the "poor old man," the "creature of the Hamiltonians," and the "Duke of Braintree."

Abigail's rage mounted as war seemed more and more inevitable. In the spring of 1798 when it became known that the American envoys had been told that they would not be received by the French government until they had repudiated the militaristic policy expressed in the president's inaugural address and until they had paid the French Directory a substantial sum of money, Abigail fired off a letter to Mercy Warren with a copy of the dispatches (the so-called XYZ papers) which should, in case Mercy needed persuading, be sufficient proof of the "pitch of venality, Rapacity and avarice, the present Rulers of France have arrived at." Actually, the publication of the dispatches did for a brief period bring Americans closer together. John Adams enjoyed a short spell of popularity; Congress passed bills to increase the size of the army and the navy and to empower American war vessels to capture French cruisers and privateers found in American waters. But instead of finding strength in such signs of unity and resolution, Abigail (along with many Federalists) merely became more sensitive to dissent, more susceptible to abuse.

In April Abigail was infuriated to see the president referred to in

the *Aurora* as "old, querilous, Bald, blind, Toothless Adams."
"Nothing," she declared, "will have an effect on Bache until they
pass a Sedition Bill." In May she wrote: "If that fellow [Bache]
. . . is not surpressed, we shall come to a civil war." In July she
turned her wrath on Congress. Frustrated that it had not openly declared war, she demanded, "Why, when we have the thing, should
we boggle at the Name?"

When Congress adjourned a few weeks later, it had not declared
war. It had, however, imposed a direct federal property tax. And it
had passed the Alien Act, by which the president was empowered to
deport aliens who were citizens of an enemy nation in case of war or
the threat of war, and the Sedition Act, which forbade writing or
speaking against the government or the president with the purpose
of bringing them into contempt or stirring up sedition. As a further
step in preparation for war, John Adams had appointed George
Washington commander in chief of the army.

In Plymouth the Warrens observed the proceedings in Philadelphia with despair. For James, who once said that he hoped to live to
see the downfall of kings and conquerors everywhere, it was a great
grief to see America ranged on the side of the kings. No matter
what insults France had offered, England (to judge by Jay's treaty
alone) was still the enemy and would one day, James predicted,
have to be fought again. James was used to being on the losing side
of issues. Ever since the war, he had been a lone voice crying about
first principles; he was the forgotten man — or so he viewed himself
— but never had he felt so lonely, so defeated, as he did in his small
corner in Plymouth, fulfilling his one public duty as justice of the
peace while John Adams was in Philadelphia, as the president of the
United States, preparing to lead the country to war beside George
III. So bitter did James feel about his old friend that he refused to
sign a bipartisan address of loyalty that Plymouth, like so many
towns throughout the country, sent John Adams after the disclosure
of the XYZ dispatches. Henry Warren apparently felt no such com-
punction, but the absence of James's name was conspicuous and

Mercy, still unwilling to sacrifice her friendship with the Adamses, tried to smooth matters over. The general sent the government his best wishes, she wrote Abigail, but these days he addressed "no being below the supreme."

Yet Mercy was no less disillusioned with public policy than James was and no less annoyed by the Federalist party line. She was particularly incensed to find herself as a Republican automatically pushed by the Federalist press into the camp of the infidels. Had she not for years been denouncing Voltaire and his followers? she asked. And what of Gibbon? Did anyone castigate British partisans because of Edward Gibbon's infidelity? Besides, the brutalities that the French had committed were not the result of their infidelity, she insisted; they were the reaction to years of monarchic oppression — the kind of oppression, moreover, that was even now showing up in America. Like most Republicans, Mercy considered the passage of the Alien and Sedition bills to be final proof that the Federalists would do anything, even violate the Constitution, to keep their power and have their way. The one freedom left to the minority in America, she observed in a letter to George, was the freedom to think. "Silence is the only medium of safety for those who have an opinion of their own that does not exactly square with the enthusiasms of the times."

·   ·   ·

The summer of 1798 was generally unhappy for the country and especially unhappy for John Adams. On the way to Quincy after the adjournment of Congress, Abigail took sick and remained sick all summer. She suffered chronically from a combination of diabetes and diarrhea but this time her life seemed to be in danger. John hovered at her bedside, distraught, helpless, finding no comfort in the farm (the wagons loaded with salt hay, the barrels filled with barley went unnoted), and feeling no disposition to fight wars or Republicans. Indeed, without Abigail's companionship, the weight and loneliness of his office seemed almost insupportable. Yet because of his anxiety and perhaps because of his comparative isolation in

Quincy, removed from both the source of his opposition and the source of his political support, John Adams was thrust into an independent frame of mind and into a mood of introspection and reappraisal. And the circumstances, as it turned out, warranted a reappraisal.

In the first place, it seemed uncertain whether the country, divided as it was, would be willing to fight a war with France, at least without more dramatic provocation. The Alien and Sedition bills, which John Adams defended as necessary wartime measures, would have caused less alarm had the country been basically united (as Federalists may have supposed it to be) but as it was the indignation aroused by the passage of the bills and their subsequent operation made it clear that the dissenters were not just a small, vocal minority but a substantial part of the American people. The Federalists did manage to arrest some editors and intimidate others (Benjamin Bache, never silenced, died of yellow fever before his case came to court), but far from making the nation secure the Federalists simply made themselves and their cause more unpopular.

In the second place, there were reports that made John Adams question if a war with France was really going to be necessary. Letters from Europe, particularly those from his son John Quincy, minister to Prussia, informed him of a new attitude of appeasement in the French government; Elbridge Gerry, one of the members of the famous three-man peace mission to France (in fact the infamous member, for he had violated his instructions, stayed in France, and had attempted to negotiate on his own after his colleagues had left), returned to America and reported privately that the French were, indeed, eager to make peace; and, as further evidence that France did not want war, the French government had issued orders that put an end to much of the harassment of American shipping.

Finally, however, John Adams had to ask himself: now that the wheels of war had been set in motion, could he stop them even if he wanted to? By appointing Washington commander in chief of the wartime army, had he stripped himself of the power to make peace?

John had not wanted to elevate Washington again before the people, but actually it was Hamilton, not Washington, whom he feared. If Hamilton succeeded in becoming the second in command, which he was obviously determined to do, he would for all practical purposes, as Washington's long-time protégé and adviser, be head of the army. And John did not like it. He was still enough of an old republican at heart, in spite of what the Warrens might think, to feel uncomfortable about the idea of a large standing army. Certainly he recognized the dangers that could arise from having the army in the wrong hands; and Alexander Hamilton, with his enormous ambition, his lust for military glory, his affinity for intrigue, and his absolute conviction that only he knew what was right for America, was not the man John Adams cared to trust as second in command.

John did his best to persuade Washington to name his three major generals in order of their actual rank at the close of the war: Knox, Charles Pinckney, and Hamilton; but Washington insisted that if he was to serve as commander in chief, Hamilton must have second place. In the end John had to submit, but as the matter dragged on through the summer, with correspondence not only from Washington but from various members of the cabinet, it became increasingly clear that Hamilton himself was manipulating the strings behind stage and at least three members of Adams' cabinet (James McHenry, secretary of war; Timothy Pickering, secretary of state; Oliver Wolcott, secretary of the treasury) were in constant communication with Hamilton and took their orders from him. Under such conditions, not only was the president's authority undermined but there was a distinct possibility that the country, once in danger (so John Adams thought) from the overly democratic forces on the far left, might now be threatened by an aristocratic clique on the far right — the High Federalists, as they came to be known. It also seemed possible that John Adams might have to put his theory of presidential power to the test.

In November John returned to Philadelphia alone (Abigail was much improved but unable to make the journey); in December he delivered an address to Congress which gave no indication that he might be considering a change in foreign policy. Talking to High Federalists in Congress and in his cabinet, he realized that although there was no move at the moment to declare war openly, the word from the Hamilton headquarters was: no appeasement, no concessions, no relaxation of militancy. So in January when John Adams received a letter which stated the French government's willingness to negotiate with America, he kept his counsel. Unfortunately the letter, delivered through roundabout diplomatic channels, was not the direct, unequivocal reassurance that he had sought, yet it was an overture. On February 18, without previously consulting or informing anyone, John Adams sent to the Senate a nomination for a minister plenipotentiary to be sent to the French republic, provided that France would offer more formal assurances of a proper reception.

John had always rather enjoyed shocking people with his outspoken manner and his independent point of view and, while the question before the nation was far too serious for him to be much diverted, still he must have had moments when he was amused at the extent to which he had "electrified the public," as Abigail put it. He was prepared, of course, for opposition in the Hamilton wing of his party and, indeed, the opposition never let up. When the High Federalists could not stop the mission, they tried to delay it and it was eight months before the new envoys (two new members had been added to Adams' original nomination) finally left the country with the prescribed letter from France and even then they left on private orders from Adams that did not have the concurrence or prior knowledge of the three recalcitrant members of the cabinet. But the mission was successful, the war fever gradually subsided, the wartime army was disbanded, and Adams quite rightly took the credit. To the end of his life he found satisfaction in the fact that, no matter how poorly his administration might be judged by posterity, he had as president taken upon himself the responsibility for peace with France.

At the time, however, this may have been small comfort since it brought him few new friends. He did have the support of moderate Federalists, but Republicans, however pleased they may have been with peace, would never forgive him for the Alien and Sedition Acts, and the High Federalists became increasingly hostile, particularly after Adams in a burst of temper replaced two of Hamilton's men (McHenry and Pickering) in his cabinet. So the president spent the last year of his administration, just as he had the first years, plagued by what he called "the two Jugglers behind the Scene": Hamilton, working deliberately to destroy him, and Washington, through no fault of his own casting his shadow relentlessly across John's path. Washington died on December 14, 1799, and his image, awesome enough in life, assumed godlike proportions in death. Replicas of his funeral were held throughout the country, statues commissioned, streets renamed for him, and for months the press was swollen with elegies, tributes, poems, and extravagancies in his honor. (Washington's name was invariably accompanied in print by such epithets as "sainted," "peerless," "revered," "heroic," "immortal.") Actually, John Adams had always liked and admired Washington, but he was discomfited by the myth. Indeed, he grumbled, in time people would be celebrating Washington's birthday as a national holiday and would be making pilgrimages to Mount Vernon as they did to Mecca and Jerusalem. As for John Adams' administration, it would be forever dwarfed by the figure of the first president. The "impious Idolatry to Washington," he declared, "destroyed all [its] Character."

John had been well aware that when he broke with the High Federalists, he jeopardized his chances at a second term, but he found it no easier than he ever had to face the prospect of defeat. Although he was the Federalist candidate for president (Charles Pinckney for vice president), the party never united behind him and Hamilton worked openly to put Pinckney in Adams' place. It was not yet thought proper for a presidential candidate to campaign for himself and so John sat on the sidelines, watching Hamilton ("the bastard Bratt of a Scotch Pedlar," John called him) throw the Federalist party into confusion. In November, a month before the electors were to meet, the Adamses moved to the new federal city on the banks of the Potomac — named, of course, Washington. Here in the damp, unfinished presidential mansion John and Abigail tried to keep warm as they waited for the election results ("No woodcutters nor carters to be had at any rate," Abigail reported. "Congress poured in, but shiver, shiver"). They tried to keep calm while attacks, lies, and rumors surged around them (John was accused of trying to marry one of his sons to a daughter of George III); and in the closing days of their ordeal they tried to comfort each other. On December 8 when the votes were just beginning to come in, the Adamses received word that their son Charles, a once promising lawyer who had recently fallen into debt and taken to drink, had died in New York the ugly death of an alcoholic. For John this was, as he said, "the deepest affliction of my Life"; the prospect of defeat could hardly make him feel more desolate than he felt now.

· · ·

In Plymouth Mercy and James had recently suffered a similar tragedy — their third loss, however, rather than their first. George had died in Maine some months before, following a five-week illness. As always, it was separation from a son when he had needed her that was so hard for Mercy to bear. There was nothing on earth that they would not do for him, she wrote, "but alas! what can we?" Oranges, tamarinds, lemons, confectionary — she longed to send him something, but there was nothing that she had that was not also available in Maine. In January George had submitted to several "tapping" operations and on February 5, after listening to a letter from his mother that was read to him, he died.

Perhaps if it had not been winter Mercy might have attempted to see George during his last illness. For the last two years she had tried to convince James that they should visit Maine. "I tell him he is not too old for such a journey," she wrote, but James felt old and he did not like to leave home. A few years before he had agreed to accompany Mercy to Barnstable, where he had been only once in the last eighteen years, but he had thought it a "mighty business," Mercy said. James was seventy-four years old now, afflicted with palsy as well as gout. Yet in spite of his trembling hands, he did manage on good days to get off letters, shaky as the writing might be; he continued to make commercial transactions; he worked about the farm when he was able, although there came a day when he had to contract for his hay to be cut. (How many hands were necessary to cut and put the hay on board a sloop? he asked Joseph Otis.) But no matter how old he grew, James never lost his interest in politics.

The election of 1800 assumed particular significance for him. His days, he felt, were numbered and if he could not see the kings of the world deposed before he died, he at least wanted to see the Tories (or Federalists) defeated in his own country. Indeed, he was as eager to see John Adams brought low as he was to see Jefferson elevated and when the word came that the Federalists were out and the Republicans were in, James Warren considered it a personal victory.

"I have sat like a Man under the shade of Tree unnoticed," James wrote to Jefferson at his inauguration. "I have seen principles sacrificed to ambition, and consistency of sentiment to the Interest of the Moment."

Not only was James vindicated; rewards were forthcoming. Henry Warren was appointed the Collector of the Port at Plymouth; James Warren, Jr., who had moved back to Plymouth to live with his parents, was made the postmaster.

With the country so obviously on the right tack, Mercy Warren returned to her desk and took up the writing of her history.

XIV

HERE ENDS the 18th Century," a New England diarist wrote on December 31, 1800. "The 19th begins with a fine clear morning wind at S.W."

Neither the new century nor the new administration in Washington, however, changed the character of American thinking. Indeed, it would be another fifteen or twenty years before the nineteenth century would show its colors — particularly in Massachusetts, the stronghold of conservatism and last battleground of the Federalist party. The eighteenth-century man was still in control, less Puritanical but still involved in the same basic conflicts that had engaged him since colonial days, still pursuing, it seemed, the same conversations. He wrote odes to sensibility, essays on purity, diatribes on inebriation; he upheld natural law, debated the advantages and disadvantages of studying a dead language, reviewed the fine points of baptism, paid homage to reason while indulging in the most violent political rhetoric, and bent every effort to acquire the material prosperity that threatened, as he was forever pointing out, to corrupt his soul. Styles had changed, of course: women had given up hoop skirts for décolleté gowns amid much talk of "loose and indecent attire"; young men argued whether straight hair or curled, long hair or short ("à la Brutus") was more republican. There were new turnpikes, toll bridges, and water carts to lay the dust in Boston's streets, a new State House designed by Charles Bulfinch, but these were improvements rather than changes. Actually, the people in Massachusetts felt no need for change. The eighteenth century had been superior, they agreed, to any century and the condition of the human race was tending, as one writer put it, to as "high [a] degree of perfection as the weakness and wickedness of man will allow."

The most conspicuous change was not in the scene but in the cast of characters. Some of the old patriots — Elbridge Gerry, for instance — were still playing their part in politics, but John Hancock had been dead for seven years now, his old ailments having finally caught up with him, and Samuel Adams, although still on hand with another two years to live, was already offstage. Physically helpless, mentally impaired, he spent his time fighting old battles and wandering among old arguments — an "object of compassion," John Adams said. But there were new faces to replace the old. Among the most notable was Harrison Gray Otis, who was known as one of his party's most eloquent spokesmen and as Boston's most gracious host. The youthful rebellion of his Sans Souci days had been a revolt against Puritanism and no more. Politically he was, as he had always been, conservative; socially he was what was termed "a gentleman of the old school," courtly and elegant in the tradition of the Hutchinsons and Olivers of colonial days. His home on Beacon Street was the center of generous hospitality, but unlike the hospitality offered in John Hancock's home a generation before, Otis' was exclusive. Federalists entertained Federalists in the early 1800s, and it was for them that Harrison Gray Otis kept his blue and white Lowestoft punch bowl filled, and for them that he stocked his special ice chest with jellies, whips, and syllabubs.

But as gay and prosperous as Boston society might appear, there were deep strains of insecurity that ran through it, especially on the upper levels. Jefferson could speak confidently in his inaugural address of the country being in the full tide of successful experiment and could call up a picture of America a thousand years in the future, but in Massachusetts men were not at all sure about that experiment and were generally more disposed to look behind them than they were to look ahead. Always enamored of their past, they took comfort now in going over familiar ground as if they sensed but did not want to face the changes that inevitably lay ahead for a country perched as the United States was on the edge of an untamed continent. At the moment they simply did not care to make history; in their time they had rolled a revolution across the stage and now they wanted to read and write about it. Mercy Warren may have been one of the first to begin work on a new history, but she had been joined by a host of others — some attempting, as she was, to bring the record up to date, some retelling and garnishing the old colonial story. Indeed, in New England there were so many histories coming off the press that a disgruntled critic observed that it was not necessary for every New Englander "capable of putting sentences together" to become the historian of his country. Mercy, however, was the only contemporary woman to write a full-scale history of the American Revolution, the only member of the revolutionary generation to write from the Massachusetts point of view, and most significantly she was the only Republican to write such a history.

She had three principal competitors: William Gordon, who had traveled extensively over battlefields during the war and had interviewed many of the leading characters, but who had forfeited the consideration he might have expected from the American public by publishing his history first in England and adjusting it to British taste; David Ramsay, a doctor from South Carolina, a moralist and a moderate Federalist, known as the first native historian of the Revolution; and John Marshall, the first volume of whose *Life of George Washington* appeared in 1804, a year before Mercy's history, and was its most serious competitor. In trying to raise subscriptions for Mercy's history, a lady in Boston wrote apologetically that she had met with little success; *The Life of George Washington,* she said, "forestals, if not wholly precludes" the sale of Mrs. Warren's work.

John Marshall had several advantages over Mercy: he was a man and so was automatically taken more seriously; he was the Chief Justice of the United States; and he was a Federalist who represented Federalism at its most statesmanlike level and who at a time when they were on the defensive gave to Federalists a renewed feeling of their place in history and a sense of their identity. (Federalists, he said, were those who grasped the organic nature of the country and acted in response to the total requirements of a situation rather than in accordance to a set of preconceived, fixed principles.) Moreover, Marshall's book came out first, it had a greater appeal to Boston society, which was at the moment largely Federalist, and finally it had a better title. *The Life of George Washington* was a misleading title (Washington was the star of his story, not the subject) but it sold books.

Mercy's history was, of course, totally Republican and filled with principles. How else, she asked, could a nation maintain its direction? To reject principles, to say — as John Marshall did — that principles might have been useful in founding a nation but were of no value, possibly even injurious, in the running of a nation, was to reject history itself, for principles were the product of history, the invariables that remained when the past had been sifted for truth. And truth was Mercy's goal. In writing her history, she determined, she said, "that the strictest veracity should govern her heart, and the most exact impartiality be the guide of her pen"; and indeed she did display standards of accuracy as high as any of her competitors, perhaps an even broader appreciation of the total pattern of the Revolution (she covered the diplomatic aspects far more thoroughly than her competitors did). And in spite of the diffidence she expressed because of her sex, she showed a keen understanding of military strategy. As for her sources, her information came directly from "many of the first patriots and most influential characters of the continent" and, like all historians of her day, she checked facts with the *Annual Register,* a British magazine which summarized news year by year. For the body of her work, however, she relied on the *Annual Register* less than many historians, some of whom actually copied sections word for word.

But impartial Mercy was not. On every issue from the Stamp Act to the French Revolution, she took her stand firmly and if she persuaded herself that she was impartial it was because she found that, for herself, public questions generally shook down in short order to a matter of right and wrong. Besides, from her point of view she must have seemed extraordinarily objective; one has only to compare the overwrought rhetoric of some of her letters to the considered prose of her history to realize how much she restrained herself. When she wrote of Shays's Rebellion, for instance, she could not be too hard on the insurgents — ignorant men for the most part, she believed, rather than malicious — but on the other hand she was far less critical of the General Court than she and James had been at the time. On the subject of the Constitution, she used ten pages to defend her original objections but concluded that "the experiment proved salutary, and has ultimately redounded as much to the honor and interest of America, as any mode or form of government that could have been devised by the wisdom of man." She did not hesitate to denounce the Indian War, condemn John Jay, expose monarchic tendencies wherever she saw them, and criticize Washington (gently) for being partisan in his appointments, but Mercy also had techniques for retreating from a subject when it was convenient. Let the "future historian" investigate the matter further, she would say; let posterity decide. Still, tactful as she might try to be, Mercy Warren was clearly a Republican and the political opinions in her history exhibited, as Harrison Gray Otis told a Federalist friend, a decided "tincture of democracy."

But if her text was biased and often abstract, returning as it so frequently did to ground itself in morality, it was lively when dealing with individual people, particularly people whom Mercy did not like. Mercy had always been astute at "drawing characters," as John Adams had long ago testified ("I dread her history," he had laughed), and now she indulged herself. Friends and enemies, heroes, despots, traitors, bunglers — they were all there, sometimes in full portrait, sometimes in a thumbnail sketch: Washington, who "in most instances," she said, ". . . presided with wisdom, dignity, and moderation, but complete perfection is not to be attributed to man"; Gage, who came off better than one might have expected — "naturally a man of humane disposition . . . but he had not the intrigue of a statesman"; Samuel Adams, "a quick understanding, a cool head, stern manners, a smooth address, and a Roman-like firmness"; General Howe, "a man of pleasure and a soldier"; Governor Bernard, "a man of little genius and some learning"; John Hancock, "a gentleman of fortune of more external accomplishments than real abilities"; and Thomas Hutchinson, who was still the complete villain. "Dark, intriguing, insinuating, haughty and ambitious" — so began the long list of his unhappy attributes. The only concession that Mercy would make was to acknowledge that Hutchinson had been raised in "reverential ideas of monarchic government," the implication being that perhaps he could not help himself.

It was John Adams' character, however, that Mercy struggled most with. How could she pass over the ambitious vice president with his penchant for titles, or the president willing to sanction an act that abridged a man's freedom of speech? On the other hand, how could she expose this particular old friend to the condemnation she felt he deserved? Yet John himself had once told Mercy: "The faithfull Historian delineates Characters truly, let the Censure fall where it will." In the same letter, however, he had also said that the "Desire of Esteem and the dread of Scorn" was the principle that governed a man's life; the difficulty was that neither Mercy nor John was immune to this principle. Certainly in the major literary effort of her life Mercy was eager for John's esteem; certainly John would be stung by her scorn.

In the earlier sections Mercy, of course, had no trouble praising John Adams for his many services to the country (although she might have given him credit for his part in framing the Massachusetts constitution), but when she came to the period when she felt that he had "forgotten the principles of the American Revolution" she stated her dilemma frankly, addressing, one feels, John Adams himself:

The veracity of the historian requires that all those who have been distinguished, either by their abilities or their elevated rank, should be exhibited through every period of public life with impartiality and truth. But the heart of the annalist may sometimes be hurt by political deviations which the pen of the historian is obliged to record.

Then Mercy proceeded to discuss Mr. Adams' recent "partiality for monarchy" in as "charitable" terms as she could, referring to his defection (or what she considered his defection) as a "political phenomenon" almost in the nature of an illness — the result, she said, of "living long near the splendor of courts and courtiers." She admitted that his "prejudices and passions were sometimes too strong for his sagacity and judgment," that his character combined "pride of talent and much ambition," but, as if she wished to take the edge off her words, she added: "time and circumstances often lead so imperfect a creature as man to view the same thing in a very different point of light." In private life, she hastened to say, John Adams' character was unimpeachable, notwithstanding "any errors in public conduct." She did not detail those errors; rather than explore the events of his administration, she simply called on that accommodating "future historian."

Mercy was handicapped in writing her history by chronic trouble with her eyes which in 1801 was so serious that she was often forced to stay in bed in a darkened room with her eyes covered. James, Jr., acted as Mercy's secretary during these spells, and indeed to the end of her life, but when she was ready for help in the final phases of work, she turned to an old family friend, Dr. James Freeman, pastor of King's Chapel in Boston. He found her a printer, solicited for subscriptions (more successfully than Mercy's lady friend), advised her how to set up a title page, instructed her how to make an index, and even took the responsibility for reading proof.

The correspondence continued for three years. What about a motto for the title page? Dr. Freeman asked. Generally a motto was in Latin, he told her, and he noted several he thought would be appropriate but Mercy had selected her own — one from St. Paul, and one from Shakespeare: "O God! Thy arm was here . . . And not to us, but to thy arm alone, Ascribe we all." (Mercy had long ago decided on her title: *History of the Rise, Progress, and Termination of the American Revolution, Interspersed with Biographical, Political, and Moral Observations.*) What about spelling? Dr. Freeman asked. In words such as *honor,* did she prefer the *our* ending which the purists (and Dr. Samuel Johnson) insisted upon or would she take *or* as some Americans were now advocating? (Mercy decided to leave the *u* out in all words of Latin origin as *honor* and *error* but retain it in Anglo-Saxon words such as *endeavour.*) What about type? Dr. Freeman sent her a sample of pica typeface and reported that the total cost of publishing 1500 copies of the three volumes of her history (about 400 pages a volume) would be $2882 ($1325 for paper, $1107 for printing, $450 for binding) or 64 cents a volume. The printer recommended that each volume be sold at $2 and offered to publish the history at his own risk, provided that he would not pay Mercy any money until 800 copies had been sold. Dr. Freeman advised Mercy to accept the proposal.

When all three volumes of Mercy's history were finally off the press, it was 1806. Thomas Jefferson had been elected to a second term (James Warren had presided over the Massachusetts electoral college); the Louisiana Territory had been purchased in spite of the violent opposition of Federalists who wanted to restrict the size of the nation to the thirteen original states; and England and France were back at war. Mercy was seventy-seven years old now. She was described by a visitor as being as eloquent in conversation as she had ever been and as erect in stature. She was wearing, the visitor recalled, "a steel-colored gown, with short sleeves and a very long waist; the silk skirt being covered in front with a white lawn apron. She wore a lawn mob-cap, and gloves covering the arms to the elbows cut off at the fingers." Undoubtedly she entertained in her favorite "elbow chair" (one with upholstered arms) in what she called "the old corner," where the Adamses and the Warrens used to gather during the early days of the Revolution.

Because Mercy's volumes appeared one at a time, beginning in 1805, reaction to the complete history came slowly. A Boston monthly, the *Panoplist,* carried one of the first reviews, a particularly frustrating kind of criticism, as it turned out, for an author to read. The reviewer, less interested in history than in sentence structure, did not give Mercy's books the overall evaluation that they deserved but instead moved in quickly for close-quarters attack. Opening with a supercilious reference to Mercy's sex, he quoted the statement in her preface in which she said she had not "yielded to the assertion, that all political attentions lay out of the road of female life." This was evident, the reviewer said slyly; every page offered additional proof of it. Yet she had reason to be diffident — a woman entering territory already occupied by such prominent men as William Gordon and David Ramsay!

Having thus put Mercy in her place, the reviewer combed the three volumes for awkward phrases, overlong sentences, misused words. Actually, he was not discriminating against Mercy. This myopic procedure was standard practice in reviewing and reflected the current preoccupation of literary circles with language itself. (Marshall's and Ramsay's histories and indeed Wordsworth's poems underwent the same type of scrutiny.) American writing and speech were under such constant attack in England that while a few men — notably Noah Webster — maintained that Americans could have an independent language as well as an independent government, most educated Americans were determined to prove that they were as sensitive to correct English as the English themselves. So the *Panoplist* reviewer took Mercy to task for "the improper use of some words and the introduction of others totally unknown to the English language." He cited these examples: "a principle producing *benevolent* effects," "needless to adduce *innumerable* instances," "the voice of the people *breathes.*" He objected to her phrase "flying like fugitives" as a tautological expression "the impropriety of which will immediately be perceived"; he took issue with her use of *retrospect* as a verb; he was disgusted at her reference to Plymouth "at the bottom" of Massachusetts Bay.

The reviewer could find nothing to praise without also finding fault. "Although the reader is often charmed," he said, "with elegant expression and the polished period, yet he is frequently disgusted by the heavy sentence, rendered tedious, and almost unintelligible by parenthesis." (He cited three sample sentences, none of which contained parentheses.) He admitted Mercy had a devout mind but complained that she was too often distracted by irrelevant material. Finally, however, he acknowledged that "although we cannot bestow unqualified commendation on the work before us . . . we have derived considerable pleasure, and, we hope, some profit, from a perusal of it."

In general, Mercy felt that her history was well received and for a while she even hoped that it might go into a second edition. That there was not enough demand to warrant this was, of course, disappointing, but on the other hand there continued to be a response to the books that Mercy found gratifying. She received letters from Jefferson, Joel Barlow (one of America's most distinguished writers), Elbridge Gerry, James Winthrop, who found her history "a well digested and polished narrative," and John Dickinson in Pennsylvania, who reminisced about the old days and reported that he was now in his seventy-fifth year — such an age, he said, as "could hardly be expected by a Man born in the Middle part of Maryland." But although Mercy and Abigail Adams exchanged letters in the spring of 1807, there was no evidence that either Abigail or John had read Mercy's history yet.

. . .

Actually, in the last few years John Adams had also been setting down the history of his times, but he kept his writing secret, perhaps even from Abigail. He wrote almost involuntarily, it seemed, in response to his brooding, for ever since his retirement — busy as he had been on the farm and happy as he might appear on the surface — John Adams had brooded over the past, returning again and again to his defeat, like a man with an open wound who probes to see if it has healed. John's wound never did heal completely, but

what tormented him most was the question of his long-range reputation. How would he be remembered by future generations? What
would history say about him, he who had been so maligned by his
contemporaries? John had no faith in historians. Most of those who
had written on the American Revolution wrote to make money, he
said, as Gordon and Marshall had done. (Marshall's *Life of George
Washington* he called a "Mausolaeum, 100 feet square at the base,
and 200 feet high.") But who could write an adequate history of
the Revolution? "Who will ever be able to write it?" he asked
again and again. He had long ago come to the conclusion that perhaps faithful history had never been written — nor ever could be.

Various people over the years had tried to persuade Adams himself to write such a history or at least to write his autobiography. He
had different excuses: he did not have enough time; he could not go
through all the trunks, letter books, and papers; he would not be
believed even if he did write something; he did not wish to be reminded of his "Mortifications, Disappointments or Resentments" —
they would set him "on fire." Once he confessed to a friend: "I look
so much like a small boy in my own eyes, that with all my vanity, I
cannot endure the sight of the picture." His most compelling reason,
however, was his belief that the very fact that he was writing about
himself would be misinterpreted. "Washington and Franklin," he
said, "could never do anything but what was imputed to be pure,
disinterested patriotism; I never could do anything but what was
ascribed to sinister motives."

Yet as early as 1802 John Adams began to write a private autobiography, to vindicate himself not before the public but before the
eyes of his children and their children after them. He completed
Part One, which he called "John Adams," in June 1805. In December 1806 he began Part Two, "Travels and Negotiations," and it was
while writing this section that he read Mercy Warren's history or at
least those parts that related to him. That he had finished most of
her history by the early part of 1807 and was highly irritated by it,
he revealed in his own text. With obvious ill humor he referred to

his "quondam Friend Mrs. Warren," who in her third volume asserted that Mr. Adams was "not beloved by his colleague doctor Franklin." This was, as it turned out, only one of a multitude of offenses he charged to Mercy, but he bided his time in confronting her. Perhaps he did not intend to write until he was sure he could control his temper; perhaps he did not even confide his anger to Abigail, for her letter to Mercy in March 1807 was especially cordial; perhaps when John actually did write, he was responding not only to the indignities he imagined that he suffered at Mercy's hands but to the frustrations of the times.

On June 30, 1807, Boston received the news that the British frigate *Leopard,* in an attempt to recover deserters believed to be aboard the United States frigate *Chesapeake,* fired on the *Chesapeake,* killed three American sailors, impressed three others (plus one British subject), and wounded eighteen more. The whole country was of course aroused and no one more than John Adams, who had sacrificed so much to maintain American neutrality. It was as if the events of the Federalist administrations were being replayed except that this time he was on the sidelines and Thomas Jefferson, a man whom John believed to be impractical and whose theories he distrusted, was in charge. Assailed by feelings of helplessness, as he so frequently was in his retirement, John flung aside the third part of his autobiography which he had titled "Peace" and never returned to it. Instead on July 11 he began a series of letters to Mercy Warren in which he listed his grievances in order, he said, for her to make corrections in her next edition. Actually, these letters — ten in six weeks, some running to twenty pages — were his long pent-up cry of outrage at the world in general, at his age which had reduced him to the role of a spectator, at his enemies who had defeated him, at his friends who had misunderstood him, at himself for not being sufficiently dignified (like Washington) or sufficiently genial (like Franklin) to be forgiven his foibles, and at all historians, present and future, who would not write history as he would have it written, who would not let him play his part as he knew he had played it.

One by one, John Adams descended on the objectionable statements, beginning with Mercy's comment that Mr. Adams' "passions and prejudices were sometimes too strong for his sagacity and judgment."

"If I had acted from passion or prejudice," John replied, ". . . the public affairs of this country would have been in a much less prosperous condition than they are." He categorically denied any partiality for monarchy, claimed that he took no pride in his talents — indeed, he had "no talents beyond mediocrity," reviewed at length his whole philosophy of government, and concluded in an injured tone. "If I were to measure out to others the treatment that has been meted to me, I could make wild work with some of your party. Shall I indulge in retaliation or not?"

Mercy thought that the "irritation of the times" must surely have agitated John's mind. "It is true," she said, "that I have asserted that you were subject to passions and prejudices like other men; your warmest friends and acquaintance will never contradict this; nor do I think a natural irritability of temper any impeachment of character." But Mercy was not yet aware of the extent of John's grievances nor the depths of his bitterness and apparently she still hoped that in his next letter he would become again the friendly critic. "Were you to write with the same eye of candor and friendship with which you once viewed her compositions," she said, "the author might have little to fear from your strictures."

Once started, however, John could not stop. Whatever mention Mercy had made of him, he rejected. When she wrote, "In his diplomatic character, Mr. Adams had never enjoyed himself so well as while residing in the Dutch Republic," John chose to ignore the phrase "in his diplomatic character." "I know not what foundation Mrs. Warren had for this observation," he said. "In Holland, I had a fit of sickness, the most severe I ever experienced." When Mercy referred to his plain, straightforward manner ("His genius was not altogether calculated for a court life," she wrote; he was "deficient in the 'je ne sais quoi,' so necessary in polished society"), John ex-

ploded. "Franklin, Jay, Laurens, Jefferson . . . I suppose were not
deficient in this *je ne sais quoi.*" "Why am I singled out to be stig-
matized as a clown?" When Mercy (inadvertently, she insisted)
placed Franklin's and Jay's names before his in the list of peace
commissioners of which he had been the head, he accused Mercy of
a "determined resolution" to strip him of his laurels. He was angry
that she had not given him credit for the work he had done prior to
1774, not even assigning him, he grumbled, the role "of a doorkeeper, a livery servant, a dancer, a singer, or a harlequin . . . I
ought not to have been shoved off the theatre and kept behind the
screen for fourteen years." And although he believed Mercy should
have terminated her book at the end of the war, he resented the fact
that "not the least notice is taken of my repeated elections as Vice
President" nor any attention given to the peace he had made with
France. Finally John accused her not only of writing "to the taste of
the nineteenth century . . . to gratify the passions, prejudices, and
feelings of the party who are now predominant" but also of writing
out of spite because John Adams as vice president had not found
offices for members of her family.

For a time Mercy tried to counter his attacks, to remind him of
the compliments that he had overlooked, to point out that he put a
"perverse construction on every passage" where he was named, but
in the end she simply threw up her hands. "It was not in the design
of my historic work," she said, "to write a panegyric on your life and
character, though fully sensible of your virtues and your services."
To his repeated demands that she retract her errors, she asked what
would he have her do? Did he want her to "tell the world that Mr.
Adams was no monarchist . . . that he was a man of fashion . . .
that his passions were always on a due equipose; that he was beloved by every man, woman, and child in France . . . that he 'had
no talents to be proud of' . . . that his name was always placed at
the head of every public commission; that nothing had been done,
that nothing could be done, neither in Europe nor America, without
his sketching and drafting the business, from the first opposition to

British measures in the year 1764 to signing the treaty of peace with England in the year 1783"? Mercy was weary of the whole affair; at her time of life, she said, it was just too much to read ten long letters of accusation and reproach. And so, for now, ended the correspondence and so, it seemed, the long friendship.

John Adams' anger was of course highly personal, yet its roots went deep into the long, bitter party hostility that had cut through families, alienated friends, and divided towns in Massachusetts. When Mercy said that John had lapsed from republican principles, she was expressing what Republicans in general felt about Federalists; when John Adams snapped back that Mercy did not know what she meant by republicanism, he was voicing the standard Federalist rejection of such criticism. At the heart of the conflict in Massachusetts there lay a deep sense of having been betrayed, party by party, friend by friend; nor was there any hope that people could be reconciled as long as Europe insisted on drawing America into its quarrels, as long as America continued to think of Europe in partisan terms, Federalists nursing anti-French grudges, Republicans fanning their hatred of England. Indeed, both parties were motivated less, it seemed, by their pro sentiments than by their anti sentiments. James Warren had lost confidence in France when, as he said, Napoleon went whoring after the fleshpots of Egypt, but his antipathy for England was as intense as it had ever been. And it was this unswerving anti-British, antimonarchy sentiment that helped to keep the Warrens and so many like them faithful to their party in the dark days ahead.

If the clash between the *Leopard* and the *Chesapeake* introduced the dark days, certainly Jefferson's Embargo Act in December 1807 deepened the darkness. From the Republican point of view, the Embargo Act, an experiment in using peaceful means to force Britain to recognize the freedom of the seas, was the only alternative to war. From the Federalist point of view, however, any act that stopped all American ships from going to and from foreign ports was not only a violation of their principles but an insufferable inva-

sion of their purses. Up and down the coast of New England ships
lay at anchor with their topmasts housed, sailors loafed on the wa-
terfronts, fish rotted in fish houses, maritime industries stood idle, and
Federalists howled. The administration was against New England,
they said; Southerners were running the country; Jefferson was secretly in league with Napoleon and wanted to destroy American
commerce; America would fare better in the long run if England
won the war with France, so why challenge England?

This was a new chapter in the long, seesawing Federalist-
Republican feud and one in which the two almost evenly matched
parties were pushed into new positions, inevitably also into contradictions. For ideologies to remain consistent or "pure," as Mercy
once said, they had to stay in the "philosopher's closet," and both the
Federalist and Republican parties were showing the effects of
weather. The Federalists were declaring now that they had never
fought the war for any purpose except to be independent from England, yet at the same time they were demonstrating that they were
still far from independent and, indeed, that they did not believe they
could survive without England. The Republicans replied that the
war had been fought, as everyone knew, not only to free America
from English tyranny but to form a government that would keep
America free from all tyranny; yet now, as creators rather than crit-
ics of national policy, the Republicans had sponsored the Embargo
Act, as arbitrary an act as any sponsored by the Federalist administration. The High Federalists, on the other hand, were making a
complete turnabout from nationalism to localism. Many of the same
men who had once been so outraged by Shays's Rebellion were
whispering now that New England would always be discriminated
against by the national government; perhaps it should secede.

In Plymouth Mercy Warren claimed that she had laid aside "all
political attentions . . . as a waste of time at my advanced period,"
yet she was no more immune to the effects of the Embargo Act than
anyone else. James had investments at stake; Henry was Collector
of the Port at Plymouth, surely one of the most unpopular jobs a

man could hold at the moment; Joseph Otis, assisted by his son William, was Collector at Barnstable. Their letters went back and forth between the two ports. "I give you my decided opinion," Henry wrote, "that this vessel is intended on a voyage in violation of the Embargo — you will take such measures in consequence as you may think proper." To live in a coastal town in the days of the embargo was to be at the scene of intrigue and at the center of party bitterness. To be a Republican was to be on the defensive or, if one was discreet, quiet. But when Mercy heard rumors that a group of High Federalists, including possibly Harrison Gray Otis, was talking about forming a separate government, she did not hesitate to speak up. What, she asked her nephew bluntly, was he about?

Harrison replied in a light vein, addressing Mercy affectionately but firmly. He had made it a policy long ago not to discuss politics with his aunt, he said, and he was not going to break it now. "You may well suppose that there is no individual of your political party, whom I would prefer for a confessor to your much respected self. But it certainly must occur to you that if I have really turned conspirator against the State, I ought not to put it even in your power to hang me."

James Warren defended the embargo as he would any act to curb England, but in the end war with England was bound to come, he believed, although he did not expect to see it. His health was failing; indeed, he was at that stage in life when a man is often impelled to assess his total experience. John Adams in his old age reached a point when he could say that he had experienced more comfort than distress, more pleasure than pain, "ten to one, nay if you please an hundred to one," but even such momentary ebullience was not in James Warren's style. Certainly his public life had brought him more pain than pleasure, but this was due less to ill fortune and political inequities than to the peculiarities of his temperament.

James's pleasures had come mainly from his private life and these he enjoyed in his last years without the obtrusion of other responsibilities. Still, when he came, like John Adams, to make a final assessment, he decided characteristically that his greatest satisfaction came from a solid sense of duty well done — in other words, from the knowledge that he had lived a life of public service, no matter how disagreeable, and lived it in conformity to a set of fixed principles. James perhaps had not been able to change the world as much as he would have liked, but he took considerable pride in saying that the world had not changed him. Indeed, he had become more strict, rather than less, in the interpretation of his principles. Having fought in the revolution to take power from the few and give it to the many, he had spent the years since the war fighting Federalist elitism so fiercely that he had come to think of the "many" in ever more literal terms.

In the fall of 1808 James wrote a friend: "I do not expect ever to recover more health — the season of year is against it — my age is against it . . . I have uniformly endeavored to do my duty — I think I have generally done it — and wherein I have erred, I shall be forgiven."

On November 27 James Warren died, leaving Mercy, who had once dreaded even the shortest separation, alone. There had been so many final farewells for Mercy, however, that she had loosened her hold on life and, although she grieved, she did not think this separation would be for long. Meanwhile she took comfort in the expressions of sympathy and respect for James, for the people of Massachusetts venerated their Revolutionary leaders and mourned the departure of each as part of a dying species. Actually they had shown James more honor in his life than he had acknowledged, and although he had not been a popular man in his last years, the people would have agreed with his own verdict: he had done his duty and where he had erred he would probably be forgiven. Harrison Gray Otis once characterized James and Mercy in this way: "Though well born & a real lady," he said, referring to Mercy, "and as proud a woman as lives, she is the wife of a disappointed patriot . . . and is too much under his influence altho' vastly his superior in every sort of literary attainment." There was truth in his statement, but Mr. Otis obviously did not appreciate how much Mercy owed James. Intellectually inferior perhaps, James nevertheless provided Mercy with exactly what she needed for her own growth. His support was unfailing, his respect for her freedom was unqualified, his admiration for her talents was selfless, and his tenderness defied even age. Mercy's final tribute to him was her choice of an epitaph for his tombstone: "Mark the perfect man, and behold the upright: for the end of that man is peace."

The old patriots were aging, slipping away; of the Massachusetts signers of the Declaration of Independence ("Signers," they were called — the most cherished of their kind), there remained only John Adams, Robert Treat Paine, and Elbridge Gerry. With every year the surviving patriots were treated with more respect, yet they did not need to be told that they were members of an uncommon generation; they had always known it, and to the end they maintained as fresh as ever, their sense of having participated in a great drama. Just as in the early days when they had reached for phrases to show that the curtain was going up, so now they reached for the phrases which would acknowledge that the actors were going off-stage, the drama was closing, the curtain was coming down. Most had complete faith in a future life. John Adams, who had grown increasingly liberal in his religion, asked what there was in life to attach people to it "but the hope of a future and a better? It is a Cra(c)ker, a Rocquett, a Firework, at best." Yet so impressed was this generation with the extraordinary events they had witnessed that they seemed unwilling to let their particular segment of time go without establishing its special significance. Surely, they felt, their drama was unique in history; might it not even be the first link between this world and the next?

And so they talked of the millennium, sometimes jokingly, sometimes seriously. This particular wave of talk had begun in the 1790s, partly in response to a revival that had swept through New England, partly out of excitement for the French Revolution, and as the talk increased, it had been implemented by definite steps to prepare for the great day. Missionary societies were formed, Bibles were distributed in the "benighted corners of the world," and books were published which attempted to prove that the Biblical prophecies were already being realized. In Republican circles the king of France was reputed to be the first of the Ten Horns of the Great Beast; more recently, especially among the Federalist clergy, Napoleon was represented as Antichrist. John Adams had little use for the latter-day prophets, but John Dickinson wrote that, according to the best commentators he had talked to, the coming of the millennium would be "two or three centuries remote."

Among Mercy's friends, James Winthrop was the most serious student of the prophecies. In 1794 he had translated the prophetic part of the Apocalypse of St. John into familiar language, and since then he had been preparing a calendar that showed when the fulfillment of the prophecies would take place. An eccentric, given to strange outbursts of "levity" which Mercy reproved him for, James Winthrop was recognized as a scholar; yet twice he had launched what he claimed were scientific discoveries, only to be suspected each time of outright fraudulency. Once he had offered a solution to the problem of trisecting an angle and duplicating a cube, but this was proved to be completely false; then he wrote an article with new, but — as it turned out — unconfirmed and perhaps unconfirmable information on ancient history. Undaunted, James Winthrop worked on his prognostications and informed Mercy of his findings: the judgment on Antichrist, he figured, would take place in 1821; Mohammedanism would be "diverted, and the Messiah's Kingdom established at Jerusalem" in 1866. Mercy argued occasionally with Winthrop and once, when he seemed especially worked up, she asked if he never relaxed with a glass of wine, but Mercy herself was making a study of the prophecies. With the help of her sons, she was reading about the Asiatic world and the "prospect of the expansion of truth and righteousness through the dark corners of the globe."

Speculation on the prophecies may, indeed, have reduced the mysteries of the next world for the patriots, but in the meantime their days in this world were passing all too swiftly. The strawberries in Mercy's garden scarcely ripened, it seemed, before the apples were dropping and winter was closing in. The days were not long enough to satisfy all one's curiosities. Mercy would have sudden urges — to reread Newton, for instance, or to order a book on Hindu mythology. And when she heard that a neighbor of James Winthrop in Cambridge, a Mr. Craigie, had grown a passionflower in his famous greenhouse, she was seized by a desire to see what a passionflower looked like. She was not one of those who condemned Mr. Craigie for going against nature by turning winter into summer in his glass house; on the contrary, she was excited by the idea and asked James Winthrop to send her one of the flowers. As it turned out, Mrs. Craigie had pressed the last bloom in a book and had forgotten which book it was in, so Mercy had to wait a few months until the plant produced a fresh blossom which could be sent to Plymouth.

Nor were the days long enough for Mercy to say all that she wanted to say, particularly to the new generation of Otises and Warrens. For Marcia, she wrote a book of alphabetical maxims in which she rolled off virtues and vices for each letter with appropriate commentaries: *A* for Admiration, *B* for Beauty, *C* for Care, *D* for Duty. She paused only when she came to *X* and then called upon Xantippe to illustrate "the horrors of an ungoverned temper in a woman." Presumably the moral lessons were cautionary as far as Marcia was concerned, but with Joseph Otis' sons, John and William, her lessons were intended to be corrective. Mercy apparently alienated John with her advice, but William always came back for more. And, indeed, he had need to. As erratic, fiery, and troublesome an Otis as the family had ever produced, William was constantly in difficulty and forever threatening to quit his job, get even with his enemies, or move west. He spent his life, it seemed, teetering on the brink of emergencies while Mercy exhorted him to maintain his self-command.

Meanwhile war with Britain loomed just offstage. Forced by public opinion in New England, Jefferson had finally revoked the Embargo Act just before leaving office, and for three years his successor, James Madison, had been trying to ward off the war that England either did not think would take place or did not care to avoid. On a cold January day, John Adams might contend that the "blustering and bullying of France and England" disturbed him less than the freezing and thawing of winter, but this was only because he had long ago accepted the fact (unlike most Federalists) that war with England would be necessary — a second war of independence, in effect, to validate the first.

The danger, however, was not only external but internal. The Federalists, particularly in Massachusetts, were as wildly antiwar as they had been antiembargo, and having just survived a Republican administration in Boston, they had never been more anti-Republican, nor in fact had they had better reason to be. The Republicans and Governor Elbridge Gerry had pushed through one piece of legislation after another in a frenzied attempt to maintain control of the state: a new suffrage act, a bill to allow dissenting religions to receive tax money, and, most reprehensible from the Federalist point of view, an act that provided for the redistricting of the state to the Republicans' advantage. So aroused were the Federalists that in the spring elections of 1812 they turned out 11,000 new voters and captured both the governor's chair and the leadership in the House. From this base, they prepared to oppose the war.

They did not have long to wait. On June 18 war was declared and one week later the Federalists fired their first fusillade.

"Organize a *peace party* throughout your Country," the people were advised in an address published by the Massachusetts House of Representatives. ". . . Express your sentiments without fear, and let the sound of your disapprobation of this war be loud and deep . . . If your sons must be torn from you by conscriptions, consign them to the care of God; but let there be no volunteers except for defensive war." The Massachusetts Senate went on record denouncing the war as "founded in falsehood, declared without necessity."

By midsummer emotions had erupted fitfully into violence. "For myself, indeed," Mercy Warren wrote, "I do not feel nor fear much from the world — yet I have much at stake as regards my children, my friends, my country and posterity." In Plymouth a large portion of the inhabitants were, in Mercy's words, "so virulent" that the least spark could flare up into a fire. On the night of August 5 that spark was lighted and, as it happened, the fire was on Mercy Warren's own doorstep.

Congressman Charles Turner, Jr., of Plymouth, a Republican who had voted for the war, arrived in town that evening to attend the Court of Sessions, which was to meet the next day and of which he was the Chief Justice. According to his own account, Colonel Turner put up his horse and went to the home of David Bacon where he "tarried until a few minutes before 9 o'clock, when I left with a view to call on Madame Warren." On the way, he was recognized by a group of men in the street who began to shout. "'. . . here he is . . . here is the damned rascal!' . . . One dressed in dark clothes," the colonel said, "came on my right side and put his hand around my body, and held my right arm . . . another struck . . . another said, kick him . . . kick him." James Warren, Jr., hearing the commotion, went to the door and held it open until Colonel Turner was able to make his escape inside.

News of the Plymouth disturbance swept through the state and surely those who heard the story felt almost as much sympathy for Mrs. Warren inside the house as they did for Charles Turner outside, for Mercy was respected as an old patriot in Massachusetts — a frail little lady who had fought the Revolution as fiercely as many men and who could still stand up to the best of them and speak her mind if she wanted to. In her time she and her family had been accused so often by the Federalists of supporting the Shaysites and encouraging anarchy that even the Federalists must have felt the irony in the story of this old republican giving refuge to another Republican being attacked by a Federalist mob. Certainly Abigail Adams was affected by the story, for it was about this time that she broke her long silence and traveled to Plymouth, along with her daughter and granddaughter, to visit Mercy. For several years Elbridge Gerry had been trying (with Mercy's encouragement) to effect a reconciliation between Mercy and John Adams, but John, although mellowed sufficiently to have resumed his friendship with Thomas Jefferson, was slow to respond to Gerry's overtures. At least Mercy had Abigail back though, and she was delighted. The two old friends picked up their conversation enthusiastically; now they could even agree on major political issues, for both supported the war. As a sign of friendship, Mercy gave Abigail a lock of her hair and after Abigail had gone, Mercy renewed the correspondence jubilantly. "Blessed are the Peace-makers!" she cried.

Abigail had the lock of hair placed in a handkerchief pin and set with pearls; at the same time she had a matching ring made. "I forward to you," she wrote Mercy in December, "a token of love and friendship. I hope it will not be the less valuable to you for combining, with a lock of my own hair, that of your ancient friend's, at his request."

"*A token of love and friendship,*" Mercy replied. "What could be more acceptable to a mind of susceptibility? . . . I shall with pleasure wear the ring as a valuable expression of your regard; nor will it be the less valued for combining with yours a lock of hair from the venerable and patriotic head of the late President of the United States. This, being at his own request, enhances its worth in my estimation. It is an assurance that he can never forget former amities. For this I thank him."

Letters went back and forth regularly between Mercy and Abigail after this. Abigail expressed her indignation at the "disgraceful outrages" committed upon Henry Warren by Federalist hotheads who continued to make life difficult for Republicans in Plymouth; Mercy consoled Abigail on the loss of her daughter. But John, although willing to have Abigail remember him to Mercy, did not write. Perhaps he was afraid that a correspondence would open up old arguments, perhaps he simply did not know how to begin without either apologizing for his intemperance, which he would not do and might not even admit, or without assuming an air of forgiveness, which of course would be fatal to any reconciliation. Time was passing, however, friends were dying, and Abigail was obviously urging him to take the first step. In the spring of 1813 John reread parts of Mercy's history and although he grumbled to Elbridge Gerry that history was not the "Province of the Ladies," he was able to view the work with a bit more tolerance. Her volumes, in spite of their faults — the "Little Passions and Prejudices, want of Information, false Information . . . and frequent Partiality" — did contain, he admitted, "many Facts, worthy of Preservation."

In September John Adams found the opening he had been waiting for. He had just received a letter from Governor Thomas McKean of Pennsylvania, one of the veterans not only of the Continental Congress but of the Stamp Act Congress, in which he reminisced about James Otis. "In the Congress of 1765 there were several conspicuous characters," Governor McKean wrote. "Mr. James Otis appeared to me to be the boldest and the best speaker." John Adams put the letter in a fresh envelope, added a piece he had written at the time of Franklin's death, "Dialogue of the Dead," in which James Otis had figured as one of the characters, and he enclosed a note. As it happened, two of the Adams' granddaughters were making a trip to visit Mercy, and John gave them the envelope to deliver.

On September 12 Mercy replied: "I was much gratified by seeing your signature affixed to a Letter addressed to Mm. Warren."

John Adams had, of course, been astute to draw upon memories of James Otis at this delicate stage in his friendship with Mercy, for Mercy knew how deeply John had been attached to her brother, how often he had reminded the country of its debt to James Otis, whom he considered the first patriot and earliest spokesman of the Revolution. Mercy was grateful; no American had known her brother better than John Adams, she said, and no one was "more capable of portraying his character."

The breach had been crossed, the friendship reestablished. "I know not, Madam," John wrote two months later, "what your Father, your Husband, or your Brother, would think of these times."

Now even the last bitterness was overcome, for in this letter ("a very important letter," Mercy said) John had referred to James Warren as though he too had been restored to the old terms and readmitted to the "old corner" where the two couples had enjoyed each other in earlier days. "It is truly a satisfaction to me," Mercy wrote, "to receive letters from a Gentleman with whom I have corresponded for near half a century, and to find therein the same flow of esteem, friendship and confidence."

However lively Mercy's letters were, she had to dictate them to James, Jr., and she signed them with increasing difficulty. "We are as usual," James would say when he wrote to the family at Barnstable, "my mother feeble." And because they recognized how feeble Mercy was, her brother Samuel Allyne Otis went to Plymouth in the spring of 1814 on the way from Boston to Washington to make what even Mercy realized was his last call. After the visit, she reported, he backed away from the doorway toward his carriage, as if he were loath to take his eyes from her as she stood at the window, waving to him surely for the last time.

Twelve years Mercy's junior, Samuel at seventy-four still served as secretary to the Senate, just as he had for the last twenty-five years, never missing a day's work, so it was said. But soon after he returned to Washington, Samuel died suddenly — possibly from overexertion. For Mercy, the loss of this younger brother was a profound shock, not only because she had seen him so recently in good health but because with his death, all her brothers and sisters were gone. Joseph had died in 1810 and was buried beside his father — two graves so close to the road, it was as if these Otis men still could not resign their interest in Barnstable business. Scattered around them were graves of sisters, wives, and the short mounds for Otis babies, some not even named. Mercy was alone, she said, "the last of my father's house. I stand a wonder to myself and all around me."

In the summer of 1814 Mercy felt closer to her friends than she ever had before. "Is it because I am about to leave them," she asked, "or is it because the circle is so circumscribed?" Yet there was one piece of unfinished business that nagged at her all summer. She had long ago checked to see if a copy of her history was in the Library of Congress and had been assured that it was on the same shelf with Marshall's and Gordon's histories, but a friend had recently reported to her that her Revolutionary play *The Group* was being attributed to another author. The copy at the Boston Athenaeum gave its author as Mr. Samuel Barrett.

"If the author of the 'Group' ever deserved half the encomiums you have lavished on her talent," Mercy wrote John Adams, "it ought to be rescued from oblivion. I know of no one living who can or will do this but yourself."

John having reached "three score and nineteen years" was at the point when nothing could induce him to sleep out of his own bed, but he did go to Boston occasionally and he made it a point to go when he heard from Mercy. Within two weeks he wrote her, "I have certified in the book in the Athenaeum that to my certain knowledge, The Group was written by Mrs. Warren."

Mercy wanted the record set straight; she would have been just as unhappy to be given credit for writing something which in fact she had not written as to be denied credit which was rightfully hers. Unfortunately in recent years it has been suggested that she was the author of a Revolutionary satire called *The Blockheads,* an answer to General Burgoyne's play, *The Blockade of Boston,* which was performed in the winter of 1776–77. *The Blockheads,* a prose play, coarse in tone and filled with examples of broad sexual humor and lavatory language, was not written in Mercy's style and absolutely out of keeping with her character. That Mercy might have heard such language or that her brothers may have indulged in it is no indication that she would have used it (as has been argued); indeed, to believe that she was the author when in fact there were many Whigs trying their hands at satire is to discount the evidence of her entire life. Blood and gore she was not averse to, for this was in the epic tradition, but Mercy Warren would not have allowed a character in a play of hers to say that he had "shit" his "breeches." Besides, in April 1776 Abigail Adams sent Mercy a copy of the "parody written in Boston," which indicates that Abigail certainly did not think that Mercy had written it. Mercy would have found little satisfaction in writing something that had to be kept a profound secret even from her best friends (surely even from her sons). She was simply too proud to write anything that she could not or would not claim. (For this reason it is also doubtful that she wrote *The Motley Assembly*, which has also been attributed to her — a satire about the so-called moderate Whigs of 1778.)

But Mercy, like John Adams, had no control over what posterity would say. At the moment she felt that her life was in order and she sat tranquilly in her "elbow chair — patiently awaiting the destination of providence with regard to myself, my family, my friends, & my Country." The war had come close to Plymouth. There were alarms; shots had been exchanged with British ships at sea; soldiers walked the streets. The atmosphere was as tense as it had been in the days after the Battle of Lexington when Mercy had hourly expected the British to descend on Plymouth and commit all the atrocities that they were said to commit. Yet in June she wrote, "I would not have you think me alarmed by womanish fears or the weakness of old age. I am not."

By early September the situation was even more alarming. The British had captured Washington and burned the Capitol; the eastern part of Maine had fallen, Castine was occupied, Bangor raided, and of course it was assumed that Boston would be the next target. While the people of Massachusetts worked frantically to prepare for their defense, the High Federalists began talking again, as they had sporadically over the last years, about calling a New England convention to seek national and perhaps constitutional reforms, to explore ways to counteract what Harrison Gray Otis called "the destructive policy" of the national government which had reduced Massachusetts to a state of "humiliation, of danger, and distress."

The Republicans claimed that the secret purpose of such a convention was to plan secession, but the Federalists maintained a convention would appease radical antiwar groups and prevent wide-scale disorder. On October 12 the Massachusetts Senate approved a resolution to initiate such a convention at Hartford, but Mercy, who would of course have disapproved, did not know this. Nor did she know that Harrison Gray Otis was appointed a delegate.

On Thursday, October 13, Mercy entertained some visitors from Boston and when they had left, she went to bed, apparently feeling well. In the early morning, however, she was "suddenly and violently attacked." For five days she continued in great pain, Henry Warren wrote, and although on Monday she got up from her bed and went to the breakfast table, it was a momentary effort. On Wednesday morning at two o'clock Mercy died. "She expired with great calmness & perfect recollection of mind."

"And thus," Henry said, "the *last* frail reed is broken."

Had Mercy lived a few months longer, she would have seen the end of the war, but this would hardly have mattered to her. She had committed the future to Providence long ago and if, as she would have said, the curtain had come down before peace was actually established, she had nevertheless stayed onstage to the very brink of a new era. With the war over, America was able to turn her back on Europe, at least long enough to explore her own potentialities, to look west, test new freedoms, try her power. Change was already in the wind; *democracy* had become an acceptable word; the Federalist party was dying of its own elitism; General Andrew Jackson, who had just defeated the British at the Battle of New Orleans, was a new national hero.

But if Mercy could have foreseen the future, she would not have changed her message to posterity. Like all the old patriots, she had recognized that America, because of its geography if nothing else, was destined for power and subject to pride. That she herself, as she sought to build John Winthrop's "citty upon a hill" higher and yet higher, might in any way have contributed to a dream of American superiority probably did not occur to her. Her business was fighting tyrants and it was tyranny that she had in mind when she sat down at her desk to address her final words of advice to remote generations who would be living in an America that she could not begin to envision.

Let not the frivolity of the domestic taste of the children of Columbia, she said, nor the examples of strangers of high or low degree . . . or the imposing attitude of distant nations, or the machinations of the bloody tyrants of Europe . . . rob them of their character, their morals, their religions, or their liberty.

The partiality to military honor has a tendency to nourish a disposition for arbitrary power.

Any attempt, either by secret fraud, or open violence, to shake the union, to subvert the constitution, or undermine the just principles, which wrought out the American revolution, cannot be too severely censured.

The principles of the revolution ought ever to be the polestar of the statesman.

It will be the wisdom, and probably the future effort of the American government, for ever to maintain . . . the present neutral position of the United States.

America may with propriety be styled a land of promise . . . a fair and fertile vineyard, which requires only the industrious care of the laborers to render it for a long time productive of the finest clusters in the full harvest of prosperity and freedom.

The people may again be reminded, that the elective franchise is in their own hands; that it ought not to be abused, either for personal gratifications, or the indulgence of partisan acrimony.

They therefore cannot be too scrutinous on the character of their executive officers. No man should be lifted by the voice of his country to presidential rank, who may probably forget the republican designation, and sigh to wield a sceptre, instead of guarding sacredly the charter from the people.

There was nothing new in Mercy's advice, nothing that she had not been saying all her life. She was not innovative or in fact very flexible, but she was an able spokesman for her generation and, like the other patriots, she worried about the ability of future Americans to manage the country. "Am I mistaken," she had asked John Adams ". . . that the generations of men which have since arisen . . . with few exceptions . . . appear a very ignorant and narrow minded people." Mercy was of course viewing the new generation from the perspective of old age, but she was also viewing it from the perspective of a passionately political generation, for the old patriots had been absorbed by politics, both selfishly and unselfishly; they had been stimulated by the philosophy of politics, pushed to the edge of endurance by the practice of politics, driven by politics to exhibit the weakest traits in human nature, and inspired by politics to display the finest. Committed to preserving the rights of the individual, they had thought in terms of the body politic, their sense of self springing directly from their sense of community and their sense of community rooted in their religion. Government, they had insisted, was created to serve the people, but at the same time they had felt themselves *to be* the government in a deeply personal, almost a visceral way that was perhaps unique to a people founding a nation. Of course the new generation appeared to them painfully inexperienced and inept, but then the patriots had never had much faith in man, a perverse creature bound to live with his fellows but too selfish to be able to do it with grace.

In their last years the patriots, although still interested in politics, became more detached. They had long since stopped looking for vines to sit under and accepted the fact that the important battles of this world would always be fought, as theirs had, on the fields of compromise. The perfect state, if it existed, would be in the next world and it was to this world that they turned as their time thinned out.

"The Day is far spent with Us all," John Adams once wrote Mercy. "It can not be long before We must exchange this Theatre for some other.

"I hope," he added, "it will be one, in which there are no Politicks."

Notes
Bibliography
Index

ABBREVIATIONS

AFC   *Adams Family Correspondence*

GOP   Gay-Otis Papers

JAD   *Diary and Autobiography of John Adams*

MHS   Massachusetts Historical Society

MWH   *History of the Rise, Progress, and Termination of the American Revolution, Interspersed with Biographical, Political, and Moral Observations.* Mercy Warren

MWLB   Mercy Warren Letter Book

MWP   Mercy Warren Papers

MW Poems   *Poems, Dramatic and Miscellaneous*

OFM   Otis Family Manuscripts

OP   Otis Papers

WAL   Warren-Adams Letters

WAP   Warren-Adams Papers

WFLP   Warren Family Letters and Papers

NOTES

CHAPTER I

page
3 "For wee must consider." *Collections,* 3d ser., 7, p. 47.
4 "He is vastly." JAD, 1, p. 227.
5 "If to be had." OP, 1, n.d.
9 "Out a whalon"; "gitton." OP, 1, Christopher Stuart to James Otis, Sr., Mar. 12, 1735.
10 "A Commonwele." W. Bradford, p. 49.
10 "So Orpheus fiddled." Tudor, p. 9.
11 "He springs." JAD, 1, p. 84.

CHAPTER II

13 "Naturally and constitutionally." *Gazette,* May 13, 1765. James Otis, Jr.
13 "I Have all so sent." OP, 1, n.d.
15 "To resist the Supreme Magistrate." J. C. Miller, *Sam Adams,* p. 16.
16 "To make a Great commencement." OFM, #16, James Otis, Jr., to James Otis, Sr., May 9, 1743.
18 "When Hutchinson came." Freiberg, p. 38.
18 "If you serve." Sibley and Shipton, 8, pp. 152–53.
19 "We are fond." Hutchinson, *History,* 2, p. ix.
19 "A pleasant situation." Hosmer, *Hutchinson,* p. 116.
19 "About as large as." Freiberg, p. 32.
20 "Like selling the skin." Schutz, *Shirley,* p. 90.

20 "As for my Writing." OP, 1, James Otis, Jr., to James Otis, Sr., July 1745. OP, 1.

21 "We got the goose." Schutz, *Shirley,* p. 101.

CHAPTER III

24 "Mountains of Eel River." MWP, Mercy Warren to James Warren, 1775.

24 "He is blessed." MWP, James Warren to Mercy Warren, 1778.

24 "Were you to look." WAL, 2, p. 8, Mercy Warren to James Warren, Mar. 10, 1778.

25 "His attachments." WAL, 2, p. 254. Mercy Warren to John Adams, Apr. 27, 1785.

25 "The book and the pen." GOP, Mercy Warren to Mary Otis, Apr. 29, 1800.

26 "Your Lemons & wine." OP, 2, James Warren to James Otis, Sr., Jan. 2, 1762.

27 "Thank God." Allan, p. 64.

27 "The house seemed." JAD, 1, p. 1.

28 "Since the earthquake." Sibley and Shipton, 9, p. 250.

30 "The world Is filled." OFM, #21, Joseph Otis to James Otis, Sr., Jan. 8, 1749.

31 "One hundred Whaleboats." OFM, #45, Thomas Pownall to James Otis, Sr., Apr. 25, 1757.

31 "About the Publick affairs." OFM, #44, Memo by James Otis, Sr., Aug. 1757.

31 "Wt David Gorham told Me." Ibid.

31 "Had a Bad Opinion." Ibid.

32 "Was an Old Pirate." OFS, #67, Copy of evidence by Ebenezer Chipman, Aug. 8, 1758.

33 "Vines." The reference is to 1 Kings 4:25, "every man under his vine and under his fig tree," but New Englanders used the expression loosely, often shortening it simply to "vines" or "vine trees."

33 "Before the Chief Justice." *News Letter,* Apr. 7, 1763.

33 "Drovers, horse jockies." R. E. Brown, p. 181.

34 "Mr. Otis, the son." *News Letter,* Apr. 7, 1763.

34 "Would set the Province." Ibid.

34 "From so small a spark." Hutchinson, *History*, 3, p. 64.
34 "A new scene." Ibid., p. 62.

CHAPTER IV

39 "Rumors were everywhere." John Adams, *Works*, 4, p. 6.
41 "Lordly man." JAD, 1, p. 83.
41 "Queer and affected." Ibid., p. 84.
41 "Musical eloquence." Ibid., 3, p. 275.
42 "This writ is against." *James Otis's Speech on the Writs of Assistance*, p. 4.
42 "I oppose the kind." G. L. Austin, p. 234.
42 "Let the consequences." Ibid.
42 "Enacted in the zenith." Ibid., p. 235.
43 "Even if the writ." Ibid.
43 "Every act repugnant." Hutchinson, *History*, 3, p. 67.
44 "I am an old Man." JAD, 1, p. 190.
45 "Wholly disapprove." Ibid., p. 196.
45 "Not employed on." Ibid., p. 47.
45 "Pigs turd." Ibid., p. 197.
45 "I was much more attentive." Ibid., 3, p. 276.
46 "All Plays are." Allan, p. 67.
46 "Be frugal." Ibid., p. 66.
46 "You mention." Ibid., pp. 68–69.
47 "To my certain knowledge." John Adams, *Works*, 10, p. 364.
48 "Out of this election." Tudor, p. 92.
48 "I know it is the maxim." Freiberg, p. 26.
49 "Despatch the fishermen." OP, 2, James Otis, Sr., to Joseph Otis, Apr. 13, 1762.
49 "Curiosity makes them." OP, 2, #74, Samuel Allyne Otis to Joseph Otis.
50 "I hear Sister." OP, 2, #75, James Otis, Sr., to Joseph Otis, Apr. 16, 1762.
50 "I had 112 votes." OFM, #92, James Otis, Sr., to Joseph Otis, May 30, 1762.
50 "Decent elegance." MWLB, Mercy Warren to Janet Montgomery, Jan. 5, 1780.

51 "The most darling privilege." J. Otis, *Political Writings,* p. 277.

51 "Kings were." Ibid., p. 278.

52 "Take the advice." Ibid., p. 44.

52 "But what he would have." Ibid., p. 300.

52 "A convert." *Collections,* 74, p. 78. James Otis, Jr., to J. Mauduit, Oct. 28, 1762.

52 "We are now convinced." Ibid.

53 "The zeal pot." AFC, 1, p. 135, John Adams to Abigail Adams, July 9, 1774.

53 "A clever fellow"; "on the right scent now." Sibley and Shipton, 11, p. 258.

53 "Unexceptionable Regulations." JAD, 1, p. 236.

53 "With a whiff." Ibid.

53 "Attacked the other day." OFM, Samuel Allyne Otis to Joseph Otis, Mar. 8, 1763.

54 "To ruin his reputation." *Gazette,* Feb. 28, 1763.

54 "I am not mad." Ibid., Mar. 14, 1763.

54 "What can a virtuous." Ibid., Mar. 28, 1763.

54 "Act as the Dutchmen." OFM, Samuel Allyne Otis to Joseph Otis, Feb. 14, 1763.

55 "I am sure I am right." *Gazette,* Feb. 28, 1763.

56 "O, poor New England." Austin, p. 239.

56 "Make 2 and 2." J. Otis, *Political Writings,* p. 334.

57 "Independence was a plant." MWH, 1, p. 54.

57 "The wisest mad." J. Otis, *Political Writings,* p. 337.

57 "Much easier." *Gazette,* Nov. 8, 1764.

57 "This place, sir." Ibid., Nov. 4, 1765.

58 "Sackcloth and ashes." Sibley and Shipton, 11, p. 262.

58 "For the least iota." J. Otis, *Political Writings,* p. 415.

58 "A little, dirty." Ibid., p. 414.

58 "It requires something." Ibid., p. 420.

58 "Undoubted power." Ibid., p. 430.

58 "The rage." John Adams, *Works,* 10, p. 295.

58 "Reprobate." Ibid.

58 "The gentleman." *Gazette,* May 6, 1765.

58–59 "As Jemmy is." *Evening Post,* May 13, 1765.

59 "The little chit chat." *Gazette,* May 13, 1765.

59 "Otis is now." E. S. and H. M. Morgan, p. 105.

59 "His integrity unimpeached." MWH, 1, p. 85.

59–60 "I should not be surprised." MWP, Mercy Warren to James Warren, Dec. 11, 1775.

60 "Susceptible of quick." MWH, 1, pp. 85–86.

60 "Running to some." WAL, 1, p. 3, James Otis, Jr., to Mercy Warren, Apr. 11, 1766.

60 "Singular Wisdom." OFM, #122, James Warren to James Otis, Sr., Dec. 27, 1765.

60 "Composing the Minds." WAL, 1, p. 4, John Dickinson to James Otis, Jr., Dec. 5, 1767.

61 "Ticklingburgs"; "oznabrigs." *Gazette,* Aug. 19, 1765. The two words, variously spelled, referred to a coarse linen cloth.

61 "Barbikue." Rowe, p. 88.

61 "As to News." OFM, #121, Samuel Allyne Otis to Joseph Otis, Aug. 16, 1765.

61 "This was an indignity." Hutchinson, *History,* 3, p. 88.

61 "Become rather popular." Hosmer, *Hutchinson,* p. 91, Thomas Hutchinson to Richard Jackson, Aug. 30, 1765.

62 "I couldn't stand." Ibid., p. 92.

62 "Some ran." Ibid.

62 "Rich India cabinet." Hutchinson, *Diary,* 2, p. 352. The complete inventory of what was lost and destroyed is contained in the appendix to this volume of the diary.

62 "One of the best." Hosmer, *Hutchinson,* p. 92.

63 "His look big." Ibid., p. 95.

63 "I call God." Ibid., pp. 95–96.

63 "The Stamp Act." OFM, #123, James Otis, Jr., to James Otis, Sr., Jan. 8, 1766.

63 "The Province was." JAD, 1, p. 312.

64 "Suited to the Occasion." Rowe, p. 95.

64 "Before the Bottles." Sibley and Shipton, 11, p. 324.

64 "Old trees don't." Freiberg, p. 135.

65 "The father's principles." OP, 2, #142, James Otis, Sr., to Joseph Otis, June 12, 1767.

CHAPTER V

67 "Lines Written after." MW Poems, p. 219.

67 "My Soul and body." MWP, Mercy Warren to ?, July 5, 1775.

67 "To adore the Hand." MWP, Mercy Warren to George Warren, 1786.

68 "Very suddenly." *Gazette,* Nov. 7, 1763.

68 "I think it proper." OFM, #119, Samuel Allyne Otis to Joseph Otis, May, 1765.

68 "I am heartily." WAL, 1, p. 1, James Otis, Jr., to Mercy Warren, Apr. 11, 1766.

68 "Pretty things." MWP, James Warren to Mercy Warren, May 17, 1763.

69 "The Irksome Methods." MWP, Mercy Warren to James Warren, Feb. 1775.

69 "In the Force of Reason"; "obligations of Duty." Ibid.

70 "The Days are so." MWP, James Warren to Mercy Warren, May 1763.

70 "My Dearest Friend." MWP, Mercy Warren to James Warren, June 1, 1779.

70 "A Whig & a Tory." MWP, Mercy Warren to James Warren, Apr. 22, 1772.

70 "Little loadstone." MWP, Hannah Winthrop to Mercy Warren, Nov. 10, 1773.

71 "If you should find me." WFLP, Hannah Winthrop to Mercy Warren, Aug. 14, 1772.

71 "Tomorrow morning I." AFC, 1, p. 48, John Adams to Abigail Adams, Sept. 30, 1764.

71 "In Coll. Warren." Ibid., p. 83, John Adams to Abigail Adams, May 1772.

71 "I have a dread." JAD, 1, p. 100.

71 "My boyish Habits." Ibid., 2, p. 64.

72 "Madam, I never." WAL, 1, p. 21, John Adams to Mercy Warren, Jan. 3, 1774.

72 "You was not made." WAL, 2, p. 216, Mercy Warren to John Adams, May 4, 1783.

72 "Invariable Attachment." AFC, 1, p. 87, Mercy Warren to Abigail Adams, July 25, 1773.

73 "I could spare." AFC, 2, p. 276, Mercy Warren to Abigail Adams, July 7, 1777.

73 "Garlick thread." Ibid., p. 314, Abigail Adams to Mercy Warren, Aug. 16, 1777. Garlick thread was a kind of linen cloth which originally came from Gorlitz, Germany.

73 "Saucy." AFC, 1, p. 320, John Adams to Abigail Adams, Nov. 4, 1775.

73 "A little seasoning." Ibid., pp. 344–45, Mercy Warren to Abigail Adams, Feb. 7, 1776.

73 "Still keeping up." OP, 2, #142, James Otis, Sr., to Joseph Otis, June 12, 1767.

74 "Like an open." J. C. Miller, *Sam Adams*, p. 106.

74 "Mighty Negative." JAD, 1, p. 325.

75 "An ingenuous writer." Hosmer, *Hutchinson*, p. 142.

75 "I am a mere cypher." Freiberg, p. 173.

76 "According to the fashion." Ibid.

76 "By surprise." J. C. Miller, *Sam Adams*, p. 123.

76 "Seditious paper." Beach, p. 144.

76 "With the contempt." Ibid.

76 "Rescind the resolution." Ibid., p. 145.

77 "Parcel of Button-makers." Sibley and Shipton, 11, p. 275.

77 *"Oppugnation to his."* MWH, 1, p. 57.

77 *"An expiring faction."* Ibid.

78 "The best blood." Ibid., pp. 57–58.

78 "Angry pedagogue." Ibid., p. 59.

78 "The experience of all." Ibid., p. 62.

78 "We expect them." OP, 2, Samuel Allyne Otis to Joseph Otis, Sept. 30, 1768.

78 "The fleet is come." Ibid., Oct. 1, 1768.

79 "Sullen silence." MWH, 1, p. 66.

79 "To be called to." Beach, p. 167.

79 "Spirit Stirring Drum." JAD, 3, pp. 289–90.

79 "Turned inside out." R. E. Brown, p. 244.

80 "Measures necessary." Hosmer, *Hutchinson*, p. 436, Thomas Hutchinson to Thomas Whately, Jan. 20, 1769.

80 "To keep secret." Ibid., p. 437, Oct. 20, 1769.
80 "Dependance." Ibid., p. 436, Jan. 20, 1769.
80 "There must be." Ibid.
81 "Felt more trouble." Hutchinson, *History*, 3, p. 192.
82 "If she was a Daughter." A. Brown, p. 101, Hannah Winthrop to Mercy Warren, Apr. 6, 1769.
82 "Curtain Lectures." JAD, 1, p. 349.
82–83 "The present measures." *Proceedings,* 43, p. 493, James Otis, Jr., to Arthur Jones, Nov. 26, 1768.
83 "Rights of the crown." Sibley and Shipton, 11, p. 277.
84 "The Cause, and End." JAD, 1, p. 342.
84 "Otis talks all." Ibid., p. 343.
84 "Superlative blockhead." Sibley and Shipton, 11, p. 277.
84 "A natural right." Ibid., p. 278.
84 "The fellow to it." Ibid., p. 277.
84 "Clubb." JAD, 1, p. 343.
84 "No Politeness." Ibid.
84 "Knock him down." *Gazette,* Sept. 25, 1769.
85 "I saw you fallen." MWLB, Mercy Warren to James Otis, Jr., Sept. 1769.
85 "I have done more mischief." Sibley and Shipton, 11, p. 280.
85 "Wondered what our parsons." Ibid.
85 "Like a Ship." JAD, 1, p. 348.
86 "Raving Mad"; "raving vs. Father." Ibid., p. 350.
86 "This shewes." Ibid.
88 "Very Bad Wine." Rowe, p. 212.
89 "Oh the Transitory." OP, 3, James Warren to Joseph Otis, Apr. 13, 1771.

CHAPTER VI

90 "Not suspected." R. E. Brown, p. 280.
90 "You say you have been spoken." Allan, p. 121.
91 "A new set of acquaintance." Ibid., p. 125.
91 "Meddle not." JAD, 2, p. 63.
91 "How easily the People." Ibid., p. 15.
91 "Every other Thing we." Ibid., p. 34.

91 "Languor and." WAL, 2, p. 399, James Warren to Samuel Adams, Nov. 8, 1772.

92 "When you *once* spoke." WAL, 1, p. 8, Samuel Adams to James Warren, Mar. 25, 1771.

92 "Nil desperandum . . . Where there." WAL, 1, p. 14, Samuel Adams to James Warren, Dec. 9, 1772.

92 "In his old way." OP, 3, Samuel Allyne Otis to Joseph Otis, 1771.

92 "If you escape." MWLB, Mercy Warren to James Warren, Jr., 1772.

92 "Glide into paths." Ibid.

92–93 "Into mazes of error." Ibid.

93 "And his little chambermate." WFLP, Hannah Winthrop to Mercy Warren, Aug. 14, 1772.

93 "I tremble." MWLB, Mercy Warren to James Warren, Jr., 1772.

93 "He trembles." JAD, 2, p. 14.

93 "All roiled." JAD, 2, p. 50.

93 "He runs into." Ibid.

94 "I fear he is." OP, 3, Samuel Allyne Otis to Joseph Otis, 1771.

94 "With grief did I behold." Hannah Winthrop to Mercy Warren, Jan. 1, 1772.

95 "I doubt not." MWLB, Mercy Warren to James Otis, Jr., Dec. 28, 1771.

95 "Behaved well." OP, 3, Samuel Allyne Otis to Joseph Otis, 1772.

95 "In one of those intervals." MWH, 1, p. 88.

95 "Cruelly." GOP, James Otis, Sr., to James Otis, Jr., Aug. 1, 1772.

95 "I must let you know my mind." Ibid.

95–96 "It is amaseing to me." Ibid.

96 "Especially when I considered." Ibid.

96 "Sett up the Worship." Ibid.

97 "Calculated to strike." Hutchinson, *History*, 3, pp. 262–63.

98 "90 to 1." Mass. Archives, 25, Peter Oliver to Thomas Hutchinson, Dec. 16, 1772.

98 "Sufficient to crush us." Hutchinson, *History*, 3, p. 255.

98 "Presume upon such." Ibid.

98 "I endeavoured to show." Hosmer, *Hutchinson*, p. 250, Thomas Hutchinson to Gambier, Feb. 14, 1773.

98–99 "It is essential." Bailyn, *Pamphlets*, p. 133.

99 "Gave a fair opening." MWH, 1, p. 114.
99 "I send you my speech." Hosmer, *Hutchinson*, p. 250, Thomas Hutchinson to Gambier, Feb. 14, 1773.
99 "Amazed at the Governor." JAD, 2, p. 77.
99 "Ruin and Destruction." Ibid.
99 "It gives me pain." Hosmer, *Hutchinson*, p. 251, Thomas Hutchinson to Lord Dartmouth, June 12, 1773.
100 "Keep secret." Ibid., p. 437, Thomas Hutchinson to Thomas Whately, Oct. 20, 1769.
100 "There must be an." Ibid., p. 436, Thomas Hutchinson to Thomas Whately, Jan. 20, 1769.
100–01 "Bone of our Bone." JAD, 2, p. 81.
101 "He flattered himself." Hutchinson, *History*, 3, p. 281.
101 "No instance." Ibid., p. 280.
102 "In character." Hosmer, *Hutchinson*, p. 285, Thomas Hutchinson to Israel Williams, July 20, 1773.
102 "The deception." Ibid.
103 "The Council say." Ibid., p. 293.
104 "I was born." JAD, 2, p. 82.
104 "I have never known." Ibid., p. 78.
104 "New covered and glased." Ibid., p. 74.
105 "Our house of Commons." WAL, 1, p. 17, Hannah Winthrop to Mercy Warren, Apr. 12, 1773.
105 "The happiness of living." G. S. Wood, p. 24.
105 "The bounds." MW Poems, p. 228.
105 "Gentleness, charity." MWLB, Mercy Warren to Samuel Allyne Otis, Dec. 22, 1772.
106 "Hell! what a night." Mercy Warren, *The Adulateur*, p. 232.
106 "Long have I wept." Ibid., p. 257.
106 "I fall unpitied." Mercy Warren, *The Defeat, Gazette*, May 24, 1773.
107 "Is the Game." Ibid., July 19, 1773.
107 "As the amusement." MW Poems, p. iii.
107 "Though . . . a Little personal." WAL, 1, p. 37, Mercy Warren to John Adams, Jan. 30, 1775.
107–08 "I should think myself." Ibid., p. 42, John Adams to Mercy Warren, Mar. 15, 1775.

108 "Of all the Genius's." Ibid., pp. 43–44.

108 "Gilden and false Lustre." JAD, 1, p. 360.

109 "One of my own Sex." AFC, 1, p. 77, Abigail Adams to Isaac Smith, Apr. 20, 1771.

109 "Like a Dutch." James Boswell, *Boswell in Search,* p. 160.

109 "She is not so much." AFC, 1, p. 72, Isaac Smith to John Adams, Feb. 21, 1771.

109 "Conscious inferiority." MWLB, Mercy Warren to Catherine Macaulay, June 9, 1773.

110 "Has the genius." Ibid.

110 "Blind trumpeter." Lewis, p. 82.

111 "The Tea that bainfull." AFC, 1, p. 88, Abigail Adams to Mercy Warren, Dec. 5, 1773.

112 "Not a pure white but next to it"; "a little life." Hosmer, *Hutchinson,* p. 287.

114 "The forlorn state." Hutchinson, *History,* 3, p. 314.

114 "Nobody suspected." Hosmer, *Hutchinson,* p. 304.

115 "You may not know." Hutchinson, *Diary,* p. 108, Peggy Hutchinson to Polly Hutchinson, Jan. 25, 1774.

116 "The ball of empire." MWH, 1, pp. 176–78.

CHAPTER VII

119 "We are all upon our oars." OP, 3, Samuel Allyne Otis to Joseph Otis, Feb. 22, 1774.

119 "It is now a very gloomy." Hulton, p. 73.

119–20 "Our brethern at Scituate." *Gazette,* Oct. 24, 1774.

120 "I think the appointment." AFC, 1, p. 138, Mercy Warren to Abigail Adams, Aug. 9, 1774.

121 "At the beat of a drum." Freeman, p. 433.

121 "Whole people." Ibid., p. 434.

122 "The whole body with their heads." Ibid., p. 446.

122 "You seem inclined to censure." MWLB, Mercy Warren to Hannah Lincoln, Sept. 3, 1774.

122 "The greater part of the species." Ibid.

123 "Irregularities"; "productive of less." Ibid.

123 "Part in the Drama." AFC, 1, p. 182, Mercy Warren to Abigail Adams, Jan. 28, 1775.

123 "Buckle on." AFC, 1, p. 139, Mercy Warren to Abigail Adams, Aug. 9, 1774.

124 "If such is Life." WAL, 2, p. 403.

124 Tea Party poem. AFC, 1, p. 102.

124 "A court of sychophants." Moses, p. 222.

125 "That state Crokedile." AFC, 1, p. 187, Mercy Warren to Abigail Adams, Feb. 25, 1775.

125–26 "I am very sensible." WAL, 2, p. 408, James Warren to Harrison Gray, Jan. 20, 1775.

128 "Ridiculous." AFC, 1, p. 182, Mercy Warren to Abigail Adams, Jan. 28, 1775.

128 "Not a robust man." Richards, 1, p. 46.

128 "The die is cast." AFC, 1, p. 183, Abigail Adams to Mercy Warren, Feb. 1775.

129 "A good fall of lambs." Moore, p. 77.

129 "My spirits have done." MWP, Mercy Warren to James Warren, Mar. 1775.

130 "I seem to want nothing." WAL, 1, pp. 44–45, James Warren to Mercy Warren, Apr. 6, 1775.

130–31 "I begin to think of the Trunks." Ibid., pp. 45–46.

131 "Full of the most painful apprehensions." MWLB, Mercy Warren to Mrs. Bowen, Apr. 1775.

132 "In pieces in her bed." Ibid.

132 "He has so great a desire." MWP, Mercy Warren to James Warren, May 3, 1775.

132 "I beg you would not suffer." MWLB, Mercy Warren to James Otis, Sr., 1775.

132 "In such a shifting." WAL, 1, p. 47, James Warren to John Adams, May 7, 1775.

132 "Fixt settled Government." Ibid., p. 48.

132 "With the same ease." Ibid.

133 "The roads filled with." WFLP, Hannah Winthrop to Mercy Warren, Apr. 1775.

133 "Desirous of seeing." Hutchinson, *Diary*, p. 491.

134 "Would astonish everyone." WAL, 1, p. 49.

134 "Hutcheson I hear flatters." WFLP, Catherine Macaulay to Mercy Warren, Sept. 28, 1774.

134 "Next to being married." Hutchinson, *Diary*, p. 275.

134–35 "We had a dispute." Ibid., pp. 276–77.

135 "I will not permit." Ibid., p. 282.

136 "I am not only free." Ibid., p. 186.

136 "Presume to say," Ibid., p. 175.

136 "I have seen Mr. Hutchinson." Ibid., p. 158.

137 "New England is wrote." Ibid., p. 283.

137 "Six or eight bushels." Ibid., p. 201.

137 "I hope none of my friends." Hutchinson, Correspondence, Nov. 1775.

137 "If there is a prospect." Hutchinson, *Diary*, p. 393.

137 "And the trees will bear." Ibid., p. 399.

137 "A fish converted." Ibid., p. 450.

138 "I see my contemporaries." Ibid.

138 "There never was a more unjust charge." Ibid., p. 504.

138 "The most distressing." Ibid., p. 477.

138 "My house at Milton." Ibid.

138 "Such instruction." Ibid., p. 526.

138 "A cruelty hard to bear." Hutchinson, Correspondence, Thomas Hutchinson to Thomas Hutchinson, Jr., June 27, 1775.

139 "Necessity will oblige." AFC, 1, p. 217, Abigail Adams to John Adams, June 1775.

139 "Than turtles." WAL, 1, p. 121, James Warren to John Adams, Oct. 1, 1775.

139 "They should be encouraged." Ibid., p. 53, John Adams to James Warren, June 10, 1775.

139 "Plans of Cities." AFC, 1, p. 252, John Adams to Abigail Adams, July 17, 1775.

140 "In case of real Danger." Ibid., p. 192, John Adams to Abigail Adams, May 2, 1775.

140 "Everything that has hapned." Hutchinson, *Diary*, p. 461.

140 "We are besieged." Ibid., p. 459.

140 "You who riot." Ibid., p. 469.

140–41 "Irish and British." MWP, Mercy Warren to James Warren, June 16, 1775.

141 "Modern Soldier." WAL, 1, p. 50, James Warren to Mercy Warren, May 18, 1775.

141 "Let your Colonel's." Ibid.

141 "If more soldiers." Thacher, *Military Journal,* p. 22.

141 "Under the pressure." MWP, Mercy Warren to James Warren, June 16, 1775.

142 "Beloved Husband." MWP, Mercy Warren to James Warren, June 16, 1775.

142–43 "Don't write." Ibid.

143 "Infatuated multitude." Massachusetts, *Journals of Each Provincial Congress,* pp. 330–31.

143 "All the natives." Ibid., p. 346.

143 "Spirituous liquors"; "particularly circumstanced." Ibid., p. 340.

143 "As we have reason to fear." Ibid., p. 342.

144 "Nothing to boast." WAL, 1, p. 62, James Warren to John Adams, June 20, 1775.

144 "It is impossible." WAL, 1, p. 59, James Warren to Mercy Warren, June 18, 1775.

144 "To add Sentences." Ibid., pp. 60–61.

CHAPTER VIII

146 "Rather too much levity." MWH, 1, p. 214.

146 "After putting on." Ibid., p. 215.

146 "Like a Coach and six." AFC, 1, p. 215, John Adams to Abigail Adams, June 17, 1775.

147 "All the Philosophy." WAL, 1, p. 232, John Adams to James Warren, Apr. 20, 1776.

147 "Content without a slice." Ibid., p. 78, James Warren to John Adams, July 7, 1775.

147 "I, poor Creature." AFC, 1, p. 226, John Adams to Abigail Adams, June 25, 1775.

147 "John the round Head." Ibid., p. 311, Abigail Adams to John Adams, Oct. 22, 1775.

148 "Certain great Fortune." WAL, 1, p. 88, John Adams to James Warren, July 24, 1775.

148 "The Fidgets." AFC, 1, p. 256, John Adams to Abigail Adams, July 24, 1775.

148 "Pay an implicit Obedience." Sibley and Shipton, 11, p. 390.

148 "I am more and more convinced." AFC, 1, p. 329, Abigail Adams to John Adams, Nov. 27, 1775.

148 "The great fish." Ibid.

149 "Propensity in human nature." MWLB, Mercy Warren to John Adams, Oct. 17, 1775.

149 "Infamous hussey." WAL, 1, p. 121, James Warren to John Adams, Oct. 1, 1775.

149 "Good God!" Ibid., p. 137, John Adams to James Warren, Oct. 13, 1775.

150 "With such symmetry." Ibid., p. 39, Mercy Warren to John Adams, Jan. 30, 1775.

150 "Exercise the powers." Continental Congress, *Journals,* 2, p. 84.

150 "I can't . . . say that I admire." WAL, 1, p. 64, James Warren to John Adams, June 20, 1775.

151 "I am sick of our." WAL, 1, p. 183, James Warren to John Adams, Nov. 14, 1775.

151 "As you ever saw pismires." WAL, 1, p. 68, James Warren to John Adams, June 27, 1775.

151 "As great as ever any man." WAP, James Warren to Mercy Warren, Aug. 9, 1775.

152 "It is enough for me." MWP, Mercy Warren to James Warren, Dec. 5, 1775.

152 "Every body either eats." WAL, 1, p. 149, James Warren to John Adams, Oct. 20, 1775.

152 "I want to know." AFC, 1, p. 302, Abigail Adams to Mercy Warren, Oct. 19, 1775.

152 "Draw the Character." WAL, 1, p. 201, John Adams to Mercy Warren, Jan. 8, 1776.

152 "Venerable person"; "the most amiable"; "to a degree of ugliness"; "a brave soldier." MWLB, Mercy Warren to John Adams, Oct. 17, 1775.

152 "What is Commonly called." WAL, 1, p. 229, Mercy Warren to Abigail Adams, Apr. 17, 1776.

153 "All political attentions." MWH, p. iv.

153 "Anything so far beyond." WAL, 1, p. 107, Mercy Warren to John Adams, Sept. 4, 1775.

153 "A Share and no Small." Ibid., p. 115, John Adams to Mercy Warren, Sept. 26, 1775.

153 "Book." Ibid., p. 229, Mercy Warren to Abigail Adams, Apr. 17, 1775.

153 "History, the deposite." MWH, p. 1.

154 "In proportion to the height." MWLB, Mercy Warren to James Warren, Jr., 1776.

154 "Well-regulated"; "pleasing prospect." WFLP, Hannah Winthrop to Mercy Warren, Dec. 13, 1775.

154 "The yellow produce"; "each one had his." MWP, Mercy Warren to James Warren, Sept. 21, 1775.

154 "In your armed chair." MWP, Mercy Warren to James Warren, Feb. 1, 1776.

155 "Every laudable." MWP, Mercy Warren to James Warren, Jan. 1776.

155 "To Fidelio." MW Poems, p. 213.

157 "Cannot Hulks." WAL, 1, p. 216, John Adams to James Warren, Mar. 29, 1776.

157 "For God's sake." Ibid., p. 221, John Adams to James Warren, Apr. 3, 1776.

157–58 "If I was there." AFC, 1, p. 406, John Adams to Abigail Adams, May 12, 1776.

158 "Is not Boston." WAL, 1, p. 239, James Warren to John Adams, May 8, 1776.

158 "As David slew." Ibid., p. 262, James Warren to John Adams, July 17, 1776.

158 "I can't describe." Ibid., p. 219, James Warren to John Adams, Apr. 3, 1776.

158 "You say the Sigh's." Ibid., p. 227, John Adams to James Warren, Apr. 16, 1776.

158 "We are certainly." Ibid., p. 240, James Warren to John Adams, May 8, 1776.

159 "That many blockheads." Ibid.

160 "Injure his country." Ibid.

160 "I cant bear the Thought." Ibid., p. 248, John Adams to James Warren, May 18, 1776.

160 "Banded about." AFC, 1, p. 404, Abigail Adams to Mercy Warren, May 8, 1776.

160 "Disordered in his mind." Ibid., p. 418, Abigail Adams to John Adams, May 27, 1776.

160 "Wound which cannot." AFC, 2, p. 80, Abigail Adams to John Adams, Aug. 5, 1776.

160 "Some Axiety." AFC, 1, p. 421, Mercy Warren to Abigail Adams, May 27, 1776.

161 "Illness"; "rise high"; "happy effect." WFLP, Hannah Winthrop to Mercy Warren, July 8, 1776.

161 "Impaired in Health." AFC, 2, p. 80, Abigail Adams to John Adams, Aug. 5, 1776.

162 "God grant." Ibid., p. 45, Abigail Adams to John Adams, July 13, 1776.

162 "No Business." WAL, 1, p. 262, James Warren to John Adams, July 17, 1776.

162 "Yesterday the greatest." AFC, 2, p. 27, John Adams to Abigail Adams, July 3, 1776.

162 "In a State little better." Ibid., p. 70, Abigail Adams to John Adams, July 30, 1776.

163 "With the Multitude." Ibid., p. 56, Abigail Adams to John Adams, July 21, 1776.

163 "Thus ends royall." Ibid., p. 56, Abigail Adams to John Adams, July 21, 1776.

CHAPTER IX

164 "Already hanker after." WAL, 1, p. 195, Samuel Adams to James Warren, Dec. 26, 1775.

164 "A distinct people." MWH, 1, p. 310.

165 "To dread the consequences." WAL, 1, p. 219, James Warren to John Adams, Apr. 3, 1776.

165 "Very unequal to." Ibid., p. 335, James Warren to John Adams, June 22, 1777.

166 "Marked with the wisdom." Ibid., p. 368, James Warren to John Adams, Sept. 17, 1777.

166–67 "At present if there." J. T. Austin, I, p. 266, Samuel Allyne Otis to Elbridge Gerry, Nov. 22, 1777.

167 "The clearest and coolest." WAL, 1, p. 243, John Adams to James Warren, May 12, 1776.

167 "Provided an equal." Ibid.

167 "Is a certain elevated." Ibid., p. 340, John Adams to James Warren, July 7, 1777.

167 "We have had two Presidents." Ibid., p. 378, Samuel Adams to James Warren, Oct. 30, 1777.

168 "The Great Man." WAL, 2, pp. 20–21, James Warren to John Adams, June 7, 1778.

168 "Why Doe we wast." Taylor, ed., *Massachusetts, Colony,* p. 69.

168 "Should be expressed." Plymouth, *Records,* 3, p. 346.

169 "If Ticonderoga." WAP, John Adams to James Warren, Apr. 29, 1777.

169 "We have lately ordered." WAL, 1, p. 323–24, James Warren to John Adams, May 5, 1777.

169 "An officer always unfortunate." MWH, 2, p. 6.

169 "How shall the disgrace." AFC, 2, p. 294, Abigail Adams to John Adams, July 30, 1777.

169 "The Nest of Hornets." WAL, 1, p. 315, John Adams to James Warren, Apr. 16, 1777.

170 "Business of the Season." Ibid., p. 349, James Warren to John Adams, Aug. 10, 1777.

170 "A Dagger in my Bosom." MWP, Mercy Warren to James Warren, Sept. 15, 1776.

170 "If you march." Ibid.

170 "It may be hard." Gardiner, p. 42, James Warren to Elbridge Gerry, July 7, 1776.

171 *"Or such other officer."* WAL, 1, p. 349, James Warren to John Adams, Aug. 10, 1777.

171 "If we have no right." Ibid.

171 "The herds at Eal-river." Ibid., p. 341, James Warren to John Adams, July 10, 1777.

171 "After a ten years." MWP, Mercy Warren to James Warren, June 14, 1777.

172 "Inglorious affair." Gardiner, p. 59, James Warren to Elbridge Gerry, Apr. 30, 1777.

172 "Common civility." MWP, Mercy Warren to James Warren, June 14, 1777.

172 "I have taken such a lurch." WAL, 1, p. 327, James Warren to John Adams, June 5, 1777.

172 "For Want of my farm." AFC, 2, p. 238, John Adams to Abigail Adams, May 15, 1777.

172 "Posterity!" Ibid., p. 224, John Adams to Abigail Adams, Apr. 26, 1777.

172 "You must not decline." WAL, 1, p. 332, John Adams to James Warren, June 19, 1777.

173 "So many thousands." MWH, 2, p. 51.

173–74 "Last Thursday." WFLP, Hannah Winthrop to Mercy Warren, Nov. 11, 1777.

175 "Rioting on the Fat." WFLP, Hannah Winthrop to Mercy Warren, Feb. 4, 1778.

175 "Once in every Age." AFC, 2, p. 393.

175 "What must be that Genius." Ibid., p. 391, Abigail Adams to John Thaxter, Feb. 15, 1778.

175 "Tis four Months." Ibid., p. 231, Abigail Adams to John Adams, May 6, 1777.

176 "I want a companion." Ibid., p. 270, Abigail Adams to John Adams, June 23, 1777.

176 "Yesterday compleated." Ibid., p. 340, Abigail Adams to John Adams, Sept. 10, 1777.

176 "Problematical"; "too Great a Regard"; "suspicious." Ibid., p. 379, Mercy Warren to Abigail Adams, Jan. 8, 1778.

176 "I don't write to the Embassador." WAL, 2, p. 50, James Warren to John Adams, Oct. 7, 1778.

177 "Fellows who would have cleaned." Ibid., p. 105, James Warren to John Adams, June 13, 1779.

177 "Crawling in." Jameson, p. 70.

177 "Follies of the Day." MW Poems, pp. 250–52.

177 "Ah, Ninevah." WFLP, Hannah Winthrop to Mercy Warren, Jan. 9, 1778.

178 "To sacrifice." Mercy Warren to Hannah Winthrop, May 29, 1778.

179 "Hid in Holes and Corners." WAL, 2, p. 42, James Warren to Samuel Adams, Aug. 18, 1778.

179 "Can a man take Fire." WAL, 1, p. 292, Samuel Adams to James Warren, Feb. 16, 1777.

179 "O America, America!" Thacher, *History,* p. 209.

180 "Swallowed it." WAL, 2, p. 52, James Warren to John Adams, Oct. 7, 1778.

180 "Endeavouring since the 19th." Plymouth, *Records,* 3, p. 329.

180 "False Lenity." Gardiner, p. 58, James Warren to Elbridge Gerry, Apr. 23, 1777.

180 "Dear Mr. Hallowell's." *Winslow Papers,* p. 25.

181 "He was suffered." WAL, 2, p. 16, Mercy Warren to James Warren, June 2, 1778.

181 "I love you should feel." WAP, James Warren to Mercy Warren, June 8, 1778.

182 "Out of sight." WAL, 2, p. 20, James Warren to John Adams, June 7, 1778.

182 "The people feel." Ibid.

182 "An old Fashioned Fellow." Ibid., p. 92, James Warren to Samuel Adams, Feb. 28, 1779.

182 "You know I have been on Deck." Ibid., p. 24, James Warren to Samuel Adams, June 26, 1778.

182 "Glass of Wine." Ibid., p. 122, James Warren to James Lovell, Dec. 1779.

183 "Sluggish." Ibid., p. 101, James Warren to Mercy Warren, June 6, 1779.

183 "That a Mind." Ibid., p. 102.

183 "Trembling Nerves." Ibid.

183 "I am sometimes Ready." MWP, Mercy Warren to James Warren, Mar. 12, 1780.

183 "Why was this such." WAL, 2, p. 85, Mercy Warren to Abigail Adams, Jan. 19, 1779.

184 "Bewildered man." JAD, 2, p. 368.

184 "Long absent son." MWP, Mercy Warren to James Warren, Mar. 15, 1780.

184 "Your son is on board." WAL, 2, p. 127, John Adams to James Warren, Feb. 28, 1780.

185 "And believe me, Sir." MWP, Charles Warren to James Warren, Dec. 23, 1780.

185 "Slender constitution." Allan, p. 285.

185 "Pen as it were." MWLB, Mercy Warren to Winslow Warren, Sept. 12, 1784.

186 "Taste for elegant." MWLB, Mercy Warren to Winslow Warren, Mar. 25, 1780.

186 "Attended with the most shameful." MWP, Mercy Warren to Winslow Warren, July 1780.

186 "I have no Quarrel." MWP, Mercy Warren to Winslow Warren, Dec. 1779.

186 "The morals of a whore." Boswell, *Samuel Johnson*, 1, p. 189.

186 "Purchasing Sailors Shares." JAD, 4, p. 192.

187 "Accidental deviation"; "beacon." MWLB, Mercy Warren to Winslow Warren, Dec. 4, 1779.

187 "Unhinged." MWP, Mercy Warren to James Warren, Mar. 12, 1780.

187 "I know not what reasons." Ibid.

187 "No Winslow yet." MWP, Mercy Warren to James Warren, Mar. 15, 1780.

187 "Do I raise my hopes." MWP, Mercy Warren to James Warren, Mar. 26, 1780.

187 "With Mr. Tillotson." WAL, 2, p. 132, Mercy Warren to James Warren, Apr. 2, 1780.

187 "I can't bear." MWP, James Warren to Mercy Warren, Apr. 2, 1780.

188 "No mortal." MWP, Mercy Warren to James Warren, Apr. 11, 1780.

188 "I dont Believe." Ibid.

188 "In a room with three windows." Moore, p. 280.

188 "Fear seized on all." Pynchon, p. 63.

188 "By which the whole people." Taylor, ed., *Massachusetts, Colony,* p. 128.

189 "You have surveyed." MWLB, Mercy Warren to Winslow Warren, June 1780.

189 "Did he do Everything." MWP, Mercy Warren to James Warren, June 5, 1780.

189 "If this Infant." WAL, 2, p. 147, Mercy Warren to John Adams, Nov. 15, 1780.

CHAPTER X

191 "I see that the ways." Hutchinson, *Diary*, 2, p. 193.

191 "Most of us expect." Ibid., p. 171.

192 "Died of Milton Hill." Sibley and Shipton, 8, p. 213.
192 "My shortness of breath." Hutchinson, *Diary*, 2, p. 347.
192 "A week passed." Ibid.
193 "With one or two gaspes." Hosmer, *Hutchinson*, p. 348.
195 "A man of pleasure." *Proceedings*, 65, p. 247.
195 "A somewhat amphibious." Ibid., p. 245.
195 "I pray God." *Proceedings*, 65, p. 237, James Warren to Winslow Warren, Sept. 27, 1780.
195 "Philosophic Hints." WAL, 2, p. 146, Mercy Warren to John Adams, Nov. 15, 1780.
195 "Explicit opinions." Ibid., p. 147.
196 "Guard against the fascinating." MWP, Mercy Warren to Winslow Warren, Sept. 11, 1781.
196 "Virtue is melted." Ibid.
196 "Why have you not." MWP, James Warren to Winslow Warren, Sept. 28, 1781.
196–97 "Lord Hillsborough asked." *Proceedings*, 65, p. 252.
197 "Has any part of his Conduct." WAL, 2, p. 181, Mercy Warren to John Adams, Oct. 24, 1782.
197 "He has been travelling." WAL, 2, p. 189, John Adams to Mercy Warren, Jan. 29, 1783.
198 "Three quarters of the Low." *Proceedings*, 65, p. 255.
198 "When shall I see." MWP, Mercy Warren to Winslow Warren, Apr. 29, 1782.
198 "If my Winslow is safe." MWP, Mercy Warren to Winslow Warren, May 4, 1783.
198 "What judicious." MWP, Mercy Warren to Winslow Warren, May 4, 1783.
199 "To a Young Gentleman Residing in France." MW Poems, p. 222.
199 "Sweet." James Warren to Winslow Warren, *Proceedings*, 65, p. 260.
199–200 "Oh, my Dear Husband." MWP, Mercy Warren to James Warren, Jan. 27, 1781.
200–01 "When you return." MWP, James Warren to Winslow Warren, June 3, 1781.
201 "Not ten men." Clark, p. 236.

202 "Bore the Stroke." MWP, Charles Warren to Winslow Warren, Sept. 30, 1781.

202 "Always fallen in pleasant places." MWP, Mercy Warren to Sally Sever, Dec. 1781.

202 "Our affairs wear." *Proceedings,* 65, p. 259, James Warren to Winslow Warren.

203 "I shall certainly take pleasure." WAL, 2, p. 178, James Warren to John Adams, Oct. 7, 1782.

203 "Do ascertain." Ibid., p. 179.

203 "I dread her History." Ibid., p. 155, John Adams to James Warren, Dec. 9, 1780.

204 "I assure you." Ibid., p. 188, John Adams to Mercy Warren, July 29, 1783.

205 "What a field for genius." *Proceedings,* 65, p. 265, Mercy Warren to Winslow Warren.

205 "A republican form." Gardiner, p. 162, Mercy Warren to Elbridge Gerry, June 6, 1783.

205 "You know I hate." *Proceedings,* 65, p. 260, James Warren to Winslow Warren.

206 "A Step which has been." MWP, James Warren to Benjamin Lincoln, Apr. 28, 1783.

206 "Super Intendant," WAL, 2, p. 248, James Warren to John Adams, Jan. 28, 1785.

206 "Old Man." Ibid., p. 231, James Warren to John Adams, Oct. 27, 1783.

206 "I never know when." Ibid., p. 209, John Adams to James Warren, Apr. 13, 1783.

206 "How long will he live?" Ibid, p. 231, James Warren to John Adams, Oct. 27, 1783.

207 "Example of one Good Man." Ibid., p. 216, Mercy Warren to John Adams, May 4, 1783.

207 "Exercise his patriotic feelings." MWP, Charles Warren to Mercy Warren, Nov. 17, 1782.

207 "Old Hands." WAL, 2, p. 189, John Adams to Mercy Warren, Jan. 29, 1783.

207 "Out of Season." Ibid., p. 231, James Warren to John Adams, Oct. 27, 1783.

207 "If you ask why." Ibid., p. 220, James Warren to John Adams, June 24, 1783.

208 "I am no longer." Ibid., p. 206, John Adams to James Warren, Apr. 9, 1783.

208 "I have this day." Tudor, p. 481.

209 "The resort of." Ibid., p. 483.

209 "Sun shorn of his beams." Ibid.

210 "State baby." Gardiner, p. 163, Mercy Warren to Elbridge Gerry, June 6, 1783.

211 "Forced . . . to dine." Tudor, p. 483.

211 "There was a visible oscillation." Ibid.

211 "He went like a lamb." Ibid.

212 "Extraordinary in Death." WAL, 2, p. 224, John Adams to Mercy Warren, Sept. 10, 1783.

212 "When God in anger." MWH, 1, p. 89.

213 "Eyes of all Europe." MWH, 3, p. 298.

213 "As a child just." Ibid., p. 323.

CHAPTER XI

217 "Alas, his Fortitude." Gardiner, p. 174, James Warren to Elbridge Gerry, Dec. 17, 1783.

218 "Compleatest Devil." *Winslow Papers,* p. 150, Sarah Winslow to Benjamin Marston, Nov. 29, 1783.

218–19 "And is my son." MWP, Mercy Warren to Winslow Warren, May 19, 1783.

219 "For reasons I will." MWP, James Warren to Winslow Warren, May 18, 1783.

219 "I hope you will be able." Ibid.

219 "It is the *world.*" MWLB, Mercy Warren to George Warren, Mar. 24, 1785.

219 "I think we are obliged." MWLB, Mercy Warren to Ellen Lothrop, 1775.

219 "I would check." MWP, Mercy Warren to Winslow Warren, May 19, 1783.

220 "It cannot be." MWLP, Mercy Warren to Winslow Warren, May 29, 1783.

220 "Most certainly and indispensably." MWP, James Warren to Winslow Warren, May 18, 1783.

220 "Where now is your philosophy?" MWLB, Mercy Warren to Janet Montgomery, Apr. 1792.

220 "Disagreeable spasms." WFLP, Mercy Warren to George Warren, Aug. 2, 1794.

220 "Statu quo." MWP, James Warren to Charles Warren, Dec. 12, 1784.

221 "Some of the scenes." Ibid.

221 "Great folks." MWP, Charles Warren to Winslow Warren, Sept. 30, 1781.

221 "No, Sir." Ibid.

221 "Tight Winter." Gardiner, p. 177, James Warren to Elbridge Gerry, Feb. 25, 1784.

221 "On the brink of eternity"; "bursting bubble." MWP, Mercy Warren to James Warren, Jr., 1785.

222 "Eligible manner." MWP, James Warren to Winslow Warren, Nov. 7, 1784.

222 "My dear Winslow." MWP, Mercy Warren to Winslow Warren, May 9, 1784.

222 "I have lived long enough." WAL, 2, p. 253, Mercy Warren to John Adams, Apr. 27, 1785.

222 "Little by experience." MWLB, Mercy Warren to Catherine Macaulay, July 1789.

223 "Eligantly situated." *Winslow Papers,* p. 150, Sarah Winslow to Benjamin Marston, Nov. 29, 1783.

223 "Ned behaved." MWP, Mercy Warren to Winslow Warren, July 18, 1784.

224 "Is it not singular." MWLB, Mercy Warren to George Warren, Jan. 9, 1785.

224 "I love your letters." MWLB, Mercy Warren to Winslow Warren, Mar. 1785.

224 "I am going to work hard." MWP, Winslow Warren to Mercy Warren, Aug. 17, 1784.

224 "I have a son." WFLP, James Warren to Thomas Jefferson, 1785.

225 "In all the cold." MWP, James Warren to George Warren, Dec. 29, 1784.

225 "Don't you think." Ibid.

225 "As rotten as an old Catherine pear." Donnelly, p. 186, said by John Wilkes.

226 "Animated severity." WAL, 2, p. 257, Catherine Macaulay Graham to Mercy Warren, July 15, 1785.

226 "Sneers at religion." MWLB, Mercy Warren to Winslow Warren, Mar. 1785.

226 "Pure republicanism." MWH, 3, p. 279.

226 "Did we consult the history." *Gazette,* Jan. 15, 1785.

227 "Arrogant stripling." *Proceedings,* 60, p. 331.

227 "Baleful comet." Ibid., p. 324.

227 "Weak-nerv'd G-n-r-l." Ibid., p. 341.

227 "Little indigested farrago." Ibid., p. 343, Mercy Warren to George Warren, Mar. 7, 1785.

227 "Rigid republicans"; "contracted minds." Ibid., p. 321.

227 "Instead of being Sans Souci." Ibid., p. 330.

228 "Throwing an undue weight." MWH, 3, p. 386.

228 "Grown grey." Ibid., p. 283.

230 "From many of the best." WAL, 2, p. 281, John Adams to James Warren, Jan. 9, 1787.

230 "I think the first Magistrates." Ibid.

230–31 "As resolute and as unchangeable." MWLB, Mercy Warren to George Warren, Nov. 2, 1793.

231 "Is there no possibility." OP, #289, Samuel Allyne Otis to Joseph Otis, 1785.

231 "If the Sheriff." OP, #290.

231 "I desire you would keep." OP, #292.

231 "Shutt up," OP, #297.

231–32 "In consequence of Mr. Warren's." Ibid.

232 "What a reverse." MWP, Mercy Warren to Winslow Warren, Aug. 28, 1785.

232 "Trembling widow." MWP, Mercy Warren to Winslow Warren, Sept. 29, 1784.

232 "You will in future consider." MWP, James Warren to Winslow Warren, Jan. 3, 1785.

232 "It is hard work." Ibid.

232–33 "Our General Court sets." WAL, 2, p. 272, James Warren to John Adams, Apr. 30, 1786.

233 "Man on Milton Hill." Ibid., p. 262, James Warren to John Adams, Sept. 4, 1785.

234 "The distress of the people." *Independent Chronicle,* Feb. 23, 1786.

235 "Every Amateur in America." MWP, Mercy Warren to Winslow Warren, Aug. 28, 1785.

235 "I should wish." WAL, 2, pp. 300–01, John Adams to Mercy Warren, Dec. 25, 1787.

235 "Several of the first." Ibid., p. 301.

235 "Dramatics to perfect." MWLB, Mercy Warren to Winslow Warren, Sept. 1785.

236 "Be guarded." MWP, Mercy Warren to Winslow Warren, Aug. 28, 1785.

236 "Well, Charles." MWLB, Mercy Warren to Charles Warren, Oct. 17, 1785.

236 "A lonely hour." MWLB, Mercy Warren to Charles Warren, Dec. 29, 1785.

237 "God grant." Ibid.

237 "Attacked alone." MWP, Mercy Warren to George Warren, 1786.

237 "Tumultous." Ibid.

237 "Strangers' tears." MW Poems, p. 241.

237 "Wealthy, flagitious villain." MWLB, Mercy Warren to John Adams, May 8, 1789.

238 "Attached the Body." *New Haven County Court Records,* Nov. 1786.

238 "We had a caning match." Knox, Papers, Henry Knox to Henry Jackson, Mar. 12, 1786.

239 "Could not, or would not." WAL, 2, pp. 278–79, James Warren to John Adams, Oct. 22, 1786.

239 "Three upper Counties." Ibid.

239 "Broke the gaol aforesaid." Massachusetts, *Circuit Court Records,* 1790.

240 "Time serving Talents." WAL, 2, p. 293, James Warren to John Adams, May 18, 1787.

240 "Peevish disposition." Ibid., p. 292.

240 "Regret the change." Ibid.

241 "The most arbitrary." Ibid., p. 293.

241 "The dread of reviving." Ibid.

354 NOTES

241 "G[eneral] Warren did differ." WAL, 2, p. 313, John Adams to Mercy Warren, May 29, 1789.
242 "Enter so far into." Bloom, p. 15.
242 "It was thought by some." MWH, 3, p. 357.
242 "Fine little plump girl." MWP, Samuel Allyne Otis to Mercy Warren, Aug. 1787.
243 "I have Faith." WAL, 2, p. 289, Abigail Adams to Mercy Warren, May 14, 1787.
243 "I am — a grand." Ibid., p. 290.
243 "Our situation." WFLP, Mercy Warren to Catherine Macaulay Graham, Sept. 28, 1787.
243 "Panting for nobility." WFLP, Mercy Warren to Catherine Macaulay Graham, Aug. 2, 1787.
244 "Does anything transpire." Proceedings, 64, p. 162.

CHAPTER XII

245 "Chinese wall." MWH, 2, p. 314.
246 "Too sublime and florid." Proceedings, 64, p. 144.
247 "Not the result of ignorance." MWH, 3, p. 360.
247 "A very warm Federalist." WAL, 2, p. 304, Catherine Macaulay Graham to Mercy Warren, Oct. 26, 1788.
250 "I often . . . take a walk." MWP, Mercy Warren to Sally Sever, Dec. 1781.
250 "Large share of malicious." Gardiner, p. 210, James Warren to Elbridge Gerry, July 20, 1788.
251 "You are the only Confidential." Ibid., p. 213, Feb. 1, 1789.
251 "Stopp'd about half an hour." John Quincy Adams, Diary, p. 413.
253 "Out of circulation." P. Smith, 2, p. 736, John Adams to Abigail Adams Smith, July 16, 1788.
253 "Honorable principles." Ibid., p. 738, Nov. 11, 1788.
254 "I am persuaded." WAL, 2, p. 309, Mercy Warren to John Adams, Apr. 2, 1789.
256 "Be assured." MWP, Mercy Warren to Winslow Warren, 1789.
256 "Sure." WAL, 2, p. 311, Mercy Warren to John Adams, May 7, 1789.
256 "Contemptible character." MWLB, Mercy Warren to Henry Knox, 1789.

257 "Equally ambitious." Abigail Adams, *New Letters*, p. 16, Abigail Adams to Mary Cranch, July 12, 1789.

257 "In the first place." WAL, 2, p. 314, John Adams to Mercy Warren, May 29, 1789.

257 "To the uninterrupted." Ibid., p. 313.

257 "What an astonishing." MWLB, Mercy Warren to Henry Knox, 1789.

258 "Inaccurately and without." Gardiner, p. 223, James Warren to Elbridge Gerry, Apr. 19, 1789.

258 "Duly sensible." WAL, 2, p. 318, George Washington to Mercy Warren, June 4, 1790.

258 "As great an admirer." MWLB, Mercy Warren to Lady Hraselevige, 1773.

259 "A dreadful thing." MWP, James Warren to Mercy Warren, June 28, 1790.

259 "I recd your letter." Ibid.

259 "Young officer." MWH, 3, p. 372.

259 "It is certain." WAL, 2, p. 326, Alexander Hamilton to Mercy Warren, July 1, 1791.

259 "Elegant letter." MWLB, Mercy Warren to George Warren, 1794.

260 "Though the vice-president." WAL, 2, p. 323, Mercy Warren to John Adams, Sept. 24, 1790.

260 "However foolishly." Ibid., p. 324, John Adams to Mercy Warren, Dec. 26, 1790.

260 "In the stile of my old friend." Ibid., p. 325, Mercy Warren to John Adams, Jan. 14, 1791.

261 "A Civil war, Madam." WAL, 2, p. 325, John Adams to Mercy Warren, Feb. 14, 1791.

261 "There should be." Ibid., p. 326.

261 "A monster." MWH, 3, p. 372.

261 "It ill becomes." MWLB, Mercy Warren to Catherine Macaulay Graham, July 1789.

261 "A whole Country." Gardiner, p. 235, James Warren to Elbridge Gerry, Aug. 23, 1789.

262 "I dared not disclose." MWLB, Mercy Warren to George Warren, Feb. 1792.

262 "Fly to his assistance." MWLB, Mercy Warren to Winslow Warren, May 18, 1781.

263 "Shall the citizens of America." Ibid.

263 "I wish I could entirely." MWP, Mercy Warren to Winslow Warren, May 22, 1791.

263 "Can I do anything." MWLB, Mercy Warren to Winslow Warren, May 18, 1791.

264 "What if I should send." MWP, Mercy Warren to Winslow Warren, May 29, 1791.

264 "The idea of going." MWLB, Mercy Warren to Winslow Warren, May 18, 1791.

264 "Best." MWLB, Mercy Warren to Winslow Warren, June 10, 1791.

264 "Why did you wish." Ibid.

265 "You would be surprised." MWP, Winslow Warren to Mercy Warren, July 3, 1791.

265 "The face of the Earth." MWP, Winslow Warren to Mercy Warren, Aug. 10, 1791.

265 "Notwithstanding we were." Ibid.

265–66 "In point of fertility." Ibid.

266 "Tell our countrymen." Ibid.

266 "Sufficient, unquestionably." Ibid.

266 "I viewed with different emotions." Ibid.

266 "We received yesterday." MWLB, Mercy Warren to Winslow Warren, Sept. 9, 1791.

266 "So that I shall soon." MWP, Winslow Warren to Mercy Warren, Aug. 29, 1791.

266 "Little." MWLB, Mercy Warren to Winslow Warren, Dec. 1791.

267 "I am often asked." MWLB, Mercy Warren to Winslow Warren, Nov. 30, 1791.

267 "Who & who." Abigail Adams, *New Letters*, p. 77, Feb. 5, 1792.

267 "Good God." Morison, *Harrison Gray Otis*, p. 66, Harrison Gray Otis to Sally Otis, Dec. 14, 1791.

CHAPTER XIII

268 "Forlorn." MWH, 3, p. 314.

268 "We are not forbidden." MWLB, Mercy Warren to George Warren, Jan. 5, 1792.

268 "Alas, I knew." MWLB, Mercy Warren to George Warren, July 1792.

268 "Cold philosophy." Ibid.

268–69 "May I ever remember." MWLB, Mercy Warren to George Warren, Jan. 5, 1792.

269 "The end of my walk." MWLB, Mercy Warren to George Warren, Feb. 1792.

269 "Revise & correct." MWP, Winslow Warren to Mercy Warren, July 3, 1791.

269 "Is Patrick Henry." Gardiner, p. 246, Mercy Warren to Elbridge Gerry, Mar. 24, 1791.

269 "Young, florid." MWLB, Mercy Warren to George Warren, Feb. 1792.

270 "I constantly contemplate." MWP, James Warren to Mercy Warren, Feb. 18, 1793.

270 "Magnitude." MWLB, Mercy Warren to George Warren, Nov. 1793.

270 "I cannot bear." Ibid.

270 "Is it not best." MWLB, Mercy Warren to George Warren, Mar. 22, 1795.

270 "A thousand fears." MWLB, Mercy Warren to George Warren, Nov. 11, 1796.

271 "The mistress of." MWLB, Mercy Warren to Mary Warren, Nov. 1791.

271 "There is nothing." Ibid.

271 "Marcia Otis is." MWLB, Mercy Warren to George Warren, Oct. 5, 1792.

271 "My little Marcia." MWLB, Mercy Warren to James Warren, Jr., Nov. 11, 1792.

273 "Adhered to the." MWH, 3, p. 371.

273 "Great Britain at the." James Otis, *Political Writings,* p. 330.

273 "We have such a clear." MWLB, Mercy Warren to George Warren, 1796.

274 "Freeze the soul." MWH, 3, p. 379.

275 "Distinguish between principles." Ibid., p. 414.

275 "How far our partialities." MWP, Samuel Allyne Otis to Henry Warren, Apr. 12, 1794.

275 "Supplicate at the levee." MWLB, Mercy Warren to George Warren, July 17, 1795.

276 "To establish the basis." MWH, 3, p. 386.

276 "Alas, humiliated America!" MWLB, Mercy Warren to George Warren, July 17, 1795.

277 "Water melon frolicks." J. C. Miller, *Sam Adams,* p. 396.

277 "Then for frugality." P. Smith, 2, p. 905, John Adams to Abigail Adams, Dec. 12, 1796.

277 "A foolish, mortifying." Ibid.

277 "Not above forty." Ibid., p. 890, John Adams to Abigail Adams, Mar. 11, 1796.

278 "Is not very charming." Ibid., p. 822, John Adams to Brand-Hollis, Feb. 19, 1792.

278 "Militant state." Ibid., p. 1081, John Adams to Noah Webster, Feb. 6, 1816.

278 "Supple enough." John Adams, *Letters to His Wife,* 2, p. 234, John Adams to Abigail Adams, Dec. 8, 1796.

279 "I hate speeches." Ibid., p. 207, John Adams to Abigail Adams, Mar. 1, 1796.

279 "Fastened up hand." P. Smith, 2, p. 916, Abigail Adams to John Adams, Dec. 23, 1796.

279 "Earliest Birds." JAD, 3, p. 227.

279 "A fine soft rain." Ibid., p. 228.

279 "Alas! What." Ibid., p. 238.

280 "The Lovely Marcia." WAL, 2, p. 332, Abigail Adams to Mercy Warren, Mar. 4, 1797.

280 "Was unexpected." MWLB, Mercy Warren to George Warren, Nov. 11, 1796.

280 "The sublimest thing." John Adams, *Letters to His Wife,* 2, p. 245, John Adams to Abigail Adams, Mar. 5, 1797.

282 "Spies, emissaries." Morison, *Harrison Gray Otis,* p. 104, Harrison Gray Otis to General Heath, Mar. 30, 1798.

282 "I am ready to profess." Ibid., p. 105.

283 "Rising up and sitting down." Abigail Adams, *New Letters,* p. 91, Abigail Adams to Mary Cranch, May 16, 1797.

283 "Pitch of venality." WAL, 2, p. 337. Abigail Adams to Mercy Warren, Apr. 25, 1798.

284 "Old, querilous." Abigail Adams, *New Letters,* p. 91, Abigail Adams to Mary Cranch, Apr. 28, 1798.

284 "Nothing will have an effect." Ibid., p. 165, Abigail Adams to Mary Cranch, Apr. 26, 1798.

284 "If that fellow." Ibid., p. 172, Abigail Adams to Mary Cranch, May 10, 1798.

284 "Why, when we have." Ibid., p. 201, Abigail Adams to Mary Cranch, July 9, 1798.

285 "No being below the supreme." MWLB, Mercy Warren to Abigail Adams, May 1798.

285 "Silence is the only." MWLB, Mercy Warren to George Warren, June 14, 1798.

288 "Electrified the public." P. Smith, 2, p. 1000, Abigail Adams to John Adams, Feb. 14, 1796.

289 "The two Jugglers." John Adams, *Adams-Jefferson Letters,* 2, p. 346, John Adams to Thomas Jefferson, June 30, 1813.

289 "Impious Idolatry." Ibid., p. 349, John Adams to Thomas Jefferson, July 3, 1813.

290 "No woodcutters." Abigail Adams, *Letters,* p. 384, Abigail Adams to Mrs. Smith, Nov. 27, 1800.

290 "The deepest affliction of my Life." John Adams, *Adams-Jefferson Letters,* 1, p. 264, John Adams to Thomas Jefferson, Mar. 24, 1801.

290 "But alas!" MWLB, Mercy Warren to George Warren, Jan. 8, 1800.

290 "I tell him he is not." MWLB, Mercy Warren to George Warren, June 18, 1797.

291 "Mighty business." Ibid.

291 "I have sat like a Man." MWP, James Warren to Thomas Jefferson, Mar. 4, 1801.

CHAPTER XIV

292 "Here ends." Ames, p. 158.

292 "Loose and indecent." *The Ordeal,* June 17, 1809.

292 "A la Brutus." Winsor, 4, p. 14.

293 "High degree of perfection." *The Monthly Anthology,* Apr. 1805.

293 "Object of compassion." J. C. Miller, *Sam Adams,* p. 400.

294 "Capable of putting sentences together." *The Monthly Anthology,* Oct. 1805, p. 341.

294 "Forestals, if not precludes." WAL, 2, p. 346, Mrs. Judith Sargent Murray to Mercy Warren, June 1, 1805.

295 "That the strictest veracity." MWH, 1, p. vi.

295 "Many of the first patriots." Ibid., p. iii.

296 "The experiment proved." Ibid., 3, p. 369.

296 "Future historian." Ibid., p. 395.

296 "Tincture of democracy." Morison, *Harrison Gray Otis,* p. 207, Harrison Gray Otis to John Rutledge, 1805.

296 "I dread her history." WAL, 2, p. 155, John Adams to James Warren, Dec. 9, 1780.

296 "In most instances." MWH, 3, p. 375.

296–97 "Naturally a man." MWH, 1, p. 241.

297 "A quick understanding." Ibid., p. 211.

297 "A man of pleasure." Ibid., p. 242.

297 "A man of little genius." Ibid., p. 42.

297 "A gentleman of fortune." Ibid., p. 212.

297 "Dark, intriguing." Ibid., p. 79.

297 "Reverential ideas." Ibid., p. 126.

297 "The faithfull Historian." WAL, 1, p. 42, John Adams to Mercy Warren, Mar. 15, 1775.

297 "Desire of Esteem." Ibid., p. 43.

297 "Forgotten the principles." MWH, 3, p. 392.

297–98 "The veracity of the." Ibid., p. 391.

298 "Partiality for monarchy." Ibid., p. 392.

298 "Charitable." Ibid., p. 394.

298 "Political phenomenon." Ibid., p. 393.

298 "Living long near the." Ibid., p. 394.

298 "Prejudices and." Ibid., 392.

298 "Pride of talent." Ibid., p. 393.

298 "Time and circumstances." Ibid., p. 392.

298 "Any errors." Ibid., p. 395.

299 "A steel-colored gown." Ellet, p. 126.

299 "Elbow chair"; "the old corner." WAL, 2, p. 394, Mercy Warren to John Adams, July 10, 1814.

299 "Yielded to." *The Panoplist,* 2, #8, p. 380.

300 "The improper use." Ibid., p. 382.

300 "A principle producing." Ibid.

300 "Needless to adduce." Ibid.

300 "The voice of the." Ibid.

300 "Flying like fugitives . . . the impropriety of." Ibid.

300 "At the bottom." Ibid., p. 383.

301 "Although the reader." Ibid., p. 381.

301 "Although we cannot bestow." Ibid., p. 432.

301 "A well digested." WAL, 2, p. 350, James Winthrop to Mercy Warren, Feb. 4, 1807.

301 "Could hardly be." Ibid., p. 348, John Dickinson to Mercy Warren, Dec. 22, 1806.

302 "Mausolaeum." John Adams, *Adams-Jefferson Letters*, 2, p. 349, John Adams to Thomas Jefferson, July 3, 1813.

302 "Who will ever." Ibid., p. 451, John Adams to Thomas Jefferson, July 30, 1815.

302 "Mortifications, Disappointments." JAD, 1, p. lxix.

302 "I look so much." John Adams, *Papers,* p. 305.

302 "Washington and Franklin." Ibid., p. 308.

303 "Quondam Friend." JAD, 4, p. 118.

304 "Passions and prejudices." MWH, 2, p. 392.

304 "If I had acted." *Collections,* 5th ser., 4, p. 322, John Adams to Mercy Warren, July 11, 1807.

304 "No talents beyond." Ibid., p. 470, John Adams to Mercy Warren, Aug. 19, 1807.

304 "If I were to measure." Ibid., p. 328, John Adams to Mercy Warren, July 11, 1807.

304 "Irritation of the times." Ibid., p. 328, Mercy Warren to John Adams, July 16, 1807.

304 "It is true." Ibid., p. 330.

304 "Were you to write." Ibid., p. 329.

304 "In his diplomatic character." MWH, 3, p. 176.

304 "I know not what foundation." *Collections,* 5th ser., 4, p. 407, John Adams to Mercy Warren, Aug. 3, 1807.

304 "His Genius was not." MWH, 3, p. 176.

304 "Deficient in the *'je ne sais quoi.'* " Ibid., p. 177.

305 "Franklin, Jay." *Collections,* 5th ser., 4, p. 408, John Adams to Mercy Warren, Aug. 3, 1807.

305 "Why am I singled." Ibid., p. 428, John Adams to Mercy Warren, Aug. 8, 1807.

305 "Determined resolution." Ibid., p. 429.

305 "Of a doorkeeper." Ibid., p. 358, John Adams to Mercy Warren, July 27, 1807.

305 "Not the least notice." Ibid., p. 432, John Adams to Mercy Warren, Aug. 8, 1807.

305 "To the taste." Ibid., p. 463, John Adams to Mercy Warren, Aug. 15, 1807.

305 "Perverse construction." Ibid., p. 360, Mercy Warren to John Adams, July 28, 1807.

305 "It was not in the design." Ibid., p. 449, Mercy Warren to John Adams, Aug. 15, 1807.

305–06 "Tell the world." Ibid., p. 423, Mercy Warren to John Adams, Aug. 7, 1807.

307 "All political attentions." Ibid., p. 456, Mercy Warren to John Adams, Aug. 5, 1807.

308 "I give you my decided." GOP, Henry Warren to William Otis, Aug. 21, 1808.

308 "You may well suppose." WAL, 2, p. 361, Harrison Gray Otis to Mercy Warren, Feb. 4, 1809.

308 "Ten to one." John Adams, *Adams-Jefferson Letters*, 2, p. 469, John Adams to Thomas Jefferson, May 3, 1816.

309 "I do not expect." MWP, James Warren to ?, 1808.

309 "Though well born." Morison, *Harrison Gray Otis*, p. 207, Harrison Gray Otis to John Rutledge, 1805.

310 "But the hope of a." John Adams, *Adams-Jefferson Letters*, 2, p. 471, John Adams to Thomas Jefferson, May 3, 1816.

311 "Benighted corners of the world." WAL, 2, p. 370, James Winthrop to Mercy Warren, Feb. 8, 1812.

311 "Two or three centuries." Ibid., p. 348, James Winthrop to Mercy Warren, Dec. 22, 1806.

311 "Levity." Ibid., p. 364, James Winthrop to Mercy Warren, Nov. 1, 1809.

311 "Diverted, and the Messiah's." Ibid., p. 371, James Winthrop to Mercy Warren, Feb. 8, 1812.

311 "Prospect of the expansion." MWP, Mercy Warren to Catherine Macaulay Graham, Mar. 29, 1812.

312 "The horrors of an." MWP, "Book of Alphabetical Maxims."

313 "Blustering and bullying." Quincy, p. 215, John Adams to Josiah Quincy, Jan. 15, 1811.

313 "Organize a *peace party.*" Morison, *Harrison Gray Otis,* p. 326.

313 "Founded in falsehood." Ames, p. 252.

314 "For myself, indeed." MWP, Mercy Warren to Elbridge Gerry, Aug. 16, 1812.

314 "So virulent." Ibid.

314 "Tarried until a few minutes." *Weekly Messenger,* Aug. 12, 1812.

315 "Blessed are the Peace-makers!" MWP, Mercy Warren to Abigail Adams, Sept. 1812.

315 "I forward to you." *Collections,* 5th ser., 4, p. 502, Abigail Adams to Mercy Warren, Dec. 30, 1812.

315 "*A token of love.*" Ibid., p. 503, Mercy Warren to Abigail Adams, Jan. 26, 1813.

315 "Disgraceful outrages." WAL, 2, p. 384, Abigail Adams to Mercy Warren, July 11, 1813.

316 "Province of the Ladies." Ibid., p. 380, John Adams to Elbridge Gerry, Apr. 17, 1813.

316 "Little Passions." Ibid.

316 "In the Congress." Ibid., p. 386, Governor McKean to John Adams, Aug. 20, 1813.

316 "I was much gratified." Ibid., Mercy Warren to John Adams, Sept. 12, 1813.

316 "More capable of." Ibid., p. 387.

316–17 "I know not, Madam." Ibid., p. 388, John Adams to Mercy Warren, Nov. 24, 1813.

317 "A very important letter." Ibid., p. 390, Mercy Warren to John Adams, Mar. 31, 1814.

317 "It is truly a satisfaction." Ibid.

317 "We are as usual." GOP, James Warren, Jr., to Maria Otis Colby, May 9, 1814.

317 "The last of my father's." MWP, Mercy Warren to Mrs. Samuel Allyne Otis, Aug. 16, 1814.

318 "Is it because." Ibid.

318 "If the author." *Collections,* 5th ser., 4, p. 509, Mercy Warren to John Adams, Aug. 4, 1814.

318 "Three score." WAL, 2, p. 396, John Adams to Mercy Warren, Aug. 17, 1814.

318 "I have certified." Ibid.

319 "Parody written." AFC, 1, p. 379, Abigail Adams to Mercy Warren, Apr. 14, 1776.

319 "Elbow chair." MWP, Mercy Warren to ?, June 30, 1814.

319 "I would not have you." Ibid.

319 "The destructive policy." Morison, *Harrison Gray Otis,* pp. 256–57.

320 "Suddenly and violently." GOP, Henry Warren to Maria Otis Colby, Oct. 19, 1814.

320 "She expired." Ibid.

320 "And thus the *last* frail." MWP, Henry Warren to Mary Otis Colby, Oct. 19, 1814.

321 "Let not the frivolity." MWH, 3, p. 414.

321 "The partiality to military." Ibid., p. 420.

321 "Any attempt." Ibid., p. 431.

321 "The principles." Ibid.

321 "It will be the wisdom." Ibid., p. 433.

321 "America may with propriety." Ibid., p. 434.

321 "The people may again." Ibid., p. 432.

322 "They therefore cannot be." Ibid., p. 424.

322 "Am I mistaken." WAL, 2, p. 395, Mercy Warren to John Adams, July 10, 1814.

323 "The Day is far spent." Ibid., p. 345, John Adams to Mercy Warren, Aug. 30, 1803.

BIBLIOGRAPHY

———— ◆◦◆ ————

MANUSCRIPTS

Adams, Samuel. Adams Papers. New York Public Library.
Bernard, Francis. Letters, 1768–1769. Washington, D.C. Library of Congress, Division of Manuscripts. Force Transcripts.
Gay-Otis Papers. New York. Columbia University, Butler Library. Special Collections.
Hancock, John. John Hancock Papers. Boston. MHS.
Harvard University Faculty Records. Cambridge. Harvard University Archives.
Hutchinson, Elisha. Diary of Elisha Hutchinson. Washington, D.C. Library of Congress Transcripts. Egerton Manuscripts. Vol. 2669.
Hutchinson, Thomas. Correspondence, 1772–1779. Microfilm. Boston. MHS.
Hutchinson and Oliver Papers. Boston. MHS.
Knox, Henry. Henry Knox Papers. Boston. MHS.
Massachusetts Archives. Boston. State House.
Otis Family Manuscripts. New York. Columbia University, Butler Library. Special Collections.
Otis Papers. Boston. MHS.
Oliver, Peter. The Origin and Progress of the American Rebellion to the year 1776 in a letter to a Friend. Boston. MHS.
Paine, Robert Treat. Robert Treat Paine Papers. Boston. MHS.
Shays's Rebellion. Papers relating to Shays's Rebellion. Boston. MHS.
Tudor Flynt's Diary. Cambridge. Harvard University Archives.
Warren, James. Miscellaneous Manuscripts. New York. New-York Historical Society.

Warren, Mercy. Mercy Warren Letter Book. Boston. MHS.
———. Mercy Warren Papers. Boston. MHS.
Warren, Winslow. Letters to his mother from Lisbon, Portugal, 1784. Boston. MHS.
Warren-Adams Papers, 1750–1814. Boston. MHS.
Warren Family Letters and Papers, 1763–1814. Compiled and arranged by Charles Warren. Plymouth, Mass. Pilgrim Museum.
Williams, Israel. Israel Williams Papers. Boston. MHS.
Winthrop, Hannah. Diaries. Cambridge. Harvard University Archives.
Winthrop, William. Papers. Cambridge. Harvard University Archives.

NEWSPAPERS AND MAGAZINES

The Boston Evening Post
The Boston Gazette
The Boston Independent Chronicle
The Boston News-Letter
Columbian Centinel
The Emerald or Miscellany of Literature
The Monthly Anthology and Boston Review
The Ordeal, a Critical Journal of Politics and Literature
The Panoplist or the Christian's Armory
The Weekly Messenger, Boston

BOOKS AND ARTICLES
Primary Sources and Early Histories

Adams, Abigail. *Letters of Mrs. Adams.* Edited by Charles Francis Adams. Boston: Wilkins, Carter & Co., 1848.
———. *New Letters of Abigail Adams, 1788–1801.* Edited by Stewart Mitchell. Boston: Houghton Mifflin Co., 1947.
Adams, John. *Adams Family Correspondence.* Edited by L. H. Butterfield. 2 vols. New York: Atheneum, 1965.
———. *The Adams-Jefferson Letters.* Edited by Lester J. Cappon. 2 vols. Chapel Hill: University of North Carolina Press, 1959.
———. "Correspondence between John Adams and John Winthrop." *Collections,* MHS. 5th ser., vol. 4: 287–313.

————. "Correspondence between John Adams and Mercy Warren Relating to Her 'History of the American Revolution,' July–August, 1807." *Collections,* MHS. 5th ser., vol. 4, pt. 3: 315–511.

————. *Diary and Autobiography of John Adams.* Edited by L. H. Butterfield. 4 vols. New York: Atheneum, 1964.

————. *The Earliest Diary of John Adams.* Edited by L. H. Butterfield. Cambridge: Harvard University Press, Belknap Press, 1966.

————. *Familiar Letters of John Adams and His Wife Abigail Adams, during the Revolution.* Edited by Charles Francis Adams. New York: Hurd and Houghton, 1876.

————. *The John Adams Papers.* Selected, edited, and interspersed by Frank Donovan. New York: Dodd Mead & Co., 1965.

————. *Letters of John Adams Addressed to His Wife.* Edited by Charles Francis Adams. 2 vols. Boston: Charles C. Little & James Brown, 1841.

————. *The Spur of Fame: Dialogues of John Adams and Benjamin Rush, 1805–1813.* Edited by John A. Schutz and Douglas Adair. San Merino, Calif.: Huntington Library, 1966.

————. *The Warren-Adams Letters, Being chiefly a correspondence among John Adams, Samuel Adams, and James Warren.* *Collections,* MHS. Vols. 72, 73.

————. *The Works of John Adams.* Edited by Charles Francis Adams. 10 vols. Boston: Little, Brown and Co., 1850–56.

Adams, John Quincy. *Diary of John Quincy Adams.* *Proceedings,* MHS. 2d ser., vol. 16.

Adams, Samuel. *The Writings of Samuel Adams.* Edited by Harry Alonzo Cushing. 4 vols. New York: G. P. Putnam's Sons, 1904–1908.

Ames, Nathaniel. *Jacobin and Junto, or Early American Politics as viewed in the Diary of Dr. Nathaniel Ames, 1758–1822.* Edited by Charles Warren. Cambridge: Harvard University Press, 1931.

Blockheads: or the Affrighted Officers, a Farce, The. Boston: Printed in Queen Street, 1776.

Bowdoin, James. *The Bowdoin and Temple Papers.* *Collections,* MHS. 6th ser., vol. 9; 7th ser., vol. 6.

Bradford, William. *Of Plymouth Plantation: The Pilgrims in America.* Edited by Harvey Wish. New York: G. P. Putnam's Sons, Capricorn Books, 1962.

Burnett, Edmund D., ed. *Letters of Members of the Continental Congress.* 8 vols. Washington, D.C.: Carnegie Institute of Washington, 1921–36.

Continental Congress. *Journals of the Continental Congress, 1744–1789.* 34 vols. Washington, D.C.: Library of Congress ed., 1904–1937.

Cooper, Samuel. "Letters of Samuel Cooper to Thomas Pownall, 1769–1777." *American Historical Review* 8 (Jan. 1903): 301–30.

Copley, John S. "Letters and Papers of John Singleton Copley and Henry Pelham, 1739–1776." *Collections,* MHS. Vol. 71.

Crèvecoeur, Hector St. John de. *Letters from an American Farmer.* Edited by Ernest Rhys. New York and London: E. P. Dutton & Co., Everyman's Library, 1940.

Force, Peter, ed. *American Archives.* 9 vols. Washington, D.C.: Prepared and published under authority of an Act of Congress, 1837–53.

Gage, Thomas. *The Correspondence of General Thomas Gage.* 2 vols. New Haven: Yale University Press, 1931, 1933.

Gardiner, C. Harvey, ed. and commentator. *A Study in Dissent: The Warren-Gerry Correspondence, 1776–1792.* Carbondale: Southern Illinois University Press, 1968.

Gordon, William. *The History of the Rise, Progress, and Establishment of the Independence of the United States of America.* 3 vols. New York: John Woods, 1801.

Hulton, Ann. *Letters of a Loyalist Lady, Being the Letters of Ann Hulton, Sister of Henry Hulton, Commissioner of the Customs at Boston, 1767–1776.* Cambridge: Harvard University Press, 1927.

Hutchinson, Thomas. *The Diary and Letters of His Excellency Thomas Hutchinson.* Edited by Peter Orlando Hutchinson. 2 vols. Boston: Houghton, Mifflin & Co., 1884, 1886.

———. *The History of the Colony and Province of Massachusetts-Bay.* Edited by Lawrence S. Mayo. 3 vols. Cambridge: Harvard University Press, 1936.

Lynde, Benjamin, and Lynde, Benjamin, Jr. *The Diaries of Benjamin Lynde and Benjamin Lynde, Jr.* Edited by Fitch Edward Oliver. Boston: Private printing [Cambridge: Riverside Press], 1880.

Mann, Mary Lee, ed. *A Yankee Jeffersonian: Selections from the Diary and Letters of William Lee of Massachusetts, 1796–1840.* Cambridge: Harvard University Press, Belknap Press, 1958.

Marshall, John. *The Life of George Washington.* 2 vols. Philadelphia: Crissy, 1850.

Massachusetts. *Circuit Court Records.* U.S. Circuit Court for the District of Massachusetts. Vol. 1, 1790–99.

———. *Journal of the Convention for Framing a Constitution of Government for the State of Massachusetts Bay . . . Sept. 1, 1779 to the Close of Their Last Session, June 16, 1780.* Boston: Dutton and Wentworth, 1832.

———. *Journal of the House of Representatives.* 25 vols. 1715–77.

———. *The Journals of Each Provincial Congress of Massachusetts in 1774 and 1775, and of the Committee of Safety.* Boston: Dutton and Wentworth, 1838.

Massachusetts Historical Society. *Collections.* Vols. 1– . 1792– . Special collections as cited; other references as specified in Notes.

———. *Proceedings.* Vols. 1– . 1859– .

Massachusetts Soldiers and Sailors in the Revolutionary War. Boston: Wright and Potter, 1907.

Mauduit, Jasper. *Jasper Mauduit, Agent in London for the Province Massachusetts-Bay, 1762–1765. Collections,* MHS. Vol. 74.

Moore, Frank. *Diary of the American Revolution: From Newspapers and Original Documents.* New York: Charles T. Evans, 1863.

Motley Assembly, a Farce, The. Published for the Entertainment of the Curious. Boston: Nathaniel Coverly, 1779.

New Haven County Court Records, November, 1786. Hartford: Connecticut State Library.

Otis, James. *James Otis's Speech on the Writs of Assistance.* American History Leaflets, 33. New York: A. Lovell & Co., 1902.

———. *Some Political Writings of James Otis.* Collected by Charles E. Mullett. 2 vols. *University of Missouri Studies.* Columbia: University of Missouri Press, 1929.

Plymouth. *Plymouth Church Records, 1620–1859.* Boston: The Colonial Society of Massachusetts, 1920. Vols. 22, 23.

———. *Records of the Town of Plymouth.* 1903. Vol. 3.

Pynchon, William. *The Diary of William Pynchon of Salem: A Picture of Salem Life, Social and Political, a Century Ago.* Edited by

Fitch Edward Oliver. Boston and New York: Houghton, Mifflin and Co., 1890.

Ramsay, David. *The History of the American Revolution.* London, 1793.

Rhys, Ernest, ed. *Chronicles of the Pilgrim Fathers.* New York: E. P. Dutton & Co., Everyman's Library, 1910.

Rowe, John. *Letters and Diary of John Rowe, Boston Merchant, 1759–1762, 1764–1779.* Edited by Anne R. Cunningham. Boston: W. B. Clarke Co., 1903.

Sewall, Samuel. *Diary of Samuel Sewall. Collections,* MHS. 5th ser., vol. 7.

Stiles, Ezra. *Extracts from the Itineraries and Other Miscellanies of Ezra Stiles, D.D., L.L.D., 1775–1794, with a Selection from His Correspondence.* Edited by Franklin Bowditch Dexter. New Haven: Yale University Press, 1916.

Thacher, James. *A Military Journal During the Revolutionary War.* Boston: Cottons & Bernard, 1827.

Tyler, Mary Palmer. *Grandmother Tyler's Book: The Recollections of Mary Palmer Tyler, 1775–1866.* Edited by Frederick Tupper and Helen Tyler Brown. New York: G. P. Putnam's Sons, 1925.

Warren, Mercy. *The Adulateur, a Tragedy.* Pamphlet. First published in *The Massachusetts Spy,* 1772. Reprinted in *The Magazine of History,* 63, Tarrytown, N.Y., 1918.

———. *The Defeat, a Play.* First published in the *Boston Gazette,* 1773.

———. *The Group, a Farce.* Pamphlet. Boston: Edes and Gill in Queen Street, 1776.

———. *History of the Rise, Progress, and Termination of the American Revolution, interspersed with Biographical, Political, and Moral Observations.* 3 vols. Boston: Ebenezer Larkin, 1805.

———. *Observations on the New Constitution, and on the Federal and State Conventions. By a Columbian Patriot.* Pamphlet. Boston, 1788.

———. *Poems, Dramatic and Miscellaneous.* Boston: T. Thomas and E. T. Andrews, 1790.

Winslow Papers, The. Edited by W. O. Raymond. St. John, New Brunswick: Sun Printing Co., 1901.

Winthrop, John. *A Modell of Christian Charity. Collections*, MHS. 3d ser., 7: 31–48.

Secondary Sources (selected)

Adams, Brooks. *The Emancipation of Massachusetts*. Boston and New York: Houghton, Mifflin and Co., 1887.

Adams, Henry. *The United States in 1800*. Ithaca, N.Y.: Cornell University Press (1889), 1955.

Adams, James Truslow. *New England in the Republic, 1776–1850*. Boston: Little, Brown and Co., 1926.

———. *Revolutionary New England, 1691–1776*. Boston: Atlantic Monthly Press, 1923.

Alden, John Richard. *The American Revolution, 1775–1783*. New York: Harper and Brothers, 1954.

———. *General Gage in America: Being Principally a History of His Role in the American Revolution*. Baton Rouge: Louisiana State University Press, 1948.

Allan, Herbert S. *John Hancock, Patriot in Purple*. New York: Macmillan, 1948.

Anthony, Katherine. *First Lady of the Revolution: The Life of Mercy Otis Warren*. Garden City, N.Y.: Doubleday & Co., 1958.

Austin, George Lowell. *The History of Massachusetts*. Boston: B. B. Russell, 1884.

Austin, James T. *The Life of Elbridge Gerry. With Contemporary Letters. To the Close of the American Revolution*. 2 vols. Boston: Wells and Lilly, 1828–29.

Bailyn, Bernard. *The Ideological Origins of the American Revolution*. Cambridge: Harvard University Press, 1967.

———. *Pamphlets of the American Revolution, 1750–1776*. Cambridge: Harvard University Press, Belknap Press, 1965.

Bancroft, George. *History of the United States of America*. 6 vols. New York: D. Appleton & Co., 1884.

Banner, James J., Jr. *To the Hartford Convention: The Federalists and the Origin of Party Politics in Massachusetts, 1789–1815*. New York: Alfred A. Knopf, 1970.

Barry, John S. *History of Massachusetts*. 3 vols. Boston: Phillips, Sampson & Co., 1855–57.

Beach, Stewart. *Samuel Adams: The Fateful Years, 1764–1776.* New York: Dodd, Mead & Co., 1965.

Becker, Carl Lotus. *The Declaration of Independence, a Study in the History of Political Ideas.* New York: Alfred A. Knopf, 1942.

———. *Freedom and Responsibility in the American Way of Life.* New York: Alfred A. Knopf and the University of Michigan, 1945.

Berky, Andrew S., and Shenton, James P., eds. *The Historians' History of the United States.* 2 vols. New York: G. P. Putnam's Sons, 1966.

Bloom, Sol. *History of the Formation of the Union under the Constitution.* Washington, D.C.: United States Constitution Sesquicentennial Commission, 1943.

Boorstin, Daniel J. *The Americans: The Colonial Experience.* New York: Random House, 1958.

Boswell, James. *Boswell in Search of a Wife, 1766–1769.* Edited by Frank Brady and Frederick A. Pottle. (Copyright, 1956, Yale University.) New York: McGraw-Hill Book Co., n.d.

———. *The Life of Samuel Johnson, L.L.D.* 3 vols. London: Macmillan & Co., 1912.

Bowen, Catherine Drinker. *John Adams and the American Revolution.* Boston: Atlantic–Little, Brown and Co., 1950.

———. *Miracle at Philadelphia: The Story of the Constitutional Convention, May to September, 1787.* Boston: Atlantic–Little, Brown and Co., 1966.

Bowen, Francis. "Life of James Otis." In *Library of American Biography.* Edited by Jared Sparks. Boston: Charles C. Little and James Brown, 1847.

Bradford, Alden. *History of Massachusetts from July, 1775, to the Year 1789.* Boston: Wells and Lilly, 1825.

Brennan, Ellen E. "James Otis: Recreant and Patriot." *New England Quarterly* 12 (Dec. 1939): 691–725.

———. *Plural Officeholding in Massachusetts, 1760–1780: Its Relation to the Separation of Departments of Government.* Chapel Hill: University of North Carolina Press, 1945.

Brooks, Van Wyck. *The World of Washington Irving.* New York: E. P. Dutton & Co., 1944.

Brown, Alice. *Mercy Warren.* New York: Charles Scribner's Sons, 1896.
Brown, Robert E. *Middle-Class Democracy and the Revolution in Massachusetts, 1691–1780.* Ithaca, N.Y.: Cornell University Press, 1955.
Brown, Wallace. *The Good Americans: The Loyalists in the American Revolution.* New York: William Morrow & Co., 1969.
Brush, Edward Hale. *Rufus King and His Times.* New York: Nicholas C. Brown, 1926.
Burnett, Edmund Cody. *The Continental Congress.* New York: Macmillan Co., 1941.
Chidsey, Donald Barr. *The Siege of Boston.* New York: Crown Publishers, 1966.
Chinard, Gilbert. *Honest John Adams.* Boston: Little, Brown & Co., 1933.
Clark, William Bell. *Gallant John Barry, 1745–1803.* New York: Macmillan Co., 1938.
Commager, Henry Steele, and Giordanetti, Elmo. *Was America a Mistake? An Eighteenth-Century Commentary.* New York: Harper & Row, Publishers, 1967.
Crawford, Mary Caroline. *Old Boston Days and Ways.* Boston: Little, Brown & Co., 1909.
Cunningham, Noble E., Jr. *The Jeffersonian Republicans: The Formation of Party Organization, 1789–1801.* Chapel Hill: University of North Carolina Press, 1957.
Cushing, Harry Alonzo. *History of the Transition from Province to Commonwealth Government in Massachusetts.* Columbia University, Studies in History, Economics and Public Law, 7. New York: Columbia University Press, 1896.
Dauer, Manning J. *The Adams Federalists.* Baltimore: Johns Hopkins Press, 1953, 1968.
Davidson, Philip. *Propaganda and the American Revolution, 1763–1783.* Chapel Hill: University of North Carolina Press, 1941.
Davis, William T. *Ancient Landmarks of Plymouth.* Boston: A. Williams & Co., Old Corner Book Store, 1883.
Davol, Ralph. *Two Men of Taunton: In the Course of Human Events, 1731–1829.* Taunton, Mass.: Davol Publishing Co., 1912.

374   BIBLIOGRAPHY

Deyo, Simeon L., ed. *History of Barnstable County, Massachusetts, 1620–1890.* New York: H. W. Blake, 1890.

Donnelly, Lucy Martin. "The Celebrated Mrs. Macaulay." *William and Mary Quarterly* 3d ser., vol. 6, no. 2 (Apr. 1949): 174–207.

Douglass, Elisha P. *Rebels and Democrats: The Struggle for Equal Political Rights and Majority Rule during the American Revolution.* Chapel Hill: University of North Carolina Press, 1955.

Drake, Samuel Adams. *Old Landmarks and Historic Personages of Boston.* Boston: Little, Brown & Co., 1900.

Ellet, Elizabeth F. *The Women of the American Revolution.* Vol. 1. Philadelphia: George W. Jacobs & Co., 1900.

Fleming, Thomas J. *Now We Are Enemies: The Story of Bunker Hill.* New York: St. Martin's Press, 1960.

Forbes, Esther. *Paul Revere and the World He Lived In.* Boston: Houghton Mifflin Co., 1942.

Freeman, Frederick. *The History of Cape Cod: The Annals of Barnstable County.* Vol. 1. Boston: Privately printed, 1860.

Freiberg, Malcolm. *Prelude to Purgatory: Thomas Hutchinson in Provincial Massachusetts Politics, 1760–1770.* Thesis, Brown University, 1950.

Frothingham, Richard. *History of the Siege of Boston.* Boston: Charles C. Little and James Brown, 1851.

Furnas, J. C. *The Americans, A Social History of the United States, 1587–1914.* New York: G. P. Putnam's Sons, 1969.

Gardner, Allen. *Massachusetts Privateers of the Revolution.* Boston: MHS, 1927.

Gaustad, Edwin Scott. *The Great Awakening in New England.* Chicago: Quadrangle Books, 1957.

Gay, Peter. *The Enlightenment: An Interpretation: The Rise of Modern Paganism.* New York: Random House, Vintage Books, 1966.

Gipson, Lawrence Henry. *The Coming of the Revolution, 1763–1775.* New York: Harper and Brothers, 1954.

Goehring, Walter A. *The West Parish Church of Barnstable: An Historical Sketch.* West Barnstable, Mass.: The West Parish Memorial Foundation, 1959.

Goodman, Paul. *The Democratic-Republicans of Massachusetts: Politics in a Young Republic.* Cambridge: Harvard University Press, 1964.

Greene, Evarts B. *The Revolutionary Generation, 1763–1790.* New York: Macmillan Co., 1943.

Handlin, Oscar and Mary F. *Commonwealth: A Study of the Role of Government in the American Economy: Massachusetts, 1774–1861.* New York: New York University Press, 1947.

————. "Radicals and Conservatives in Massachusetts after Independence." *New England Quarterly* 17 (Sept. 1944): 343–55.

Haraszti, Zoltan. *John Adams and the Prophets of Progress.* Cambridge: Harvard University Press, 1952.

Harding, Samuel B. *The Contest over the Ratification of the Federal Constitution in the State of Massachusetts.* New York: Longmans, Green & Co., 1896.

Hickman, Emily. "Colonial Writs of Assistance." *New England Quarterly* 5 (Jan. 1932): 83–104.

Higginson, Stephen. *Ten Chapters in the Life of John Hancock.* New York, 1857.

Hofstadter, Richard. *The American Political Tradition and the Men Who Made It.* New York: Alfred A. Knopf, 1948.

Hosmer, James K. *The Life of Thomas Hutchinson.* Boston: Houghton, Mifflin and Co., 1896.

————. *Samuel Adams.* Boston: Houghton, Mifflin and Co., 1885.

Hurd, Hamilton D., ed. *History of Plymouth County.* Philadelphia: J. W. Lewis, 1884.

Jameson, J. Franklin. *The American Revolution Considered as a Social Movement.* Princeton: Princeton University Press, 1926.

Jensen, Merrill. *The Founding of a Nation.* New York: Oxford University Press, 1968.

————. *The New Nation: A History of the United States During the Confederation, 1781–1789.* New York: Alfred A. Knopf, 1950.

Kenyon, Cecilia. "Men of Little Faith: the Anti-Federalists on the Nature of Representative Government." *William and Mary Quarterly* 3d ser., vol. 12 (Jan. 1955): 3–43.

————. "Republicanism and Radicalism in the American Revolution: An Old-Fashioned Interpretation." *William and Mary Quarterly* 19 (Apr. 1962): 153–82.

Koch, Adrienne. *Power, Morals, and the Founding Fathers.* Ithaca, N.Y.: Cornell University Press, 1961.

Lewis, Wilmarth Sheldon. *Horace Walpole*. New York: Random House, Pantheon Books, 1960, 1961.

Long, J. C. *George III*. Boston: Little, Brown and Co., 1960.

Lossing, Benson J. *Field Book of the Revolution*. New York: Thomas Emmet, 1890.

Lynd, Straughton. *Intellectual Origins of American Radicalism*. New York: Random House, Pantheon Books, 1968.

Malone, Dumas. *Jefferson the President: First Term, 1801–1805*. Boston: Little, Brown and Co., 1970.

———. *Jefferson and the Ordeal of Liberty*. Boston: Little, Brown and Co., 1962.

Marble, Annie Russell. "Mistress Mercy Warren: Real Daughter of the American Revolution." *The New England Magazine* (Apr. 1903).

Mencken, H. L. *The American Language*. New York: Alfred A. Knopf, 1937.

Miller, John C. *Alexander Hamilton: Portrait in Paradox*. New York: Harper and Brothers, 1959.

———. *Crisis in Freedom: The Alien and Sedition Acts*. Boston: Little, Brown and Co., 1952.

———. *The Federalist Era, 1789–1801*. New York: Harper & Row, Publishers, 1960.

———. "The Massachusetts Convention: 1768." *New England Quarterly* 7 (Sept. 1934): 445–74.

———. *Origins of the American Revolution*. Boston: Little, Brown and Co., 1943.

———. *Sam Adams: Pioneer in Propaganda*. Boston: Little, Brown and Co., 1936.

Miller, Perry, ed. *The American Puritans: Their Prose and Poetry*. Garden City, N.Y.: Doubleday & Co., 1956.

———. *The Life of the Mind in America from the Revolution to the Civil War*. New York: Harcourt, Brace & World, 1965.

Moody, Robert E. "Samuel Ely: Forerunner of Shays." *New England Quarterly* 5 (Jan. 1932): 105–34.

Morgan, Edmund S. *The American Revolution: Two Centuries of Interpretation*. Englewood, N.J.: Prentice-Hall, 1965.

———. "Thomas Hutchinson and the Stamp Act." *New England Quarterly* 12 (Dec. 1948): 459–92.

Morgan, Edmund S. and Helen M. *The Stamp Act Crisis: Prologue to Revolution.* Chapel Hill: University of North Carolina Press, 1953.

Morison, Samuel Eliot. "The Formation of the Massachusetts Constitution." *Massachusetts Law Quarterly* 40 (Dec. 1955).

――――. *Harrison Gray Otis 1765–1848: The Urbane Federalist.* Boston: Houghton Mifflin Co., 1969.

――――. *John Paul Jones: A Sailor's Biography.* Boston: Little, Brown and Co., 1959.

――――. *The Maritime History of Massachusetts: 1783–1860.* Boston: Houghton Mifflin Co., 1941.

――――. "The Struggle over the Adoption of the Constitution of Massachusetts, 1780." *Proceedings,* MHS. Vol. 50 (1916–17): 353–412.

――――. *Three Centuries of Harvard.* Cambridge: Harvard University Press, 1936.

Morison, Samuel Eliot, and Commager, Henry Steele. *The Growth of the American Republic.* 2 vols. New York: Oxford University Press, 1950.

Morris, Richard. *The American Revolution Reconsidered.* New York: Harper & Row, Publishers, 1967.

――――, ed. *The Era of the American Revolution.* New York: Columbia University Press, 1939.

Moses, Montrose J., ed. *Representative Plays by American Dramatists, 1765–1819.* Vol. 1. New York: E. P. Dutton & Co., 1918.

Nevins, Allan. *The American States During and After the Revolution, 1775–1789.* New York: Macmillan Co., 1924.

Otis, Amos. *Genealogical Notes of Barnstable Families: Reprint of the Amos Otis Papers published in "The Barnstable Patriot."* Barnstable, Mass.: The Patriot Press, 1888–90.

Otis, William A. *A Geneological Historical Memoir of the Otis Family in America.* Chicago, 1924.

Parrington, Vernon L. *The Colonial Mind, 1620–1800.* Main Currents in American Thought. Vol. 1. New York: Harcourt, Brace & World, 1927, 1954.

Paullin, Charles O. "Admiral Pierre Landais." *Catholic Historical Review* 17 (Oct. 1931): 296–307.

Perkins, Bradford, ed. *The Causes of the War of 1812.* New York: Holt, Rinehart and Winston, 1962.

Phillips, James Duncan. *Salem in the Eighteenth Century.* Boston: Houghton Mifflin Co., 1937.

Pickering, Octavius. *The Life of Timothy Pickering.* Vol. 1. Boston: Little, Brown and Co., 1867.

Quincy, Edmund. *Life of Josiah Quincy of Massachusetts.* Boston: Ticknor and Fields, 1867.

Richards, Lysander Salmon. *History of Marshfield.* 2 vols. Plymouth: Memorial Press, 1901.

Ritcheson, Charles R. *British Politics and the American Revolution.* Norman: University of Oklahoma Press, 1954.

Robinson, G. Frederick, and Wheeler, Ruth Robinson. *Great Little Watertown: A Tercentenary History.* Cambridge: The Riverside Press, 1930.

Roebling, Washington A. *Richard Warren of the* Mayflower *and Some of His Descendants.* Boston: D. Clapp and Son, 1901.

Rossiter, Clinton. *The First American Revolution.* New York: Harcourt, Brace & World, 1953, 1956.

———. *The Political Thought of the American Revolution.* New York: Harcourt, Brace & World, 1953, 1963.

Sabine, Lorenzo. *Biographical Sketches of Loyalists of the American Revolution, with an Historical Essay.* 2 vols. Boston: Little, Brown and Co., 1864.

Schlesinger, Arthur M. *The Birth of a Nation.* New York: Alfred A. Knopf, 1968.

———. "Colonial Newspapers and the Stamp Act." *New England Quarterly* 8 (Mar. 1935): 63–83.

———. *Prelude to Independence: The Newspaper War on Britain, 1764–1776.* New York: Alfred A. Knopf, 1958.

Schutz, John A. *Thomas Pownall, British Defender of American Liberty: A Study of Anglo-American Relations in the Eighteenth Century.* Glendale, Calif.: A. H. Clark Co., 1951.

———. *William Shirley, King's Governor of Massachusetts.* Chapel Hill: University of North Carolina Press, 1961.

Sibley, John Langdon, and Shipton, Clifford K. *Biographical Sketches of Graduates of Harvard University in Cambridge, Massachusetts.* Boston: MHS, 1873– .

Smith, Page. *John Adams*. 2 vols. Garden City, N.Y.: Doubleday & Co., 1962.

Smith, William Raymond. *History as Argument: Three Patriot Historians of the American Revolution*. The Hague and Paris: Mouton & Co., 1966.

Stark, James Henry. *The Loyalists of Massachusetts*. Boston: W. B. Clarke Co., 1910.

Starkey, Marion L. *A Little Rebellion*. New York: Alfred A. Knopf, 1955.

Taylor, Robert J., ed. *Massachusetts, Colony to Commonwealth*. Chapel Hill: University of North Carolina Press, 1961.

————. *Western Massachusetts in the Revolution*. Providence: Brown University Press, 1954.

Thacher, James. *History of the Town of Plymouth*. Boston: Marsh, Capen & Lyon, 1832.

Thompson, Elroy S. *History of Plymouth, Norfolk and Barnstable Counties*. New York: Lewis Historical Publishing Co., 1928.

Trayser, Donald G. *Barnstable, Three Centuries of a Cape Cod Town*. Hyannis, Mass.: F.B. & F.B. Goss, 1939.

Trevalyn, George Otto. *The American Revolution*. Abridged and edited by Richard B. Morris. New York: David McKay Co., 1964.

Tudor, William. *The Life of James Otis of Massachusetts*. Boston: Wells and Lilly, 1823.

Tyler, Moses Coit. *The Literary History of the American Revolution, 1763–1783*. 2 vols. New York and London: G. P. Putnam's Sons, 1897.

Van Doren, Carl. *The Great Rehearsal: The Story of the Making and Ratifying of the Constitution of the United States*. New York: The Viking Press, 1948.

Van Tyne, Claude H. *The Loyalists of the American Revolution*. New York: Macmillan Co., 1902.

Walpole, Horace. *Memoirs of the Reign of George III*. 4 vols. London: Lawrence & Bullen, 1894.

Warren, Charles. "Elbridge Gerry, James Warren, Mercy Warren and the Ratification of the Federal Constitution in Massachusetts." *Proceedings,* MHS. Vol. 64 (Mar. 1931): 143–64.

————. *Odd Byways in American History*. Cambridge: Harvard University Press, 1942.

————. "Samuel Adams and the Sans Souci Club in 1785." *Proceedings*, MHS. 3d ser., vol. 6 (May 1937): 318–44.

————. "A Young Man's Adventures in England and France During the Revolutionary War: Winslow Warren in Europe." *Proceedings*, MHS. Vol. 65 (Jan. 1934): 234–67.

Waters, John J., Jr. *The Otis Family in Provincial and Revolutionary Massachusetts*. Chapel Hill: University of North Carolina Press, 1968.

Waters, John J., Jr., and Schutz, John A. "Patterns of Massachusetts Colonial Politics: The Writs of Assistance and the Rivalry between the Otis and Hutchinson Families." *William and Mary Quarterly* 3d ser., vol. 24 (Oct. 1967): 543–67.

Welch, Richard E., Jr. *Theodore Sedgwick, Federalist: A Political Portrait*. Middletown, Conn.: Wesleyan University Press, 1965.

Wells, William V. *The Life and Public Services of Samuel Adams*. 3 vols. Boston: Little, Brown and Co., 1865.

Wertenbaker, Thomas Jefferson. *The Puritan Oligarchy: The Founding of American Civilization*. New York: Charles Scribner's Sons, 1947.

Weyl, Walter E. *The New Democracy*. New York: Harper & Row, Publishers, 1912.

White, R. J. *The Age of George III*. New York: Walker & Co., 1968.

Willison, George F. *Saints and Strangers*. New York: Reynal & Hitchcock, 1945.

Winsor, Justin. *The Memorial History of Boston*. 4 vols. Boston: Ticknor & Co., 1880.

Wolford, Thorp Lanier. "Democrat-Republican Reaction in Massachusetts to the Embargo of 1807." *New England Quarterly* 15 (Mar. 1942): 35–61.

Wood, George A. *William Shirley, Governor of Massachusetts, 1741–1756: A History*. New York: Columbia University Press, 1920.

Wood, Gordon S. *The Creation of the American Republic, 1776–1787*. Chapel Hill: University of North Carolina Press, 1969.

Woodbury, Ellen. *Dorothy Quincy*. Washington, D.C.: Neale Publishing Co., 1901.

Zobel, Hiller B. *The Boston Massacre*. New York: W. W. Norton & Co., 1970.

INDEX

INDEX   389